Wireless XML
Developer's Guide

About the Author

Mikael Hillborg is a consultant specializing in wireless application development. Currently, he's working with mobile Internet application development, as a consultant and project manager for one of the world's largest mobile communication companies.

Hillborg has almost 10 years of experience in the wireless industry and has participated in a wide range of projects as a developer, project manager, test engineer, and analyst.

He is the author of the very successful book, *WAP: Mobile Internet, An Introduction to WAP Programming* (ISBN 91-636-0600-3) which was published in Sweden and Finland. In the book, Hillborg's practical approach was highly appreciated among the developers who struggled to put together the first generation of mobile Internet applications. Now, with *Wireless XML Developer's Guide*, Hillborg releases the definitive guide to developing wireless applications using XML based technologies in general.

Wireless XML
Developer's Guide

Mikael Hillborg

McGraw-Hill/Osborne

New York   Chicago   San Francisco
Lisbon   London   Madrid   Mexico City   Milan
New Delhi   San Juan   Seoul   Singapore   Sydney   Toronto

McGraw-Hill/Osborne
2600 Tenth Street
Berkeley, California 94710
U.S.A.

To arrange bulk purchase discounts for sales promotions, premiums, or fund-raisers, please contact **McGraw-Hill**/Osborne at the above address. For information on translations or book distributors outside the U.S.A., please see the International Contact Information page immediately following the index of this book.

Wireless XML Developer's Guide

1234567890 FGR FGR 0198765432

ISBN 0-07-219536-3

Publisher	Brandon A. Nordin
Vice President & Associate Publisher	Scott Rogers
Editorials Director	Wendy Rinaldi
Project Editor	Monika Faltiss
Acquisitions Coordinator	Timothy Madrid
Technical Editor	Ryan Fife
Copy Editor	Marcia Baker
Proofreader	Mike McGee
Indexer	Jack Lewis
Computer Designers	Carie Abrew, Tara Davis
Illustrators	Michael Mueller, Lyssa Wald
Series Design	Roberta Steele
Cover Series Design	Greg Scott
Cover Illustrator	Eliot Bergman

This book was composed with Corel VENTURA™ Publisher.

Contents at a Glance

Part I **XML in a Wireless Context**

Chapter 1 **Introduction to Wireless Applications** **3**

Chapter 2 **Wireless Networks and Protocols** **17**

Chapter 3 **XML Primer** **47**

Part II **The Developer's Quick Reference Guide**

Chapter 4 **XHTML** **103**

Chapter 5 **Voice** **123**

Chapter 6 **Synchronized Multimedia** **133**

Chapter 7 **Geography** **149**

Chapter 8 **Translations and Optimizations** **171**

Chapter 9 **Profiles** **185**

Chapter 10 **Synchronization** **195**

Chapter 11 **Low-level Communication** **205**

Part III **Use Cases: The Developer's Detailed Guide**

Chapter 12 **Building XHTML Applications** **217**

Chapter 13 **Building WML 2.0 Applications** **271**

Chapter 14 **Building a Voice Portal** **327**

Chapter 15 **Building Multimedia Applications** **365**

Chapter 16   **Using SVG with GML to Represent the Real World** **395**

Chapter 17   **Mobile Commerce** **433**

Part IV   **The Future of XML in Wireless**

Chapter 18   **Proximity** **459**

Chapter 19   **The Future of Personalization** **475**

Chapter 20   **Instant Messaging and Presence Applications** **487**

Chapter 21   **Databases** **497**

Index **505**

Contents

Introduction . . . .   *xv*

Part I   **XML in a Wireless Context**

Chapter 1   **Introduction to Wireless Applications** **3**

Application Types   4

    Connected All the Time   4

    Instant Messaging and Presence   4

    Personalization   7

    Location   11

    Synchronization   12

Applications   14

    Environments   14

    Applications   15

Chapter 2   **Wireless Networks and Protocols** **17**

Network Topologies   18

    Cells   18

    Wireless Does Not Imply Mobility   19

Circuit Switching and Packet Switching   19

    Circuit-switched Networks   19

    Packet-switched Networks   20

From the First to the Fourth Generation   20

    The First Generation   21

    2G   21

    2.5G   21

    3G   22

    4G   25

Protocols and Interfaces 26
    Protocol Stacks 27
    Application Protocols 27
    Network Protocols 33

Chapter 3   **XML Primer** **47**

XML Documents 48
    Content Types 49
    Elements, Tags, and Attributes 50
    Grammars 52
    The XML Declaration 54
    Character Encoding 54
    The Formal Public Identifier 55
Validation 55
    Document Type Definitions 56
Namespaces 71
Schemas 72
    The Structure of a Schema 72
    Simple and Complex Types 72
    Sequences 75
    Attributes 76
    Rewriting a DTD as a Schema 77
Links 80
    Link Types 81
Paths 86
    Tree Structures 86
XSL Transformations 88
    Structure 89
Cascading Style Sheets 92
    CSS Basics 93
    Block and Inline-level Elements 93
    Font Properties 95
    Space 96
    Units 97
    Colors 98
    Matching 99
XML Tools 100

Part II   **The Developer's Quick Reference Guide**

Chapter 4   **XHTML** **103**

XHTML and the Modularization of HTML4   104
    Document Type Definitions   104
    Closed Tags (Well-Formed XML)   105
    The XHTML Modules   106
    The Modules of XHTML Basic   107
    Structure, Text, Hypertext, and Lists   108
    Applets and Scripting   109
    Presentation, Edit, and Bidirectional Text   110
    Forms and Basic Forms   111
    Tables and Basic Tables   113
    Image Maps and Embedded Objects   117
    Frames, iframes, and Targets   118
    Intrinsic Events and Metainformation   119
    Style Sheets and the Style Attribute   120
    Links and Base   120
    Name Identification and Legacy Constructs   121

Chapter 5   **Voice** **123**

VoiceXML   124
    Document Structure   125
    Forms   126
    Menus   128
    Play Audio Files   129
Alternatives to VoiceXML   131
    CallXML   131
    VoxML   131
    Other   132

Chapter 6   **Synchronized Multimedia** **133**

SMIL 2.0   135
    The Structure of a SMIL Presentation   135
    Graphics   136
    Audio   136
    Sequential Presentations   137

Parallel Presentations 138

Combinations of Sequential and Parallel Presentations 139

Links 141

Practical Issues 143

The SMIL Modules 145

The SMIL 2.0 Basic Profile 147

Modules 147

Chapter 7   **Geography** **149**

Geography Markup Language (GML) 150

SVG 164

The Drawing Board 165

Shapes 167

Paths 167

Text 168

The Map in SVG 169

Chapter 8   **Translations and Optimizations** **171**

Binary XML 172

The Start of a WBXML Document 173

The String Table 176

The Document Body 177

Summary 181

A Few Words About WAX 183

One Language 183

Chapter 9   **Profiles** **185**

RDF — Resource Description Framework 186

CC/PP 189

UAProf 190

Using the Profile 193

Chapter 10   **Synchronization** **195**

SyncML Messages 197

The Source and Target Elements 199

SyncML Commands 200

Chapter 11   **Low-level Communication** **205**

Distributed Wireless Systems 206

Procedure Calls 207

XML-RPC	. . . .	208
Using Data Types	. . . .	210
Further Reading	. . . .	213

Part III	**Use Cases: The Developer's Detailed Guide**	

Chapter 12	**Building XHTML Applications**	**217**
	Examples in XHTML	218
	Converting HTML to XHTML	218
	Dealing with Frames	225
	Things to Avoid	226
	Examples in XHTML Basic	230
	Creating a Site for Small Devices and Desktop Computers	230
	Converting i-mode HTML to XHTML Basic	235
	A Sample XHTML Basic 1.0 and i-mode Site	249
	Working with XHTML Basic, the Presentation, and Style Sheet Modules	259
	Development Tools	264
	XML Spy	264
	HTML-Kit	267
	XHTML Support in the Nokia Mobile Internet Toolkit	268

Chapter 13	**Building WML 2.0 Applications**	**271**
	Basics	272
	HTML Body vs. a Deck of Cards	273
	Formatting	276
	Links	278
	Tables	280
	Images	282
	Making Navigation Easier	284
	Using Access Keys	284
	Using Variables	286
	Reading the Value of a Variable	286
	Writing Parameterized Code Using Variable References	287
	Setting a Variable	287
	Free Text Input	288
	Sending Variable Values to a Server Script	291
	Setting Variables to Change Attribute Values	293
	Selection Lists	294

Jumps 297
   Jumping Forward 297
   Setting Variables in a Jump 301
   Jumping Back 302
   Detecting Forward and Backward Jumps 304
Using the Timer 306
   A Start Page 307
   Simple Animations 307
Integrating Phone Functionality 309
   Dialing a Number 309
   Managing the Phone Book 310
Using Scripts 310
   Functions 311
   The Standard Libraries 314
   Using the Libraries 315
Building WML 1.*x*-compliant Sites 324
   Namespaces and the Header 324
   Widgets and Roles 325
   Templates 326

Chapter 14   **Building a Voice Portal** **327**
Functionality 328
   A Welcome Message 328
   A Top Menu of Choices 329
   Services 330
Implementation 331
   The Welcome Message 331
   The Navigation System 331
   The Services 337

Chapter 15   **Building Multimedia Applications** **365**
Preparations 366
   Development Tools 366
   Formats and Content Types 367
   Document Submission 367
Layouts and Regions 368
   Image and Text Regions 368
   Making It Fit Particular Screen Types 371

Slide Show Timings 377
Text Messages 378
    Static Text 379
    Animated Text 381
Graphics and Animation 384
    Animation with Pictures 385
    Animation Using Sequences 386
    Combined Text and Graphics Animations 387
    Optimizations and Adjustments 388
Audio 388
    Embedding Audio 388
    iMelody 390

Chapter 16   **Using SVG with GML to Represent the Real World** **395**
Advanced Object-oriented Models 396
    Modeling Tools 396
    Models 399
A Map 399
    Representation in GML 401
    Transformation to SVG 423
    About Batik 431

Chapter 17   **Mobile Commerce** **433**
Digital Signatures 434
    Signing a Document and Sending It to a Server 434
ECML 438
    Shipping 439
    Shipping Content to a Mobile Phone Number 441
    Billing 443
    Receipts 446
    Cards Details 449
    Merchant and Transaction Information 452

Part IV   **The Future of XML in Wireless**

Chapter 18   **Proximity** **459**
Navigation with NVML 460
    Document Structure 461

Routes 462

Guides 464

Specifying Points of Interest with POIX 466

Formats 467

The Position 468

Mobility 469

Extending the Point of Interest with Start and End Points 471

Chapter 19   The Future of Personalization **475**

CSS Mobile Profile 1.0 476

Adding Style 476

Selectors 476

Properties 479

Virtual Personal Information 480

Using the vCard Format 480

Using the vCalendar Format 483

Future Representations of Business Cards and Calendars 485

Chapter 20   Instant Messaging and Presence Applications **487**

RFC2778 and RFC2779 488

The Instant Messaging and Presence Protocol 489

CPIM Messages 489

CPIM Instant Inboxes 490

CPIM Presentities 491

APEX 493

The APEX Core 493

The APEX Presence Service 494

Make It SIMPLE 495

Watchers 495

Chapter 21   Databases **497**

XQuery 498

A Basic Query 498

Conditional Queries 499

For, Let, Where, Return Queries 501

XQL 502

Other Alternatives 504

Index **505**

Introduction

Wireless applications based on technologies such as SMS, i-mode, HDML, and WAP have been in use for a couple of years. So far it's been a trial because infrastructures, concepts, and applications had to be tried out by service providers, content providers, and end users. The industry learned a lot, and now the map is starting to become much clearer than it was just one or two years ago. Many of the technologies that are playing, or in the future will play, an important role for application developers are based on XML.

XML is used today to build personalized services, voice portals, multimedia messaging services, hypertext documents with phone functionality, and a variety of applications that are described in this book. In addition, the book outlines where wireless and XML is heading and what you, as an application developer, or technically oriented manager, or analyst might expect of the future of XML in wireless.

Who Should Read This Book

This book is for readers who want to learn how to implement wireless applications based on XML. It contains several examples which can serve as catalysts for new services and a comprehensive coverage of important technologies such as XHTML, MMS, ECML, VoiceXML, and so on. Although, there are many examples that describe the nuts and bolts of creating wireless applications, even technical managers and analysts will find the book useful, since it gives a good idea of which wireless technologies and concepts play an important role now and will in the future.

How This Book Is Organized

This book is divided into four parts. Part I, "XML in a Wireless Context" contains three chapters that cover wireless networks and XML based applications. Part II, "The Developer's Quick Reference Guide" teaches you the essentials of technologies such as XHTML Basic, VoiceXML, MMS SMIL, GML, SVG and so forth. Part III, "Use Cases: The Developer's Detailed Guide" goes into the details of building wireless applications using XML. Part IV, "The Future of XML in Wireless" examines areas and technologies that might play an important role for the future wireless applications of XML.

Chapter 1, "Introduction to Wireless Applications" presents different platforms and applications types such as IM applications and location based services. Circuit switching, packet switching, and the terms 2G, 2.5G, 3G and 4G are discussed in Chapter 2, "Wireless Networks and Protocols." The part ends with Chapter 3, an XML primer.

Part II begins with Chapter 4, "XHTML" which explains how HTML4 was modularized. The modularization of HTML4 makes it easier for vendors to create languages, such as XHTML Basic, that are adapted for wireless handheld devices. Chapter 5, "Voice" describes how wireless applications can be created on arbitrary networks using voice recognition and voice synthesis. The Multimedia Messaging Service (MMS) uses SMIL and Chapter 6, "Synchronized Multimedia" explains how these messages are laid out and designed in SMIL. Chapter 7, "Geography" shows how technologies such as GML and SVG can be used to implement location-based services. To use the wireless network as efficient as possible, binary XML can be used to compress XML applications. How Wireless Binary XML (WBXML) works is explained in Chapter 8, "Translations and Optimizations." Because many handheld devices have a limited display and keyboard, it's important that the user can personalize the application with respect to the capabilities of different types of devices. Chapter 9, "Profiles" explains how that can be achieved. SyncML is presented in Chapter 10, "Synchronization." SyncML can be used to keep information on a desktop computer synchronized with a wireless handheld device. XML can be used to implement low-level communication routines in a distributed application. Chapter 11, "Low-level Communication" describes how XML-RPC works and how it can be used to distribute your application over several computers connected in, for example, a Wireless LAN.

Part III begins with Chapter 12, "Building XHTML Applications." This chapter presents a number of examples designed in XHTML and XHTML Basic. i-mode applications are listed, explained and compared with similar applications created in XHTML Basic. In Chapter 13, "Building WML 2.0 Applications" XHTML is used in a WAP 2.0 environment. In addition, elements and attributes that provide telecom functionality unique for WML 2.0 are presented and easily explained. A voice portal is built in Chapter 14, "Building a Voice Portal." The portal contains a game, a news section, and a variant of the classic AI program, *Eliza*. The applications are controlled with voice recognition only, and all replies are made with synthesized speech. The applications and the portal's main page are listed and, as with all examples in the book, the code is discussed. In Chapter 15, "Building Multimedia Applications" the implementation of multimedia messages that contain text, graphics, samples and ring tones are listed. The Multimedia Messaging Service (MMS), content types, character sets, clipping, animations and so forth are discussed. Maps and the representation of real world objects are discussed in Chapter 16, "Using SVG with GML to Represent the Real World." Chapter 16 also shows how a representation in GML can be transformed to a representation in SVG and displayed on a device with a small display. In Chapter 17, "Mobile Commerce" ECML is used to provide a merchant with all the information necessary to complete a business transaction with a mobile customer. Chapter 17 also shows how a document can be given a digital signature to authorize a business transaction.

Part IV begins with Chapter 18, "Proximity." This chapter explains how technologies such as POIX and NVML might be used to provide routes and the position of a user who is traveling in a vehicle. Chapter 19, "The Future of Personalization" explains the foundations of future IM and presence applications. Concepts such as watchers and instant inboxes are discussed. In Chapter 20, "Instant Messaging and Presence Applications" XML based query languages that might become recommendations (or influence upcoming recommendations) are presented and discussed, in particular XQuery. Finally, Chapter 21, "Databases" deals with the CSS Mobile 1.0 profile. The chapter also gives an insight into how calendar information and business cards are represented today and how they might be represented in the future, using XML.

XML in a Wireless Context

OBJECTIVES

▶ Be familiar with the most common operating systems and platforms that execute wireless applications

▶ Be familiar with the terms 2G, 2.5G, 3G, and 4G

▶ On a high level, understand how Bluetooth works

▶ Understand how the HTTP and OBEX protocols work

▶ Write well-formed and valid XML documents

▶ Create and use schemas

▶ Write XML documents that use links, paths, and namespaces

Introduction to Wireless Applications

IN THIS CHAPTER:

Application Types

Applications

Exactly what is a wireless application? Wireless applications execute on wireless devices, which are normally small handheld devices, and these have a number of limitations. The most obvious limitation is that handheld devices are small and a small display cannot display the same amount of information (simultaneously) as a large one. Small devices usually also have a limited amount of memory available, which makes it impossible to incorporate all the fine features that are part of a full-fledged web browser.

Application Types

In the following sections, you learn which types of wireless applications are most common today and which will be available in the near future. You learn about the characteristics of these applications, as well as their advantages and problems. Then you look at the applications themselves, discover which platforms they execute on, and learn the main differences between the platforms.

Connected All the Time

Using so-called packet-switched networks, users get the impression they are connected all the time. This is because the network sends packets of data only when a need occurs to transfer information. As opposed to traditional circuit-switched data communication, which dials a number to set up a connection before data can be exchanged, this method of communicating is practical for several reasons.

Suddenly, the user can use browser-based services, as if they were menus in the phone or on the personal data assistant (PDA). The vendors and operators can provide an additional set of virtual menus, which can be tailor-made for the customer, depending on which category of user he represents for them. An interesting consequence is menus and functionality, which previously were associated with the manufacturers of the operating system, and can be provided by vendors and operators by changing the address of the start page in the phone or PDA's browser.

Instant Messaging and Presence

Instant messaging and presence applications belong to a category of applications which lets the user stay in contact with friends or colleagues in a special way. Instant messaging and presence applications usually provide an integrated environment for messaging, presence polling, security, naming, chat, and other functions. By providing this integrated environment for, say, a work group, no one needs to care about which tools he or she should use to communicate with her colleagues. And the user also needn't have to care about details, such as encryption, presence polling, and where the colleague is currently located.

Instant Messaging

The idea behind instant messaging and presence applications is that the user should be able to reach one of his colleagues instantly, preferably wherever they are at that moment. For this purpose, e-mail fills an important function. Because few people are always online in front of their desktop computers, however, instant messaging involves alternative interfaces, such as i-mode and Wireless Application Protocol (WAP), as well as the capability to send brief notes, such as Short Message Service (SMS) messages. In the future, you might also see instant messaging and presence applications, which support the Enhanced Messaging Service (EMS) and the Multimedia Messaging Service (MMS). These services are described in detail in Chapter 2.

Presence

The capability to sense if one or several colleagues are present is an important feature of instant messaging (IM) and presence applications. The application should handle the polling of presence automatically. Alternative solutions exist but, in general, the user should be able to add and remove colleagues from a hot list, which is supervised. A colleague can signal that he or she is present and the application then broadcasts this information to all users in the work group. With wireless technologies, like Bluetooth or Wireless LAN, it's possible to create IM and presence applications, which indicate presence as the user moves into the proximity of the radio interface. Other solutions exist to the presence problem. For example, the application can sense if the user touches the computer keyboard or the mouse.

Location

While presence functions indicate if a user is present, nothing says they should provide the location of the user. However, this is an attribute that could be helpful for a group of people who are traveling and need to stay updated about where people are located. The hot list would then display not only presence information, but also information about the colleague's location.

Security

An application that continuously transmits information about where people in a project are located is vulnerable to industrial espionage. Therefore, IM and presence applications always need to provide functions for secure communication. This means they should provide functions for encryption of the exchanged messages information that is exchanged about the work group as a whole and the user information. Another important aspect is authentication. It should be impossible for an unauthorized person to connect with an arbitrary work group. Integrity issues are also involved. An unauthorized person shouldn't be able to filter any of the messages that are exchanged in the work group.

Naming

Instant messaging and presence applications have various solutions for naming and addressing colleagues in the work group. Ultimately, it should be possible to establish a communication link to a colleague by referring to a nickname, no matter where the colleague's located. The application could send an SMS, EMS, or MMS message if the colleague isn't in front of the computer, but has the phone switched on. This scenario requires that the application keep track of not only where the user is located, but also at which addresses the user can be reached and which of these addresses should be used for each message.

Chat

Instant messaging isn't only about sending short messages like SMS messages and e-mails, it also involves chat functionality. Users who collaborate in work groups over the Internet need to reach each other instantly, regardless of where the colleague is located and which type of device he's using. However, single short messages usually aren't sufficient to maintain a creative discussion and to exchange a number of messages in a relatively short time.

SMS servers use a technique called *store-and-forward,* which means when one user sends a message to another user, the message is first stored on a server before being forwarded to the receiver. If the server is extremely busy, then it can take some time before the message reaches the receiver. Even short delays, like 20 seconds, are too long for normal conversion. Useful chat services, therefore, must be implemented using infrastructure and techniques other than message centers and store-and-forward solutions. In 3G networks, like UMTS and WCDMA networks, it's possible to send messages between clients without passing through a persistent server. Therefore, instant messaging and presence applications are more suitable for these types of networks.

The second generation of mobile networks doesn't support user-to-user messaging without passing through a store-and-forward server.

Personalization

Personalization, personalized services, and personalized applications are often mentioned in white papers and tutorials, which are related to wireless devices and the mobile Internet. This means the end user should be able to make drastic changes to how the application behaves with respect to content (what information is displayed), input (how the user may interact), and output (how the information is presented).

Display Size

At the moment, the market is invaded by a number of small handheld devices, which are different when it comes to their display capabilities. Some phones are only capable of displaying two or three lines of text with 12 characters on each line. Phones equipped with larger displays are usually capable of displaying from 5–7 lines of text, each with 15–20 characters per line. Personal digital assistants usually have a slightly larger display, but they're far from the capabilities of a desktop computer.

Applications that are designed to work in a web browser, as well as on a PDA and a phone, need to implement basic features to personalize the display. An application that lets the user subscribe to stock rates could display the rate only if the user accesses the service over SMS on a limited phone. Another user who uses a PDA could get some additional information, such as a simple graph, which shows the progress of stock for the past few days, while the PC user could access even more data and more advanced graphs.

Personalization with respect to the display size can be done in various ways. You learn about the nuts-and-bolts of this in Part 3, including using cascading style sheets (CSS) and XSL transformations.

Fonts

Fonts can add a lot to the impression of the service and sometimes even make messages easier to read. When different font styles are used, you can also reduce the chance that a message is being misinterpreted. For example, boldface or italics can be used to emphasize certain words. Personalized applications will try to make the message as clear as possible regarding the device you're using.

Simple phones seldom use more than one font face, but some use two or three different sizes. If neither i-mode nor WAP is supported, and if no support exists for a messaging service other than SMS, then there's no need to support different font sizes or more than one font face. SMS is a pure message service, which doesn't even deal with the ASCII character set, and the technology doesn't let you change fonts. The character set in SMS is even smaller than that; it allows only characters, numbers, and a few additional characters.

Personalized applications take font sizes into account. For example, an application that lets the user subscribe to news can present the headline in a slightly bigger font and provide an abstract of the article in a smaller font. However, if the user accesses the application over SMS using the simplest phone, then it might only distribute the headline and not the abstract.

Graphic Capabilities

A picture is worth a thousand words. This, of course, is only true if the device has graphic capabilities. Personalized wireless applications, which are designed to run on a variety of handheld devices, must enable the user to specify which graphical capabilities the device has. I-mode supports color pictures in the GIF format, while only the second generation of WAP (not the first generation) supports color pictures (for example, through the MMS service, supported by WAP 2.0). The sizes of the pictures also must be adapted to the terminal. A Pocket PC can display larger images than a small phone.

If the application uses SMS to distribute content to the user, then only Nokia phones can receive pictures over the smart messaging protocol. Other manufacturers need to use EMS, for example, to send and receive pictures. The EMS automatically concatenates SMS messages, so pictures can be packaged into, and sent in, a number of SMS messages.

Consequently, applications that support a variety of terminals must enable the user to make personal adjustments concerning how the content looks on the user's terminal from a graphical point of view.

Input Device

Some phones and PDAs have limited input devices. Phones are usually equipped with a numeric keyboard, which is primarily used with one hand to dial a phone number. A technology called T9 makes it easier for the user to type words on a phone keyboard. The *T9* technology uses a database stored in the phone's memory to predict what the user is going to type. Then the user needn't press a key several times to type a certain character. Although technologies such as T9 make typing letters on a phone keyboard easier, certain applications that are executed on phones require substantial text input from the user. A solution to this problem can be to let the user make personalized settings, like shortcuts. These shortcuts can use certain keys to trigger longer text sentences, such as "I'll contact you tomorrow," "Best regards," or the user's full name, which are often used in e-mail or messaging applications.

Personalized shortcuts can be made accessible even for users of devices, which are equipped with handwriting recognition and smaller keyboards.

Memory Capabilities

A huge variety exists in memory capacities, so when handheld devices are compared, the user should be able to make personal adjustments concerning how much memory the application consumes. The size of the graphics can be reduced either by reducing the number of colors or removing some of the more space-consuming graphics and replacing them with text. Applications that are downloaded from a server can be split into several units where the rare and seldom-used functions are kept in a separate module which is downloaded when needed. Messaging applications that distribute the content in SMS, EMS, or MMS messages can split the content into several messages. The user can then be given the freedom to make personal adjustments concerning how the information should be split.

Palm devices have different memory capabilities depending on the model and how much the user has expanded it. The same applies to the Pocket PC platform, where many devices are equipped with 8 or 16MB of primary memory. However, it's quite common with 64MB or more. Phones that execute Java 2 ME applications have a maximum size for the *Jar* file, which is the file in which the application is packaged and transported over the network. This maximum size varies among vendors, models, and even operators. The user can then be given the option to download and run the application as one physical unit or to download the main application, without all the fancy functions, if the handheld device has limited memory capabilities. Additional modules would then be downloaded on demand.

Message Length

When content is distributed to the handheld device in SMS or EMS messages. Then the application, which generates the content, should always let the user specify what the message should contain. The SMS only allows between 150 and 160 characters of text. Consequently, if the user doesn't prefer a space-consuming headline, but is well aware of the message's content, more room can be given for the actual message. Abbreviations can also be used but, in most cases, they should be optional and personalized.

The EMS sends the content in several SMS messages, which are automatically concatenated by the receiver's phone before it's displayed. The number of SMS messages that can be concatenated varies among different manufacturers, so this is also a factor the user should be able to adjust.

Language

Personalized settings involve regional settings and language settings. A news service that retrieves information from the Internet and sends it in a message to a wireless subscriber could discard messages that aren't related to a certain region or in the user's language. Applications that are downloaded and executed on the handheld device could be made available in several languages. The basic idea with personalized applications, though, is the user shouldn't have to specify this every time an application is downloaded or executed. Instead, it should be set in a preferences menu—for example, at the web site on which the application is accessed—and then the transformation should be done automatically. In Part 3, you see a similar scenario where XSL transformations are used to provide different versions of the same source material. Profiles can also be stored on the device, and the idea with profiles, such as UAProf and the CSS Mobile Profile, is that the user shouldn't have to specify the preferences on every site he or she visits.

Time and Date Representation

A number of variations exist on how time and date should be displayed. In this global world, an application that's accessed over the Web can be available for a huge number of countries with different traditions concerning how time and date should be expressed. In certain regions of the world, time is expressed using the 12-hour clock (A.M. and P.M.), while in other regions, such as Europe, the 24-hour clock system is used (22:00 equals 10 P.M.). Dates can be written using the "-" character as a separator. 1967-01-11 means January 11, 1967 and, in other regions, 67/01/11 or 67/11/01 has the same meaning. Through personal settings, the user could be allowed to specify which syntax should be used.

Time

The latest version of the second generation of mobile networks (often referred to as *2.5G*) and the third generation of mobile networks use packet switching as the means for data communication. Users get the impression they're always online with their handheld devices (as long as they're switched on). No charges per minute occur; instead, charges are per byte, kilobyte, or megabyte, or there's a flat rate, depending on the operator's charging policies, so it's no problem for the user to stay connected all the time. Data that consumes bytes in the network are transferred as soon as the user accesses the Web, a service, or a portal in the mobile network. With this evolution, we'll most likely have our phones and PDAs switched on and connected for a long time before the batteries are recharged. Standby times of up to hundreds of hours aren't uncommon for small handheld devices.

In the global economy, applications can be provided worldwide by small service providers located anywhere. Time differences then become a bit of a problem. Applications and messages can be distributed from the service provider in the daytime, which is in the middle of the night for a large number of users. First, the user doesn't want her phone to beep in the middle of the night just because a subscribed newsletter has arrived. Second, in many cases, the user wants these messages to arrive when he or she's doing something else, such as sitting on a commuter train or having a 10 A.M. coffee break at work.

To reach as many users as possible, the application or the framework that surrounds the application could make it possible for the user to personalize how the content should be displayed on his handheld device and how it should be distributed, as well as when it should be distributed to the user at his local time.

Location

Location-based services and applications retrieve the position of the user and use it to add a certain extra value to the application. This added value can result in a simplified navigation menu or more relevant information for the end user.

An application that provides a city map, needn't provide an interface in which the user types in where she is located. Consequently, that menu or input field can be removed and more room can be given for maps on the handheld device's small display. Other uses exist as well. A search engine might determine the user searches for local information and can then immediately remove hits that aren't relevant regarding the user's current location.

Client-Centric Solutions

The *client-centric solution* to location-based services assumes the client takes all the initiatives to retrieve the position from a server in the mobile network. This server is usually provided by the network operator and the application developers are given an interface, which can be used to send queries about the user's position. However, there are handheld devices with built-in GPS receivers. In this case, the application would have to execute calls toward an API in the client to retrieve the position of the user, meaning the operator of the mobile network wouldn't be involved at all. GPS modules are available for the Pocket PC platform. The major telecommunication vendors provide servers that can be used by applications to determine the position.

Server-Centric Solutions

The *server-centric solution* to location-based services assumes the client doesn't take any implicit actions into account to retrieve location-based information. Instead, a gateway provided by the operator works as the source of information. In this case, the location data is sent back in response messages, together with the results of ordinary HTTP requests and web documents.

Physical Retrieval

As an application developer, you don't have to determine exactly how the position of the user is retrieved. This is a task for the operator. Several techniques retrieve the position. GPS was mentioned earlier, but there are also techniques such as observed time difference that use so-called triangulation methods to compute the user's current location.

The Location Interoperability Forum (LIF) and the Wireless Application Protocol Forum are working on interfaces for application developers that can be used by an application to send queries about the user's current position. This is a complicated problem because a number of security issues exist that must be taken into account, such as encryption, authenticity, and integrity. Encrypting the user and position information should be possible. LIF has developed the Mobile Location Profile (MLP), which can be used to retrieve the position of a mobile subscriber. If you'd like to know more about MLP, you can download the specification from http://www.locationforum.org.

Synchronization

An interesting category of wireless applications is the application that synchronizes and transfers data. Synchronization is, rather, a feature that is part of some application and lets the user transfer information between, say, a handheld device and a computer. Synchronization protocols are important for wireless handheld devices because these devices are often used as complements to desktop computers and laptops. When information, like a new phone number, is stored on one of these devices, the user needs to transfer this change to the other device and continue from there.

SyncML

SyncML has emerged as a reasonably new technology that can be used to synchronize a handheld device with a computer. The synchronized data is put in a so-called object store. With SyncML, the content of the object store in the handheld device is compared with the content of the computer's object store to determine which type of synchronization should be performed.

Content in one object store can be replaced by the content of the other. Ordinary updates, rather than replacements, can also be executed. One-way updates and two-way updates can be performed. A *one-way update* means SyncML only checks if one of the devices has any information that should be transferred to the other. A *two-way update* means SyncML checks to see if a need exists to perform updates in both directions, transferring information from and to each of the two synchronized devices. With SyncML, you can also perform a *slow update,* which means all records in the object stores are examined in detail to see which updates should be performed.

Synchronized Data

With synchronization technologies, like SyncML, updates to the address book on your handheld device can easily be transferred to the desktop computer. Also, e-mails can be transferred from the desktop computer to the handheld device for offline reading. However, more applications of synchronization technologies exist than that. It's possible to work on text documents on two different devices and let the synchronization protocol keep track of which device used to perform the latest updates.

Formats

With SyncML, the capability of the device that will be part of the synchronization is described in an XML document, referred to as the *device information document.* This information is necessary for the sync engine to verify that the information, which is exchanged, is compatible with the other device.

The representation protocol of SyncML deals with how the information exchanged is represented as one or several XML documents. In addition to the mandatory calendar, contacts, and message types, ordinary MIME types are supported by SyncML. This means practically any registered Multipurpose Internet Mail Extensions (MIME) type can be exchanged over the SyncML protocol.

The Actual Exchange

You can synchronize wireless handheld devices in several ways when it comes to the actual networks used for transfer. Bluetooth supports synchronization. The Bluetooth specifications include a profile that specifies how the synchronization between a handheld device and a PC should be carried out. Unfortunately, no programming APIs are specified yet for Bluetooth. At press time, consequently, programmers can't write applications that use the synchronization features of Bluetooth without using hardware emulators and the APIs implemented for these specific platforms.

The IrDA protocol developed by the Infrared Data Association is still the way to go when it comes to synchronization and transfer of data in general. Most PCs and many handheld devices are equipped with hardware and software that supports infrared communication over IrDA.

Applications

So far so good. You've seen a number of different types of applications. But which execution environment and frameworks do the applications require?

Environments

A number of environments, frameworks, and application platforms are out there that are used to execute wireless applications and are more or less popular in different regions of the world.

Pocket PCs use a small version of Microsoft Windows to run applications and several advantages are inherent with this approach. Developers can use similar development tools as are used when they develop applications for desktop computers that run Windows. In addition, the Pocket PC platform includes a smaller version of the Internet Explorer, which can browse ordinary HTML and XHTML pages. A number of browser plug-ins, like Flash, are also available for this platform.

The Symbian platform and the EPOC operating system are used by smartphones like Ericsson's R380 and PDAs from Psion. Applications developed for the Symbian platform have access to a number of powerful APIs, such as databases, interfaces to the address book, and a set of graphical user-interface elements. The Opera web browser is available for this platform, which makes it possible to browse ordinary web applications on these devices.

Sun Microsystems created Java 2 Platform, Micro Edition (J2ME) technology. Part of this platform is the Connected, Limited Device Configuration and the Mobile Information Device Profile (MIDP). This configuration and profile together form a basis for the development of *MIDlets,* which are extremely small applications transferred in Jar files from a server to a wireless handheld device, like a mobile phone. The applications are then executed in the phone's virtual machine. Because a virtual machine is used, it doesn't matter which microprocessor the manufacturer uses for the phone. As long as they're compliant with the instruction set of the virtual machine, and follow the configuration and the profile, they'll be compatible.

Mobile Linux isn't a single solution or product, but a collective name for a number of projects that aim to put the Linux operating system on small handheld devices. With Linux on your handheld, it's possible to run powerful applications developed using ordinary UNIX development tools, such as Perl and Python scripts and advanced programming languages. Browsers are also available for Linux, which should be possible to port for this platform. And work is in progress that tries to get handwriting recognition applications running on Mobile Linux.

Palm OS is an operating system that executes applications created for the Palm handheld PDAs and other handheld devices that use this operating system, such as Visor Handspring devices. A number of different languages can be used to develop applications for this platform and a set of powerful APIs can be used by application developers to create different types of applications.

Links to Web Sites

The following is a list of links to various technologies mentioned in this chapter. Note, many of these sites have a links section with pointers to many more sites.

Pocket PC   You can read more about Pocket PC development at http://www.pocketpc.com and http://www.pocketprojects.com.

Symbian   Information about the Symbian platform and application development on the Symbian platform can be obtained from http://www.symbian.com and http:// www.symbiandevnet.com.

Opera Software A/S   Opera Software A/S is the company behind the Opera web browser. You can obtain more information about the browser at http://www.opera.com.

Java 2 ME   Sun Microsystems has plenty of information about Java 2 ME, MID Profile, and CLDC at http://java.sun.com/j2me, http://java.sun.com/products/midp, and http://java.sun.com/products/cldc.

Mobile Linux   If you're interested in Mobile Linux, check the site at http://www.mobilelinux.com.

Palm OS   Information about the Palm OS, Palm, and Visor Handspring devices can be obtained from http://www.palm.com and http://www.visor.com.

Applications

The applications that execute in the previously mentioned environments are created and executed in slightly different ways.

Ordinary HTML applications can be executed on the Pocket PC platform and on the Symbian/EPOC platform. If these applications are developed with certain restrictions in mind, such as limited display size, limited available memory, and limitations for input of large amounts of text, then you can create web applications that can be executed using an ordinary desktop computer, as well as a wireless handheld device over a mobile network. The number of plug-ins is much less on the handheld device than on the distributions of the browser software, which is adapted for desktop computers. If you need to stay compatible with as many devices as possible, you should implement your application in HTML or XHTML only, with a minimum number of plug-ins or scripts. If you need to use scripts, you should use server-side scripts, like JSP or ASP.

Applications that are implemented using XHTML are compatible with desktop computers as well as browsers for the Pocket PC platform and for the Symbian/ EPOC platform (Opera) as well as the next generation of WAP phones. WAP Next Generation –(NG) is based on XHTML Basic, which is a subset of the elements and attributes of XHTML. Although most tags are still there, there are no frames and no support for file uploads in forms. Displaying frames on a small handheld device could create problems, so the choice to exclude frames from the XHTML Basic specification was probably good.

Using the Quartz reference implementation, developers can create applications for handheld devices, which use a tablet as the input device and execute on the Symbian platform. Quartz applications can be developed using Java and C++; development kits are available.

MIDlets, which execute on the Java 2 ME platform, are programmed in Java, but there's also a substantial support for XML in Java. XML parsers are available, which means Java applications can request XML documents from a server, and then parse the information therein and use it for arbitrary purposes.

Applications for Palm OS can be downloaded from the Web, and then run offline on the PDA. In addition, another type of application, called a *web-clipping application,* is based around a GUI, which has the look and feel of a web application. The application gets access to the Internet through a special gateway provided by Palm. The gateway receives the request, which has been packed in a compact form before it entered the gateway, and then forwards it on to the Internet as an ordinary HTTP request. As the gateway gets a response, the returned web page is packed and transferred to the Palm device.

Wireless Networks and Protocols

IN THIS CHAPTER:

Network Topologies

Circuit Switching and Packet Switching

From the First to the Fourth Generation

Protocols and Interfaces

This chapter describes how some of the networks, interfaces, and protocols beneath your XML application are used. Because you're an XML developer, you don't have to know exactly how the underlying networks and protocols work; you can probably manage fine without that knowledge. You're more interested in learning how to use the wireless XML-based technologies described in this book, but it won't hurt to have a reasonably good understanding of wireless networks, which protocols are used, and which standards exist. This chapter gives you a quick and easy understanding of the most common acronyms and concepts in the wireless world.

Network Topologies

Different network topologies exist, depending on which type of network you're using. Some networks only allow a certain number of wireless devices to connect to it at the same time, others don't have any limitations, while still other networks are wireless, and are tailor-made for communication between two devices only.

Cells

In a cellular network, base stations communicate with the phones to send and transmit voice or data. *Cell planning* is an activity led by the operator when the system is deployed. During this process, the operator decides where the base stations should be positioned to obtain the maximum coverage. Few operators provide 100 percent coverage in all areas of the region in which they operate. Typically, they provide less good coverage in areas where few people live to maximize income and reduce expense.

When the coverage is computed, the concept of cells is used. The cells are hexagons, which are put together in a mosaic-like pattern, as in the following illustration.

Each cell corresponds to a base station, which is positioned in the middle of the cell. The radio signal of the base station is strong enough to reach the border of the cell—in all directions—and even across the border and a bit into the nearby cell. Consequently, a slight overlap exists for neighbor cells.

Handover

As the user moves around in the cellular network and travels across the border from one cell to another, *handover* occurs. The mobile telephony system then has to maintain the call and, at the same time, switch over to another cell and its associated base station.

Mobile telephony systems have a built-in hysteresis for determining when to hand off a call. When the user moves from a cell to another, the system doesn't change its base station immediately as the user crosses the border of the cell. Instead, the system performs a handover when the user has reached reasonably far into the cell to draw the conclusion that the user has definitely entered a new cell. If the user returned to the old cell, then he or she would have to get a certain distance into the cell before handover would occur again. Consequently, some resistance exists before handover occurs. If the system didn't have a hysteresis, then it would behave chaotically if a user stood still at the border between two cells.

Wireless Does Not Imply Mobility

Although cellular systems, like CDMA and GSM, are mobile systems, networks exist that are wireless only and don't allow users to move around. The Bluetooth technology has a limited range for radio signals and this range has been adapted for home use. Wireless LANs have a longer range, but still only for a local area. The technology of Infrared Data Associations (IrDA) is created for devices that are within a short and visible range. If some of the devices move a bit, then communication might fail.

Circuit Switching and Packet Switching

In practice, you can communicate in mobile telephone networks in two different ways: by circuit-switched data communication and a packet-switched network.

Circuit-switched Networks

Circuit-switched data communication first reserves, and then sets up, a connection in the network. Once done, the exchange of data can start—for example, transferring an XML file to a phone or PDA. When the transfer is complete, the circuit is disconnected.

Circuit-Switched Data (CSD) is based on the reservation of a certain path through the network, which can be used for data communication (or voice). This way of communicating has both advantages and disadvantages. The advantage is, once the connection is set up, the user is guaranteed a certain bandwidth until he disconnects. The disadvantage is this: the time it takes to set up the connection can be several seconds, which is too long for services when the user wants an immediate answer to a query. If the user doesn't disconnect immediately after the service has been used, he or she is charged for that period.

Bit rates are usually around 9,600 bits per second, but some techniques can boost the data rate, such as High-Speed Circuit-Switched Data (HSCSD).

Packet-switched Networks

Packet-switched communication can be considered the opposite of circuit-switched communication. *Packet switching* doesn't require a time-consuming setup and teardown phase before and after the transmission. Instead, the user gets the feeling he or she is always online because when the exchange of data starts, packets are sent immediately. No need occurs to establish a physical connection through the network.

The document that's transferred (for example, an XML document) is first divided into small packets. Each packet is then sent from one node (computer) to another, in a sequence, before it reaches the final destination. In each node, the packet is queued for delivery, which means it's stored, in some sense, before it's delivered to the next node on its way to the final destination. At the destination, all the packets are put together again to form the original document.

PDC-P, which is the Japanese system for i-mode, is a packet-switched mobile telephony system. The General Packet Radio Service (GPRS) is also a packet-switched mobile telephony system, as are the third generation systems UMTS (W-CDMA) and CDMA2000.

From the First to the Fourth Generation

In the media, there's often talk about the third and, sometimes, the fourth generation of mobile telephony systems. Let's quickly go through the mobile telephony history from the first to the fourth generation, so you can see what's happened and what you can expect in the future. We're now experiencing improvements of the second generation of mobile telephony systems. Soon, the operators will start to use the third generation, and around 2010, the fourth generation will start being used.

The First Generation

The first generation of mobile telephony systems was deployed during the eighties. In America, one of them was Advanced Mobile Phone System (AMPS), and in northern Europe, the first generation of mobile telephony systems was represented by the Nordic Mobile Telephony System (NMT). A system called Total Access Communication System (TACS) was also used in some areas.

These systems were analog. The call and the connections weren't carrying bits and bytes, but continuous analog signals. The result was a diminished sound quality (diminished because the audio was often more noisy and sensitive to interference) and the connections were much more sensitive to interference. Some people claim these systems, including the phones, had a higher electromagnetic radiation, but there hasn't been enough research done to prove this.

If you were unlucky, you could sometimes get a bad connection where hearing what the other person said was difficult. In comparison, the second generation of mobile telephony systems provided a dramatic improvement of the sound quality.

2G

The second generation of mobile telephony systems (2G) replaced AMPS, TACS, and NMT with Code Division Multiple Access (CDMA), Digital AMPS (D-AMPS), and Global System for Mobile Communications (GSM). CDMA is mostly used in America, while GSM is used in the European countries. In Japan, a Personal Digital Communications (PDC) network was deployed.

The second generation of mobile telephony systems is used often today. Small and lightweight phones with high standby times are available for the masses. Prices have come down, so mobile phones are now affordable. Compared to the first generation, the second is a big success for the operators because the first generation attracted mostly businessmen and companies. Messaging was introduced in the second generation of systems. The GSM standard includes the Short Message Service (SMS), which has been a tremendous success.

2.5G

The media often mentions 2.5G. It represents packet-switched mobile telephony systems that aren't providing broadband speed, as in the UMTS and CDMA 2000 systems (see 3G in the following). These networks can be seen as the late second generation of mobile networks. The 2.5G systems are supposed to give the user a feeling that she's connected all the time, as soon as she switches on the phone. While 2G systems use

Circuit-Switched Data (CSD) to transfer data, 2.5G systems send the data in packets. The end user is charged only for the number of bytes sent or received (or a flat rate), rather than being charged on a time basis, as is the case with the 2G systems and CSD.

The speed provided by 2.5G systems, like the General Packet Radio Service (GPRS), is slower than the third generation provides, but it's still good enough to transfer XML files (like an XHTML page with a few icons or small pictures) to a phone without any irritating delays. In practice, the user will experience around 20 kilobits per second, but in theory, GPRS can provide up to hundreds of kilobits per second. The reason there's both a theoretical speed and a practical speed is that the data is sent in time slots. If many users are online at the same time, fewer time slots are available to share, and the transfer rate is reduced for each user.

In Japan, 2.5G is represented by Personal Digital Communications Packet (PDC-P). The operator NTT DoCoMo introduced PDC-P in 1999, together with the i-mode service. With i-mode, pages can be accessed from the operator's portal or from the Internet using an i-mode phone.

3G

3G is represented by CDMA2000 and Universal Mobile Telephony System (UMTS). The latter is also sometimes referred to as W-CDMA (Wideband CDMA). Because CDMA2000 is more or less an upgrade from existing CDMA networks, many American operators are considering this path. In Europe, most of the major mobile telephony operators are building UMTS networks. UMTS and CDMA2000 systems are incompatible, but work is underway to resolve this. A number of players are involved in this activity.

Organizations

A number of organizations were involved in the creation of the 3G specifications and interoperability certifications for these networks. IMT-2000, 3GPP, and 3GPP2 play the most central roles.

IMT-2000   Because CDMA2000 and UMTS are different systems with different architectures, a need exists to coordinate the development and standardization of interfaces, protocols, and capabilities to achieve a global interoperable standard for 3G. This rather difficult task is taken care of by International Mobile Telecommunications-2000 (IMT-2000). Led by the International Telecommunication Union, IMT-2000 is also responsible for the integration of wireline and wireless networks.

IMT-2000 consists of a number of external organizations that work together with ITU. Radio aspects, such as how the radio interfaces should be designed, and network aspects, such as call control, are issues studied by the IMT-2000. The goal is that standards such as CDMA2000 and W-CDMA will be compatible in the end.

3GPP—The 3G Partnership Project   One of the many roles of the 3G Partnership Project, 3GPP, is to approve the specifications of the 3G core networks and be part of their creation. 3GPP works with the 3G networks that are migrated to from GSM. Practically, this means UMTS.

A project coordination group and a number of technical specification groups exist. The technical specification groups work with the specification of the radio access network, the core network, terminals, and services that will be provided by the network.

3GPP2—The 3G Partnership Project 2   While the 3G Partnership Project focuses on 3G systems that are evolving from the GSM world (UMTS), 3GPP2 is similar to the 3GPP project, but focuses on the North American 3G system standard, CDMA2000. In addition, a number of Japanese, Korean, and Chinese groups are involved in the 3GPP2 project.

The 3G Systems

The 3G networks deliver around 2MB per second over the air at the maximum rate. However, if the user is sitting in a moving vehicle, like a car or a train, it becomes much harder for the network to maintain these speeds. In cases like these, the requirements are much lower. Nevertheless, the 3G networks must be able to deliver at least 144 Kbps. This is fair enough for high-quality video telephony applications. Because the screens are much smaller than on a desktop computer, the bandwidth requirements become much smaller.

Both UMTS (W-CDMA) and CDMA2000 use a technology referred to as Code Division Multiple Access. CDMA provides a high-bit rate and has a good resistance against interference.

UTRAN and RAN   The radio access network in UMTS is called UMTS Terrestrial Radio Access Network (UTRAN). In CDMA2000, UTRAN is simply referred to as Radio Access Network (RAN). The RANs are connected to *core networks,* which contain all the equipment, which, in turn, controls the whole system. A problem with the 3G RANs is they aren't compatible and this is what IMT-2000 is trying to solve.

Ultimately, users will be able to travel seamlessly between these two radio networks without losing the connection.

Services   Because the 3G networks provide bit rates up to 2 Mbps, video telephony becomes possible. At the same time, prices for web cameras drop and manufacturers already have web cameras for sale that can be attached to your mobile phone and send pictures. The bit rate of 2 Mbps is theoretical, though, but even if a busy network provides 10 percent of that bandwidth, you'll get around four times as much bandwidth as on a traditional modem connection.

Multimedia messaging is already being introduced in the 2.5G networks. Because a packet-switched 2.5G network is the basis for the migration toward 3G, you can expect enhanced versions of this service in the 3G networks, which behave the same, but with an improved quality. The Multimedia Messaging Service (MMS), mentioned in this chapter and described more in detail in Chapters 6 and 15, is one of the messaging services that might become popular. This depends on which terminals appear on the market, however. The phone manufacturers focus on multimedia-based presentations that use the SMIL framework, but there are competitors who see an opportunity to increase the use of their proprietary multimedia players and formats. These competitors will probably do whatever they can to get their software into the 3G terminals.

XML in 3G

The 3G Partnership projects don't specify exactly how the services in the 3G networks shall be implemented. This is a good choice because technology evolves and it would be a less appropriate solution if they dictated that a certain markup language or application programming interface (API) should be used to implement particular services. Instead, the specifications focus on service capabilities rather than formats. The service capabilities define which capabilities you should expect from 3G network equipment, like streaming video at a certain bandwidth with a certain loss rate.

However, certain applications that are going to execute on top of the 3G networks have already been pointed out by manufacturers and operators. Most of the operators that run the infrastructure and the manufacturers of 3G handsets support the introduction of XHTML in WAP-NG. *WAP-NG* is version 2.0 of the Wireless Application Protocol. Infrastructure for WAP-NG will also be required to run MMS, which is aimed primarily for the 3G networks and handsets. MMS is the Multimedia Messaging Protocol that can be used to send rich multimedia presentations, including audio and video, to MMS-compatible handheld devices. Because SyncML is part of WAP-NG, lives a life on its own, and is already being incorporated into handsets by leading manufacturers, you can expect SyncML will also play a major role. This is because the organization has hundreds of handset manufacturers and software development companies involved in the initiative.

4G

Some claim the fourth generation (4G) of mobile telephony networks will be deployed around ten years after 3G because trials were made with the 3G networks ten years after the introduction of the 2G networks. Consequently, the standardization work hasn't begun yet. The only activities carried out today occur in the research laboratories of the manufacturers and the operators. The reason the fourth generation is so far away is not only does the technical architecture need to be developed, but all manufacturers also have to agree on a set of technologies that are interoperable. Let's look quickly at the trends and possible future scenarios.

The Wireless LAN Cloud

The Wireless LAN standard is formally referred to as 802.11b, but it's also known as WiFi. Wireless LANs are like clouds of wireless networks, which can be used immediately as you approach the proximity of the network. The radio signals for a Wireless LAN reach around 1,000 feet outdoors. There's also a technology that can be used for Internet telephony, called H.323, which can be used with the traditional TCP/IP protocol stack to set up telephone calls. Imagine building a city network that would consist of a number of Wireless LANs, placed side by side, and support seamless handover. This is a possible scenario for the fourth generation of mobile telephony networks.

The handsets would then have to support the traditional TCP/IP protocol stack in combination with future updates of the H.323 and 802.11 protocols. They would become more like computer terminals, running your favorite operating system. If you want to upgrade the software that makes the calls to support new supplementary services, you could simply download a new version of the protocol, just as you're downloading software for your computer.

A fair chance exists that the fourth generation of mobile telephony networks won't distinguish between ordinary computers and handheld "phones." A phone might be the same thing as a small computer with telecommunication software, which can also execute on an ordinary desktop computer. Moore's Law says that processor speed doubles every 12 to 18 months. This would mean that ten years from now, we'll have processors in our phones at least 64 times faster than today's speeds. Thus, the problems that must be solved for 4G aren't necessarily related to processor speed, but rather to finding standards that can unite a majority of the manufacturers.

IPv6

With version 6 of the Internet Protocol (IP), it's possible to address more hosts in the network than what's possible with version 4. In version 4 of the IP, which is used to a high degree today, the address space is too small and the Internet is running out of addresses. As we get close to the fourth generation of mobile telephony networks, we'll end up in an impossible situation if the network is based on IP version 4. The market for mobile phones is exploding and people will stay connected to the Internet using devices other than desktop computers. With the introduction of packet-switched networks, these devices will be constantly online. Consequently, a need for a larger address space will definitely exist and, here, version 6 of the IP is the solution.

32 Bits   The address space in version 6 of the IP is increased from the four 8-bit numbers, which are separated by a dot (32 bits), to 128 bits. This address space is more than enough, even if every person on Earth owned hundreds of devices and were connected to the Internet simultaneously. The addresses in version 6 of IP are written as eight 16-bit hexadecimal numbers, separated by a colon. It may look like this:

```
0F0F:1234:3333:44FF:0030:CFF9:922D:AB30
```

Each hexadecimal number has a 16-bit range. $16 \times 8 = 128$ bits.

Flows   IP version 6 also supports flow control. Almost the same way as a phone call is set up in a circuit-switched network, flows guarantee the packets, or certain amounts of the packets, are delivered to the receiver in real-time. Suddenly, version 6 of the IP becomes less connectionless compared to version 4 of IP, which is completely connectionless. The priority field of IP version 6 can be set to a value, which indicates the type of traffic the packet is carrying. Routers can check this field to determine in which order the packets should be forwarded.

Protocols and Interfaces

Protocols were, in the old days, associated with a set of signals that were sent over the network in a certain order. The protocol was the document, or the set of documents, that described in which order the signals should be sent and which replies should be expected.

Lately, the concept of a communication protocol has become much wider and more general. A communication protocol could be seen as a set of rules for how the communication should be performed. This doesn't necessarily mean the communication for a certain protocol is carried out sending signals. The mechanism to exchange information could be the invocation of methods or the existence of a set of files that describe, on a conceptual level, what should be done and in what order. Work is in progress at the World Wide Web Consortium (W3C) to define an XML-based framework for the exchange of messages. Other examples exist that indicate the telecommunication industry will move toward XML-based formats, even for low-level communication mechanisms like RPC.

Interfaces are going through the same changes. In the beginning, an interface was a collection of methods or procedures that should be called by a program using a certain set of well-defined parameters and in a certain order. The second step was to create a defined language, like the Interface Definition Language (IDL). Now these applications are adopting the XML standard. Examples are SyncML, which has the content specified in XML, and RPC, a communication mechanism and an interface.

Protocol Stacks

In technical literature, the term "protocol stack" or "stack" is often mentioned. Communicating systems are often built using a layered or stacked architecture. These systems are implemented so a fundamental, low-level routine manages the most raw form of communication with the other device. Another program uses this routine and you could then say the latter program resides on top of the low-level routine. This program is called by another and the chain of calls can then be seen as a stack.

Application Protocols

Application protocols operate just below the application. The purpose is to provide the application with fundamental mechanisms, such as low-level communication, so it can perform the tasks it's intended to perform.

Some of the most interesting application protocols now are i-mode, WAP-NG, SyncML, and Palm Web Clippings. Let's look closely at them to see how they work and how they're related to XML, if at all.

i-mode

The *i-mode* service was introduced in Japan in 1998. To introduce the service, the operator upgraded the existing PDC network to a packet-switched version of it, called *PDC-P.* Consequently, the infrastructure for the i-mode service uses proprietary protocols in the wireless network, but packets can travel through a gateway. The gateway then performs a protocol conversion so web pages written in cHTML can be retrieved from the wired Internet and transferred back to the handset. A similar solution, using a gateway that performs protocol conversion, is implemented in WAP.

The Portal   Built into the infrastructure of i-mode is the *portal,* which is located at the operator's domain. A user can access information from the portal without leaving the mobile network. External i-mode pages can also be accessed, and then a gateway performs a protocol conversion from the PDC-P protocol stack to the traditional Internet protocol stack and vice versa. This is similar to how the WAP gateway works.

Markup   The i-mode services can easily be created using compact HTML (cHTML), which is an extended subset of plain old HTML. Some elements have been removed from HTML and a few new ones have been added. In i-mode, there is also support for color graphics with GIF files. JPEG files aren't supported. JPEG is a compressed file format, which requires substantial amounts of computational power to render. Mobile phones are often limited in terms of CPU power. To provide support for JPEG pictures, the phones would have to spend serious amounts of their resources on just the decompression of a picture. This isn't a good idea because the operating system of phones often has to deal with other things as well, such as tracking incoming phone calls, displaying the battery power, and the field strength of the radio network.

WAP-NG (WAP Next Generation)

Version 1 of WAP is getting old. It didn't support color graphics, animation, or multimedia. Still WAP 1.*x* was important because it represents the first generation of mobile Internet access. As such, operators, manufacturers, and users learned a lot. But some of its drawbacks were the lack of multimedia support, the introduction of a new markup language, which was incompatible with ordinary web pages, and it wasn't possible to synchronize personal information stored in the phone with a computer.

WAP-NG is equivalent to WAP 2.0, which was released in early August 2001. Some of the key features of WAP-NG are worth a close look because they meet customers' and developers' demand for high-quality services.

MMS

The Multimedia Messaging Service (MMS) is part of the WAP-NG architecture. With the MMS, multimedia documents can be pushed on to an MMS-compatible phone or PDA, the same way SMS messages are sent from one phone to another. Messages can also be created by a server on the Internet and sent to MMS-compatible devices. MMS can be seen as the messaging service for mobile networks of the third (and late second) generation.

MMS can transfer audio, video, and text, but the most exciting feature for you as a wireless XML developer is the use of the Synchronized Multimedia Integration Language (SMIL). *SMIL* has been used for a while on desktop computers to create rich multimedia presentations and now it's being adopted by the wireless community. With SMIL, you can specify how the multimedia content should be replayed on the wireless 3G devices. Typically, the SMIL file includes tags that specify when an audio clip should be played, in which order pictures should be displayed, when text should be displayed, where the text should be displayed, which fonts should be used, and so forth. In short, the SMIL file is the glue for all the components in your wireless multimedia presentation.

One of the strengths of SMIL is that you can design your SMIL presentations on an ordinary desktop computer before they're tested on the wireless devices. Emulators are available for the most popular browsers.

Chapter 6 is an introduction to SMIL with many examples that illustrate how media can be replayed and synchronized. In Chapter 21, a more advanced example demonstrates the power of SMIL in combination with database technology.

Synchronization of PIM Data

A new feature of WAP-NG is the support for synchronization of Personal Information Management data. SyncML can be used to synchronize the Personal Information Management data in wireless devices, which are WAP-NG-compatible. However, SyncML isn't necessarily dependent on WAP-NG. Wireless handheld devices are on the market that support SyncML, but not WAP-NG.

Because SyncML is based on XML, it has several advantages. It can easily produce content specifications using ordinary elements and attributes, and can also be used in combination with the Wireless Binary XML format to boost the synchronization speed. The actual specification for what will be synchronized is then compressed and optimized for wireless transfer over the air.

WAP-NG compatible phones that are equipped with Bluetooth technology might be a killer configuration for several reasons. Then SyncML cannot only be compressed with WBXML, but the actual synchronization can also be initiated automatically when one of the Bluetooth devices enters the proximity of the other.

SyncML cannot only be used to synchronize the content of two devices. It can also be used as an ordinary information transfer service when you need to load personal information onto a device. A SyncML primer is provided in Chapter 10.

XHTML

XHTML Basic is included in the WAP-NG specifications. It can be used as the markup language for the next generation of wireless handheld terminals (for 2.5G and 3G). XHTML Basic is a subset of XHTML. The modularization of XHTML, which is a W3C recommendation, resulted in a number of modules that can be combined in various ways to produce languages within the XHTML family. XHTML Basic includes all the so-called core modules. The core modules implement elementary elements and attributes, such as the HTML, paragraph, and title elements.

If a manufacturer wants to extend the set of elements and attributes of XHTML Basic, the remaining modules of XHTML can be incorporated easily. Consequently, XHTML gives the manufacturers a controlled way of adding new features that are compatible with their handsets and still conform to the basic requirements of XHTML Basic.

The modularized framework of XHTML is based on HTML4. HTML4 was rewritten as an XML application to take advantage of all things in which an XML implementation results. All features in HTML4 are supported. XHTML Basic, though, was created for small information appliances, so several features—support for frames, scripting, advanced tables, and advanced forms—had to be omitted.

SyncML

SyncML is a protocol that makes it possible for applications to perform synchronization functions. An e-mail application can use the SyncML framework to transfer messages or virtual business cards, which have been attached to e-mails, to other clients. The purpose is so you can keep the same information on your mobile phone or other handheld device as on your desktop computer, without having to type in the same information several times. If you had to duplicate all the information, like phone numbers and addresses, there's a fair chance you'd make mistakes. It would also take some time to duplicate everything. In Chapter 10, SyncML is described in detail.

SyncML messages can be transferred over HTTP, WSP, and OBEX. As you know, *HTTP* is the protocol used by traditional web browsers to browse HTML documents. *WSP* is the implementation of HTTP for the Wireless Application Protocol. HTTP is also used by the WAP gateway to retrieve WAP content. The client uses WSP for communication in the wireless network and the task of the gateway is to convert these messages to HTTP and pass them on, using the Internet. The Object Exchange (OBEX) protocol is used to transfer objects, such as virtual business cards, over connections, like a Bluetooth radio connection or an IrDA connection.

The SyncML Representation Protocol   SyncML messages are exchanged between the devices that are going to be synchronized. A SyncML message is represented as an XML file. The XML file contains a header and a body section. The version number and other details of the document can be specified in the header, while the body section contains the actual commands that are going to be interpreted and executed by the synchronization engine. Only elements—not attributes—are used in the markup language for the SyncML representation protocol.

A document instance of the SyncML representation might look like this:

```
<SyncML>
  <SyncHdr>
    <VerDTD>1.0</VerDTD>
    <VerProto>SyncML/1.0</VerProto>
    <SessionID>42</SessionID>
    ...
  </SyncHdr>
  <SyncBody>
    <Put>
      <Item>
        ...
      </Item>
    </Put>
    <Get>
      <CmdID>2308</CmdID>
      <Item>
        ...
      </Item>
    </Get>
    <Copy>
      <CmdID>2307</CmdID>
      <Item>
        ...
      </Item>
    </Copy>
```

```
</SyncBody>
</SyncML>
```

The header must include some mandatory information, like which version of the DTD is being used and which version of the SyncML representation protocol is used. A unique identifier for the synchronization session must also be supplied by the device that initiates the synchronization. We go through all these details in Chapter 10.

In the body of the XML document, it's possible to specify a number of commands. Each command has a start and an end tag, and between the tags, details concerning what the command will do are specified. Data can be added, replaced, and deleted. It's also possible to supply a command, which performs a search for data of a certain type. Multiple commands can be grouped into an atomic command, so either all commands are executed or none of them are, if some wouldn't be possible to execute on the target device.

Device Information   Before two devices can be synchronized, they need to exchange information that describes their features and capabilities. SyncML device information documents are used for that. Here's an example:

```
<DevInf xmlns='syncml:devinf'>
<VerDTD>1.0</VerDTD>
<DevId>09348209482039</DevId>
<DevTyp>handheld</DevTyp>
<DataStore>
  <SourceRef>./pim/calendar</SourceRef>
  <Rx-Pref>
    <CTType>text/vcalendar</CTType>
    <VerCT>1.0</VerCT>
  </Rx-Pref>
  <Rx>
    <CTType>text/vcalendar</CTType>
    <VerCT>1.0</VerCT>
  </Rx>
  <Tx-Pref>
    <CTType>text/vcalendar</CTType>
    <VerCT>1.0</VerCT>
  </Tx-Pref>
  <Tx>
    <CTType>text/vcalendar</CTType>
    <VerCT>1.0</VerCT>
  </Tx>
```

```
<SyncCap>
    <SyncType>1</SyncType>  <!-- One-way sync from client. -->
</SyncCap>
</DataStore>
</DevInf>
```

In this case, the device information document describes a handheld device that can send and receive calendar data. The DevTyp element is used to specify which type of device the document describes. A number of different device types are defined in SyncML. We look more closely at them in Chapter 10.

As you can see in the previous example, the document has an introductory section followed by the DataStore element, which includes the actual capabilities of the device. The SourceRef element contains an identifier, which specifies where the calendar data can be found. Rx-Pref denotes which format and version the device *prefers* to receive, while Rx denotes which format and version the device *can* receive. Tx-Pref and Tx are similar, but with respect to the transmission of calendar data. Finally, the SyncCap element describes the actual synchronization capabilities of the data store. In this case, we specified the device is capable of performing a two-way synchronization. This is indicated by the number 1, which occurs between the SyncType tags. Seven different synchronization types exist—numbered 1 thru 7—which you learn more about in Chapter 10.

Network Protocols

Transport and network protocols are called by the lower routines of the applications or the Application Programming Interfaces. For you, as an XML developer, this happens more or less automatically, such as when an XML file is transferred over HTTP, WSP, or OBEX. Nevertheless, it can be good to know what's really happening when your file is transferred over, say, an infrared connection from your handheld to your desktop computer or vice versa. Let's look at the more common network protocols used in a wireless context.

HTTP

You're probably familiar with the Hypertext Transfer Protocol (HTTP), which is the network protocol that transfers hypertext files from a server to a client browser. In addition, HTTP can be used to transfer information from a browser to a server.

WSP, the session protocol used in WAP-NG, is, in fact, an implementation of HTTP 1.1 for wireless networks with a limited bandwidth, like the second generation of mobile telephony networks (for example, GSM and CDMA-One). Consequently,

XHTML Basic documents are transferred over both HTTP and WSP in WAP-NG. The W3C is also working on XML mappings for HTTP. This means it will be possible to transform the HTTP protocol into an XML representation. In addition, the HTTP protocol is used in i-mode, between the gateway and the Internet, when i-mode pages are retrieved from the traditional Internet. These are a few good reasons for you, as an XML developer, to know the basics of HTTP and how it operates.

Requests and Responses   Messages are a central part of the HTTP protocol and two different types of HTTP messages exist: requests and responses. Requests are sent from the client, typically a browser, and responses are sent back from the server, as a result from the request.

HTTP Requests   An HTTP Request starts with a method, a request-URI (the web address), and the version number for HTTP. The method specifies which type of HTTP Request it is. GET Requests may transfer additional parameters sent with the HTTP Request, appended at the end of the request-URI. For example, if the web server runs a server script that expects two parameters, then the address can look like this:

```
http://www.server.com?para1=abc&para2=def
```

The actual request-line then looks like this:

```
GET http://www.server.com?para1=abc&para2=def HTTP/1.1
```

Spaces are between GET, the address, and HTTP/1.1. HTTP/1.1 is the version number. In this case, we're using HTTP 1.1.

After the previous request-line is a series of header-lines. Additional information about the request and the requested document can be given to the web server here. Each header contains a parameter followed by a colon and the value of that parameter. A number of parameters are defined in the HTTP protocol and new ones might be defined in the future. Here's an example:

```
From: james@example.com
User-Agent: CoolBrowser/1.23
```

Someone who has the e-mail address james@example.com is carrying out the request for the document. He uses version 1.21 of CoolBrowser. If we assume no additional headers are transferred in the request, then the complete request can look something like this:

```
GET http://www.server.com?para1=abc&para2=def HTTP/1.1
From: james@example.com
User-Agent: CoolBrowser/1.23
```

A carriage return line and line feed should appear after each line and, after the last line, there should be an extra carriage return line feed. The first indicates the end of the last line and the second ends the whole request.

HTTP Responses   When the request has been sent from the client and the server has received it, then a response message is sent back with the requested document. Response messages are similar to request messages because they start with a status-line, which is similar to the request-line, and then a number of response headers may follow, similar to how the request headers occur after the request-line.

The status-line contains the HTTP version, a status code, and a reason phrase. Here is an example:

```
HTTP/1.1 404 Not found
```

This status-line is transferred when the server, for some reason, couldn't find (or generate) the requested document. As you can see, the version number is there, like in the request-line. It is followed by a code and some text. The text is a textual description for the code. In this case, the code 404 means the document couldn't be found. In fact, all error codes start with the numeral 4. All successful responses have codes that begin with 2. The code 200 means OK.

An arbitrary number of header lines follow the status-line. As with the header lines in the request, each line ends with a carriage return line feed. Here's an example that shows how the header lines in the response could look:

```
Location: http://www.goHereInstead.example.com
```

If the status-code in the status-line is 301, this is an indication the document has moved permanently. It's then possible to use a response header, like the previous one, which specifies the new location for the document. When the client browser receives the previous response, it can redirect the user automatically to the new address.

The response-header should indicate which content type the document has. Assume an ordinary web page was requested. If it was transferred back successfully, the status-code could be 200 and the content-type would be text/html. Then the response header, which describes the content, would include the following line:

```
Content-Type: text/html
```

The date header makes it possible for the server to specify when the document was generated. In most cases, the server must include this information in the response message. It could look like this:

```
Date: Fri, 15 Jul 2001 17:03 GMT+1
```

Web servers should also reply with the total length of the content, for example, a web page that's transferred back as the result of the request. Then the header line could look like this.

```
Content-Length: 4943
```

This is the length, in bytes, of the message body. The message body follows after all the header lines in the response.

Assume we want to retrieve the web page, which is located at http:// page.example.com/page.html. Then the following request could be sent from the client to the server:

```
GET http://page.example.com/page.html HTTP/1.1
From: james@example.com
User-Agent: CoolBrowser/1.23
```

The server could then reply with the following message to the client browser:

```
HTTP/1.1 200 OK
Date: Fri, 15 Jul 2001 17:03 GMT+1
Content-Type: text/html
Content-Length: 1895

<html>
...
</html>
```

The client browser would check the status-response to see that everything is okay. The header lines would be used to extract the message body and to show it for the user.

Judging from the date field, the server is located somewhere in middle Europe. GMT means Greenwich Mean Time (UK). GMT+1 is slightly east of the United Kingdom, for example, Berlin, Vienna, Rome, or Stockholm. In the United States and Canada, GMT-6 is Central Time and GMT-7 is Mountain Time. All dates and time stamps in HTTP are represented in relation to how far off Greenwich Mean Time they are. See the previous example, which indicates the date and time is GMT plus one hour.

WSP

The Wireless Session Protocol (WSP) provides HTTP 1.1 functionality so, in a certain sense, WSP can be seen as the WAP equivalent of HTTP. But it also incorporates new features, such as a session model. The reason a new protocol was created—to transfer content to the handheld devices—was that mobile networks of the second generation have a much more narrow bandwidth and behave slightly different. Critics argue, however, that the traditional HTTP protocol should have been used, so WAP-NG also includes a Wireless profiled verson of HTTP.

The semantics of WSP are more or less the same as HTTP and you should expect a similar behavior. The XML documents, like XHTML pages, however, are tokenized by a gateway in the network before they're sent over WSP from the origin server to the handheld devices. This is a neat little feature, which you learn about in Chapter 8. Basically, the XML document is broken down into tokens that represent common elements and text strings, like http and <p>. These elements are given codes, which are shorter than their ASCII representation. Consequently, the documents are made more compact and can be transferred faster over the air. WBXML encoding also allows the error checking to be done on the gateway and reduces the load on the mobile device.

IP

The IP is the network protocol, which is used on the Internet. The IP is also the network protocol used in the first and next generation of WAP, and by the gateways in the i-mode service. The third generation of mobile networks, like CDMA2000 and UMTS, make use of the IP.

Addresses   The IP makes it possible to send packets of data from a host, like a phone or handheld PC, to another device, which also executes the IP. All hosts that are connected to the Internet have a unique 32-bit address. The address is written as four 8-bit numbers with a dot between each number. It might look like this:

```
111.222.033.044
```

The first 8-bit number can be used to determine which class the complete address belongs to by checking the leftmost bits of the number. Five classes of IP addresses are defined: class A, B, C, D, and E. Addresses that belong to class A are given to large organizations and companies, and addresses that belong to class B are given to medium-sized ones. Class C addresses belong to small organizations and companies. Class D should be used to send multicast packets and class E is reserved for experimental use. *Multicast packets* are packets that are distributed to a large number of receivers, as opposed to a single receiver.

Packets   When an application needs to send something over the network, it passes on the data to the lower-level communication API. In most cases, the Transmission Control Protocol (TCP) or the Universal Datagram Protocol (UDP) receives the data and performs segmentation to create a number of small packets of the data. Each packet is sent to the destination, using the IP. When the host receives the packets, they're reassembled in the right order because not all packets may choose the same path in the network to reach the destination.

Each IP packet contains a header and a data section. In the header, the sender's and the receiver's IP addresses are specified. The protocol field in the header also tells the receiver which protocol the packet should be passed on to. If it was sent using UDP, then the receiver should know this so it can be passed on to the receiver's UDP routines, rather than some other protocol like TCP. When the protocol above IP, like UDP or TCP, has reassembled the packets into its original format, it is passed on to the application.

IrDA

Infrared Data Association (IrDA) is a communication protocol stack that's tailor-made for communication over infrared connections. IrDA includes a physical layer that handles the raw infrared signaling, such as the conversion of bytes into a serial stream of infrared bits, and how these bits will be communicated to guarantee a low latency, and so forth.

IrLAP   The Link Access Protocol (LAP) of IrDA resides just above the physical layer and provides the link management protocol with connection-oriented and connection-less services. This protocol also includes a discovery mechanism (a discovery feature is also part of the Bluetooth technology).

IrLMP   The Link Management Protocol (LMP) in IrDA resides above the IrLAP layer. It uses the connection and connection-less services provided by IrLAP to implement features like multiplexing of several links on to a physical infrared connection and basic information access services.

OBEX

The Object Exchange (OBEX) protocol is part of the IrDA protocol stack and can be used as an alternative to HTTP because both these protocols can be used to transfer arbitrary documents between two devices. As mentioned earlier, SyncML messages can be transferred over OBEX, as well as HTTP and its WAP-NG equivalent, WSP.

Although OBEX can be used as the communication protocol for infrared links, using the OBEX framework in other environments is also possible. Bluetooth, which is a radio interface, includes an OBEX implementation.

Transfers   With OBEX, simple objects can be pushed from one device to another using an operation called PUT. In this case, the provider of the object sends it to the inbox of the receiving device. Objects can also be pulled from one device to another using the GET operation. In this case, a client requests an object, like a phone book entry, and the serving device responds with the object. When objects are pushed, the sender can include information about the object, such as which type of object it is. This is only a guideline for the receiver, though. The sender cannot expect the receiver to handle the object in a certain way. It isn't possible for the sender to force a certain behavior on to the receiver. If this were the case, a potential security problem would exist and it could be possible for the sender to force the receiver to behave in a certain way when particular types of objects were received.

Similar to HTTP, the client can send a request and the server responds with a result code and the document. The result codes are the same as with HTTP. For example, if the server cannot find the requested document, it responds with the result code 404 (Not Found). If no problems exist at all, the server typically replies with the result code 200 (OK, Success) and the document.

Capabilities   The capabilities of an OBEX device are described in a *capability object,* which is a bit similar to the SyncML device information document. The capability object can include information such as which object types the device can respond with in a GET operation or which types the device can receive in a PUT operation. Not all formats in OBEX are based on XML, but the capability object is one of them. The following is a sample capability object, which can send and receive text files. The client can also use the folder browsing service of OBEX to see which text files are stored on the device.

```
<General>
  <SN>345987539487</SN>
  <Manufacturer>WireLess Corp.</Manufacturer>
  <Model>XE-419 Pro</Model>
  <SW-Info Version="1.02"/>
</General>
<Inbox-Objects>
  <Object Type="text/plain" Name-Ext="txt"/>
```

```
</Inbox-Objects>
<Service-Objects>
  <Object Type="text/plain" Name-Exit="txt"/>
  <Object Type="x-obex/folder-listing"
    UUID="F9EC7BC4-953C-11d2-984E-525400DC9E09"/>
</Service-Objects>
<Services>
  <Folder-Browsing UUID="F9EC7BC4-953C-11d2-984E-525400DC9E09">
    <IrDA Target="F9EC7BC4-953C-11d2-984E-525400DC9E09"/>
  </Folder-Browsing>
</Services>
```

A general section is followed by a declaration of the inbox objects, the service objects, and the supported services. In the general section, the serial number for the device is specified. This is a unique serial number, which has been defined by the manufacturer of the device. It must always be specified, as must the name of the manufacturer and the model. Specifying the version of the software the device executes is optional. In this case, it's set to 1.02.

The Inbox-Objects section specifies which types of objects the device can receive in a PUT operation. Our device can receive simple text files that have the file extension txt.

In the Service-Objects section, you can specify which types of objects the device can provide a client with in a GET operation. In our case, this section is the same as for the inbox. Our device can provide clients with text files.

The last section deals with the services the device supports. OBEX includes a Folder-Browsing service, which is specified according to the previous example. In OBEX, all services have a unique identifier. The Folder-Browsing service of OBEX is identified by setting the UUID to the previous code. When the client that retrieved the object capability file wants to use the service, it refers to that code in the request.

Folders   The Folder-Browsing service transfers information about a folder in a folder listing, which is an XML file. The *folder listing* can contain a number of folder and file specifications. When a device browses the file system of another device over OBEX, it typically sends a GET request and receives a response, which contains a status code and the folder listing, provided that the status code wasn't negative. Files and folders can be specified with a number of attributes, such as size, modification date, creation date, read, write, and delete permissions. The client can tell the server which attributes should be included in the folder listing. For example, the client might not be interested in the creation date. Then, it's possible for the server to omit that information in the response.

Here is a sample folder listing:

```
<?xml version="1.0"?>
<!DOCTYPE folder-listing SYSTEM "obex-folder-listing.dtd">
<folder-listing version="1.0">
  <parent-folder/>
  <folder name="misc"/>
  <file name="myText.txt" size="1040"/>
  <file name="tech4.txt" size="25920"/>
  <file name="notes.txt" size="15829"/>
</folder-listing>
```

As you can see, the encoding can be kept quite simple. There's a top-level element, the folder-listing. It can contain three types of elements: folders, files, and a parent-folder. The parent-folder element is used only if the folder isn't the top-level folder of the device's file system. The parent-folder element indicates it's possible to walk one step further up in the file system tree. Folders are specified using the element with the same name and files are specified with the file element. A number of optional attributes exist for these elements, although, we've only used one of them, the size element. The name attribute must always be specified together with the file and the folder elements.

IrMC

In addition to OBEX, another protocol at the top of the IrDA stack is worth some attention: the Infrared Mobile Communications (IrMC) protocol. With IrMC, it's not only possible to transfer objects using the OBEX protocol, but also to set up phone calls and establish two-way audio channels over the infrared connection. A real-time clock object is also defined, which can be transferred as an object over the infrared link. All objects in the IrMC framework can be transferred using the OBEX framework, as previously described.

Call Control   IrMC can be used to set up phone calls. For this purpose, a common command set and a system-oriented command set are available. The *common command set* includes generic commands that apply to mobile telephony networks in general. For specific systems, like GSM and PDC, *system-oriented command sets* exist that apply to these systems only. The commands are sent between the actual phone and a computer. Consequently, it's possible to create a computer application that uses the infrared link to answer calls, reject incoming calls, terminate calls, select phone book memory storage, or dial directly from the phone book.

Commands are entered using the plain old AT command syntax, which is used to program computer modems and telecommunication equipment in general.

Two-way Audio Audio can be transferred over an infrared connection using the IrMC framework. In this case, the application uses a service interface, which provides connect, disconnect, control, and audio services.

First, the user establishes a Real-time Transfer Control Protocol connection by calling the connection service. The RTCON transfers the actual audio, as well as the telephone call control data, which travels on the same infrared link as the audio. When the connection is established, the control service can be used to send control data for the telephone call, such as dial or answer. When the necessary call control information is transferred and a call is established, the audio service can be used to transmit the actual audio data over the infrared link. When the phone call is ready to be terminated, the call control service is used again to terminate the call and, finally, the disconnect service can be used to disconnect the RTCON connection.

The Real-time Clock A *real-time clock* is available as an object within the IrMC framework. Using OBEX, the clock can be transferred, using the PUT and GET operations, as mentioned earlier in the OBEX section. The real-time clock should have the name telecom/rtc.txt, which works as identification for the receiving device to verify the sender is sending only the real-time clock object and nothing else (like a text file).

Bluetooth

Bluetooth is a short-range radio-link or radio-interface that can be used for communication between a wide range of device types. Bluetooth is a low-power technology, which is continuously being refined by the Bluetooth Special Interests Group (SIG). The Bluetooth SIG has more than 1,000 members who support the development of the wireless communication framework. The development of Bluetooth was initiated by five companies: Ericsson Mobile Communications AB, Intel Corporation, International Business Machines Corporation, Nokia Corporation, and Toshiba Corporation.

With Bluetooth, devices like a printer can communicate with your PC using a wireless radio link. When you want to connect the printer temporarily to a WAP phone, a Java-enabled phone, or a personal digital assistant to print an e-mail message, assign the printer as a slave to the same wireless network as the WAP phone and print without the hassle of changing cables.

Bluetooth supports traditional file transfers. This means, for example, Word documents or audio files can be transferred between two devices. Also, a framework exists for the exchange of objects between devices. Typically, an object could be a virtual visit card, such as those commonly attached to e-mail messages, a virtual calendar, or a note.

Because Ericsson and Nokia are two of the five founders of the Bluetooth SIG, it's no surprise that much of the Bluetooth technology involves the interaction between phones and accessories consumers might want to interface with their phones. For example, a Bluetooth-enabled mobile phone can be used as a 3-in-1 phone. Under certain circumstances, the phone can be used as one of the devices in a home intercom system. Also possible is to use the Public Service Telephone Network (PSTN) and, when you're on the move, the phone automatically switches to the mobile network. The Bluetooth specifications also standardize how the communication between a headset and a mobile phone should be implemented.

All the previously mentioned use cases are referred to as profiles in the Bluetooth specifications. Each *profile* specifies a common use case that's likely to be implemented by a manufacturer. However, some use cases could be regarded as common, but they still aren't specified. Many uses for wireless communication exist and the specifications cannot outline every single use case.

Network Elements   A Bluetooth device can operate as a master or a slave, or as both master and slave if it's connected to several networks. We're dealing with a point-to-point architecture in the two-node case or a point-to-multipoint architecture when more than two devices are connected. Up to seven active slaves can be connected to one master in a network. More than seven devices can be connected to the network, but all cannot be active at the same time. Instead, they need to be parked or put on hold. A *network* element (a Bluetooth device) can be released from one network and can join another by asking permission to join the network. In this case, an authentication occurs and the user needs to input a password to be authenticated.

In the simplest case, one master is connected to one or more slaves. The network is referred to as a *piconet*. When two or more of these networks share a device, the network is referred to as a *scatternet*. At least one of the Bluetooth devices is then connected to more than one piconet.

Speed   The total available bit rate is 1 Mbps. The master and all the slaves share this bandwidth by sending the packets in well-defined time slots.

A Bluetooth network can consist of three simultaneous audio channels, each with a bit rate of 64 Kbps. If, instead, the system is used to exchange asynchronous data messages, then a bit rate of up to 723.2 Kbps can be used. In this case, however, the communication is asymmetric, meaning we get 723.2 Kbps in only one direction. In the reverse direction, we have to accept a maximum 57.6 Kbps. If we need symmetry and maximum speed, then the Bluetooth system can communicate at 433.9 Kbps in each direction.

Getting Information about which Devices Are in Range   Before a connection is established according to the previous scheme, a Bluetooth device might need to find out which other devices are close enough to the radio link to establish a connection.

Inquiry Messages   The device sends out signals at different frequencies and the message sent is an inquiry message, which is communicated over different frequencies to catch the attention of all devices within range. The inquiry message contains a description of which kind of devices the sender wants to contact. Listening devices of this type that have allowed themselves to be discovered can then send a response message back to the sender. If the inquiry message contains the General Inquiry Access Code (GIAC), all listeners can respond. Also available are 63 Dedicated Inquiry Access Codes (DIACs) that all call for specific types of devices.

Minimizing Replies   The purpose of using inquiry access codes is to minimize the number of replies when a unit scans for in-range devices. In other words, the device that sends out the inquiry message must be able to narrow the amount of potential responders to devices of a certain kind only—for example, printers or phones—to avoid chaos and congestion on the Bluetooth piconet.

Links   The Bluetooth devices connected in the piconet communicate over links. A *link* can be synchronous and connection-oriented or it can be asynchronous, and then operate in a connection-less manner. In plaintext, this means connection-oriented links have a setup and a teardown phase, while the connection-less links send packets immediately without the explicit setup of a connection in advance.

SCO Links   The Synchronous Connection-Oriented (SCO) links can be used for streaming audio. In many cases, these connections are set up to or from a phone and another device. SCO links can be used to transfer radio and music channels, implement a wireless doorbell, or be used to transfer synthetic speech. They can also be used for graphics or other streaming media. The SCO link, which is set up between the master and a slave, reserves a number of slots to obtain the necessary bandwidth for the application. A master can handle up to three SCO links to the same slave or to different slaves. A slave only supports up to two links if they originate from different masters.

ACL Links   The Asynchronous Connection-Less (ACL) link is used for data communications. Packets are sent over this link without the need to set up a connection. Typically, an ACL link is used for file transfers. Unlike the SCO link, the ACL link supports retransmission of data. Because SCO links reserve slots, ACL links have to use the remaining slots to send packets.

Held, Active, and Parked Devices   When a Bluetooth device has been connected to a piconet, it can operate in one of several well-defined modes, each specifying if, when, and how the device can communicate with the other devices in the network.

Hold Mode   When a Bluetooth device operates in Hold mode, it stays in this state for a certain time and can neither send nor receive any data packets over an ACL link during that time. When the hold time has expired, the device wakes up and can again start to communicate over an ACL link. When the device is put on hold, it keeps its 3-bit address in the network, so when it wakes up again, the communication can continue. This mode can be used as a low-power Stand by mode to disconnect the device temporarily from the communication, but still keeps it connected to the network with a unique address.

Active Mode   In Active mode, the device is active on the piconet as a master or one of the seven slaves, communicating over SCO and ACL links.

Parked Mode   Similar to Hold mode, this state is also a low-power state but, in this case, the device loses its 3-bit address and needs to retrieve a new active member address when it becomes active again. When the device is going to be operated in this mode, it instead receives two 8-bit addresses (a parked member address, and an access request address). This first address keeps track of all parked devices, while the second is used when the device leaves the parked state to become active. The device isn't active in the piconet communication in this state, with the exception that it can listen to broadcast messages.

A slave can unpark itself or be unparked by the master device. Hundreds of parked devices can exist, but there can only be eight devices active in the piconet. Still, a parked device can quickly become active and vice versa.

Bluetooth XML Applications   So far, the Bluetooth specifications don't contain any programming APIs. Instead, the manufacturers have provided the specification for the radio interface and a number of profiles that describe, on a high level, how a chosen set of use cases should be designed. In the near future, Java APIs will be available for the access and control of Bluetooth devices. The final specifications will be finished early in 2002 and will be based around the Java 2 Micro Edition (J2ME) technology.

Transferring XML files, like XHTML code, SyncML device information, SMIL applications, and so forth is possible with the file transfer functions in the Bluetooth serial port profile, the generic object exchange profile, or the synchronization profile. OBEX is also supported by Bluetooth.

CHAPTER 3

XML Primer

IN THIS CHAPTER:

XML Documents

Validation

Namespaces

Schemas

Links

Paths

XSL Transformations

Cascading Style Sheets

XML Tools

T his chapter is an introduction to XML and XML-related technologies. My goal was to keep the chapter as basic as possible and still provide explanations for the most important topics, such as DTDs, schemas, and XSL transformations.

If you have prior experience using XML in design, you might want to take a quick look to make certain you understood everything. For those of you new to XML, please take your time when you read this chapter. These pages are important and many of the examples, which are provided later in the book, assume you understood everything in this chapter.

First, you learn about XML documents in general and how they're structured. Then you learn about grammars and the Bachus-Naur Form. Next, document type definitions are explained, followed by a guide through the world of schemas. You then learn to perform basic XSL transformations, which convert one XML document to another and, finally, you learn about cascading style sheets and how documents can be formatted.

XML Documents

XML documents can be useful because an application developer might have the freedom to decide which tags and attributes should be used. The designer more or less specifies her own language, consisting of elements (tags) and attributes, which are tailor-made for a specific application. A complete framework that can handle this language is already there. This framework can handle XML files and other tools that can be used to store, communicate, convert, administrate, and extract information from the XML documents.

Although we use the term "document," the application, which generates or retrieves the document, doesn't necessarily have to provide a file. The document can be generated by a server script and transferred as a stream of data to the wireless device, where the relevant information is extracted and used by the application immediately. In fact, for small handheld devices, this might be the case, rather than receiving the document and storing it on disk. In many cases, small handheld devices have a limited amount of memory to play with. If the document is generated on the server rather than retrieved from a file system, and if the handheld device processes and uses it immediately as it's received, the word document is less relevant because we aren't talking about files any longer. This is simply a convenience.

When XML files are transferred over the network, the receiver needs to know which type of application the file should be associated with. Otherwise, it's impossible to launch an appropriate application automatically that uses the file. For this purpose, content types are used.

Content Types

Content types are specified at the beginning of the stream of data sent over the network and represent the file. The content type isn't part of the document, but is inserted before the actual document in the HTTP response message, as you learned in Chapter 2. It works as an identification mechanism for the receiver. A request for an ordinary HTML page might look like this.

```
HTTP/1.1 200 OK
Date: Sun, 22 Jul 2001 12:04:37 GMT
Server: Apache/Unix (Unix)
Last-Modified: Tue, 28 Nov 2000 09:03:49 GMT
Content-Length: 1512
Connection: close
Content-Type: text/html

<HTML>
...
</HTML>
```

Usually, the receiver first checks the content type to see which type of document was received, and then the appropriate application is launched. Ordinary HTML files use the content type text/html, as in the previous example. For JPEG images, the content type image/jpeg is reserved. GIF pictures use the image/gif type. The content type contains a type and a subtype. In the previous example, the general type is text and the subtype is HTML. The second field—the subtype—can be seen as a specialization of the left field, which is more general.

A request for a 25,671 bytes long JPEG image may generate a response that looks like this.

```
HTTP/1.1 200 OK
Date: Sun, 22 Jul 2001 12:45:35 GMT
Server: Apache/Unix (Unix)
Last-Modified: Mon, 31 May 1999 08:03:18 GMT
Content-Length: 25671
Connection: close
Content-Type: image/jpeg
...
```

XML files have different content types, depending on the application. XHTML documents use the content type application/xhtml+xml. The *subtype* indicates the document is both an XML document and an XHTML document because XHTML is an application of XML. The same goes for all applications of XML. The subtype can use the suffix +xml to indicate it's an XML application. Another example is the Scalable Vector Graphics (SVG). SVG, which you can read about in this book, uses the content type image/svg+xml.

To make the web server transfer the right content types when users access documents, the types are set up by the web master or the system administrator. This is usually a trivial task, like associating file extensions with the content types, in a text file or a dialog box. Nevertheless, if the content types haven't been defined, your application might not work with the wireless devices that check the content type before the appropriate actions are taken.

Elements, Tags, and Attributes

An XML document contains *elements,* which are made up of tags, and *attributes,* which are associated with elements.

Elements and Tags

There are elements that have a content model and there are elements that are empty. Elements that might have content are made up of a start tag and an end tag. It might look like this:

```
<p>This is an example.</p>
```

The previous XHTML code uses the paragraph and the line break elements. The paragraph element contains a start tag <p> and an end tag </p>. In XML, all elements must be closed, which means the end tag </p> must not be left out. If the end tag is left out, then the XML code isn't well formed. The whole idea with XML is it should be possible to process the documents using standard tools and environments. A requirement for this is to make the documents well formed. Here's another example:

```
<p>This is an <b>example.</p></b>
```

This is also forbidden in XML. In the previous example, the end tags for the b element and the p element have been swapped. Consequently, the b element is closed outside the scope of the paragraph, which isn't allowed. Be sure to format your XML documents so they become symmetric. You can use indentation to make it easier to read. Then it also becomes easier to check manually that the document is well formed. Here's an example that uses indentation to make the code easier to read.

```
<body>
  <p>Here are many
    <em>fine</em>
    examples.
  </p>
</body>
```

When spaces are inserted, as in the previous document, it becomes much easier to match the start tags with the end tags. But there are also empty elements in XML. Empty elements don't have a content model associated with them. That is, they don't have a start tag, an end tag, and content in between. Instead, empty elements make use of a single tag only.

Empty elements have the slash just before the greater-than symbol (>) instead of an end tag, where the slash occurs just after the less-than symbol (<). Empty elements are used when the markup should describe an instruction, rather than working as a container. The img element in XHTML is another example of an empty element that doesn't have any content associated with it.

```
<img src="http://www.someurl.com/thepic.gif" alt="my car"/>
```

The element is closed immediately by placing the slash right before the greater-than symbol. There's no end tag for the img element. Empty elements can use attributes, though, and, in some cases, external content might be associated with the element using attributes that are set to addresses where the content resides.

Attributes

The *img* element in XHTML is an example of an empty element that's associated to content by making use of attributes. It consists of a single tag only, but it has an attribute—*src*—that associates a picture with the element, as in the previous example.

Attributes augment the elements with characteristics or certain properties. While elements may describe hierarchies and sequences, attributes describe characteristics and features of each element or the content associated with that element. In the previous example, the img element is used to tell the interpreter that an image occurs at that point in the paragraph. The src attribute is used to describe the image further, where the actual image resides. An additional attribute—*alt*—provides a textual description of the image for devices that can't display graphics. Some primitive handheld devices, like pagers, might not be equipped with graphical capabilities, and then the text can be displayed instead.

Grammars

XML files contain elements that are either empty elements or elements with a start tag and an end tag. The elements may occur in a certain order and there are certain hierarchies in which the elements may also occur. A grammar describes this sequence of order and these hierarchies. For example, in XHTML, the paragraph might contain an image element and the image element might only occur inside a paragraph. The line break element must also occur inside a paragraph. We have to follow certain rules, otherwise, the document won't be a valid XML document.

Before going into the actual grammars and what they can be used for, let's look at grammars in general and a notation commonly used to specify grammars. For languages that are already specified, like XHTML, SMIL, SyncML, and SVG, you don't have to write your own grammar. However, if you want to get as much out of these languages as possible, then you should learn what a grammar is and how grammars are read. If you design your own application, you might want to write your own XML application in some situations, and then you'll have to write the grammar for your own XML language.

To make this simple, assume you have a markup language that contains an element called body. The body contains an element called start and another called end. *Start* must always occur before *end,* and both the start and the end elements must always occur inside the body element. Then these properties need to be expressed to make it clear—for the developer and for the tools that can be used to parse the file—that the elements must occur only in this order.

BNF

The Bachus-Naur Form (BNF) is the traditional way of writing grammars. If you read the detailed specifications for languages, such as XHTML or VoiceXML, it gets easier to understand these specifications if you learn the BNF syntax.

Let's continue with the previous example, which uses the body, start, and end elements, and provide a grammar for it. The markup should always start with the start tag for the body. Two elements should occur inside the body: the start element and the end element. The start element must be provided before the end element. At the end of the markup, the body element should be closed with its end tag. Neither the start element nor the end element has a content model. They are empty elements. The grammar, written on BNF, can look like this.

```
<document> ::= <bodyStart> <bodyContent> <bodyEnd>
<bodyStart> ::= "<body>" | "<BODY>" | "<Body>"
<bodyEnd> ::= "/body>" | "/BODY>" | "/Body>"
<bodyContent> ::= <text> <start> <text> <end>
<start> ::= "start/>" | "START/>" | "Start/>"
<end> ::= "end/>" | "END/>" | "End/>"
<text> ::= <char> <text> | "<"
<char> ::= ' ' | 'a'-'z' | 'A'-'Z' | '0'-'9'
```

The grammar is read like this. A document has a body start, followed by the content of the body (bodyContent) and the end of the body (bodyEnd). The start of the body is defined as the text body, or the text BODY, or the text Body. Thus, a vertical bar denotes "or." The content of the body might contain text and, at an arbitrary point in the text, there might be a start tag. Some text might follow the start tag, and then there must be an end tag. Text might be left out, though.

Assume you have the following file:

```
<body>This is my document.
<start/>That was the start of it. Here is some more text.
<end/>
</body>
```

If you can apply the previous grammar on the file, then you're sure the file belongs to your language. Let's see if the file can be "parsed" by our grammar.

Line 1 of our grammar says the file should start according to the rule bodyStart. What's a bodyStart? Line 2 in our grammar says a *bodyStart* is the text <body>, <BODY>, or <Body>. Because your file begins with <body>, there's a match. So far so good. Now we've consumed the first part of the production rule, which is named bodyStart.

According to Line 1 in the grammar, a bodyContent should always appear after a bodyStart. Line 4 in the grammar says a *bodyContent* can be a text string, which ends with a <. This is exactly how your file looks after the <body> section has been consumed. It contains the text "This is my document," followed by the < on the next line.

If you move on in the grammar, text should be followed by a start and, according to Line 5, a *start* can be the text string start/>, START/>,"or Start/>. Our file contains the text start/>, so this is a match. After a start, a text section follows again, according to Line 4, and that's exactly what our file contains: the text section "That was the start of it. Here is some more text," followed by the < on the next line. Line 4 says after the text section, an end should appear. Our file contains the characters end/>, which matches Line 6. Now Line has been matched. Line 1 says, after the bodyContent, there should be a bodyEnd and according to Line 3, a *bodyEnd* can be the text body/>. Our text contains exactly this string of characters, so Line 6 is matched and this completes Line 1. Our document has been *parsed* according to the grammar.

Grammars are used to check the validity of XML documents. In XML, grammars can be implemented using document type definitions or schemas.

The XML Declaration

XML documents, can start with an optional XML declaration. This is used by applications to check that the document is an XML document and nothing else. An XML declaration can look like this:

```
<?xml version="1.0"?>
```

The line should start with the characters <? followed by the xml element and the version attribute set to the XML version, which the document complies to. Here's another example.

```
<?xml version="1.0" standalone="yes"?>
```

Standalone is an optional attribute, which may be assigned the value "yes" or "no." It specifies whether the XML document is embedded in another XML document or if it's supposed to be used standalone.

Character Encoding

The header might contain yet another attribute, *encoding,* which can be set to the character encoding used in the document. Character sets can be encoded in a number of different ways. A *character encoding* represents all the characters in one or several character sets with codes. These codes are interpreted by the application when the markup is rendered, so the characters are displayed as they're supposed to. The most common encoding is Unicode.

Unicode

Unicode contains several substandards for how the encoding should be carried out. *UTF-8* is the default encoding for XML documents, if nothing else was specified. UTF-8 is compatible with the traditional ASCII encoding, which has been used for decades. With UTF-8, each common character is represented as a byte. For devices that have limited CPU power, like phones and simple PDAs, UTF-8 is most suitable.

If a larger number of characters will often be used in a document, though, UTF-8 is a less-appropriate choice. In this case, the Unicode UTF-16 can be used. Both UTF-8 and UTF-16 represent millions of characters. The difference is how they treat the most common characters in the Latin alphabet. With UTF-8, rare characters might occupy as much as 4 bytes, while the UTF-16 encoding standard might occupy only 2 bytes for these rare characters and 1byte for the characters in the Latin alphabet.

The character encoding can be specified in the optional encoding attribute in the XML header. After the header, an XML document might include a DOCTYPE declaration and a Formal Public Identifier.

The Formal Public Identifier

Later in this chapter, you learn about Document Type Definitions (DTDs), which define the elements and attributes allowed in the instance document (the document that contains the markup). In this case, the DTD must be referred by the instance document in the prologue. It might look like this:

```
<?xml version="1.0" encoding="UTF-8"?>
<!DOCTYPE html
SYSTEM "http://www.w3c.org/DTD/xhtml1-strict.dtd"
PUBLIC "-//W3C//DTD XHTML 1.0 Strict//EN">
. . .
```

In the DOCTYPE declaration, the PUBLIC declaration contains information about which organization maintains the DTD, which type of document it is, and which language is used. Each field in the FPI is separated by //. The first field indicates the FPI is private; a well-defined group of people will be responsible for maintenance. In this case, the maintainer is W3C, specified in the second field. The third field specifies the language, XHTML Strict, and its version number, 1.0. The last field indicates the document's default language: English.

Validation

XML documents can be validated. *Validation* is a process when the elements and attributes of the document are examined with reference to a grammar. The grammar can be implemented using either a schema or a DTD. First, let's look at what a DTD is, and then you'll learn about how the DTD can be used by tools to validate the XML document.

Document Type Definitions

Assume you're working on a portal that's supposed to provide mobile games and utilities for download. Some mobile devices use XHTML Basic, some use compact HTML, and a few PDAs use traditional HTML. Then it can be a good idea to write the download pages in XML and use a transformation technology, like XSLT or WAX, that converts to the final format. Updates can then be done at one place and the XML code will automatically be converted to the final formats.

The XML code for the download page might look like this:

```
<?xml version="1.0"?>
<applications>
  <app>
    <name>Cool-game-of-mine for mobiles.</name>
    <a href='http://www.mygame.com/g1.exe'/>
  </app>
  <app>
    <name>Alpha-X, another game.</name>
    <a href='http://www.mygame.com/g2.exe'/>
  </app>
  <app>
    <name>Zonk - my third application.</name>
    <a href='http://www.mygame.com/g3.exe'/>
  </app>
</applications>
```

You need to describe all your elements in a grammar and that's where the DTD comes in. The grammar specifies the top-level element applications, which must contain one or more app elements. Each *app* element must have a text description (name) and a link, specified using the *a* element. The latter has an attribute, which is always given with the *a* element: the *href* attribute.

Writing a Grammar

First, let's try to formulate the grammar using BNF, then we'll convert the BNF to a DTD. A grammar for the previous code written on BNF might look like this:

```
<document> ::= <xml_decl> <sp> <apps_start> <apps>
<xml_decl> ::= "<?xml version='1.0'?>"
<sp> ::= " " <sp> | "<" | CR <sp>
<apps_start> ::= "applications>"
<apps_end> ::= "</applications>"
<apps> ::= <one_app> <apps> | <apps_end>
```

```
<one_app> ::= <sp> "app>" <sp> "name>" <text> "name>" <sp> <link> <sp> "/app>"
<text> ::= <char> <text> | "<"
<char> ::= ' ' | 'a'-'z' | 'A'-'Z' | '0'-'9'
<link> ::= "a href='" <url>
<url> ::= <urlchar> <url> | "'/>"
<urlchar> ::= ' ' | 'a'-'z' | 'A'-'Z' | '0'-'9' | '.' | ':' | '/'
```

The grammar that we're going to convert to a DTD contains the xml declaration, followed by a start section, a number of app declarations, and an end section. Spaces are consumed by the rule on Line 3, which is called the *sp* rule. As you can see on Line 1, the document might start with a number of spaces consumed by the sp rule. Then, when all spaces have been consumed and the < character has been found by the sp rule, an apps_start section is expected (followed by an apps section). In the apps_start section, the keyword "applications" should appear followed by a >. At this point, the apps_start section has been parsed by the grammar. Then, a number of apps declarations are expected. As you can see on Lines 6 and 7, each apps section contains a number of spaces, followed by a <, as defined in the sp rule, followed by app>, a name, some text, a link, optional spaces, and then the closing app tag. Line 6 says an arbitrary sequence of such declarations can follow until an apps_end is encountered. An apps_end contains the end tag for the top-level applications element. Maybe you're confused at this point. You won't necessarily understand grammars the first time you're confronted with them, especially not grammars that use recursion, like the previous one. Let's look at a real example to see how the code is parsed by our grammar. This might make things more clear.

Assume someone has produced the following file:

```
<?xml version='1.0'?>
<applications>
  <app>
    <name>Cool-game-of-mine for mobiles.</name>
    <a href='http://www.mygame.com/g1.exe'/>
  </app>
</applications>
```

We'll check with the grammar to see if the file is valid regarding our language. Our language has been expressed in the grammar. If the file isn't okay according to our grammar, then it will be impossible to use a transformation later to convert the general XML code into, say, cHTML or XHTML. This is the essence of validation. Tools that perform validation check to make sure the XML document is valid regarding a formally defined grammar.

The code starts with the following text:

```
<?xml version='1.0'?>
```

Our grammar starts with the production rule on Line 1, which says an XML document that conforms to our grammar should start with an xml_decl. If you move down to Line 2 in the grammar, you see our definition of xml_decl. This is the text string <?xml version='1.0'?> and you have a match in the grammar with the start of your file. So far so good. Now we've passed the <xml_decl > part of Line 1 in the grammar. According to the rule on Line 1, an xml_decl should be followed by an sp. What's an sp? Check at Line 3 in the grammar to find out that an *sp* might be a space or a carriage return followed by an sp again, or just the < character. Because the line with the xml declaration ends here, you encounter a carriage return. A carriage return can be here because you expect this in the sp rule. Because you consumed an sp_or_cr, Line 3 says that an sp should be expected again. In your XML file, the carriage return is followed by this line.

```
<applications>
```

Because this line begins with a <, you have a match in the sp rule at Line 3 in your grammar. So, now you've consumed <xml_decl> and <sp> at Line 1 of your grammar. You've now moved one character position into Line 2 of your XML file. In the grammar, you expect an apps_start. The *apps_start* is defined on Line 4 and is the text string applications>. You have a perfect match here because your XML file contains exactly that text. According to the grammar, the XML file must now contain an apps. Line 6 defines what an apps is: one_app followed by an apps again, or an apps_end, which is the end tag for the applications declaration. The *one_app* rule is defined on Line 7 as a number of spaces or carriage returns, followed by the text app>, a name, >, some text, a link, optional spaces, and the end tag for the app element. Our XML file contains an app declaration like this:

```
<app>
  <name>Cool-game-of-mine for mobiles.</name>
  <a href='http://www.mygame.com/g1.exe'/>
</app>
```

This is parsed successfully by the one_app rule. Line 6 has now consumed the one_app rule and what remains is the apps rule on the same line. In this case, the apps rule is matched on its right-hand side—as an apps_end—because what remains of our XML file is this line.

```
</applications>
```

An apps_end is defined as the text </applications>, the XML file contains exactly that sequence of characters and the file is now parsed successfully.

Writing the DTD

Now you've practiced to write a simple grammar on Bachus-Naur Form and you've also seen how you can check to make sure the grammar works. You start with the top production rule and apply it to the right-hand side of the file, which you're going to parse.

Writing a DTD is similar to writing a BNF grammar. but another syntax is used. You still have to know your grammar, though, so it's a good idea to start with a BNF grammar before you go on and code it as a DTD. Let's code our grammar as a DTD. Because our XML file now has to refer to a more formal grammar—as opposed to the BNF—the XML file must start with a DTD. This declaration points out where the grammar (DTD) is located. The DOCTYPE declaration is preceded by the XML declaration. It might look like this:

```
<?xml version="1.0"?>
<!DOCTYPE applications SYSTEM "mobileApps.dtd">
...
```

The filename mobileApps.dtd might be a full URL, which points out where the grammar resides. This is an elegant solution because a grammar can be defined by a large organization or corporation and put up on a web server. All XML documents that are applications of that grammar (use the grammar), can specify the URL in the SYSTEM reference, and then an automatic validation can be performed.

You needn't make any more additions to the XML file itself (the instance document). Now XML tools know that if the document is going to be validated, they should check in the same directory where the XML file was found. A file that's called mobileApps.dtd is supposed to be located there and this file should be used during the validation process as the formal grammar.

The mobileApps.dtd file should contain the grammar, as well as all the elements and attributes that are referred to in the grammar. Our file uses elements called applications, apps, and *a*. The latter element has a mandatory attribute, which is called href. Let's add a required attribute—id—to the app element. Now, let's move on to the DTD and define these attributes and elements. It might look like this and needs to be explained:

```
<!ELEMENT applications (app*)>
<!ELEMENT app (name, a)>
```

```
<!ATTLIST app
    id      CDATA      #REQUIRED
>
<!ELEMENT name (#PCDATA)>
<!ELEMENT a EMPTY>
<!ATTLIST a
    href     CDATA      #REQUIRED
>
```

This first line declares the applications element. Because an *application* element has a start tag and an end tag, and can contain a number of apps declarations, you write (app*) to indicate zero or more app elements might be inside the applications tags. The asterisk means zero or more, so the first line in the DTD says an element called applications can contain zero or more app elements.

If you move down to the second line, we find the declaration of the app element. This line says the *app* element contains a name followed by an *a*. What name and *a* are defined as is specified at the following lines. A *name* is a piece of text. PCDATA means Parsed Character Data and is plain text, which is checked to see that it doesn't contain any tags. An *a* is specified as an empty element. An *empty element* is a tag that occurs on its own, without any content and with the slash located just before the >, as opposed to elements, which have start and end tags. The *href* attribute, which comes with the *a* element, is mandatory. It must not be left out.

The Validation Mechanism

When tools are used to examine the XML file, the elements therein, and their attributes, then the URL in the DTD is followed to find the DTD. Let's look at the XML document that contains the markup again.

```
<?xml version='1.0'?>
<!DOCTYPE application SYSTEM "moblieApps.dtd">
<applications>
  <app id='mGame 1'>
    <name>Cool-game-of-mine for mobiles.</name>
    <a href='http://www.mygame.com/g1.exe'/>
  </app>
</applications>
```

At the beginning of the file is a DOCTYPE declaration and a SYSTEM reference, which contains the URL, or address. This address is used by the tools to retrieve the DTD. In this case, you use a small DTD, which has only ten lines. Nevertheless, it is a DTD that can be used by tools to verify the markup doesn't contain any obvious errors.

When validation is performed, the tool, which performs the validation, first processes the XML file, which contains the markup. It discovers the XML declaration on Line 1. Then, on Line 2, it finds the DOCTYPE declaration, which contains the SYSTEM reference. The system reference contains an address to a DTD, so the tool retrieves the DTD from that address and uses the DTD to parse the rest of the document.

Applications is the first element in the document. The tool, which performs the validation, checks with the DTD and notices the applications element is the top-level element. When the tool continues to parse the XML code, the start tag for the app element is found. In the DTD, the content model for the applications element is specified like this:

```
<!ELEMENT applications (app*)>
```

Because the app element is part of the content model for the applications element, the tool can draw the conclusion that the code, which contains an app element inside the applications element, is correct from a grammatical point of view.

As the tool continues to read the markup, it reaches the app element's id attribute. Then it needs to find a suitable rule in the DTD that says the app element can have an attribute called *id*. In the DTD, the following rule is found.

```
<!ATTLIST app
    id    CDATA    #REQUIRED
>
```

This confirms the XML code is valid so far. Inside the app element, the tool reaches a link that's specified using the *a* element and the attribute href. In the DTD, the following two rules are used by the tool to draw the conclusion that the name, the link, and the href attribute can be specified as they are, inside the app element:

```
<!ELEMENT app (name, a)>
<!ATTLIST a
    href    CDATA    #REQUIRED
>
```

The element declaration says the name must be provided inside the app tags and the link (*a*) must occur inside the app element. The attlist declaration, for the *a* element, says href is an attribute that's associated with the *a* element and contains character data—in this case, an address. Because *a* is declared as an empty element, that is, an element that doesn't have a content model, the element is considered closed.

As the tool continues with the validation process, the end tag for the app is found. The app element is then closed. To make this possible, the tool checks that all elements inside the app element are closed. The only element inside app is the link *a,* which has an empty content model and the element is closed.

If the end tag for the applications element had been found before the end tag for the app element, then the app element wasn't properly closed and the validation should fail. The tool knows this because it uses the following rule:

```
<!ELEMENT applications (app*)>
```

When the tool reaches the end tag for the applications element, then the rule is used to check that the app element was properly closed. This means if there was a start tag, there must be a matching end tag for the element.

Because the app element has been specified correctly—with a start tag and a matching end tag, both inside the applications element—the validation process continues. The end tag for the applications element, which is the last element in the file, is found and the applications element is closed. Because the app element is allowed to occur inside the applications element, according to Line 1 in the DTD, and the app element has been parsed successfully, the whole file has now been validated with success.

The DTD in Detail

You've written a basic DTD that can be used to validate an associated XML file. Now let's look closely at the more advanced DTD format and constructs.

Element Declarations   Tags or, more precisely, elements, are declared in the DTD using the ELEMENT keyword. In our example, it looks like this:

```
<!ELEMENT applications (app*)>
```

The ELEMENT keyword is followed by the name of the element and a description about which elements can be written between the tags for that element. In the previous case, the following XML code would be allowed.

```
<applications>
  <app>
    ...
  </app>
</applications>
```

The following code would also be allowed, however:

```
<applications>
</applications>
```

If this were our intention, the ELEMENT declaration should be kept as it is. However, if you wouldn't allow zero app declarations, but you would allow at least one, then you'd have to change the ELEMENT declaration in the DTD, so it looks like this:

```
<!ELEMENT applications (app+)>
```

The plus (+) symbol means at least one occurrence of, as opposed to the asterisk (*) symbol, which means zero or more occurrences of the element can exist.

In some cases, you don't want to allow more than one occurrence of a certain element. In this example, you might allow an additional occurrence inside the applications element, which gives an overall name to the set of applications. This name is optional, though, so the person writing the markup is free to include it. The DTD then looks like this:

```
<!ELEMENT applications (fullname?, app*)>
```

The question mark tells the interpreter of the DTD that the element, referred to as fullname, can be left out or it can be specified once before the app elements. Because the app elements are specified with an asterisk, though, there might be no app elements at all inside the applications element. Using the previous declaration, the following pieces of code would be allowed.

```
                    <!-- Variant 1 -->
<applications>
</applications>
                    <!-- Variant 2 -->
<applications>
  <fullname>
    ...
  </fullname>
</applications>
                    <!-- Variant 3 -->
<applications>
  <app>
    ...
  </app>
</applications>
```

```
                    <!-- Variant 4 -->
<applications>
  <fullname>
    . . .
  </fullname>
  <app>
    . . .
  </app>
  <app>
    . . .
  </app>
</applications>
```

Let's look at something more interesting. Try to find out if the following piece of code is valid according to the DTD. Note, this time, that the DTD is in the same file as the markup, instead of using the SYSTEM reference to point out a separate file.

```
<?xml version="1.0"?>
<!DOCTYPE applications [
<!-- ********** The rules ********** -->
<!ELEMENT applications (fullname?, (expired | app)+, prov?)>
<!ELEMENT fullname (#PCDATA)>
<!ELEMENT expired EMPTY>
<!ATTLIST expired
    id      CDATA    #REQUIRED
    date    CDATA    #REQUIRED
    reason  (expired|updated) "expired"
>
<!ELEMENT app (name, a)>
<!ATTLIST app
    id      CDATA    #REQUIRED
>
<!ELEMENT name (#PCDATA)>
<!ELEMENT a EMPTY>
<!ATTLIST a
    href    CDATA    #REQUIRED
>
<!ELEMENT prov EMPTY>
<!ATTLIST prov
    year    CDATA    #REQUIRED
    month   CDATA    #REQUIRED
    day     CDATA    #REQUIRED
>
```

```
]>
<!-- ********** The markup ********** -->
<applications>
  <fullname>Download applications.
  </fullname>
  <app id='qb14'>
    <name>QBrowser 1.4</name>
    <a href='http://www.qb.com/qbrowser1.4.exe'/>
  </app>
  <expired id='qb13' date='2000-03-07' reason='updated'/>
  <app id='mGame35'>
    <name>Mobile Game v1.5</name>
    <a href='http://www.mobgame.com/mgame15.exe'/>
  </app>
  <prov year='2001' month='06' day='23'/>
</applications>
```

The markup is, indeed, valid according to its DTD, but the previous example needs to be explained. Note, the DTD is written in the same document as the markup. If the DTD were provided in a separate file, you would have used the SYSTEM reference to let it point out the file. Instead, the DTD is provided right after the DOCTYPE declaration in the same file as the markup. As you can see, all the rules are specified inside square brackets, right after the DOCTYPE name. The markup starts after the closing]> characters.

In addition, four new constructs are used here, as in the following line:

```
<!ELEMENT applications (fullname?, (expired | app)+, prov?)>
```

We discussed the ?, the *, and the + syntax earlier. ? means "optional," * means "zero or more" and + means "one or more." However, the vertical bar (|) hasn't been mentioned yet. The | denotes "or." In this case, the | means a fullname can be followed by a number of elements (the asterisk), which are either expired or app elements (the vertical bar). At least one element must be in this sequence because we used the + symbol to indicate at least one. The prov element can follow this sequence, but this is optional.

The tags and attributes of the expired element are defined like this:

```
<!ELEMENT expired EMPTY>
<!ATTLIST expired
    id      CDATA      #REQUIRED
    date    CDATA      #REQUIRED
```

```
reason    (expired|updated) "expired"
>
```

Two of the three attributes are declared as #REQUIRED, which means they are mandatory. When the expired element is used, these attributes must also be provided. The third attribute, named reason, is a bit special. The reason attribute can only have two values: expired or updated. When this attribute is used, it must be set to one of these two values. If the attribute isn't used, the program, which interprets the markup, should treat the attribute as if it were set to expire. The reason attribute is the default value and is specified at the end of the previous last line. As you can see, the | is used again but, in this case, for attribute values. The | has more or less the same meaning, however, which is "or." In this case, the reason attribute can be set either to expired or updated.

Finally, look at this code. The DTD is the same as the previous, but the markup is slightly different. Is the markup valid regarding the associated DTD?

```
<?xml version="1.0"?>
<!DOCTYPE applications [
<!-- ********** The rules ********** -->
<!ELEMENT applications (fullname?, (expired | app)+, prov?)>
<!ELEMENT fullname (#PCDATA)>
<!ELEMENT expired EMPTY>
<!ATTLIST expired
    id       CDATA      #REQUIRED
    date     CDATA      #REQUIRED
    reason   (expired|updated) "expired"
>
<!ELEMENT app (name, a)>
<!ATTLIST app
    id       CDATA      #REQUIRED
>
<!ELEMENT name (#PCDATA)>
<!ELEMENT a EMPTY>
<!ATTLIST a
    href     CDATA      #REQUIRED
>
<!ELEMENT prov EMPTY>
<!ATTLIST prov
    year     CDATA      #REQUIRED
    month    CDATA      #REQUIRED
    day      CDATA      #REQUIRED
>
```

```
]>
<!-- ********** The markup ********** -->
<applications>
  <app id='mGame35'><name></name><a href='mgame15.exe'/>
  </app>
</applications>
```

Validation will also succeed for this file. In this case, all the optional elements and attributes were left out, and only the mandatory elements and attributes were provided. The applications element must always be provided, but the fullname can be left out. No need exists to provide an expired element because at least one app or expired element must be specified. Because the app element is used, the id attribute is required and can't be left out. The name tags must be there, but they don't have to contain any text.

Attribute Declarations   So far, we've only looked at the more basic ways attributes can be used in markup and declared in a DTD. More possibilities exist, such as using implied, fixed, and default attributes. There are only a handful of options for how an attribute can be used together with an element.

The attribute must always be provided together with a certain element. In our example, it can look like this:

```
<prov year='2001' month='07' day='4'/>
```

All the three attributes must be provided. Otherwise, the provision date isn't complete. This attribute list from the DTD, which specifies the grammar and the attributes for the date element, can look like this:

```
<!ATTLIST prov
    year    CDATA    #REQUIRED
    month   CDATA    #REQUIRED
    day     CDATA    #REQUIRED
>
```

All attributes are required. However, depending on how the code is going to be used, some of the attributes might be considered optional. The application, which performs the validation or processes the result, might take for granted that the year is the current year. In this case, you can make the year attribute optional. It might look like this:

```
<!ATTLIST prov
    year    CDATA    #IMPLIED
```

```
    month    CDATA    #REQUIRED
    day      CDATA    #REQUIRED
>
```

You can provide a default value for the application that validates or processes the result. The default value can work as a hint that the year shall be interpreted as the current year if it's left out in the markup. The attribute list can then be declared like this:

```
<!ATTLIST prov
    year     CDATA    "2001"
    month    CDATA    #REQUIRED
    day      CDATA    #REQUIRED
>
```

It can be provided with the prov element, but it needn't. If the year is left out, tools that use the code will treat it the same way as if the attribute has been provided in the code and set to 2001. Instead of declaring the year attribute as implied, tools will know the default value.

Occasions might occur when an attribute must always be provided with a certain value. For example, it can be used as a hint for the person writing the markup or the tool that provides it. In this case, the code can look like this:

```
<!ATTLIST prov
    year     CDATA    #FIXED "2001"
    month    CDATA    #REQUIRED
    day      CDATA    #REQUIRED
>
```

In this case, the year attribute must always be provided and it must be set to 2001. A fixed attribute declaration is used to achieve this.

Entities In our example, you can see the expired and app elements have attributes, which are called id. Instead of specifying the same thing at several places in the DTD, a good idea is to reuse the same declaration as a so-called entity. The DTD might then look like this:

```
<!ENTITY     %idData
    "id       CDATA     #REQUIRED">
<!ELEMENT applications (fullname?, (expired | app)+, prov?)>
<!ELEMENT fullname (#PCDATA)>
<!ELEMENT expired EMPTY>
<!ATTLIST expired
```

```
    %idData;
    date    CDATA    #REQUIRED
    reason  (expired|updated) "expired"
>
<!ELEMENT app (name, a)>
<!ATTLIST app
    %idData;
>
<!ELEMENT name (#PCDATA)>
<!ELEMENT a EMPTY>
<!ATTLIST a
    href    CDATA    #REQUIRED
>
<!ELEMENT prov EMPTY>
<!ATTLIST prov
    year    CDATA    #REQUIRED
    month   CDATA    #REQUIRED
    day     CDATA    #REQUIRED
>
```

All the occurrences of %idData; are then replaced by what is declared inside the double quotes. If some constructs are used many times in a DTD—for example, a set of attributes—then the DTD might become easier to read. Assume you want to extend the DTD, so all places where an id attribute occurs also have an optional desc attribute, which gives a textual description for the id attribute. Then, the ENTITY declaration could look like this:

```
<!ENTITY     %idData
    "id      CDATA    #REQUIRED
     desc    CDATA    #IMPLIED">
```

The expired element, as well as the app element, can then use the desc attribute, although the change was only made at one place in the DTD. The concept is called *representation independence* when it's used in traditional programming languages. Changes can be made fast and elements can be specified independent of what an idData entity really contains.

Note, if you use parameter entities, as previously described, you can't use them inside markup declarations in an internal subset. Instead, you must put the DTD in a document of its own. The XML document then looks something like this:

```
<?xml version="1.0"?>
<!DOCTYPE applications SYSTEM "myDTD.dtd">
```

```
<!-- ********** The markup ********** -->
<applications>
  <app id='mGame35'><name></name><a href='mgame15.exe'/>
  </app>
</applications>
```

Note, the document refers to an external subset—myDTD.dtd—in the SYSTEM reference. This file lists all the rules almost the same way as when the DTD was part of the instance document. Anyway, it might look like this:

```
<!-- ********** The rules. This is the file myDTD.dtd ********** -->
<!ELEMENT applications (fullname?, (expired | app)+, prov?)>
<!ELEMENT fullname (#PCDATA)>
<!ELEMENT expired EMPTY>
<!ENTITY    % idData
 "id       CDATA    #REQUIRED">
<!ATTLIST expired
    %idData;
    date    CDATA    #REQUIRED
    reason  (expired|updated) "expired"
>
<!ELEMENT app (name, a)>
<!ATTLIST app
    %idData;
>
<!ELEMENT name (#PCDATA)>
<!ELEMENT a EMPTY>
<!ATTLIST a
    href    CDATA    #REQUIRED
>
<!ELEMENT prov EMPTY>
<!ATTLIST prov
    year    CDATA    #REQUIRED
    month   CDATA    #REQUIRED
    day     CDATA    #REQUIRED
>
```

The elements, attributes, and entities here are specified as an external subset, a separate document, instead of at the beginning of the instance document.

An alternative to DTDs is called *schemas*. Because schemas make heavy use of namespaces, let's look at XML namespaces first.

Namespaces

XML namespaces can be used if several applications of XML must reside in the same document. For example, you can define your own XML language using a DTD where all the elements and all the attributes in your language are listed. In the DTD, you also specify which elements and attributes are mandatory and in what order they must occur. However, assume you want to use a vocabulary that's already been defined. Then you can get into difficult situations if your own language has been specified using the same names, such as body, head, title, or type, which are quite common names.

With XML namespaces, it's possible to declare a document that should be used by the XML parser when the document is interpreted. This document contains all the definitions for a certain namespace. You specify where in your document you want to refer to this namespace and you declare a prefix, which indicates you're referring to this specific namespace. Because the prefix is always used to qualify the namespace, you can't get any name clashes. Here's a simple example that illustrates the use of a namespace:

```
<elm xmlns:nam="http://www.example.com/path/someSchema">
   ...
</elm>
```

All elements and attributes inside elm can use the namespace, which we gave the local name "nam." This is the prefix. Assume you defined an element, called send, and an attribute, called media. Then the code might look like this:

```
<elm xmlns:nam="http://www.example.com/path/someSchema">
  <nam:send nam:media="fax">Hello
  </name:send>
</elm>
```

We refer to the element and the attribute by writing nam in front of their names. It's also possible to define a default namespace. This is the namespace to be searched by the XML processor when elements and attributes are found that have no namespace prefix and are "unknown." Such a namespace declaration might look like this:

```
<elm xmlns="http://www.example.com/path/someSchema">
  <send media="fax"/>Hello
  </send>
</elm>
```

Because the send element and the media attribute are part of the default namespace, you needn't write a prefix when they're used. Correct use of the namespace prefix and all the namespace definitions are examined when a document is validated.

Schemas are alternatives to DTDs and they make heavy use of namespaces.

Schemas

An alternative to the DTD is called a *schema.* Schemas will probably replace DTDs in the future because they support data types and can be extended. You needn't use the syntax of DTDs, which isn't too easy to use and remember. Instead, the grammar can be written in XML, a bit similar to how the instance document is written.

The Structure of a Schema

Schemas make heavy use of namespaces. When a grammar is written as a schema, all the rules should use a suitable prefix for the schema. Usually, xsd is the namespace associated with a schema. Technically, though, you're free to use whichever prefix you prefer. A simple schema might look like this:

```
<xsd:schema xmlns:xsd="http://www.w3.org/2001/XMLSchema">
  <xsd:element name="fullname" type="xsd:string">
  </xsd:element>
</xsd:schema>
```

The previous schema defines a single element, called *fullname,* which is supposed to contain a text string only. Before the declaration of the element, the schema declaration points to the definition of XML schema and sets the prefix we'll use in our schema. The prefix can be used to refer to simple types, like the xsd:string type, which is used in the previous example.

In addition to element declarations, attributes can also be declared. Then the element declaration and the attribute declaration need to be grouped together in a complex type.

Simple and Complex Types

Simple types are types that aren't broken into several components. *Complex types,* on the other hand, need to be broken into smaller units or components.

Simple Types

A *simple text string* is the simple type xsd:string. Other simple types are xsd:date, which specifies a date on the form yyyy-mm-dd, and xsd:boolean, which can be used for attributes that require only the true or false values. There is a variety of types available for you to represent numbers. For example, xsd:decimal can be used to represent a decimal number, like 3.14 or 10.0. Look at the following declaration:

```
<xsd:schema xmlns:xsd="http://www.w3.org/2001/XMLSchema">
  <xsd:element name="doc">
    <xsd:element name="name" type="xsd:string"/>
    <xsd:element name="age" type="xsd:positiveInteger"/>
    <xsd:element name="homepage" type="xsd:anyURI"/>
  <xsd:element/>
</xsd:schema>
```

Using the schema, the following markup can be produced.

```
<doc>
  <name>Joe Stephens</name>
  <age>75</age>
  <homepage>http://www.myhomepage.com/m.html</homepage>
</doc>
```

The name, age, and homepage elements are surrounded by the doc element. This is why the doc element is declared using a start and end tag in the schema, as opposed to the other elements, which have empty content models.

Because the name element is declared as type xsd:string, the content of the element can be Joe Stephens. The content of the age element is supposed to be a positive integer, so 75 is fine. Another number, such as 2,500, would also be fine. However, 0 wouldn't be allowed because it doesn't count as a positive integer. If you want to allow 0, then you'd have to use the type xsd:nonNegativeInteger. The homepage element contains any URI that includes the address given in the previous example. Short relative addresses, such as index.html or fragments, like #next, are also allowed because they're URIs.

Complex Types

Complex types, on the other hand, are types that are composed of several subcomponents, such as an element and an attribute, or several elements. Let's go back to our example—the DTD—which specifies a number of applications that can be downloaded from a portal. The applications element and the fullname element can be declared like this in a schema:

```xsd
<xsd:schema xmlns:xsd="http://www.w3.org/2001/XMLSchema">
  <xsd:element name="applications" type="applicationsType"/>
  <xsd:complexType name="applicationsType">
    <xsd:element name="fullname" type="xsd:string"/>
    <xsd:element name="app" type="xsd:string"/>
  </xsd:complexType>
</xsd:schema>
```

Line 2 contains the actual declaration of the applications element, while Lines 3–6 declare the applications element as a complexType because it contains two elements. Inside the complexType both elements are declared as elements of the type xsd:string. Because the fullname and app elements are supposed to contain a text string only (a text string is a simple type), they needn't be declared as complexTypes. So, basically, we've declared the element itself, which is Line 2 and what will be possible to write between the tags of the element. This is specified on Lines 3–6. The following XML code can be produced with the previous schema:

```xml
<applications>
  <fullname>This is the download page.</fullname>
  <app>Here is an app.</app>
</applications>
```

However, you need to specify that the fullname element can be left out or occur, at most, once inside the applications element. If you checked the DTD again, you'd recall we can express this property using the ? character. With XML schemas, two attributes can be used for this purpose.

Minimum and Maximum Number of Occurrences   Using the minOccurs and maxOccurs attributes, you can specify how many times an element can occur where it's declared. The minOccurs attribute is set to the number of times an element must occur and maxOccurs is set to the maximum number of times an element does occur. The following example shows how minOccurs and maxOccurs can be used in a schema:

```xsd
<xsd:schema xmlns:xsd="http://www.w3.org/2001/XMLSchema">
  <xsd:element name="week">
    <xsd:complexType mixed="true">
      <xsd:element name="Monday" type="xsd:string" minOccurs="0"/>
      <xsd:element name="Tuesday" type="xsd:string" minOccurs="0"/>
```

```
         <xsd:element name="Wednesday" type="xsd:string" minOccurs="0"/>
         <xsd:element name="Thursday" type="xsd:string" minOccurs="0"/>
         <xsd:element name="Friday" type="xsd:string" minOccurs="0"/>
         <xsd:element name="Saturday" type="xsd:string" minOccurs="0"/>
         <xsd:element name="Sunday" type="xsd:string" minOccurs="0"/>
      </ xsd:complexType>
   </xsd:element>
</xsd:schema>
```

Because all elements have been declared using the minOccurs attribute set to "0", they needn't be provided in the instance document. Note, the declaration of the xsd:complexType doesn't use the name attribute. Instead, the name attribute has been moved from the xsd:complexType declaration and put in an element declaration. The xsd:complexType declaration uses the mixed attribute, set to true. Now, the instance document can contain a mix of text and elements. Here's an example:

```
<week>My personal schedule.
   <Monday>Time report.</Monday>
   <Monday>Meeting with Sysadm.</Monday>
   <Wednesday>Day off</Wednesday>
   <Thursday>Release 1.4.</Thursday>
   <Friday>Cake at 2PM</Friday>
   <Saturday>Theater.</Saturday>
   <Sunday>Jogging at 7PM.</Sunday>
   <Sunday>Yoga.</Sunday>
</week>
```

A text string is immediately after the start tag for the week element. Because the complex type, week, was declared to contain a mix of characters and elements, this is possible. Note, some of the week elements, like Monday, are specified more than once and there is no Tuesday element. The minOccurs attribute only specifies the minimum number of occurrences. Because you haven't used the maxOccurs attribute, there's no limit to how many times an element may be provided.

Sequences

In some cases, it can be relevant to force the person (or tool) who produces the markup to write the elements in a certain order. For example, in the previous case, it can be argued that the weekdays must be provided in a fixed order to make it easier to read the markup. To force a fixed order, you can declare the content of the week element as a sequence. Then the schema will look like this:

```
<xsd:schema xmlns:xsd="http://www.w3.org/2001/XMLSchema">
  <xsd:element name="week">
    <xsd:complexType mixed="true">
      <xsd:sequence>
        <xsd:element name="Monday" type="xsd:string" minOccurs="0"/>
        <xsd:element name="Tuesday" type="xsd:string" minOccurs="0"/>
        <xsd:element name="Wednesday" type="xsd:string" minOccurs="0"/>
        <xsd:element name="Thursday" type="xsd:string" minOccurs="0"/>
        <xsd:element name="Friday" type="xsd:string" minOccurs="0"/>
        <xsd:element name="Saturday" type="xsd:string" minOccurs="0"/>
        <xsd:element name="Sunday" type="xsd:string" minOccurs="0"/>
      </xsd:sequence>
    </ xsd:complexType>
  </xsd:element>
</xsd:schema>
```

The elements must then be provided in the same order in the instance document as they are declared in the schema. Consequently, if the following markup is provided, validation will fail instead of succeed.

```
<week>My personal schedule.
  <Monday>Time report.</Monday>
  <Tuesday>Jogging at 7PM.</Tuesday>
  <Wednesday>Day off</Wednesday>
  <Thursday>Release 1.4.</Thursday>
  <Friday>Cake at 2PM</Friday>
  <Sunday>Jogging at 7PM.</Sunday>
  <Saturday>Party at Wendy's.</Saturday>
</week>
```

Attributes

So far, we've only written simple schemas that use elements and mixed content. In most cases, however, you want to add attributes to your grammar. Attributes are declared using the xsd:attribute declaration. Let's add an attribute—reminder—to the week element:

```
<xsd:schema xmlns:xsd="http://www.w3.org/2001/XMLSchema">
  <xsd:element name="week">
    <xsd:complexType mixed="true">
      <xsd:sequence>
```

```
        <xsd:element name="Monday" type="xsd:string" minOccurs="0"/>
        <xsd:element name="Tuesday" type="xsd:string" minOccurs="0"/>
        <xsd:element name="Wednesday" type="xsd:string" minOccurs="0"/>
        <xsd:element name="Thursday" type="xsd:string" minOccurs="0"/>
        <xsd:element name="Friday" type="xsd:string" minOccurs="0"/>
        <xsd:element name="Saturday" type="xsd:string" minOccurs="0"/>
        <xsd:element name="Sunday" type="xsd:string" minOccurs="0"/>
      </xsd:sequence>
      <xsd:attribute name="reminder" type="xsd:string"/>
    </ xsd:complexType>
  </xsd:element>
</xsd:schema>
```

The default value for minOccurs is 1, so the attribute reminder must always be provided and it must be a string. Empty strings are allowed. Here's an example:

```
<week reminder="Book a meeting with Joe this week!">
My personal schedule.
  <Monday>Time report.</Monday>
  <Tuesday>Jogging at 7PM.</Tuesday>
  <Wednesday>Day off</Wednesday>
  <Thursday>Release 1.4.</Thursday>
  <Friday>Cake at 2PM</Friday>
  <Saturday>Party at Wendy's.</Saturday>
  <Sunday>Jogging at 7PM.</Sunday>
</week>
```

If you want to make the reminder attribute optional, you'd change the attribute declaration in the schema like this:

```
    <xsd:attribute name="reminder" type="xsd:string" minOccurs="0"/>
```

Rewriting a DTD as a Schema

To compare schemas with DTDs, let's go back to the example for which we developed the DTD and rewrite the grammar as a schema. This time, we'll make it slightly more complicated at the same time. The name element is removed and it will be possible to write the text between the app or expired element, but before the link, *a*. The schema should describe the following syntax:

```
<applications>
  <fullname>Download applications.
  </fullname>
  <app id='qb14' desc='One of our most popular downloads.'>
```

```
    QBrowser 1.4
    <a href='http://www.qb.com/qbrowser1.4.exe'/>
  </app>
  <expired id='qb13' date='2000-03-07' reason='updated'/>
  <app id='mGame35'>
    Mobile Game v1.5
    <a href='http://www.mobgame.com/mgame15.exe'/>
  </app>
  <prov year='2001' month='06' day='23'/>
</applications>
```

Let's start with the schema header, the top-level element, called applications, and the element called fullname. It might be coded like this:

```
<xsd:schema xmlns:xsd="http://www.w3.org/2001/XMLSchema">
<xsd:element name="applications" type="applicationsType">
<xsd:complexType name="applicationsType">
<xsd:element name="fullname" type="xsd:string" minOccurs="0"/>
...
</xsd:complexType>
```

Note, the previous code isn't finished yet. We only provided code for the applications element and the fullname element. The applications element is first declared with its name and type. We use the applicationsType to describe that the applications element can contain a fullname. Because the fullname element has a simple type as its content—a text string—we needn't define a complexType just for the fullname element. Instead, it's specified as you saw previously, using the simple type xsd:string. Note, the attribute minOccurs is used to indicate the fullname element is optional. Let's extend the previous code and provide the definitions for the app end expired elements:

```
<xsd:schema xmlns:xsd="http://www.w3.org/2001/XMLSchema">
  <xsd:element name="applications" type="applicationsType">
  <xsd:complexType name="applicationsType">
    <xsd:sequence>
      <xsd:element name="fullname" type="xsd:string" minOccurs="0"/>
      <xsd:element type="appOrExpiredType" minOccurs="1"/>
    </xsd:sequence>
    <xsd:attribute name="reminder" type="xsd:string"/>
  </xsd:complexType>
  <xsd:complexType name="appOrExpiredType">
    <xsd:choice>
```

```
        <xsd:element name="expired" type="expiredType"/>
        <xsd:element name="app" type="appType"/>
      </xsd:choice>
    </xsd:complexType>
</xsd:schema>
```

Now the code has become slightly more complex, so let's stop for an explanation before more code is provided.

As you can see, a new element has been declared after the fullname element. However, you don't use a name for this element, but only provide the type for it. This is because the element that follows after the fullname can be either an expired element or an app element. You then have to refer to the part of the grammar that specifies either an app or an expired element will follow. That rule is specified as a complexType with the name appOrExpiredType using a choice declaration. The choice declaration enables us to express that one of the listed elements can be chosen. Note the line that refers to this type uses the minOccurs attribute set to 1, so at least one occurrence of an appOrExpiredType must be provided. In other words, at least one occurrence of an expired or app element must be provided. Let's continue now and add more code. The schema then looks like this:

```
<xsd:schema xmlns:xsd="http://www.w3.org/2001/XMLSchema">
  <xsd:element name="applications" type="applicationsType"/>
  <xsd:complexType name="applicationsType">
    <xsd:sequence>
      <xsd:element name="fullname" type="xsd:string" minOccurs="0"/>
      <xsd:element type="appOrExpiredType" minOccurs="1"/>
      <xsd:element name="prov" type="provType" minOccurs="0"/>
    </xsd:sequence>
    <xsd:attribute name="reminder" type="xsd:string"/>
  </xsd:complexType>
  <xsd:complexType name="appOrExpiredType">
    <xsd:choice>
      <xsd:element name="expired" type="expiredType"/>
      <xsd:element name="app" type="appType"/>
    </xsd:choice>
  </xsd:complexType>
  <xsd:complexType name="appType" mixed="true">
    <xsd:complexType>
      <xsd:element name="a">
        <xsd:complexType>
          <xsd:attribute name="href" type="xsd:anyURI"/>
        </xsd:complexType>
      </xsd:element>
```

```
    </xsd:complexType>
    <xsd:attribute name="id" type="xsd:string"/>
    <xsd:attribute name="desc" type="xsd:string" minOccurs="0"/>
  </xsd:complexType>
  <xsd:complexType name="expiredType">
    <xsd:element name="expired"/>
    <xsd:attribute name="id" type="xsd:string"/>
    <xsd:attribute name="date" type="xsd:date"/>
    <xsd:attribute name="reason">
      <xsd:simpleType>
        <xsd:restriction base="xsd:string">
          <xsd:enumeration value="expired"/>
          <xsd:enumeration value="updated"/>
        </xsd:restriction>
      </xsd:simpleType>
    </xsd:attribute>
  </xsd:complexType>
  <xsd:complexType name="provType">
    <xsd:attribute name="year" type="xsd:positiveInteger" minOccurs="1"/>
    <xsd:attribute name="month" type="xsd:positiveInteger" minOccurs="1"/>
    <xsd:attribute name="day" type="xsd:positiveInteger" minOccurs="1"/>
  </xsd:complexType>
</xsd:schema>
```

We use several new constructs in the previous code. As you can see, the expiredType contains an element—expired—and three attributes: id, date, and reason. The last attribute—reason—is declared as a simple type, which is based on an already existing type: xsd:string. In this case, you use xsd:string as a base type. The type is specialized by enumerating the possible values the attribute can be assigned. As you can see, the attribute can be assigned the value expired or updated.

In the schema, we declared an element—a—that has an href attribute. The element is supposed to work as a link to a file where the application is stored. Links are common in XML-based languages, so let's look more closely at how they can be used.

Links

The XML Linking Language (XLink) was created to overcome the limitations of the links seen so far on the wired and mobile Internet. XLink became a W3C recommendation on June 27, 2001.

As you probably know, links in HTML are hard coded to a specific destination and, if the link points at anything other than the start of the document, then the target must define an anchor. The purpose of providing a linking language is to make hyperlinks more sophisticated. For example, it'll be possible to link anywhere in a target document, without the need to define anchors in the target document. It's also possible to define multiple destinations, several optional documents, to which the link leads. Several ways also exist to show the linked resource—for example, embedding it in the document that links to it or replacing the document that links to it.

Link Types

If you're going to write XML code that includes links, then it can be a good idea to use the framework of XLink instead of reinventing the wheel. An alternative solution is to create your own element and attributes for the link, as we did when we wrote the DTD and the schema. However, because linking is so fundamental for the Internet, it would be nice if all XML documents used the same syntax and semantics for linking. Tools could then be developed that traverse links and administrate content in a uniform way.

Whichever solution you choose to define your link element in your own DTD or schema, or to use the XLink framework, you have to transform your XML code to the target devices that are going to use it. The XLink framework lets you specify simple links and extended links. Transforming simple links to languages like XHTML and SMIL is easy because they have much in common. Extended links are different from the traditional hypertext links we're used to on the Internet. It's more difficult to write XSL files that transform these types of links to some of the mentioned languages. Software is available, however, that does this job for you.

Simple Links

When you create an XLink, a number of predefined attributes are used to express the properties of the link, while the element in which they occur is one of your own. This element can be defined in your DTD or schema, as usual. The attributes are also listed in your DTD or schema as an ordinary attribute, but they have predefined names and special meanings. Because all the attributes use the xlink namespace, you must refer to that namespace in your DTD or schema. A simple link with an accompanying DTD can look like this:

```
<?xml version="1.0"?>
<!DOCTYPE writerLink [
<!ELEMENT writerLink ANY>
<!ATTLIST writerLink
  xmlns:xlink  CDATA    #FIXED "http://www.w3.org/1999/xlink"
  xlink:type   (simple) #FIXED "simple"
```

```
   xlink:href    CDATA     #REQUIRED
>
]>

<writerLink
  xmlns:xlink="http://www.w3.org/1999/xlink"
  xlink:type="simple"
  xlink:href="http://www.myownsite.com/writers/StephenHawking.xml">
      Information about my favorite writer.
</writerLink>
```

Two attributes from the XLink namespace are used: xlink:type and xlink:href. In
the code, the xlink:type attribute has been set to simple, which indicates the link isn't
an extended link, but a simple link. Xlink:href is also called the *locator* attribute. This
is the attribute that makes it possible to locate the resource. It's similar to the href
attribute in XHTML.

The URL to the definition of the XLink namespace is declared in the attribute list.
You must specify this before you can start to use the predefined XLink attributes.
Because the previous code uses simple links only, the xlink:type attribute is declared
as fixed. The last attribute declares the href attribute as a required attribute that can
contain an ordinary web address.

Extended Links

Extended links are more advanced than simple links. They're specified using a
number of components, such as locators, arcs, and resources.

Associated to a link is the element(s) that points out the other document. The link
itself is called the *arc* in the XLink framework and the elements that participate in the
link—either on the source or destination side of it—are called resources and locators.

Each arc in the link connects a locator or resource with another locator or resource.
Resources are local information elements and are provided in the same document
in which the link is defined. *Locators* are used to address remote resources. These
resources do not point at any objects, but objects point at the resources. Consequently,
to create a basic extended link, you can define a locator, an arc, and a resource.
Here's an example:

```
<?xml version="1.0"?>
<myLibrary xmlns:xlink="http://www.w3.org/1999/xlink">
  This is my library.

  <!-- ********* Link to books by Stephen Hawking. ********* -->
```

```
  <link xlink:type="extended">Books written by my favorite writer.
    <shelf xlink:type="resource" xlink:label="res">Look here.
    </shelf>

    <!-- ********* Connect the "link" with the books. ********* -->
    <connect xlink:type="arc" xlink:from="res" xlink:to="abrief"/>
    <connect xlink:type="arc" xlink:from="res" xlink:to="bholes"/>

    <!-- ********* Books written by Stephen Hawking. ********* -->
    <book author="Stephen Hawking"
      xlink:type="locator"
      xlink:label="abrief"
      xlink:href="http://www.somewebsite.com/dir/abrief.xml"
      xlink:title="A brief history of time.">
    </book>
    <book author=" Stephen Hawking"
      xlink:type="locator"
      xlink:label="bholes"
      xlink:href="http://www.somewebsite.com/dir/bholes.xml"
      xlink:title="Black Holes and Baby Universes and Other Essays.">
    </book>
  </link>
</myLibrary>
```

In this example, we defined a link that goes from a section of our document—the resource—to two remote web sites. The web sites are addressed by the two locators. Locators are used to point at the remote addresses where the information is stored, while resources are local information that's provided in the same document. The resource and the two locators are connected with an arc. Because we have a single resource, which points at two remote information objects, we have to provide two arcs. One of the arcs goes from the resource to the first book, while the other arc goes from the same resource, but to the other book. This is what makes extended links special. It's possible to create links that connect multiple information objects and it's also possible to create bidirectional links. The following example illustrates this:

```
<?xml version="1.0"?>
<myLibrary xmlns:xlink="http://www.w3.org/1999/xlink">
  This is my library.

  <!-- ********* Link to books by Stephen Hawking. ********* -->
  <link xlink:type="extended">Books written by my favorite writer.
    <shelf xlink:type="resource" xlink:label="res">Look here.
```

```
  </shelf>

  <!-- ********* Connect the "link" with the books. ********* -->
  <connect xlink:type="arc" xlink:from="res" xlink:to="abrief"/>
  <connect xlink:type="arc" xlink:from="abrief" xlink:to="res"/>
  <connect xlink:type="arc" xlink:from="res" xlink:to="bholes"/>
  <connect xlink:type="arc" xlink:from="bholes" xlink:to="res"/>
  <connect xlink:type="arc" xlink:from="bholes" xlink:to="abrief"/>
  <connect xlink:type="arc" xlink:from="abrief" xlink:to="bholes"/>

  <!-- ********* Books written by Stephen Hawking. ********* -->
  <book author="Stephen Hawking"
    xlink:type="locator"
    xlink:label="abrief"
    xlink:href="http://www.somewebsite.com/dir/abrief.xml"
    xlink:title="A brief history of time.">
  </book>
  <book author=" Stephen Hawking"
    xlink:type="locator"
    xlink:label="bholes"
    xlink:href="http://www.somewebsite.com/dir/bholes.xml"
    xlink:title="Black Holes and Baby Universes and Other Essays.">
  </book>
  </link>
</myLibrary>
```

We've added a number of arcs to make navigation possible in all directions. The previous code says it should be possible to navigate from "the shelf" to both books, as well as from both books back to the shelf. Also, we provide navigation facilities between the two books in both directions.

To indicate how the link will be traversed, the attributes called "actuate" and "show" may be used. The following examples illustrate this:

```
<?xml version="1.0"?>
<myLibrary xmlns:xlink="http://www.w3.org/1999/xlink">
  This is my library.

  <!-- ********* Link to books by Stephen Hawking. ********* -->
  <link xlink:type="extended">Books written by my favorite writer.
    <shelf xlink:type="resource" xlink:label="res">Look here.
    </shelf>
```

```
<!-- ********* Connect the "link" with the books. ********* -->
<connect xlink:type="arc" xlink:from="res" xlink:to="abrief"
  xlink:actuate="onRequest"
  xlink:show="replace"/>
<connect xlink:type="arc" xlink:from="abrief" xlink:to="res"
  xlink:actuate="onRequest"
  xlink:show="replace"/>
<connect xlink:type="arc" xlink:from="res" xlink:to="bholes"
  xlink:actuate="onRequest"
  xlink:show="replace"/>
<connect xlink:type="arc" xlink:from="bholes" xlink:to="res"
  xlink:actuate="onRequest"
  xlink:show="replace"/>
<connect xlink:type="arc" xlink:from="bholes" xlink:to="abrief"
  xlink:actuate=" onRequest"
  xlink:show="embed"/>
<connect xlink:type="arc" xlink:from="abrief" xlink:to="bholes"
  xlink:actuate="onLoad"
  xlink:show="embed"/>

<!-- ********* Books written by Stephen Hawking. ********* -->
<book author="Stephen Hawking"
  xlink:type="locator"
  xlink:label="abrief"
  xlink:href="http://www.somewebsite.com/dir/abrief.xml"
  xlink:title="A brief history of time.">
</book>
<book author=" Stephen Hawking"
  xlink:type="locator"
  xlink:label="bholes"
  xlink:href="http://www.somewebsite.com/dir/bholes.xml"
  xlink:title="Black Holes and Baby Universes and Other Essays.">
</book>
</link>
</myLibrary>
```

If the xlink:actuate attribute is set to onRequest, then the user must interact to trigger the traversal of the link. As you can see, all connect elements except one have the xlink:actuate attribute set to onRequest. The last connect element, though, uses the xlink:actuate attribute set to onLoad. In this case, the link traversal occurs when the document is loaded. Because the xlink:show attribute is set to embed, the result of the link traversal will also be embedded in the same window, rather than replacing the existing content. New windows can be allocated by setting the xlink:show attribute to new. The result of the traversal is then displayed in a new window, rather than being embedded or replacing the old window.

Paths

XPaths can be used with XLinks to address small components of an XML document, such as individual elements or a piece of text in an element. XPaths can also be used with extensible style sheets and XSL transformations, which you'll see soon. XPath is a W3C recommendation.

Tree Structures

Assume we've written the following XML document, which we'll address later on, using the XPath syntax:

```
<?xml version="1.0"?>
<doc name="mydoc">
  <info>
    <title>My document.
    </title>
  </info>
  <text info="basic introduction">
    <heading>Welcome!
    </heading>
    <bodyText>This is the introduction.
    </bodyText>
  </text>
  <text info="text chunk">
    <bodyText>The document contains text.
    </bodyText>
  </text>
</doc>
```

The code can be represented as a tree structure where the root of the tree is located above the top-level element, and the subelements and attributes are branches. In the previous example, doc is located one level below the root. The info and text elements are branches from the root element—the doc element—and they're both located one level below doc because they occur inside the doc element in the code. Title occurs under (branches from) the info element, so it's located one level below the info element. The info attribute is a child of the text element, so it's located one level beneath the text element. Let's summarize all the elements and attributes to see where they're located in the tree structure:

```
Level 1:
  doc                          (top level element)
  name="mydoc"                 (attribute in top level element)
Level 2:
  info                         (child of doc)
  text                         (child of doc)
  text                         (child of doc)
  info="basic introduction"    (child of doc)
  info="text chunk"            (child of doc)
Level 3:
  title                        (child of info)
  heading                      (child of text)
  bodyText                     (child of text)
  bodyText                     (child of text)
Level 4:
  My document.                 (child of title)
  This is the introduction.    (child of bodyText)
  The document contains text.  (child of bodyText)
```

If you want to refer to the contents of the first bodyText element, then you can write the following:

```
/doc/text[info = "basic introduction"]/bodyText/
```

The path matches the top-level doc element and the child element, which has set the info attribute to "basic introduction" followed by the bodyText element. It's also possible to formulate a path, which has the same meaning, using the following syntax:

```
/doc/text[1]/bodyText/
```

This expression chooses the doc element, which should be the top-level element, and then the first occurrence of a text element, followed by the bodyText element. Note, if someone changes the order of the two bodyText elements in the XML code, then the latter syntax is less good because it will return another result.

The following path also has the same meaning as the previous.

```
/doc/text[2]/../text[1]/bodyText
```

Two dots (..) indicate you should move one step up in the tree. If you're familiar with this, it's the same syntax as for filenames. In this case, first choose the doc element and the second text element, which is inside the doc element. Then move back again to the doc element and, instead, choose the first text element, which occurs inside the doc element. Then the bodyText element is finally chosen. The following path selects all text elements in the code.

```
//text
```

Two slashes (//) indicate "all occurrences of" in the document. The following path returns all attributes in the document.

```
//@*
```

The @ symbol means "attribute" and the asterisk (*) is a wild card that means "all." When you're providing an XPath, you needn't start with a / or //. If you write @* or text[2], the path will apply to the context node. Let's discuss that in the next section.

Now that you know the basics of the XML Path language, let's look at how they can be used with XSL Transformations.

XSL Transformations

XSL transformations (XSLT) are useful when you want to convert your XML document to a format that can be interpreted by a device, such as a PDA or a mobile phone. An XSLT takes an input document and converts the elements, attributes, and text in that document to an output document, which can contain a completely different set of elements, attributes, and text. The Extensible Stylesheet Language (XSL) is used to express how the XML document will be transformed, which input it expects, and what the output should be.

An XSLT processor is required for the conversion. The XSLT processor reads the XML document and the .XSL file, which contains the style sheet. The rules in the style sheet are applied to the XML document and an output document is generated by the XSLT processor. HTML documents can be generated as well as arbitrary XML documents. In fact, even text or binary documents, such as MS Word, can be generated using XSLTs. This is what makes this technology so powerful. A generic language can be defined using a schema or a DTD. Instance documents are created and validated according to the schema or DTD. The information can finally be adapted for a wide range of devices, which speak different languages, using a set of style sheets and an XSLT processor.

Structure

The style sheet begins with an XML header and uses the xsl namespace. The complete style sheet is specified between the xsl:stylesheet tags. This is a simple style sheet, which takes a simple XML file and transforms it to an XHTML document. Here is the XML file:

```
<?xml version="1.0"?>
<doc>
  <purpose>Description
  </purpose>
  <text>This is the first page of the manual.
It describes all the features and how the device is operated.
  </text>
</doc>
```

The style sheet looks like this:

```
<?xml version="1.0"?>
<xsl:stylesheet version="1.0"
xmlns:xsl="http://www.w3.org/1999/XSL/Transform">
  <xsl:output
      method="xml"
      doctype-public = "-//W3C//DTD XHTML 1.0 Strict//EN"
      doctype-system = "http://www.w3c.org/DTD/xhtml1-strict.dtd"/>

  <xsl:template match="/">
    <html xmlns="http://www.w3.org/1999/xhtml" xml:lang="en" lang="en">
      <head>
        <title>Manual
        </title>
      </head>
      <body>
        <xsl:apply-templates/>
      </body>
    </html>
  </xsl:template>

  <xsl:template match="doc">
      <xsl:apply-templates/>
  </xsl:template>
```

```
<xsl:template match="purpose">
  <h1>
    <xsl:apply-templates/>
  </h1>
</xsl:template>

<xsl:template match="text">
  <p>
    <xsl:apply-templates/>
  </p>
</xsl:template>

</xsl:stylesheet>
```

Because the output is XML code, you need to specify the PUBLIC and SYSTEM strings in the DOCTYPE declaration. As you can see, the xsl:output element is used for that.

The xsl:template element is used with the attribute match to detect where you are in the transformation process. If you are at the root of the document, indicated by /, then the following code will be produced, but not output yet:

```
<?xml version="1.0" encoding="UTF-8"?>
<!DOCTYPE html
SYSTEM "http://www.w3c.org/DTD/xhtml1-strict.dtd"
PUBLIC "-//W3C//DTD XHTML 1.0 Strict//EN">
<html xmlns="http://www.w3.org/1999/xhtml" xml:lang="en" lang="en">
  <head>
    <title>Manual
    </title>
  </head>
  <body>
  </body>
</html>
```

When this code is generated by the XSLT processor, internally, it knows when it continues to make the code complete, it will insert more code between the body tags. This is indicated by the xsl:apply-templates element, which the XSLT processor reaches when the previous code is produced. Because the processor has now generated the code it should generate when it starts to read the XML document, it continues with the top-level elements in the XML code. The first element it reaches is the purpose element. In the style sheet, it finds the following rule:

```
<xsl:template match="purpose">
  <h1>
```

```
      <xsl:apply-templates/>
    </h1>
</xsl:template>
```

The purpose element in the XML code matches the xsl:template element in the style sheet, so the XSLT processor then refines the code further by inserting the previous code between the body tags. This is where the processor was before this rule was applied. Now the code looks like this internally in the XSLT processor's memory (it hasn't been output yet).

```
<?xml version="1.0" encoding="UTF-8"?>
<!DOCTYPE html
SYSTEM "http://www.w3c.org/DTD/xhtml1-strict.dtd"
PUBLIC "-//W3C//DTD XHTML 1.0 Strict//EN">
<html xmlns="http://www.w3.org/1999/xhtml" xml:lang="en" lang="en">
  <head>
    <title>Manual
    </title>
  </head>
  <body>
    <h1>Description
    </h1>
  </body>
</html>
```

The tags for the h1 element are inserted at the right place. If you check your XML file again, you can see the purpose element and the text element are on the same level, just below the root of the XML document. None of these elements is inside another element; they are on the same level: the top-level. Consequently, the processing done so far—generating the code for the h1 element—is done in parallel with the generation of the code for the text element. The result of processing the purpose element and the result of processing the text element are inserted at the same time to generate code. The following rule is also applied.

```
<xsl:template match="text">
  <p>
    <xsl:apply-templates/>
  </p>
</xsl:template>
```

This generates the following code. Included is the result of processing the purpose element as well.

```
<?xml version="1.0" encoding="UTF-8"?>
<!DOCTYPE html
SYSTEM "http://www.w3c.org/DTD/xhtml1-strict.dtd"
PUBLIC "-//W3C//DTD XHTML 1.0 Strict//EN">
<html xmlns="http://www.w3.org/1999/xhtml" xml:lang="en" lang="en">
  <head>
    <title>Manual
    </title>
  </head>
  <body>
    <h1>Description
    </h1>
    <p>This is the first page of the manual.
It describes all the features and how the device is operated.
    </p>
  </body>
</html>
```

Finally, you have generated an XHTML document from your simple XML document. The text between the purpose and text elements is provided as is, and the document has been augmented with the right XHTML prologue and suitable elements. You could have chosen other elements. For example, you hard coded the title. Instead, the purpose element could have been translated to the title. You could also have written the description in boldface or with another font using the font face attributes in XHTML.

Cascading Style Sheets

While XSLTs are used to transform a set of elements, attributes, and text to another set of elements, attributes, and text, cascading style sheets (CSS) are used to format a document for a certain device or application. The word format isn't good, though, because it's often misinterpreted. You can format a document using elements and attributes. For example, you might write an XHTML document that introduces a line break and selects a particular font for a paragraph. This way you've introduced a certain amount of formatting into your document, although you only provided the markup itself. An XMLT can introduce such elements and attributes in the output document, and, in that case, the XSLT has dealt with issues like formatting, in addition to the transformation. CSS, on the other hand, is the technology you should use when you need to specify how the markup should be displayed in terms of pixels, colors, and general layout. XSLT should transform the set of elements and attributes from one language to another, while CSS should express the meaning of the output document in terms of rendering.

CSS Basics

Your XML document refers to the CSS document using a processing instruction where you provide the content type—in this case, text/css—and an address to where the CSS file resides. The address can be relative. For example, if you want to store the CSS file in the same directory as the XML file, the XML document can look like this:

```
<?xml version="1.0" encoding="UTF-8"?>
<?xml:stylesheet type="text/css" href="css1.css"?>
<doc>
  <purpose>Description
  </purpose>
  <text>This is the first page of the manual.
    It describes all the features and how the device is operated.
  </text>
</doc>
```

The CSS document, which is associated with the previous XML document, might look like this:

```
doc { display: block }
purpose { display: block }
text { display: block }
```

Elements that are used in the XML document are listed to the left of the curly brackets. Selectors are listed inside the curly brackets. Each selector has a value and the curly brackets can contain a semicolon-separated list of selectors and values.

Block and Inline-level Elements

All elements in the previous example are declared as block elements. The opposite of a block element is an inline element, which is used for an element that's part of a block and shouldn't cause line breaks. Assume you want to display the purpose with a bigger font, then the style sheet might look like this:

```
doc { display: block }
purpose {
     display: block;
     font-family: Courier;
     font-size: 24pt
}
text {
     display: block;
     font-family: Courier;
     font-size: 12pt
}
```

A 24-point Courier font is used to display the text inside the purpose element's block. The text inside the purpose element's block will be displayed with the same font, but at a 12-point size. A line break is introduced between block elements. This is the difference between block elements and inline elements. It's up to you, though, to decide the gap between the purpose block and the text block. If you don't specify how much space you want between the blocks, there won't be any space at all.

Here's an example that uses an inline declaration:

```
<?xml version="1.0" encoding="UTF-8"?>
<?xml:stylesheet type="text/css" href="css1.css"?>
<doc>
  <purpose>Description
  </purpose>
  <text>This is the <strong>first</strong> page of the manual.
  It describes all the features and how the device is operated.
  </text>
</doc>
```

The following CSS document is associated with the previous XML document:

```
doc { display: block }
purpose {
     display: block;
     font-family: Times New Roman;
     font-size: 24pt
}
text {
```

```
        display: block;
        font-family: Times New Roman;
        font-size: 12pt
}
strong {
        display: inline;
        font-family: Times New Roman;
        font-size: 14pt
}
```

The element surrounded by the strong tags in the XML document will be rendered using the 14pt Times New Roman font. No line break will appear because the display property is declared as inline.

Font Properties

Because the normal font size can be adjusted by most browsers, it's a less-appropriate idea to use hard-coded sizes, as in the previous example. If possible, try to express your font sizes in relative terms.

Size

Let's keep our XML file as it is and only change the CSS file. The 24pt and 12pt values are removed and replaced by relative values:

```
doc { display: block }
purpose {
        display: block;
        font-family: Courier;
        font-size: 150%
}
text {
        display: block;
        font-family: Courier
}
```

No value at all is given for the text block, which means it will use the browser's current setting for the normal size. The font size for the purpose block is 150 percent of the browser's current setting for the normal size.

Inherited Properties

The font-style property can be used to render your XML document using boldface and italics style Times New Roman font:

```
doc {
     display: block;
     font-family: Times New Roman;
     font-style: bold
}
purpose {
     display: block;
     font-size: 150%
}
text {
     display: block;
     font-style: italic
}
```

The top-level element—doc—sets the font style to boldface and the font family to Times New Roman. These properties are inherited by all the child elements: in this case, purpose and text. One of the settings is overridden by the text element, however, because a new value—italic—is provided for the font-style property. Consequently, the text for the purpose element is displayed using the boldface Times New Roman font.

Because the font-size property hasn't been specified for the top-level doc element, the font-size for the purpose element will be 150 percent of the normal font size. If a value had been provided for the top-level doc element, such as 12pt, then the font size for the purpose element would have been been calculated to 150 percent of 12 = 18.

Space

If you watch the result of the previous examples in a browser, you can see no space exists between the purpose element and the text element. Maybe you also want to introduce some space in the left and right margins. The following code uses the margin properties to add space:

```
doc {
     display: block;
     font-family: Times New Roman;
     font-style: bold
}
purpose {
```

```
        display: block;
        font-size: 150%;
        margin-top: 16pt;
        margin-bottom: 12pt;
        margin-left: 1pc;
        margin-right: 1pc
}
text {
        display: block;
        font-style: italic
        margin-top: 12pt;
        margin-bottom: 12pt;
        margin-left: 12pt;
        margin-right: 12pt
}
```

The top, bottom, left, and right margins are defined for the purpose and text elements. *Margin-left* specifies the space between the border of the browser and the first character. Using the *margin-right* property, you can specify the space between the last character and the border to the right. *Margin-top* is used to express the space between the previous block and the block where the property is defined. *Margin-bottom* applies to the space below the block and the next block. Two units have been used: *pt,* which means points, and *pc,* which means picas.

Units

One pica equals 12 points. You can also use the unit *in* for inches, *cm* for centimeters, or *mm* for millimeters.

Although we used picas and points in the previous example, you might not know which physical properties are used for the target device. Again, many different types of wireless devices, phones, and PDAs exist with small, medium, and large displays. Consequently, it's a better idea to use a percentage to specify the margins. Then the style sheet might look like this:

```
doc {
        display: block;
        font-family: Times New Roman;
        font-style: bold
}
purpose {
        display: block;
```

```
      font-size: 150%;
      margin-top: 7%;
      margin-bottom: 5%;
      margin-left: 5%;
      margin-right: 5%
}
text {
      display: block;
      font-style: italic
      margin-top: 5%;
      margin-bottom: 5%;
      margin-left: 5%;
      margin-right: 5%
}
```

In this example, we specify all margins as percentage values. The values apply to the size of the browser. Because margin-left is set to 5 percent, the text will start 5 percent to the right of the leftmost edge. If each line has 100 pixels, it means 5 pixels.

Colors

The property list for an element may contain color specifications. Using the property color, the foreground color may be specified. Background-color is the property used to express the background color for the element. The value can be specified using the traditional hexadecimal notation, as you might recognize from HTML. A hash character followed by the number specifies the color. Colors can also be expressed using RGB values. The RGB values are given either as integers between 0–255 or as percentages. Here's an example that illustrates this:

```
doc {
      display: block;
      font-family: Times New Roman;
}
purpose {
      display: block;
      font-size: 150%;
      color: RGB(255, 0, 0);
      background-color: #000000
}
text {
      display: block;
```

```
        color: #00FF00;
        background-color: RGB(50%, 50%, 50%)
}
```

The purpose element has the foreground color set to red because the RGB (Red Green Blue) value uses the red portion of the color mix only. If the RGB value has been changed to RGB(255, 64, 0), then you would have added 25 percent green to the color. The background color is set to black because none of the color components has any value. In the text block, the foreground color is green because the green component is set to its maximum hexadecimal value, FF. The background color for the text block is gray.

Matching

You can write style sheets that analyze the XML document, and then choose property rules, depending on what the XML document contains. Assume you want to indicate that a piece of text is meant to be a comment. If the class attribute is set to comment, the text is rendered using italics. The following example illustrates this. Here's the XML code:

```
<?xml:stylesheet type="text/css" href="mycss.css"?>
<doc>
  <purpose>Description
  </purpose>
  <text>This is the first page of the manual.
  </text>
  <text class='comment'>It describes all the features and how the device is
operated.
  </text>
</doc>
```

Here's the style sheet:

```
doc {
     display: block;
     font-family: Times New Roman;
}
purpose {
     display: block;
     font-size: 150%;
}
text.comment {
     display: block;
```

```
        font-style: italic;
}
text {
        display: block;
}
```

Note, the text element is mentioned twice in the style sheet. The first rule is more specific, though, because it refers to the case when the class attribute has been set to the value comment. If that rule isn't matched, the last one works as a default. You can also match attributes in other ways that have been specified in version 2 of the CSS specification. However, the previous technique is supported by WCSS, an extended subset of CSS2 that's part of WAP-NG. If you need to do attribute matching and be compatible with as many devices as possible, I recommend you go for an implementation, which is similar to the previous.

XML Tools

You can choose from many XML tools depending on what you need to do. A few of these tools should be mentioned.

Microsoft has implemented an XML parser, released in version 4 at press time. The XML parser can be used from the Internet Explorer web browser in Windows. Just drag-and-drop XML files to the Internet Explorer window and they'll be displayed.

Mozilla and Netscape Navigator 6—based on Mozilla—have extensive XML support. Mozilla supports CSS and is available with an XSLT implementation.

Napa and Saxon are two XSLT processors that can transform XML documents using XSL style sheets. *Saxon* is a general collection of tools that can be used to process XML documents and includes an XSL processor. *Napa* is a small, but easy to use, XSLT processor.

XML Writer is a simple and useful shareware tool that can perform validation. It can also transform documents using XSL.

Many plug-ins are available for HTML-Kit that can be used to write XSL, CSS, XHTML, SMIL, and other XML documents.

XML Spy is one of the most professional and comprehensive commercial XML- editing tools on the market. If you work with XML, consider this tool.

The Developer's Quick Reference Guide

OBJECTIVES

► Write documents for mobile devices using XHTML Basic

► Design services that use voice recognition and voice synthesis

► Create multimedia presentations using SMIL 2.0

► Understand how maps are specified with GML

► Translate an XML file to WBXML

► Understand how profiles can be used to adapt content for different types of devices

► Know the basics of XML-RPC

XHTML

IN THIS CHAPTER:

XHTML and the Modularization of HTML4

X HTML is a modularization of HTML4 and a translation of the language to XML. Making HTML4 an XML application has many benefits, one of which is that the documents can be validated and checked if they're well formed. This is not only helpful for the developer, but also makes it possible to use HTML (or, more precisely, XHTML) code in a mobile Internet context. Because many of the wireless handheld devices are limited when it comes to CPU power and memory, documents can be validated before they're transferred to the wireless device. Thus, parts of the error-handling routines can be moved from the wireless device to gateway or server software.

XHTML Basic is included in WAP 2.0 and future versions of the i-mode service will most likely be based on XHTML.

XHTML and the Modularization of HTML4

When HTML4 was defined in terms of XML, it was also modularized. A number of modules were defined, and each element and attribute in HTML4 was put in a specific module.

With XHTML 1.0, each module specifies a set of elements and attributes associated with a certain use case, such as the execution of scripts, formatting text, or embedding an object in the XHTML page. One of the reasons to define XHTML as a number of modules is to make it easier for vendors and software developers to specify the software's compliance with the XHTML specification. By listing all the supported modules, finding out what the software can do and which tags are supported or left out becomes much easier.

Document Type Definitions

Three Document Type Definitions (DTDs) have been defined for XHTML 1.0. They're called Transitional, Frameset, and Strict.

Transitional XHTML Documents

Transitional XHTML documents are documents that include elements and attributes that are about to be phased out and replaced by others. In particular, this applies to style sheets.

Frameset XHTML Documents

The *frameset* XHTML document is used for documents that contain frames. Because frames are less suitable for small mobile devices, and because they're based on a layout that's adapted for reasonably large screens, this DTD is rarely used by mobile applications. As the screens on handheld devices become larger and achieve better resolution, it might become possible to browse web pages originally created for a desktop computer.

Strict XHTML Documents

Strict XHTML documents are neither transitional nor refer to a number of frame documents. You'll use this document type, unless you're implementing a frame document or a document that uses elements about to be phased out.

Closed Tags (Well-Formed XML)

Because many people make the same errors when they move from HTML to XHTML, let's look at the most common mistakes. All elements must be closed or, in other words, the XML code must be well formed. This means elements that have an empty content model must contain a slash and elements that don't have an empty content model must have a closing end tag. Here's an example that contains a number of errors. See if you can find them.

```
<?xml version="1.0" encoding="UTF-8"?>
<!DOCTYPE html PUBLIC "-//W3C//DTD XHTML 1.0 Strict//EN"
    "http://www.w3.org/TR/xhtml1/DTD/xhtml1-strict.dtd">
        <html xmlns="http://www.w3.org/1999/xhtml">
<head>
  <title>Hello
  </title>
</head>
<body>
  <h1>Welcome!</h1>
  <p>Hello<br>
  <p>my friends.
</body>
</html>
```

First, the p elements have no end tags. Some HTML coders use the p element to introduce a small line break. However, the intention is that the element should encapsulate a piece of text, referred to as a *paragraph*. The end tags must be included. Secondly, the br element doesn't have a slash.

Errors like these can cause a lot of trouble in a wireless environment for several reasons. If a gateway exists in between the wireless network and the fixed Internet, then it might do an error check to see if the document is well formed. In the WAP case, it might also tokenize the markup into Wireless Binary XML (WBXML). This is only possible if the code is well formed. A simple error, such as leaving out an end tag for the paragraph element, might result in the document not being transferred to the handset. Instead, the gateway could send another document in its place, a completely valid document that describes the error. If no gateway exists between the wireless network and the fixed network, as when you're using a simple dial-up connection to a modem pool, and if the handheld device is limited in terms of CPU power, then it might be unable to perform detailed error checks. Consequently, the document might not be displayed at all on the device or some portions might be impossible to display.

The XHTML Modules

Each of the modules of XHTML is defined in a file of its own. All the modules are available to XHTML authors if you simply use the full DTD, as in the latest example. To combine different modules, a DTD for all modules in the language points at the DTDs for all the individual modules.

For you to know which modules are part of the modularized XHTML framework is relevant because some technologies, like WAP 2.0, are based on a limited subset of all modules in XHTML and this subset can be extended by independent vendors. Understanding that XHTML Basic is the foundation is important, but manufacturers might exist that support more modules than these, depending on which industry or application they're targeting. For example, a manufacturer might develop a small handheld device with one purpose: to measure and collect temperatures and display it in a table on a 96×144 pixel screen. In this case, manufacturers gain a lot if they include support for the tables module.

If you read a specification that says a browser supports XHTML Basic plus the presentation and edit modules, then you'll have a good feeling for what the browser can do. Remember, one of the reasons for modularizing HTML was a number of different devices—such as phones, PDAs, and hybrids of these—were expected to appear on the market. Manufacturers can then base their development on a core, like XHTML Basic, and add modules on top of that to support the capabilities of individual devices.

Using modules has many of the advantages object-oriented software has. Modules make it possible to encapsulate data. Each module defines a certain set of elements and attributes. If some modules need to be updated, only those modules must be changed. Modules make reuse possible. Some of the modules, such as text and links, can be part of many languages in the XHTML family, including XHTML Basic. Other modules, such as frames, might only be used in browsers that execute on a traditional desktop computer.

Remember, XHTML Basic will probably be the foundation for limited handheld devices. In the near future, though, devices and browsers might be on the market that can browse XHTML pages. This means it's a good idea to be acquainted with XHTML as a whole and not only the modules in XHTML Basic. The modules of XHTML Basic can be seen as a foundation for services with a graphical user interface (GUI) based on XHTML.

The idea with the modularization of XHTML is also to make it easier for manufacturers to add modules with which their devices and browsers are compatible. In this case, a good understanding of XHTML as a whole is motivated. Let's go through all the modules and look at some examples.

The Modules of XHTML Basic

Before we start with the details of each module, let's look at XHTML Basic. The modules in XHTML Basic 1.0 are base, basic forms, basic tables, hypertext, image, link, list, metainformation, object, structure, and text. The rest of this chapter explains this in more detail but, in general, each module stores a number of elements or/and attributes.

As you can see, the style sheets module isn't supported, however, external style sheets can be used with the link element and the link module. This module is explained later in the chapter. Frames aren't supported because frames were created with a desktop computer in mind. Displaying frames on a small handheld device isn't recommended, even if the browser on the device would support it. Only basic forms and tables, and not the more extensive modules for tables and forms, are supported.

There is a module called presentation, which isn't part of XHTML Basic 1.0. The presentation module must be added if you want to format the text using elements like *i* for italics, *b* for boldface fonts, *sub* for subscript, and *sup* for superscripts. This is the case with WAP 2.0, where the presentation module has been added to the set of modules in XHTML Basic to provide a useful framework for the creation of wireless services based on XHTML. Remember, though, the preferred way of formatting content is through *style sheets,* which make it possible to separate content and presentation.

Avoid mixing elements that describe how things are rendered with elements used to describe the structure of things.

Here's an example in XHTML Basic 1.0:

```
<?xml version="1.0" encoding="UTF-8"?>
<!DOCTYPE html PUBLIC "-//W3C//DTD XHTML Basic 1.0//EN"
    "http://www.w3.org/TR/xhtml-basic/xhtml-basic10.dtd">
<html xmlns="http://www.w3.org/1999/xhtml">
<head>
  <title>Hello</title>
</head>
<body>
  <h1>Welcome!</h1>
  <p>Hello <br/>my friends.</p>
</body>
</html>
```

This is the previous example, which wasn't well formed. It has been corrected and the DOCTYPE declaration now refers to XHTML Basic 1.0. The example uses elements and attributes from the structure and text modules.

Structure, Text, Hypertext, and Lists

The following example uses elements from the structure, text, hypertext, and lists modules only:

```
<?xml version="1.0" encoding="UTF-8"?>
<!DOCTYPE html PUBLIC "-//W3C//DTD XHTML 1.0 Strict//EN"
    "http://www.w3.org/TR/xhtml1/DTD/xhtml1-strict.dtd">
      <html xmlns="http://www.w3.org/1999/xhtml">
<head>
  <title>Structure, text, hypertext and lists
  </title>
</head>
<body>
  <h1>List of applications</h1>
  <p>These are <strong>beta</strong> versions.</p>
  <ul>
    <li><a href="./lib/cpro09.html">CalendarPro v0.9</a></li>
    <li><a href="./lib/game10.jad">Gamer v1.0</a></li>
    <li><a href="./lib/sprs08.exe">SpreadSheetPlus v0.8</a></li>
  </ul>
```

```
</body>
</html>
```

The code can be validated according to the XHTML Basic DTD because it uses elements and attributes that are part of modules in the XHTML Basic language only. So, if the code was created for devices that support XHTML Basic 1.0 only, you'd have to change the DOCTYPE declaration so it looks like this:

```
<?xml version="1.0" encoding="UTF-8"?>
<!DOCTYPE html PUBLIC "-//W3C//DTD XHTML Basic 1.0//EN"
    "http://www.w3.org/TR/xhtml-basic/xhtml-basic10.dtd">
```

Let's return to the body of the code. The body, head, html, and title elements belong to the structure module. Text container elements were put in the text module. *Text containers* are elements used for the inclusion of text, such as paragraphs, quotes, headings, and the strong and the elements. The list module contains elements for ordered and unordered lists.

Applets and Scripting

Program code sorts under the applets and scripting modules. These modules aren't supported by XHTML Basic 1.0. However, if a manufacturer has created a mobile phone or an application supports the execution of scripts or applets in an XHTML environment, then the applets and scripting modules can be added to the set of modules in XHTML Basic 1.0. In this case, the code shouldn't be validated according to the XHTML Basic DTD but, instead, according to the XHTML 1.0 strict DTD or a DTD that includes the DTDs for XHTML Basic 1.0 and the additional modules. The following example adds a small JavaScript to the previous code and the code should be displayed on a device that supports the full XHTML 1.0 strict DTD.

```
<?xml version="1.0" encoding="UTF-8"?>
<!DOCTYPE html PUBLIC "-//W3C//DTD XHTML 1.0 Strict//EN"
    "http://www.w3.org/TR/xhtml1/DTD/xhtml1-strict.dtd">
      <html xmlns="http://www.w3.org/1999/xhtml">
    <head>
        <title>Structure, text, hypertext, list and scripting.
        </title>
    </head>
    <body>
        <script type="JavaScript">
          alert("All applications are in beta versions. Use at your own
risk!!!");
```

```
        </script>
        <h1>List of applications</h1>
        <p>(<strong>beta</strong> versions)</p>
        <ul>
            <li>
                <a href="./lib/cpro09.html">CalendarPro v0.9</a>
            </li>
            <li>
                <a href="./lib/game10.jad">Gamer v1.0</a>
            </li>
            <li>
                <a href="./lib/sprs08.exe">SpreadSheetPlus v0.8</a>
            </li>
        </ul>

    </body>
</html>
```

The module's structure, text, hypertext, links, and scripting were used. The structure module is needed because the head and body elements are used. The paragraph element is part of the text module. To use the *a* element, you need the links module; to use an embedded JavaScript, you need the scripting module.

Presentation, Edit, and Bidirectional Text

The *presentation* module deals with how the content is rendered. It doesn't follow the principles of XML to separate content and presentation but, instead, is a heritage from HTML4. The elements for boldface and italics were put in that module. WAP 2.0 supports the presentation module, but because the presentation module isn't part of the modules in XHTML Basic, this module has been added.

Inserted or deleted text can be specified using the del and ins elements. They were put in the edit module, on their own, when HTML4 was modularized. If someone has made an update to a document and wants the additions or deletions to be specified in the document, these elements can be used. The edit module isn't part of XHTML Basic.

The *bidirectional* text module and its only element, *bdo,* can be used when languages are used that require the text to be interpreted, for example, right-to-left. A rather odd and rarely used module, the bidirectional text module isn't part of the XHTML Basic set of modules.

The following example extends the previous example with elements from the presentation and edit modules. The code is designed for devices that support the full XHTML 1.0 strict DTD.

```xml
<?xml version="1.0" encoding="UTF-8"?>
<!DOCTYPE html PUBLIC "-//W3C//DTD XHTML 1.0 Strict//EN"
    "http://www.w3.org/TR/xhtml1/DTD/xhtml1-strict.dtd">
      <html xmlns="http://www.w3.org/1999/xhtml">
    <head>
        <title>Structure, text, hypertext, list, scripting, presentation and
               edit.
        </title>
    </head>
    <body>
        <script type="JavaScript">
          alert("All applications are in beta versions. Use at your own risk!!!");
        </script>
        <h1>List of applications</h1>
        <p><small>(<strong>beta</strong> versions)</small></p>
        <ul>
            <li>
                <a href="./lib/cpro09.html">CalendarPro
                       <del>v0.9</del><ins>v1.0</ins></a>
            </li>
            <li>
                <a href="./lib/game10.jad">Gamer v1.0</a>
            </li>
            <li>
                <a href="./lib/sprs08.exe">SpreadSheetPlus v0.8</a>
            </li>
        </ul>
    </body>
</html>
```

The small element, which is part of the presentation module, was inserted into the paragraph. To indicate that one of the applications was updated from version 0.9 to version 1.0, the del and ins elements were used. Usually, browsers render the del element as a dash through the text and the ins element is displayed as normal text.

Forms and Basic Forms

Elements related to forms reside in two modules: forms and basic forms. In basic forms modules, some elements and attributes have been left out to provide support for simple forms, which don't demand the support for uploading of files, option groups, and so forth. The following example adds a form to the example. Just for fun, try to figure out which element or attribute belongs to the forms module and not the basic forms module. Remember, one of the basic ideas is basic forms are used by devices and applications that have no use for complex forms or simply cannot use the more complex elements and attributes because of their limited CPU power and I/O functions.

```
<?xml version="1.0" encoding="UTF-8"?>
<!DOCTYPE html PUBLIC "-//W3C//DTD XHTML 1.0 Strict//EN"
    "http://www.w3.org/TR/xhtml1/DTD/xhtml1-strict.dtd">
<html xmlns="http://www.w3.org/1999/xhtml">
    <head>
        <title>Structure, text, hypertext, lists, scripting, presentation, edit
            and forms.
    </title>
    </head>
    <body>
        <script type="JavaScript">
          alert("All applications are in beta versions. Use at your own risk!!!");
        </script>
        <h1>List of applications</h1>
        <p>
            <small>(<strong>beta</strong> versions)</small>
        </p>
        <ul>
            <li>
                <a href="./lib/cpro09.html">CalendarPro <del>v0.9</del>
                    <ins>v1.0</ins>
                </a>

            </li>
            <li>
                <a href="./lib/game10.jad">Gamer v1.0</a>
            </li>
            <li>
                <a href="./lib/sprs08.exe">SpreadSheetPlus v0.8</a>
            </li>
        </ul>
        <form action="www.thereceiver.com/script.cgi">
          <p>
            Your name <input name="yourName" type="text"/><br/>
            Image of you <input name="yourImage" type="file"/><br/>
            Gender <select name="gender">
                        <option value="male">Male</option>
                        <option value="female">Female</option>
                    </select><br/>
            Email <input name="emailAdr" type="text"/><br/>
```

```
                <input type="submit" value="Submit!"/>
            </p>
        </form>
    </body>
</html>
```

The previous code goes beyond the basic forms module because it uses an input element that has the type attribute set to "file." Only the forms module—not the basic forms module—supports file input types. In XHTML Basic, the basic forms module is used and not the forms module. Consequently, uploading files and using other sophisticated form elements, such as option groups, isn't possible in XHTML Basic.

Tables and Basic Tables

Similar to how forms have been provided in two modules, two table modules were defined during the modularization of XHTML. As with forms, one of the modules—basic tables—is a subset of the other—tables. Thus, the tables module contains the same elements and attributes as the basic tables, plus some additional elements, for more complex tables. The following example uses elements and attributes from the most complex of the two modules, the tables module:

```
<?xml version="1.0" encoding="UTF-8"?>
<!DOCTYPE html PUBLIC "-//W3C//DTD XHTML 1.0 Strict//EN"
    "http://www.w3.org/TR/xhtml1/DTD/xhtml1-strict.dtd">
<html xmlns="http://www.w3.org/1999/xhtml">
    <head>
        <title>Structure, text, hypertext, list, scripting, presentation, edit,
           forms and tables.
        </title>
    </head>
    <body>
        <script type="JavaScript">
          alert("All applications are in beta versions. Use at your own risk!!!");
        </script>
        <h1>List of applications</h1>
        <p>
            <small>(<strong>beta</strong> versions)</small>
        </p>
        <ul>
            <li>
                <a href="./lib/cpro09.html">CalendarPro <del>v0.9</del>
                    <ins>v1.0</ins>
```

```
            </a>
        </li>
        <li>
            <a href="./lib/game10.jad">Gamer v1.0</a>
        </li>
        <li>
            <a href="./lib/sprs08.exe">SpreadSheetPlus v0.8</a>
        </li>
    </ul>
    <form action="www.thereceiver.com/script.cgi">
        <p>
        Your name <input name="yourName" type="text"/>
            <br/>
        Image of you <input name="yourImage" type="file"/>
            <br/>
        Gender <select name="gender">
                <option value="male">Male</option>
                <option value="female">Female</option>
            </select>
            <br/>
        Email <input name="emailAdr" type="text"/>
            <br/>
            <input type="submit" value="Submit!"/>
        </p>
    </form>
    <table>
      <thead>
          <tr>
            <td>Name</td>
            <td>Desc</td>
          </tr>
      </thead>
      <tbody>
        <tr>
            <td>Calendar Pro</td>
            <td>A small XHTML-based calendar app.</td>
        </tr>
        <tr>
            <td>Gamer</td>
            <td>A fun Java game.</td>
        </tr>
        <tr>
            <td>SpreadSheetPlus</td>
            <td>One of the best spreadsheets for Pocket PCs.</td>
        </tr>
      </tbody>
    </table>
```

```
    </body>
</html>
```

In this case, you use elements from the more complex tables module. The thead and tbody elements reside in the tables module, not in the basic tables module. Other elements that are part of only the tables module are the column (col) and colgroup column group (colgroup) elements.

If you want to browse the previous XHTML 1.0 strict code on a device that supports XHTML Basic, it wouldn't work. You're using the tables module and it isn't part of XHTML Basic 1.0. The tables module is more comprehensive than the basic tables module. For example, the tbody element is part of the tables module, but it isn't part of the basic tables module. So, to stay XHTML Basic 1.0-compatible, you'd have to simplify the table. Elements from the presentation, edit, and scripting modules are also used. So, you'd have to replace the table with a basic table, remove presentation-related markup, such as the small element, remove the ins and del elements, rewrite the form so it becomes a basic form, and remove the script. The code would then look like this:

```
<?xml version="1.0" encoding="UTF-8"?>
<!DOCTYPE html PUBLIC "-//W3C//DTD XHTML Basic 1.0//EN"
    "http://www.w3.org/TR/xhtml-basic/xhtml-basic10.dtd">
<html xmlns="http://www.w3.org/1999/xhtml">
    <head>
        <title>Structure, text, hypertext, list, scripting, presentation, edit,
          forms and tables.
        </title>
    </head>
    <body>
        <h1>List of applications</h1>
        <p>
            <strong>beta</strong> versions!
        </p>
        <ul>
            <li>
                <a href="./lib/cpro09.html">CalendarPro v1.0
                </a>
            </li>
            <li>
                <a href="./lib/game10.jad">Gamer v1.0</a>
            </li>
            <li>
                <a href="./lib/sprs08.exe">SpreadSheetPlus v0.8</a>
            </li>
        </ul>
```

```
<form action="www.thereceiver.com/script.cgi">
    <p>
    Your name <input name="yourName" type="text"/>
        <br/>
    Gender <select name="gender">
            <option value="male">Male</option>
            <option value="female">Female</option>
        </select>
        <br/>
    Email <input name="emailAdr" type="text"/>
        <br/>
        <input type="submit" value="Submit!"/>
    </p>
</form>
<table>
        <tr>
            <td>Name</td>
            <td>Desc</td>
        </tr>
        <tr>
            <td>Calendar Pro</td>
            <td>A small XHTML based calendar app.</td>
        </tr>
        <tr>
            <td>Gamer</td>
            <td>A fun Java game.</td>
        </tr>
        <tr>
            <td>SpreadSheetPlus</td>
            <td>One of the best spreadsheets for Pocket PCs.</td>
        </tr>
    </table>
    </body>
</html>
```

Now the document can be validated successfully, according to the XHTML Basic DTD, but we had to make several changes. The small element was removed because it's part of the presentation module and not included in XHTML Basic 1.0. The ins and del element, part of the edit module, were removed, as was the script. The table was rewritten, so it uses elements from the basic tables module only. Thus, we had to remove the thead and tbody elements. Also, the file type input element in the form was removed because it's part of the forms module. You must use basic forms only to stay XHTML Basic 1.0-compatible.

Image Maps and Embedded Objects

As in HTML, images are referred to in an XHTML document using the img element. This is the only element in the image module. Image maps can be managed in two ways: by using client-side image maps or by having the coordinates sent to a server, using server-side image maps. One module is called client-side image maps and the other is called server-side image maps. The client-side image maps module depend on the images module, so the images module must always be used when client-side image maps are used.

Embedded objects can be used when there's a need to use a browser plug-in on a web page. A module called *objects* is associated with the object and param elements. The *object* element is the container for the embedded object and the *param* element is used to specify the parameters sent as arguments to the object. So far, browsers in mobile devices, such as phones, smartphones, and PDAs, have had few, and in most cases, no plug-ins, but that's about to change. For example, Macromedia Flash is now available for the Pocket PC platform.

The following example uses elements and attributes from the structure, text, hypertext, images, and client-side image maps modules.

```
<?xml version="1.0" encoding="UTF-8"?>
<!DOCTYPE html PUBLIC "-//W3C//DTD XHTML 1.0 Strict//EN"
    "http://www.w3.org/TR/xhtml1/DTD/xhtml1-strict.dtd">
<html xmlns="http://www.w3.org/1999/xhtml">
    <head>
        <title>Structure, text, hypertext, images and client-side image maps.
        </title>
    </head>
    <body>
        <p>
            <img src="myImage.gif" usemap="#csideimap" alt="a simple image for the
                image map."/>
            <map id="csideimap">
              <p>
                <a href="page1.html" shape="rect" coords="0, 0, 50, 50">Page 1</a>
                <a href="page2.html" shape="rect" coords="50, 0, 100, 50">Page
2</a>
              </p>
            </map>
        </p>
    </body>
</html>
```

The html, head, title, and body elements belong to the structure module. The paragraph element is part of the text module and the *a* element, for links, resides in the hypertext module.

The *img* element is the only element in the images module, but the *usemap* attribute in the img element resides in the client-side image map's module. Other elements and attributes for the image map, such as the map element and the coords and shape attributes for the *a* element, are part of the client-side image map's module. Here you can see that although some elements, such as the *a* element, reside in a specific module, they can have certain attributes that are put in other modules. This is because they're used in a certain context, such as when a client-side image map is created.

Note, in XHTML, including XHTML Basic 1.0, the alt attribute for the img tag is required. Some wireless devices have limited support for graphics, and then the value of the alt attribute can be used instead, to provide a textual description of the picture. Image maps aren't supported by XHTML Basic 1.0.

Frames, iframes, and Targets

The frameset, frame, and noframes elements were put in the module called frames. Two additional modules are related to frames: the iframes module and the targets module. The *iframes* module contains a single element, iframe, which can be used to create inline frames. The *targets* module supports the target attribute, which can be used with the *a* element.

The following example uses the structure and frames modules to implement a simple web page that uses frames:

```
<?xml version="1.0" encoding="UTF-8"?>
<!DOCTYPE html PUBLIC "-//W3C//DTD XHTML 1.0 Strict//EN"
    "http://www.w3.org/TR/xhtml1/DTD/xhtml1-frameset.dtd">
<html xmlns="http://www.w3.org/1999/xhtml">
    <head>
        <title>Structure, frames and targets.
        </title>
    </head>
    <frameset cols="25%, 75%">
      <frame src="left.html"/>
      <frameset rows="25%, 75%">
        <frame src="top.html"/>
        <frame src="main.html"/>
      </frameset>
    </frameset>
</html>
```

To the left is a navigation bar—left.html—which occupies 25 percent of the screen. There's an area at the top of the web page, top.html, and a main area, main.html. Note, we refer to the frameset DTD in the DOCTYPE declaration because this is a document that contains a number of framesets. XHTML pages like this aren't suitable for wireless handheld devices because frames are used and frames were created with desktop computers in mind. In addition, most XHTML-compatible handheld devices expect a DOCTYPE declaration that contains a pointer to the XHTML Basic DTD, rather than the frameset DTD we've used in this example.

Intrinsic Events and Metainformation

The intrinsic events module doesn't contain any elements, instead, it contains a number of attributes used with elements in other modules. The module isn't part of XHTML Basic 1.0. *Intrinsic events* are events that occur when the user interacts with the browser in a certain way. The onload and onreset attributes were put in this module. They can, for example, be used with frames and forms the same way as they're used in HTML4.

The *metamodule* contains a single element, the *metaelement. Metadata,* such as author information and creation date, can be specified using this element. Here's an example that uses the structure, text, and metamodules:

```
<?xml version="1.0" encoding="UTF-8"?>
<!DOCTYPE html PUBLIC "-//W3C//DTD XHTML 1.0 Strict//EN"
    "http://www.w3.org/TR/xhtml1/DTD/xhtml1-strict.dtd">
<html xmlns="http://www.w3.org/1999/xhtml">
    <head>
        <meta name="Author" content="Mikael Hillborg"/>
        <title>Structure, text and meta information.
        </title>
    </head>
    <body>
      <p>This XHTML file includes meta information.
      </p>
    </body>
</html>
```

The metaelement can contain information about the document itself, such as expiration date, author information, or content types. Note the slash at the end of the metaelement. The metaelement in HTML4 works the same way but, because you're dealing with XML now, you must forget to insert the slash at the end.

Metatags are supported by XHTML Basic 1.0. In fact, metainformation can be used by WAP proxies to determine the expiration time and date for the document. The expiration time and date can be used to determine how long it should cache the document.

Style Sheets and the Style Attribute

The *style sheet* module can be used when a need exists to use internal style sheets and the style element. There's also a module called *style,* which works as a container for the style attribute. The *style* attribute can only style single elements, as opposed to the style element, which can be used to style more than one element. Here's an example that uses the structure, text, and style sheet modules:

```
<?xml version="1.0" encoding="UTF-8"?>
<!DOCTYPE html PUBLIC "-//W3C//DTD XHTML 1.0 Strict//EN"
    "http://www.w3.org/TR/xhtml1/DTD/xhtml1-strict.dtd">
<html xmlns="http://www.w3.org/1999/xhtml">
    <head>
        <style type="text/css">
          p {text-align: center}
        </style>
        <title>Structure, text and style sheet.
        </title>
    </head>
    <body>
        <p>This text is centered.
        </p>
    </body>
</html>
```

In this case, we use the style element, not the style attribute, so only the style sheet module is used (not the style module). Neither the style sheet nor the style modules are supported by XHTML Basic 1.0. When you need to style your documents so they're optimized for a certain handheld device's characteristics, then you should use an external style sheet and the link element, which is part of the link module.

Links and Base

The *link* element can be used in the header of the XHTML document when a need exists to use an external resource, such as an external style sheet. If relative URLs are used in a document, the *base* element can be used to specify the base address that should be used to assemble the complete URL (relative address appended to the end of the base address). Cases exist when relative URLs cannot be relative to the document in which they occur. In those cases, this element comes in handy. The base element resides in a module on its own, called the *base* module. The following example uses the structure, text, hypertext, and base modules:

```
<?xml version="1.0" encoding="UTF-8"?>
<!DOCTYPE html PUBLIC "-//W3C//DTD XHTML Basic 1.0//EN"
"http://www.w3.org/TR/xhtml-basic/xhtml-basic10.dtd">
<html xmlns="http://www.w3.org/1999/xhtml">
    <head>
        <base href="http://www.domain1.com"/>
        <title>The structure, text, hypertext and base modules.
        </title>
    </head>
    <body>
        <p><a href="doc.html">This link</a>
                is relative but will lead to
http://www.domain1.com/doc.html
                although this document resides at
http://www.domain2.com.
        </p>
    </body>
</html>
```

When the user follows the link, the browser computes the complete address. The complete address is obtained by appending the relative address in the link's href attribute to the address given in the href attribute of the base element in the head. Note the slash at the end of the base element.

Links and bases are supported by XHTML Basic 1.0. In fact, if you check the previous document again, you can see we used the XHTML Basic 1.0 DTD in the DOCTYPE declaration. This document can easily be displayed on limited handheld devices that support XHTML Basic 1.0.

Name Identification and Legacy Constructs

Only one attribute—*name*—and no elements are in the name identification module. The name attribute has been replaced by the id element. It was used in the same way: to give some elements a name, so they can be referred from another place in the code.

Don't use this attribute unless you must be backwards-compatible in some way with older tools or browsers that require this attribute.

Other old constructs have been put in the legacy module. For example, the u and strike elements and the clear attribute—used by the br element—were put in the legacy module.

IN THIS CHAPTER:

VoiceXML

Alternatives to VoiceXML

For wireless networks, voice is still the killer application. The application, which makes it possible for you to call a friend wherever you are, is the one that generates the most money for the operators. Wireless Internet services are important for operators and vendors, but the market for voice has always been, and probably will be, the biggest revenue. Consequently, it isn't strange that infrastructure for services that use voice for navigation is being deployed.

In Chapter 14, you learn to build a complete voice portal that uses voice synthesis, voice recognition, and prerecorded audio to guide the user through the content of a portal. A *voice portal* enables anyone to call a number and retrieve information from the portal by speaking into the phone and answering a number of questions. The voice portal is like a portal on the World Wide Web, but all navigation is carried out using voice commands (there are other ways as well, which are explained later).

The VoiceXML forum has created *VoiceXML,* an XML-based language that lets you design services based on voice for navigation. Ordinary phones can be used and voice recognition technology identifies what the user says and takes the appropriate actions, according to the spoken word or sentence. Voice synthesis can also be used. In addition to recording audio samples, which are replayed depending on what the user says, you can also synthesize speech from a textual description. VoiceXML is based on server-side technology. The markup is interpreted on the server side, while the user, with an ordinary phone, triggers the actions, which are executed on the VoiceXML interpreting server. The server listens to the incoming audio and tries to recognize what the user says. In addition, DTMF tones can be sent from the user's phone and will be detected by the server. When the server replies to the user, speech can be synthesized or replayed from an audio file. Consequently, the dialogue between the user and the server is an audio-only dialogue (including DTMF tones) with the benefit that any phone may be used.

In this chapter, you're introduced to applications that use voice recognition and voice synthesis using the framework of VoiceXML. Chapter 14 gives you a detailed tour through a couple applications, how they're designed and how they work. This chapter also mentions a couple languages that exist in parallel with VoiceXML, CallXML, VoxML, and PML.

VoiceXML

A VoiceXML application consists of one or more documents that execute on a VoiceXML supporting server. The elements and attributes are provided in files with the vxml extension. One of the documents serves as the top document: this is the document launched when the application starts. The other vxml documents can be called from this document. You can also store grammars as separate documents or the grammars can reside in any of the vxml documents. Grammars are used to describe how the user may respond to queries that are replayed or synthesized.

When you're developing applications for a VoiceXML-enabled server, you can use some of the available service development kits. Several kits can be installed on your desktop computer. In addition, a number of Web-based development kits exist. Both alternatives are useful. As you prototype your application, a system development kit installed on your computer might be the best solution. Some of the Web-based services let you dial-in and hear exactly how your service sounds and behaves. Motorola has excellent support for the creation of VoiceXML services in the Wireless IDE. Using Motorola's Mobile Application Development Kits, which is an option to the Wireless IDE, you can test-run your applications with full support for voice recognition and voice synthesis. BeVocal Café and HeyAnita! provide Web-based service development kits. You can use these to test your application in environments that are similar to fully deployed target environments.

Document Structure

Let's look at the VoiceXML document structure. A VoiceXML document starts with an XML header because VoiceXML is an application of XML. The vxml element is the top-level element and must always reside in a VoiceXML document. Here's an example:

```
<?xml version="1.0"?>
<vxml version="1.0" lang="en" application="root.vxml">
  ...
</vxml>
```

The vxml element has a required attribute—version. This attribute specifies which version of VoiceXML the application conforms to. If you create a VoiceXML application that's divided over a number of files; then all these files must refer to the root document, using the application attribute. Normally, you can manage just fine with only one document, but cases occur when there is a need to distribute the application logic over several documents. If you're creating a large application and you can add new features without making too many changes in the existing documents, then you might want to use several documents.

Forms

Under the vxml element, you can provide a number of forms or menus. A form is filled in by the user, while a menu lets the user choose among a number of alternatives.

A form contains a number of fields. Each field can include a prompt that is synthesized or replayed. When the form has been filled in, the filled element is executed. Here's a simple example:

```
<?xml version="1.0"?>
<vxml version="1.0">

  <form id="theForm">
    <field name="field1" type="boolean">
      <prompt>Hello. Would you like to buy some of our products?
      </prompt>
    </field>
    <filled>
      <if cond="field1">
        <prompt>How nice. Welcome to our shop.</prompt>
      <else/>
        <prompt>I am sorry.</prompt>
      </if>
    </filled>
  </form>
</vxml>
```

Each field is executed one at a time from the top to the bottom. In the previous example, only one field exists. The filled element, after the field, is executed after the user answers the question. As you can see, the filled element contains a logical expression and an if-else statement. If you're familiar with a programming language, such as C, Java, or some script language, then you probably understand that the if statement checks the logical condition inside the cond attribute. In this case, the statement is simple: it checks if the variable is true. If it is true, then the prompt that says "How nice…" is synthesized. If the user answers "no," then the else element is executed and the sentence "I am sorry" is synthesized.

This example has two fields:

```
<?xml version="1.0"?>
<vxml version="1.0">
  <form id="form_name">
    <field name="col">
```

```
            <prompt>Do you want to buy a blue, red or yellow car?
            </prompt>
            <grammar type="application/x-jsgf">
                blue | red | yellow
            </grammar>
        </field>
        <field name="turbo" type="boolean">
            <prompt>We have a very nice <value expr="col"/> car for you.
            Do you want a turbo engine?
            </prompt>
        </field>

        <filled>
            <if cond="turbo">
            <prompt>Ok. So you have decided to buy a
                <value expr="col"/> colored turbo.</prompt>
            <else/>
            <prompt>Ok. So you have decided to buy a

                <value expr="col"/> colored car and
                you don't want a turbo engine.</prompt>
            </if>
        </filled>
    </form>
</vxml>
```

This example uses a form that has two input fields. The first field asks which color the user wants. Here we use a grammar to specify we expect only the replies blue, red, or yellow. The vertical bar is a logical "or" operator. Depending on what the user answers, col will be set to red, blue, or yellow.

In this case, we used a Java Speech API Grammar Format (JSGF), which has become somewhat of an industry de facto standard to specify grammars for speech applications.

In the second field, the result of the first question—the reply—is used. As you can see, you can reference variables that have been set in previous fields. The value element and the expr attribute can be used for that purpose. In this case, you refer to the color when you ask the user if he or she wants a turbo engine. If the user answers blue on the first question, then the word "blue" is synthesized in the second question, right after the word "nice" and before the word "car" is spoken. When the user has filled in the two fields, the filled element is executed and, here, the if element is checked if a turbo engine was chosen. Two different sentences are synthesized depending on what the user chose.

Menus

While a form is the best choice when you have several fields for which you want to provide values, a menu can be used when the user is supposed to select an option. Forms collect information and set a variable for each form field. Menus don't set variables. Instead, menus are used as logical branches in the code. If a certain menu item was selected, go on to a particular task. Or, if another menu item was selected, then do something else.

The following example illustrates how a simple menu can be implemented.

```
<?xml version="1.0"?>
<vxml version="1.0">

  <menu>
    <prompt>Please say the information you want to access.
        <enumerate/>
    </prompt>
    <choice next="#bala">
        Balance
    </choice>
    <choice next="#rate">
        Interest rate
    </choice>
    <choice next="#tran">
        Transactions
    </choice>
    <noinput>Please say one of the following phrases:
        <enumerate/>
    </noinput>
  </menu>

  <form id="bala">
    <block>The balance on your account is three bucks.
    </block>
  </form>
  <form id="rate">
    <block>Current interest rate for your account is 5 percent.
    </block>
  </form>
  <form id="tran">
    <block>Latest transaction was last friday.
    </block>
  </form>

</vxml>
```

This is a simple example because we hard coded the result of the three services, but it illustrates how simple designing a menu is. All menu choices are specified inside the menu tags, using the choice element for each possible choice. The choice element has an attribute—next—which specifies the address to where we should jump if that choice is made. Note, this address can be a full URL, such as http://www.example.com/lib/myFile.vxml, or you can specify a simple anchor, as in the previous example. The pound symbol (#) followed by the name indicates we're going to jump internally in the document when that choice is made. In this case, the jumps lead to some of the forms. Each form contains a simple block of speech. The synthesized voice will say, "Please say the information you want to access: balance, interest rate, or transactions."

Play Audio Files

So far you've seen examples that use voice recognition in combination with synthesized speech. Synthesized speech means the speech isn't the result of an audio file playing back what someone has previously recorded. Instead, each word is generated using a set of rules that might depend on a number of things, such as where the word occurs in the sentence and which combinations of syllables and letters the word contains.

Today, synthesized speech can sound very human but, still, a slight touch of cold is associated with synthesized speech. Many applications can be designed using prerecorded audio files. If a large number of files are used and replayed in a sequence, a good result might be achieved.

No specific audio formats are required. Instead, the VoiceXML forum suggests a number of well-known audio formats. The WAV/RIFF format, using 8 KHz sample rate and an 8-bit resolution, is one of the suggestions.

The following code is an implementation of the latest example, but this time we use prerecorded audio only instead of synthesizing the speech:

```
<?xml version="1.0"?>
<vxml version="1.0">

   <menu>
     <prompt>
        <audio src="audiolib/say_access.wav">
           Please say the information you want to access.
        </audio>
        <enumerate/>
     </prompt>
     <choice next="#bala">
```

```
            <audio src="audiolib/balance.wav">
                Balance
            </audio>
        </choice>
        <choice next="#rate">
            <audio src="audiolib/interest_rate.wav">
                Interest rate
            </audio>
        </choice>
        <choice next="#tran">
            <audio src="audiolib/transactions.wav">
                Transactions
            </audio>
        </choice>
        <noinput>
            <audio src="audiolib/please_say.wav">
                Please say one of the following phrases:
            </audio>
            <enumerate/>
        </noinput>
    </menu>

    <form id="bala">
      <block>
            <audio src="audiolib/the_balance_is.wav">
                The balance on your account is three bucks.
            </audio>
      </block>
    </form>
    <form id="rate">
      <block>
            <audio src="audiolib/the_interest_rate_is.wav">
                Current interest rate for your account is 5 percent.
            </audio>
      </block>
    </form>
    <form id="tran">
      <block>
            <audio src="audiolib/last_transaction_was.wav">
                Latest transaction was last friday.
            </audio>
      </block>
    </form>

</vxml>
```

The text has been replaced by the audio element. Using the src attribute, you can specify where the audio files remain on disk. This might be a complete URL or, as shown previously, a relative URL. In this case, a folder called audiolib is supposed to remain in the same directory as the VoiceXML file. This is where the wav files are stored. If, for some reason, the VoiceXML server cannot find any of the files, then the text between the audio tags is synthesized instead.

In Chapter 14, we build a voice portal. That chapter gives you more details about the VoiceXML language and how it may be used. The VoiceXML code you've seen in this chapter is quite simple, but it should have given you a good introduction to how simple voice applications can be designed using the VoiceXML language and a VoiceXML-enabled server.

Alternatives to VoiceXML

VoiceXML is emerging as the de facto standard language for implementing voice applications. A number of languages are similar to VoiceXML but, in most cases, they're developed by single companies, as opposed to VoiceXML, which is the outcome of a forum with over 500 member companies. If you don't want to use VoiceXML, then some of the following languages might provide the solution you want.

CallXML

CallXML is developed by the company Voxeo. CallXML is similar to VoiceXML because it supports DTMF tones, can play and record audio, establish calls, hang up a call, and interact with traditional web servers to post and retrieve information. Variables can be assigned values and referred to in the code, as in VoiceXML. CallXML supports any type of calls, for example, calls that use voice over IP (VoIP) technology.

VoxML

VoxML was created by Motorola and the language divides a VoxML application into *steps,* which are part of a dialogue. A step might prompt the user with speech, as in VoiceXML. Different types of inputs are supported, such as money, digits, and option lists. If the speech recognition engine doesn't recognize the spoken word or sentence, then the error can be caught and the user can be prompted to say it again, and so forth.

Other

In addition to the previously mentioned languages, there's Phone Markup Language (PML), SpeechML, and TalkML. These were created before VoiceXML and most of the companies involved in the creation of the language are sponsors, promoters, or supporters of the VoiceXML forum.

Synchronized Multimedia

IN THIS CHAPTER:

SMIL 2.0

The SMIL Modules

The SMIL 2.0 Basic Profile

A s GPRS, WCDMA, and CDMA 2000 networks are built, a new application is being deployed at the same time: the Multimedia Messaging Service (MMS). With MMS, you can send multimedia presentations from one phone to another or from a server on the Internet to a phone. The presentations can be developed using the Synchronized Multimedia Integration Language (SMIL) as the presentation format. This chapter introduces SMIL 2.0 and the SMIL 2.0 Basic profile. The latter is a subset of the first, which has been tailored for limited constrained devices, such as mobile phones. SMIL has been used for a while to create multimedia presentations on ordinary computers. Thus, you can test your applications in a SMIL player—on a PC or a Mac—before the application is tested using MMS.

NOTE

SMIL in MMS is based on SMIL 1.0. This introduction to SMIL shows you the latest version of SMIL: version 2.0.

This chapter serves as a quick introduction to the subject, while Chapter 15 gives you a more detailed description of how multimedia applications for mobile handheld devices can be created using SMIL 1.0.

When you develop MMS services using SMIL, check with the technical manual of your MMS-compatible phone concerning which constructs in SMIL are supported. The manufacturers are working on common support but, until they agree on a common and stable framework, the support for certain elements or attributes might not be the same depending on which phone you're using.

SMIL presentations can be sent in MMS messages in two different ways. The first way is to have a user compose an MMS message using functions in her handheld devices. The message is then sent to a receiver, who owns an MMS- compatible device, and the presentation is replayed. However, the message isn't sent directly from the sender to the receiver. Instead, it's first transferred to a server owned by the operator. There, a check is made if the receiver has the phone switched on. If this is the case, the message is forwarded to the receiver. If not, then the message is kept on disk until he or she switches on the phone.

The second way of sending MMS messages is by having the message composed by a program. The composed message is sent over the Internet to an MMS server, owned by the network operator. The MMS server then forwards the message to the user—that is, the receiver—but only if she has her phone switched on. If not, then the message is kept on disk at the operator's premises until the user switches on the phone.

SMIL 2.0

The purpose of SMIL is to synchronize and integrate multimedia. Synchronization in this case means that media—audio, video, and text—can be replayed at the same time or in a sequence exactly as you specified in the SMIL file. For instance, an audio file can be replayed before a video clip is shown, and some text can be displayed at the same time a video is presented.

The Structure of a SMIL Presentation

Since SMIL 2.0 is an XML application, the document starts with an XML header and a DOCTYPE declaration. A simple SMIL 2.0 document might look like this:

```
<?xml version="1.0" encoding="UTF-8"?>
<!DOCTYPE smil PUBLIC "-//W3C//DTD SMIL 2.0//EN"
    "http://www.w3.org/2001/SMIL20/SMIL20.dtd">
<smil xmlns="http://www.w3.org/2001/SMIL20/Language">
  <head>
    <layout>
        <root-layout width="200" height="200"/>
        <region id="textArea" top="12" left="12"/>
    </layout>
  </head>
  <body>
    <text region="textArea" src="myText.txt" dur="10s"/>
  </body>
</smil>
```

SMIL documents have a head and a body. The head describes the layout, in other words, where text and graphics should appear on the screen. In the previous example, only one region exists, which is located 12 pixels below the top of the window and 12 pixels from the left border. The window, in this case, is 200 pixels wide and 200 pixels high. This is specified using the root-layout element. The body section contains references to the actual media objects. In this example, only one media object exists: a text file. All objects, like text and pictures, are referred to and not included in the SMIL file itself. Remember, SMIL is an integration language. It integrates all the media types and doesn't contain any descriptions of the media itself.

Graphics

To show a picture, like a GIF file, in your SMIL presentation, the img element is used.
Here's an example:

```
<?xml version="1.0" encoding="UTF-8"?>
<!DOCTYPE smil PUBLIC "-//W3C//DTD SMIL 2.0//EN"
    "http://www.w3.org/2001/SMIL20/SMIL20.dtd">
<smil xmlns="http://www.w3.org/2001/SMIL20/Language">
  <head>
    <layout>
        <root-layout width="200" height="200"/>
        <region id="pics" top="12" left="12"/>
    </layout>
  </head>
  <body>
    <img region="pics" alt="picture of me." src="pic.gif" dur="10s"/>
  </body>
</smil>
```

The region attribute is used to specify where the picture will be rendered on the
display, and the src attribute is set to the URL, which points at the picture. To make
the information available for devices that don't support the img object, you should
always use the alt attribute to specify an alternative textual description of the graphic
object. If a device supports SMIL, a language for multimedia presentations, then a
fair chance exists that it supports the img object. However, some handheld devices
might not support all image formats, like transparent GIFs or JPEG images. This is
why you should always use the alt attribute.

Some additional attributes can be used to specify even more properties for graphics
objects. Chapter 15 goes into more detail about this.

Audio

With SMIL, audio clips can be replayed. The audio element is used to specify the
audio file.

```
<?xml version="1.0" encoding="UTF-8"?>
<!DOCTYPE smil PUBLIC "-//W3C//DTD SMIL 2.0//EN"
    "http://www.w3.org/2001/SMIL20/SMIL20.dtd">
<smil xmlns="http://www.w3.org/2001/SMIL20/Language">
  <head>
    <layout>
```

```
        <root-layout width="200" height="200"/>
        <region id="pics" top="12" left="12"/>
    </layout>
  </head>
  <body>
    <seq>
        <audio src="chime.wav"/>
        <img region="pics" alt="Welcome picture." src="welcome.gif" dur="10s"/>
    </seq>
  </body>
</smil>
```

In this case, a WAV file, which is a recording of a simple chime sound, is replayed. The src attribute should contain a URI, which points at the WAV file. A relative URL points at the file. Thus, the WAV file must be located in the same directory as the SMIL file, on the server. When the chime sound has been played, a picture is displayed using the img element. Thus, they are replayed in a sequence.

Sequential Presentations

You can show text, graphics and video in a sequence using the seq element. For example, you can play a sound, show some text, and, finally, play a video for the user. Here's a simple example that displays a sequence of pictures:

```
<?xml version="1.0" encoding="UTF-8"?>
<!DOCTYPE smil PUBLIC "-//W3C//DTD SMIL 2.0//EN"
    "http://www.w3.org/2001/SMIL20/SMIL20.dtd">
<smil xmlns="http://www.w3.org/2001/SMIL20/Language">
  <head>
    <layout>
        <root-layout width="200" height="200"/>
        <region id="pics" top="12" left="12"/>
    </layout>
  </head>
  <body>
    <seq>
        <img region="pics" src="welcome.gif" dur="4s"/>
        <img region="pics" src="intro.gif" dur="4s"/>
        <img region="pics" src="message.gif" dur="4s"/>
        <img region="pics" src="end.gif" dur="4s"/>
    </seq>
  </body>
</smil>
```

The duration for each image can be set using the dur attribute. Each GIF file is displayed for four seconds before it disappears and the next image in the sequence is shown. The first picture shown is welcome.gif.

Parallel Presentations

While sequences are useful to create slide-show type applications, you need more constructs to create rich multimedia presentations. Typically, graphics are rendered, sound is replayed, and text is shown more or less at the same time, or in parallel. This is where the par element comes in. It can be used to specify media objects that are rendered or replayed at the same time or with an overlap. The following example shows a picture and some text at the same time:

```xml
<?xml version="1.0" encoding="UTF-8"?>
<!DOCTYPE smil PUBLIC "-//W3C//DTD SMIL 2.0//EN"
    "http://www.w3.org/2001/SMIL20/SMIL20.dtd">

<smil xmlns="http://www.w3.org/2001/SMIL20/Language">
  <head>
    <layout>
        <root-layout width="200" height="200"/>
        <region id="texts" top="12" left="12" width="176" height="96"/>
        <region id="pics" top="120" left="12"/>
    </layout>
  </head>
  <body>
    <par>
        <text region="texts" src="myText.txt" />
        <img region="pics" src="welcome.gif" />
        <audio src="narrator.wav" />
    </par>
  </body>
</smil>
```

Two regions are specified to make the image appear under the text. Note, the region for the text has a limited width and height. The par element has been used to specify that the audio is replayed in parallel with the rendering of the text and the image.

Overlaps

In the previous example, all objects are replayed and rendered immediately as the application is executed. Media objects needn't start at exactly the same time, though. The media objects can be rendered in parallel, but only a minor overlap occurs. For example, a two-minute long sound file can be played for ten seconds only and, when nine seconds have elapsed, an image can be displayed. The following code shows such a scenario:

```
<?xml version="1.0" encoding="UTF-8"?>
<!DOCTYPE smil PUBLIC "-//W3C//DTD SMIL 2.0//EN"
    "http://www.w3.org/2001/SMIL20/SMIL20.dtd">
<smil xmlns="http://www.w3.org/2001/SMIL20/Language">
  <head>
    <layout>
        <root-layout width="200" height="200"/>
        <region id="texts" top="12" left="12" width="176" height="96"/>
        <region id="pics" top="120" left="12"/>
    </layout>
  </head>
  <body>
    <par>
        <text region="texts" src="myText.txt"/>
        <img region="pics" src="welcome.gif" begin="9s"/>
        <audio src="narrator.wav" dur="10s"/>
    </par>
  </body>
</smil>
```

A piece of text is displayed using the text element. At the same time the text is shown, when the application is started, the audio file starts to play. The total playing length of the audio file is ten seconds. When nine seconds of the audio file have been played, an image is rendered to the screen.

Combinations of Sequential and Parallel Presentations

In many cases, you want to display a sequence of images at the same time an audio file is being replayed. Or, you might want to display a sequence of images at the same time a sequence of text is rendered to the screen. In this case, you should use nested par and seq elements, as the following code illustrates.

```
<?xml version="1.0" encoding="UTF-8"?>
<!DOCTYPE smil PUBLIC "-//W3C//DTD SMIL 2.0//EN"
    "http://www.w3.org/2001/SMIL20/SMIL20.dtd">
<smil xmlns="http://www.w3.org/2001/SMIL20/Language">
  <head>
    <layout>
        <root-layout width="200" height="200"/>
```

```
        <region id="texts" top="12" left="12" width="176" height="96"/>
        <region id="pics" top="120" left="12"/>
    </layout>
  </head>
  <body>
    <par>
        <seq>
            <text region="texts" src="text1.txt" dur="4s"/>
            <text region="texts" src="text2.txt" dur="4s"/>
            <text region="texts" src="text3.txt" dur="4s"/>
        </seq>
        <seq>
            <img region="pics" src="pic1.gif" dur="4s"/>
            <img region="pics" src="pic2.gif" dur="4s"/>
            <img region="pics" src="pic3.gif" dur="4s"/>
        </seq>
    </par>
  </body>
</smil>
```

This sequence has one par element and two seq elements. The par element
contains the text sections and the images that should be rendered in parallel. Each
of the three text sections is shown in a sequence, so they are enclosed by the seq
element. Also, each of the three images is shown in a sequence. To make this even
more complex, look at the following presentation:

```
<?xml version="1.0" encoding="UTF-8"?>
<!DOCTYPE smil PUBLIC "-//W3C//DTD SMIL 2.0//EN"
    "http://www.w3.org/2001/SMIL20/SMIL20.dtd">
<smil xmlns="http://www.w3.org/2001/SMIL20/Language">
  <head>
    <layout>
        <root-layout width="200" height="200"/>
        <region id="texts" top="12" left="12" width="176" height="96"/>
        <region id="pics" top="120" left="12"/>
    </layout>
  </head>
  <body>
    <par>
        <seq>
            <text region="texts" src="text1.txt" dur="4s"/>
            <text region="texts" src="text2.txt" dur="4s"/>
            <text region="texts" src="text3.txt" dur="4s"/>
```

```
        </seq>
        <seq>
            <par>
                <audio src="comment1.wav" dur="4s"/>
                <img region="pics" src="pic1.gif" dur="4s"/>
            </par>
            <par>
                <audio src="comment2.wav" dur="4s"/>
                <img region="pics" src="pic2.gif" dur="4s"/>
            </par>
            <par>
                <audio src="comment3.wav" dur="4s"/>
                <img region="pics" src="pic3.gif" dur="4s"/>
            </par>
        </seq>
    </par>
  </body>
</smil>
```

An outermost par element specifies two sets of media objects rendered in parallel. The first set is a sequence of texts and the other set contains audio and images. The text messages are shown in a sequence. Each text has a duration of four seconds.

The second seq element encloses three events. First, the audio file comment1.wav is replayed while the image pic1.gif is shown. Four seconds later, the audio file comment2.wav starts to play at the same time pic2.gif is shown for four seconds. Finally, comment3.wav is played at the same time pic3.gif is shown for four seconds.

Links

Anchored links can be used similarly to the way the same element—a—is used in XHTML. In addition, you can link from an element in one presentation to another element in another presentation, using fraction identifiers. The following two files illustrate this:

```
<?xml version="1.0" encoding="UTF-8"?>
<!DOCTYPE smil PUBLIC "-//W3C//DTD SMIL 2.0//EN"
    "http://www.w3.org/2001/SMIL20/SMIL20.dtd">
<smil xmlns="http://www.w3.org/2001/SMIL20/Language">
  <head>
    <layout>
        <root-layout width="200" height="200"/>
```

```
        <region id="texts" top="12" left="12" width="176" height="96"/>
        <region id="pics" top="120" left="12"/>
    </layout>
  </head>
  <body>
    <par>
      <a href="stop.smil#stop" show="replace"
              title="Follow link or press 1 to stop this presentation"
              accesskey="1">
          <text region="texts" src="myText.txt"/>
      </a>
      <img region="pics" src="welcome.gif" begin="9s"/>
      <audio src="narrator.wav" dur="10s"/>
    </par>
  </body>
</smil>
```

The link in the previous file links to the stop fragment in the following SMIL file:

```
<?xml version="1.0" encoding="UTF-8"?>
<!DOCTYPE smil PUBLIC "-//W3C//DTD SMIL 2.0//EN"
    "http://www.w3.org/2001/SMIL20/SMIL20.dtd">
<smil xmlns="http://www.w3.org/2001/SMIL20/Language">
  <head>
    <layout>
        <root-layout width="200" height="200"/>
        <region id="texts" top="12" left="12" width="176" height="96"/>
    </layout>
  </head>
  <body>
    <seq>
        <text id="stop" region="texts" src="stop.txt" dur="10s"/>
    </seq>
  </body>
</smil>
```

A link title should always be provided so the device and the application can provide the information when the cursor (if the device uses one) is moved over the object.

In our example, the show attribute was set to replace because the new text should replace the old one. Note, the whole presentation will be replaced by the new one. If you had set the show attribute to new, a new window would have been launched if the player supports it.

The accesskey attribute was used. The value specifies a key that can be used as an alternative mechanism to follow the link. Consider which type of devices the service should be deployed on: for phones, access keys—such as 1, 2, and 3—are more suitable than *x* or ?.

Practical Issues

A number of elements and attributes in SMIL can be used to adapt the presentation for different types of device capabilities and network properties. For example, GPRS networks won't give you broadband speed. Because of this, you might have to buffer media before it's used. If you want a picture to appear immediately or if you want to avoid dropouts for the audio, media can be prefetched.

Prefetch

The following application has been optimized to display the image and play the sound when they are completely downloaded, as opposed to being drawn and played during the download:

```xml
<?xml version="1.0" encoding="UTF-8"?>
<!DOCTYPE smil PUBLIC "-//W3C//DTD SMIL 2.0//EN"
    "http://www.w3.org/2001/SMIL20/SMIL20.dtd">
<smil xmlns="http://www.w3.org/2001/SMIL20/Language">
  <head>
    <layout>
        <root-layout width="200" height="200"/>
        <region id="texts" top="12" left="12" width="176" height="96"/>
        <region id="pics" top="120" left="12"/>
    </layout>
  </head>
  <body>
    <seq>
        <prefetch id="welcome" src="welcome.gif"/>
        <prefetch id="narrator" src="narrator.wav"/>
        <par>
          <text region="texts" src="myText.txt" dur="3s"/>
          <img region="pics" src="#welcome" dur="3s"/>
          <audio src="#narrator" dur="3s"/>
        </par>
    </seq>
  </body>
</smil>
```

First, the welcome image and the narrator's voice are downloaded completely. Thus, the application fetches the media before it's shown. Not even the first part of the image is displayed until the complete file is downloaded. Remember, prefetching media requires that the device can store the prefetched media in its primary memory. Handheld devices, like phones, usually have a limited amount of primary memory available. If you use the prefetch element, you should check with the devices you're targeting to make certain they support the element.

System Bit Rate

While the prefetch element can be used to download media to the device before it's displayed, the system-bitrate attribute can be used in combination with the switch element to check if the network connection is fast enough for your application. Thus, the prefetch element downloads the media to the device before it's displayed, regardless of which network connection you're on. The system bit rate can be used to select the best alternative to optimize your application for the user's current system bit rate. The following code has been optimized for 9.6 Kbps, which is a speed used often by wireless devices that transmit and receive over Circuit-Switched Data (CSD) connections. In addition, a 28.8 Kbps option is available for users who might be using GPRS, WCDMA, or CDMA2000 connections to access the application.

```xml
<?xml version="1.0" encoding="UTF-8"?>
<!DOCTYPE smil PUBLIC "-//W3C//DTD SMIL 2.0//EN"
    "http://www.w3.org/2001/SMIL20/SMIL20.dtd">
<smil xmlns="http://www.w3.org/2001/SMIL20/Language">
  <head>
    <layout>
        <root-layout width="200" height="200"/>
        <region id="texts" top="12" left="12" width="176" height="96"/>
        <region id="pics" top="120" left="12"/>
    </layout>
  </head>
  <body>
    <par>
        <prefetch id="welcome" src="welcome.gif"/>
        <text region="texts" src="myText.txt"/>
        <img region="pics" src="#welcome" begin="9s"/>
        <switch>
            <audio src="narrator1.wav" dur="10s" system-bitrate="24000"/>
            <audio src="narrator2.wav" dur="10s" system-bitrate="8000"/>
```

```
      </switch>
    </par>
  </body>
</smil>
```

The image is prefetched and the text consumes almost no bandwidth at all, which leaves all the available bandwidth for the audio file. Two audio files have been put on the server and each audio file is an 8-bit sample. The first has been sampled at 3 KHz, which means the bit rate gets $8 \times 3,000 = 24,000$ bps. The second file was sampled at 1 KHz. Thus, the necessary bandwidth to play the file, before it has been completely downloaded from the server, is $8 \times 1,000 = 8,000$ bps. A user who sits on a 28.8 Kbps will get the more high-quality file, while a user who is using a modest 9.6 Kbps connection will have to live with a lower sound quality. In the latter case, the second of the two audio elements will be used. The device will choose the highest quality choice it can.

SMIL doesn't specify how, and if, the device should determine the available bandwidth. The user might have to type it in manually, it might be hard coded, or it can be measured by the device.

The SMIL Modules

As you know, XHTML contains a number of modules to make it easier for manufacturers to state the compliance, and combine and add modules that are important for a certain type of device. Modularization also makes creating profiles of the language easier for certain types of devices that can support only a subset of all modules.

For the same reasons, the SMIL 2.0 specification is divided into a number of modules. This makes providing profiles of the language easier for, say, constrained devices like mobile phones.

Because so many modules have been defined in SMIL 2.0, they've been sorted in a number of groups. The groups are animation, content control, layout, linking, media object, metainformation, structure, timing, time manipulations, and transition effects. Knowing these groups of modules can be good because some profiles, such as the SMIL 2.0 Basic profile, don't support all modules.

Animation

The modules in this group contain elements and attributes for different types of animations. Some basic animations, however are more complex. *Complex animations* make use of spline equations to create smooth transitions between the different stages of the animation. Animations and the animate element are covered in more detail in Chapter 15.

Content Control

Elements and attributes related to the actual control of media are located in the *content control* group of modules. The prefetch and switch elements and the system-bitrate attribute are also part of this group of modules.

Layout

The root layout, layout, and region elements are part of the *layout* group of modules. This group of modules also encapsulates advanced functions, such as the elements and attributes in the MultiWindowLayout module. These elements and attributes can be used to provide presentations that include multiple windows.

Linking

The *linking* group of modules contain the *a* element and various attributes that can be used together with this element. For example, the show and accesskey attributes are defined in this group of modules. So are the more exotic sourceLevel and destinationLevel attributes. These attributes can be used to adjust the volume of the source and destination documents when a link is activated.

Media Object

Media objects, represented by elements like audio, img, and text are located in the *media object* group of modules. Related attributes, such as the src, alt attribute and title attributes, are also defined in this group of modules.

Meta Information

A metaelement in SMIL 2.0 is similar to the metaelement in XHTML. The metaelement and its attributes are defined in the metainformation module. Metainformation in SMIL is used the same way as in XHTML. You can specify the author of the document by setting the name attribute to the value "author" and the content attribute to the actual name of the author.

Structure

This module defines the elements and attributes used to provide basic structures for SMIL 2.0 documents. The top level smil element is defined in this module, as are the head and body elements.

Timing

In the *timing* group of modules, elements and attributes related to the triggering and display of media objects for a certain period are defined. The seq and par elements are part of this group of modules.

Time Manipulations

The *time manipulations* module encapsulates a number of elements and attributes that change properties, such as speed and replay direction, for the presentation. The presentation can be accelerated, decelerated, or replayed at different speeds using elements and attributes from this module.

Transition Effects

Media objects can be given alternative transitions. For example, one image can fade into another. Elements and attributes from the *transition effects* module can be used to achieve this.

The SMIL 2.0 Basic Profile

Now you should have a good understanding about SMIL 2.0. Small handheld devices, such as mobile phones, are usually equipped with microprocessors that are limited in terms of CPU power. In addition, the display capabilities of handheld devices are also limited. Handheld devices typically have screens, which have 96 vertical pixels and an even smaller horizontal number. Implementing all the features in SMIL 2.0 for these types of devices would probably be a nightmare or, at the very least, a difficult or nearly impossible task.

Modules

The SMIL 2.0 Basic profile is a profile for constrained devices, like mobile phones. It contains a subset of all modules defined in SMIL 2.0. All examples presented so far in this chapter comply with the SMIL 2.0 Basic profile.

The following modules, or groups of modules, aren't part of SMIL 2.0 Basic:

► Animation
► Metainformation

▶ Time manipulations

▶ Transition effects

The SMIL 2.0 Basic profile uses the same DOCTYPE declaration as SMIL 2.0. If a certain module that isn't part of SMIL 2.0 Basic is going to be used, then the system-required attribute can be used to specify the name of that module. The module's namespace is also declared in the smil element, using the xmlns attribute.

Say you're implementing a presentation that uses a transition effect to fade out a picture. The transition effects group of modules isn't part of SMIL 2.0 Basic. The code might look like this:

```
<?xml version="1.0" encoding="UTF-8"?>
<!DOCTYPE smil PUBLIC "-//W3C//DTD SMIL 2.0//EN"
    "http://www.w3.org/2001/SMIL20/SMIL20.dtd">
<smil xmlns="http://www.w3.org/2001/SMIL20/Language"
      xmlns:BasicTransitions="http://www.w3.org/2001/SMIL20/BasicTransitions"
      systemRequired="BasicTransitions">
  <head>
    <layout>
        <root-layout width="200" height="200"/>
        <region id="texts" top="12" left="12" width="176" height="96"/>
        <region id="pics" top="120" left="12"/>
    </layout>
    <transition id="fadeToGray" type="fade" subtype="fadeToColor"
        fadeColor="#555555" dur="2s"/>
  </head>
  <body>
    <seq>
        <img region="pics" src="pic1.gif" transOut="fadeToGray" dur="3s"/>
    </seq>
  </body>
</smil>
```

An additional namespace is specified using the xmlns attribute and the system-required attribute is set to transition to indicate the device must support the transition module. The transition module isn't part of SMIL 2.0 Basic.

The transition element can be used to fade in and out of pictures, as in the previous example. The transition is given an ID, and then the ID is used by the img element's transOut or transIn attribute. A number of transition types are defined in SMIL 2.0. Examples are barWipe, with the subtype leftToRight, or snakeWipe, with the subtype topLeftHorizontal. But, remember, the transition module isn't part of SMIL 2.0 Basic. If you use the transition module, you should refer to it in the system-required attribute and the XML namespace declaration.

CHAPTER
7

Geography

IN THIS CHAPTER:

Geography Markup Language (GML)

SVG

Location-based services is a category of mobile Internet applications that either makes use of the user's position to retrieve information or render nearby locations. For example, the user might use a service that senses the user's current position, and then presents a map of nearby streets or roads. A service that lets the user type the position, and then displays location-specific data would also count as a location-based service.

If a company provides more than one application of this kind, these services need to represent the locations in a condensed and consistent way. Time and bugs can be saved if a clearly defined language exists for how the geography is supposed to be represented and finally rendered. It's also likely that a company implements the application, renders the graphics, and presents the information for the user, and the administration of, and access to, the location data that's used by the application is outsourced.

Assume you're going to implement an application that lets the user type in the city and street, and then a picture is displayed for that specific area. In this case, you'd have to buy location data from a provider of such information because it would be an enormous task to do it yourself from scratch. That wasn't the scope of your application, was it?

The Geography Markup Language (GML) and Scalable Vector Graphics (SVG) are two languages with the potential to become de facto industry standards for representing and rendering location data. In this chapter, you look at GML and learn how it can be used to represent locations, such as city maps or offices. While GML can be used to represent the locations, Scalable Vector Graphics can be used to render them onto a screen, such as an ordinary desktop PC or a handheld device, which runs an SVG-compatible plug-in or a Java applet, which parses the SVG code and displays it.

The section about GML is followed by a look at SVG. In Part 3 of the book, you will learn how to make more complex GML models and SVG renderings. In that section, you will also become familiar with the nuts-and-bolts of transforming a GML specification into an SVG file. Those of you who aren't familiar with object-oriented models, GML, or SVG should read this chapter carefully before you get into the advanced details in Part 3.

Geography Markup Language (GML)

GML is a language based on XML that can be used to specify locations and other geography-related data, such as roads and routes. OpenGIS, or OGC, is the consortium that created GML. Most of the companies and organizations in the consortium work with geo processing and location-based applications.

If all these companies and organizations would work on their own on proprietary interfaces and formats, the world would soon end up with an enormous amount of incompatible data that would be difficult to exchange. The companies and organizations would then have to implement filters or conversion utilities that would convert geographic data from one format to another. There'd probably be no end to the conversion work that had to be done. Consequently, it would cost these companies and organizations much time and money. Instead, the consortium has been formed to make the exchange of geographic data easier.

OGC has defined what it calls the Abstract Specification. This specification is the foundation of the GML. I won't go through the Abstract Specification because it's rather formal. Instead, this subchapter is devoted to practical uses of GML. In Chapter 16, you will learn about object-oriented models.

GML can be used to represent maps, roads, corridors, or any object it's possible to describe in terms of lines, points, and shapes. The whole purpose with GML is to specify real worlds, rather than to express how they're drawn. The same principle applies with XML itself, which is used to describe information and not necessarily how it's drawn on a screen.

Your Objects

The best way to illustrate how GML can be used is to show an example. Here's a simple GML file that specifies a territory containing a house and a road:

```
<?xml version="1.0" encoding="UTF-8"?>
<Model
xmlns="http://www.myExample.com/myNameSpace"
xmlns:gml="http://www.opengis.net/gml"
xmlns:xsi="http://www.w3.org/2000/10/XMLSchema-instance"
xsi:schemaLocation=". myFeatures.xsd">

    <!-- The bounds, or the box, for the model. All objects in our model are
       inside these coordinates. -->

    <gml:boundedBy>
        <gml:Box srsName="myModel:srs">
            <coordinates>0,0</coordinates>
            <coordinates>30,30</coordinates>
        </gml:Box>
    </gml:boundedBy>

    <!-- The model itself, inside the box coordinates. -->
```

```
    <ModelMember>
        <Road>
            <lanes>2</lanes>
            <desc>This streets goes from the west end to the far east of the
                town.</desc>
            <gml:MultiLineString
                srsName="myModel:srs">
                <gml:lineStringMember>
                    <gml:LineString>
                    <coordinates>3,3</coordinates>
                    <coordinates>3,29</coordinates>
                    </gml:LineString>
                </gml:lineStringMember>
                <gml:lineStringMember>
                    <gml:LineString>
                    <coordinates>3,29</coordinates>
                    <coordinates>29,20</coordinates>
                    </gml:LineString>
                </gml:lineStringMember>
            </gml:MultiLineString>
        </Road>
    </ModelMember>
    <ModelMember>
        <House>
            <desc>14 Foo Street</desc>
            <gml:Polygon srsName="myModel:srs">
                <outerBoundaryIs>
                    <LinearRing>
                        <coordinates>10,10</coordinates>
                        <coordinates>12,10</coordinates>
                        <coordinates>12,12</coordinates>
                        <coordinates>10,12</coordinates>
                        <coordinates>10,10</coordinates>
                    </LinearRing>
                </outerBoundaryIs>
            </gml:Polygon>
        </House>
    </ModelMember>
</Model>
```

Let's go through the document from top to bottom. It begins like this:

```
<?xml version="1.0" encoding="UTF-8"?>
<Model
xmlns="http://www.myExample.com/myNameSpace"
xmlns:gml="http://www.opengis.net/gml"
xmlns:xsi="http://www.w3.org/2000/10/XMLSchema-instance"
xsi:schemaLocation=". myFeatures.xsd">
```

The element Model has been defined in our own schema, which we refer to using the xsi:schemaLocation attribute. You can also see that the GML name space is used. You must include this name space because we refer to elements like gml:Polygon and gml:LineString.

The Bounds   The document begins with an element that encapsulates the whole model. In our case, we chose to call that element Model. In GML, you must provide the bounds for your objects in the model. After the Model element, you then specify the bounds, using the gml:boundedBy element, like this:

```
<gml:boundedBy>
    <gml:Box srsName="myModel:srs">
        <coordinates>0,0</coordinates>
        <coordinates>30,30</coordinates>
    </gml:Box>
</gml:boundedBy>
```

As you can see, the gml:boundedBy element contains a gml:Box that surrounds all objects in the model. In this case, the house and the road are inside the coordinates of the box. A GML file must contain a gml:boundedBy element. This can help us if the specification is going to be rendered with, say SVG, because then you know how big you must make the window in which the objects will be drawn.

Coordinates are specified using the element with the same name and two points are needed to specify the box. You can also specify coordinates in an alternative way. The previous specification might also look like this:

```
<gml:boundedBy>
    <gml:Box srsName="myModel:srs">
        <coord>
            <X>0</X>
            <Y>0</Y>
        </coord>
        <coord>
            <X>30</X>
            <Y>30</Y>
        </coord>
    </gml:Box>
</gml:boundedBy>
```

The previous code has the same meaning, but the coord, X, and Y elements have replaced the coordinates element.

Spatial Reference Systems   The box element has an attribute, srsName. This attribute is set to an address (a URI) where you can find the specification for the spatial reference system being used. Many spatial reference systems are used to represent the world, and which one you use depends on your data provider or whether you create the data yourself from scratch. Different spatial reference systems use different models of the Earth. Some reference systems are less precise, while some are much more complex than others to provide a greater accuracy. The current version of GML, version 2.0, doesn't address the details of specifying spatial reference systems, but OGC is working on it.

You can use a local reference system and use your own name space in the srsName attribute to refer to it, as we have done. Here's another example:

```
<gml:Box srsName="osgb:BNG">
```

This is how the Ordnance Survey of Great Britain (OSGB) refers to the British National Grid (BNG) in GML.

In our model, we refer to an arbitrary reference system, called myModel:srs. Because we don't intend to share the data with others, the coordinates are expressed in meters from a point to the lower left of the bounding box and the coordinates don't have any defined accuracy or scientific background. If you're using data from a geo data provider or plan to share your data, you should check which spatial reference system the data is in or should be provided as, and which units of measurement the coordinates will have.

Members of the Model   After the gml:boundedBy element, the objects in the model are listed. In this case, we have a house and a road expressed in GML. Each of these two objects must appear in an element that says they are part of the model. For this purpose, we defined an element, called ModelMember.

```
<ModelMember>
    <Road>
        . . .
    </Road>
</ModelMember>
```

The road is specified inside the ModelMember element. This also applies to the house element, which is likewise specified inside the ModelMember element. This is how you're supposed to work with GML. All objects in your model are specified inside another element, which is given certain properties. You will see these properties later when we go through the schema.

Lines   Let's move on in the code and check how the Road element has been specified.

```
<Road>
    <lanes>2</lanes>
    <desc>This street goes from the west end to the far east of the
        town.</desc>
    <gml:MultiLineString
        srsName="myModel:srs">
        <gml:lineStringMember>
            <gml:LineString>
            <coordinates>3,3</coordinates>
            <coordinates>3,29</coordinates>
            </gml:LineString>
        </gml:lineStringMember>
        <gml:lineStringMember>
            <gml:LineString>
            <coordinates>3,29</coordinates>
            <coordinates>29,20</coordinates>
            </gml:LineString>
        </gml:lineStringMember>
    </gml:MultiLineString>
</Road>
```

As you can see, the Road contains an element, called lanes, and another element called desc. These are only used to give details about the object itself and don't have much to do with GML because they're pure element declarations in the schema. GML doesn't require that these elements are specified. The gml:MultiLineString element—a geometry element—makes it possible to provide the coordinates for the road and is more interesting. A gml:MultiLineString contains a number of gml:LineString elements. All the line strings form a multiline that represents the road. Instead of using the coordinates element, it's possible to use the coord, X, and Y elements.

Polygons and Outer Boundaries   The house element is specified inside the ModelMember element, like this:

```
<House>
    <desc>14 Foo Street</desc>
    <gml:Polygon srsName="myModel:srs">
        <outerBoundaryIs>
            <LinearRing>
                <coordinates>10,10</coordinates>
```

```
        <coordinates>12,10</coordinates>
        <coordinates>12,12</coordinates>
        <coordinates>10,12</coordinates>
        <coordinates>10,10</coordinates>
    </LinearRing>
  </outerBoundaryIs>
 </gml:Polygon>
</House>
```

The house element contains a desc element, which is used to give the house a textual description. This is a simple element that we provided support for in the schema and GML doesn't require that such an element exists. The geometry element gml:Polygon can be used to provide the data for polygon objects, like squares and other objects with an arbitrary number of edges. Polygons in GML have an outer boundary and it's possible to specify an inner boundary. The outer boundary is the shape of the object or the "walls." An inner boundary can be used to specify a "hole" in the object.

Inner Boundaries   A *linear ring* is a geometry object that has a number of coordinates, where the last and the first coordinates have the same values. A linear ring must have at least four coordinates declared. If you were to provide only three coordinates, then you would specify a straight line because the third would be the same as the first. Therefore, you would have only two unique points and it couldn't possibly be a polygon.

If you want to specify an inner boundary for the previous house, it might look like this:

```
<House>
    <desc>14 Foo Street</desc>
    <gml:Polygon srsName="myModel:srs">
        <outerBoundaryIs>
            <LinearRing>
                <coordinates>10,10</coordinates>
                <coordinates>12,10</coordinates>
                <coordinates>12,12</coordinates>
                <coordinates>10,12</coordinates>
                <coordinates>10,10</coordinates>
            </LinearRing>
        </outerBoundaryIs>
        <innerBoundaryIs>
            <LinearRing>
```

```
            <coordinates>10.5,10.5</coordinates>
            <coordinates>11.5,10.5</coordinates>
            <coordinates>11.5,11.5</coordinates>
            <coordinates>10.5,11.5</coordinates>
            <coordinates>10.5,10.5</coordinates>
        </LinearRing>
      </innerBoundaryIs>
   </gml:Polygon>
</House>
```

The innerBoundaryIs element is used to provide the coordinates for the linear ring. Note, the last coordinate is the same as the first one.

Points   We haven't used points in this example, but I should mention them. *Points* can be used to provide data for objects that are very small and meaningless to model in detail. Points can also be used to model important properties of the geographic model, although they don't exist in real life. For example, if you want to provide information about a certain area, you can model it as a feature that contains a point where the point is given coordinates that fall inside that area. For example, extremely old buildings might be marked as interesting from a cultural point-of-view. This could then be carried out using points that are positioned inside the outer bound of the house. Here's a simple example where a point has been provided inside the previously discussed house:

```
<ModelMember>
    <Marker>
        <desc>This is a house from the 19th century.</desc>
        <gml:Point>
            <coordinates>11, 11</coordinates>
        </gml:Point>
    </Marker>
</ModelMember>
```

Here we used a member of the model, which is called a *marker*. The marker works as a pin, which can be put anywhere on the map. In this case, the marker is positioned over the house, to indicate the house is to be treated, or even rendered, in a special way.

Your Schema

Now, it's time to look at the schema behind the code we've listed so far. The schema has been extended to include not only the features in the original listing at the beginning of the chapter, but also the definition of the previously described marker and the inner boundaries of the house.

First, though, let's stop and repeat a few things. To understand how the schema works, you should know that GML is very much object-oriented. This means the members of your model are described not only in terms of objects, but also in terms of classes. Chapter 16 contains more information about object orientation and advanced object-oriented models. Here's a short summary.

Feature Collections and Feature Types   All objects in your GML model are part of a collection. Each object, for example, a house or a road, is referred to as a *feature*. Because you might have several houses and several roads in your model, you need to be able to identify them all as a road type or a house type. Consequently, they belong to a certain type. Feature types are used for this. A *feature type* describes an object (or feature) of a certain type. For example, a feature type might specify that a house has a description and a multiline string, which describes the geometry of the house. Each house, though, has different settings for the description and the multiline string.

Inheritance   You must also know what inheritance is. Inheritance is described more in detail in Chapter 16 but, to summarize, *inheritance* makes it possible to say a certain feature type is like another one, and it also contains some additional content. Consequently, with inheritance, you can reuse parts of your code. You can specify a feature type—for example, a building. Then other features types, which can be considered as buildings, can inherit from that feature type and they can add additional data.

Inheritance is always used in GML schemas, including the schema you'll see soon. First, the collection—in this case, the Model—must inherit from a certain type. Each object in the model must also inherit from a specific type. This is demonstrated in the schema.

Complete Listing   This is the complete listing. I'll go through the schema from top to bottom and explain each section.

```
<!-- The schema declaration. -->
<schema targetNamespace="http://www.myExample.com/myNameSpace"
xmlns:xlink="http://www.w3.org/1999/xlink"
```

```
xmlns:myModel="http://www.myExample.com/myNameSpace"
xmlns:gml="http://www.opengis.net/gml"
xmlns="http://www.w3.org/2000/10/XMLSchema" elementFormDefault="qualified"
        version="2.03">

    <!-- Import the "standard" GML features. -->
    <import namespace="http://www.opengis.net/gml" schemaLocation="feature.xsd"/>

    <!-- The elements, which can be used in the .xml file. -->
    <element name="Model" type="myModel:ModelType"
        substitutionGroup="gml:_FeatureCollection"/>
    <element name="ModelMember" type="myModel:ModelMemberType"
        substitutionGroup="gml:featureMember"/>
    <element name="Road" type="myModel:RoadType"
        substitutionGroup="myModel:_ModelFeature"/>
    <element name="House" type="myModel:HouseType"
        substitutionGroup="myModel:_ModelFeature"/>
    <element name="Marker" type="myModel:PointType"
        substitutionGroup="myModel:_ModelFeature"/>

    <!-- The is the assocation, which is used by the ModelMemberType below. -->
    <element name="_ModelFeature" type="gml:AbstractFeatureType" abstract="true"
        substitutionGroup="gml:_Feature"/>

    <!-- The elements above use the types below, which define the "content" of the
        elements. -->
    <!-- Our model must inherit the abstract class
        gml:AbstractFeatureCollectionType.  -->
    <complexType name="ModelType">
        <complexContent>
            <extension base="gml:AbstractFeatureCollectionType"/>
        </complexContent>
    </complexType>
    <!-- The type for the association between the container class and feature
        members. -->
    <complexType name="ModelMemberType">
        <complexContent>
            <restriction base="gml:FeatureAssociationType">
                <sequence minOccurs="0">
                    <element ref="myModel:_ModelFeature"/>
                </sequence>
            </restriction>

        </complexContent>
    </complexType>
    <!-- The type for the Road class. Each Road has a certain number of lanes, a
                description and a geometric multi line string. -->
```

```
<complexType name="RoadType">
    <complexContent>
        <extension base="gml:AbstractFeatureType">
            <sequence>
                <element name="lanes" type="integer"/>
                <element name="desc" type="string"/>
                <element ref="gml:MultiLineString"/>
            </sequence>
        </extension>
    </complexContent>
</complexType>

<!-- The type for the House class. Each House has a textual description and
contains a geometric polygon.  -->
<complexType name="HouseType">
    <complexContent>
        <extension base="gml:AbstractFeatureType">
            <sequence>
                <element name="desc" type="string"/>
                <element ref="gml:Polygon"/>
            </sequence>
        </extension>
    </complexContent>
</complexType>

<!-- The type for the Marker.  -->
<complexType name="PointType">
    <complexContent>
        <extension base="gml:AbstractFeatureType">
            <sequence>
                <element name="desc" type="string"/>
                <element ref="gml:Point"/>
            </sequence>
        </extension>
    </complexContent>
</complexType>

</schema>
```

The schema is divided into a number of logical sections. It starts with the ordinary schema declaration, then follows a section that specifies all the elements used in the .xml file. The schema ends with a section that defines all types used. Note, each element declaration refers to some of the types defined in the schema.

Schema and Import   Let's start with the schema declaration and the import statement. The code looks like this:

```
<!-- The schema declaration. -->
<schema targetNamespace="http://www.myExample.com/myNameSpace"
xmlns:xlink="http://www.w3.org/1999/xlink"
xmlns:myModel="http://www.myExample.com/myNameSpace"
xmlns:gml="http://www.opengis.net/gml"
xmlns="http://www.w3.org/2000/10/XMLSchema" elementFormDefault="qualified"
        version="2.03">

    <!-- Import the "standard" GML features. -->
    <import namespace="http://www.opengis.net/gml"
schemaLocation="feature.xsd"/>
```

Here, the myModel namespace is declared. This name space is used in the
element declarations, after the schema declaration. The import element is used to
import the "standard" gml features, which are defined by OGC in the feature.xsd
schema.

The Elements in Our Model   Check the xml file again. You'll see we used the
following elements: Model, ModelMember, Road, House, and Marker. The other
elements are predefined GML elements, like gml:Polygon. Our elements are
declared like this:

```
<!-- The elements, which can be used in the .xml file. -->
<element name="Model" type="myModel:ModelType"
        substitutionGroup="gml:_FeatureCollection"/>
<element name="ModelMember" type="myModel:ModelMemberType"
        substitutionGroup="gml:featureMember"/>
<element name="Road" type="myModel:RoadType"
        substitutionGroup="myModel:_ModelFeature"/>
<element name="House" type="myModel:HouseType"
        substitutionGroup="myModel:_ModelFeature"/>
<element name="Marker" type="myModel:PointType"
        substitutionGroup="myModel:_ModelFeature"/>

<!-- The is the assocation, which is used by the ModelMemberType below. -->
<element name="_ModelFeature" type="gml:AbstractFeatureType" abstract="true"
        substitutionGroup="gml:_Feature"/>
```

Each element has a name, a type, and a substitution group. In practice, we're
saying our Model element will be handled like a gml:_FeatureCollection, and the
ModelMember element will be handled like a gml:featureType. These two types
are important. The element we use to specify the whole model—the Model element—
must belong to the substitution group gml:_FeatureCollection because it works as
a collection of objects—in our case, House and Road objects. The element we use to
enclose each object—the ModelMember element—must belong to the substitution

group gml:featureMember because it's part of the collection (Model) that manages features only. The remaining elements—Road, House, and Marker—are handled as _ModelFeature elements that inherit from their respective complex type. The last previous element declaration defines the _ModelFeature element as a _Feature. This means Road, House, and Marker are handled as _Feature elements or, in other words, objects that are part of the feature collection. In our case, the feature collection is the Model. Confused? It takes time to absorb all this information. Take your time. When you understand the previous declarations, then you'll understand much of what GML is all about: features, feature collections, and inheritance. When we continue further in the code, you'll see how inheritance is used when the types for the model members Road, House, and Marker are defined.

Extensions to the GML Types   The whole model must inherit from gml:AbstractFeatureCollectionType. Consequently, the top-level element in our mode—the Model element—must inherit from this type. This is expressed using the extension element.

```
<!-- The elements above use the types below, which define the "content" of the
          elements. -->
<!-- Our model must inherit the abstract class
          gml:AbstractFeatureCollectionType.  -->
<complexType name="ModelType">
    <complexContent>
        <extension base="gml:AbstractFeatureCollectionType"/>
    </complexContent>
</complexType>
```

The base attribute is set to the type, which ModelType inherits. A bit similar, the element, which encloses each object in the model—the ModelMember element— must extend gml:FeatureAssociationType because the ModelMember element associates each member of the model with the collection object.

```
<!-- The type for the association between the container class and
          feature members. -->
<complexType name="ModelMemberType">
    <complexContent>
        <restriction base="gml:FeatureAssociationType">
            <sequence minOccurs="0">
                <element ref="myModel:_ModelFeature"/>
            </sequence>
        </restriction>
    </complexContent>
</complexType>
```

This is the type for the ModelMember element. It inherits the gml:FeatureAssocationType because it associates the element, which is provided inside the ModelMember element, with the feature collection.

Road, House, and Marker are defined as complex types, which extend the GML type gml:AbstractFeatureType. The code that declares the types for these elements follows. Notice all these three types extend the gml:AbstractFeatureType because they're supposed to be part of a collection that manages feature types only.

```
<!-- The type for the Road class. Each Road has a certain number of lanes, a
        description and a geometric multi line string. -->

<complexType name="RoadType">
    <complexContent>
        <extension base="gml:AbstractFeatureType">
            <sequence>
                <element name="lanes" type="integer"/>
                <element name="desc" type="string"/>
                <element ref="gml:MultiLineString"/>
            </sequence>
        </extension>
    </complexContent>
</complexType>
```

Notice we only have to provide the gml:MultiLineString declaration here and not all the elements that are part of a gml:MultiLineString (coordinates and so forth). That relationship has already been defined in geometry.xsd, which is included by feature.xsd (imported in this schema). The HouseType and the PointType are defined in a similar way, but they contain a gml:Polygon and a gml:Point instead of a gml:MultiLineString.

```
<!-- The type for the House class. Each House has a textual description and
contains a geometric polygon.  -->
<complexType name="HouseType">
    <complexContent>
        <extension base="gml:AbstractFeatureType">
            <sequence>
                <element name="desc" type="string"/>
                <element ref="gml:Polygon"/>
            </sequence>
        </extension>
    </complexContent>
</complexType>

<!-- The type for the Marker.  -->
<complexType name="PointType">
    <complexContent>
```

```
        <extension base="gml:AbstractFeatureType">
         <sequence>
            <element name="desc" type="string"/>
            <element ref="gml:Point"/>
         </sequence>
        </extension>
    </complexContent>
</complexType>
```

HouseType, PointType, and RoadType inherit gml:AbstractFeatureType and include a geometry element: either a gml:MultiLineString, a gml:Polygon, or a gml:Point. Notice how the element declarations at the beginning of the schema refer to these type declarations.

If you're new to object orientation, you probably need some time to absorb this section of the chapter. Try to understand the role of the collection, feature types, and inheritance. If these topics are new for you, Chapter 16 gives you more examples that are a bit more comprehensive, but also are explained in detail. You'll see how the geometry elements of a GML file can be transformed to different SVG files to highlight different aspects of the map. To prepare you for this, let's look at some SVG basics.

SVG

Vector graphics can be used in combination with GML to render the models represented using GML. A representation in GML can be transformed into an SVG file using, for example, XSL Transformations, and then rendered on handheld devices, like personal digital assistants (PDAs) that have a Java virtual machine installed. Some of the newer Java phones can execute Java applications. How GML can be transformed to SVG is described in Chapter 16.

Vector graphics are drawn using a model of graphic objects and operations, rather than using bitmaps as the source. With SVG, you can create such a model as an XML file. As you probably know, XML content can be stored in databases without occupying too much space and an XML file can be transformed so the content can be adapted for different machines or users. Several advantages exist with an XML-based vector graphics format.

SVG files are based around the top-level tag SVG, which contains a title and a description. The body of the file can contain a number of shapes, such as rectangles, polygons, circles, and ellipses. Lines, filled areas, and strokes are also easy to create. These drawings can be defined, and then reused in different sections of the file for transformation and translation purposes. A transformation might distort the drawing in a certain way—for example, it might extend the drawing by 50 percent along the *x* axis. A translation might move the object inside what's called the view box.

Let's start with some SVG basics, and then we'll create an SVG version of the simple map we specified with GML.

The Drawing Board

The height and width of the drawing should always be declared. A number of different units are available for you, such as inches or centimeters. To simplify things, the basic structure of an SVG document goes like this:

```
<?xml version="1.0" standalone="yes"?>
<!DOCTYPE svg PUBLIC "-//W3C//DTD SVG 20001102//EN"
"http://www.w3.org/TR/2000/CR-SVG-20001102/DTD/svg-20001102.dtd">

<svg width="10cm" height="5cm">
     ...
</svg>
```

The XML header is at the top as usual. It contains the attribute standalone, which is set to yes. This means the SVG document will be used on its own rather than being part of another document. It is possible to embed SVG documents in other XML documents. But, for the moment, we'll use SVG standalone, so the attribute is set to yes. On the next line, you'll find the document type declaration, which specifies the path to the document type definition of SVG. Then follows the SVG element with a start tag and an end tag, which are supposed to surround the complete SVG specification.

The View Box

It's also possible to declare a view box in the start tag of the svg element. The *view box* works as a logical scale. While the width and height attributes specify the dimensions of the window that displays the graphics, the view box specifies which range all the graphical objects are going to use. A view box declaration can look like this:

```
<?xml version="1.0" standalone="yes"?>
<!DOCTYPE svg PUBLIC "-//W3C//DTD SVG 20001102//EN"
"http://www.w3.org/TR/2000/CR-SVG-20001102/DTD/svg-20001102.dtd">

<svg width="150px" height="100px" viewBox="0 0 150 100">
<title>An SVG example.</title>
<desc>The application renders some cool objects onto a 150x100 screen.</desc>
     ...
</svg>
```

The coordinates of the view box needn't be multiples of the values of the width and height elements. The view box should be seen as the logical drawing board, and the width and height attributes should be set to the physical dimensions of the output device.

Also notice the title and desc elements, which specify a title for the SVG file and a short textual description about what the SVG file does.

Aspect Ratios

An attribute named preserveAspectRatio can be specified together with the SVG element. If the *aspect ratio* of the view box isn't the same as the aspect ratio of the width and height attributes, then you'll have to declare how this situation should be handled. If the attribute is set to none, then nothing is done to preserve the aspect ratio: either the *x* or *y* axis is stretched and the picture becomes distorted.

If an absolute need occurs to preserve the aspect ratio, then several options are available to you. Setting the attribute to xMinYMin forces a uniform scaling, so the smallest *x* and *y* coordinates of the element are moved to the smallest *x* and *y* coordinates of the view box. Setting the attribute to xMaxYMax can move the element, so the biggest *x* and *y* coordinates of the element are moved to the biggest *x* and *y* coordinates of the view box. Here's an example:

```
<?xml version="1.0" standalone="yes"?>
<!DOCTYPE svg PUBLIC "-//W3C//DTD SVG 20001102//EN"
"http://www.w3.org/TR/2000/CR-SVG-20001102/DTD/svg-20001102.dtd">

<svg width="150px" height="100px"
     viewBox="0 0 150 100"
     preserveAspectRatio="xMinYMax">

  <title>An SVG example.
  </title>
  <desc>The application renders some cool objects onto a 150x100 screen.
  </desc>
  <rect x="5" y="10" width="145" height="90"/>
</svg>
```

The previous code produces a rectangle, which covers almost the whole view box. However, if you change the width and height attributes like this

```
<svg width="100px" height="100px"
```

and keep the rest of the code as it is, then the physical proportions aren't the same as the view box's proportions. Because the preserveAspectRatio attribute is set to something other than none, the aspect ratio is maintained and the rectangle is scaled so it fits into the view box's window. The right edge of the rectangle coincides with the right edge of the whole window because it ends at the logical point 5 + 145 = 150, which equals 100px (the width). The bottom of the rectangle is aligned with the bottom of the display window because preserveAspectRatio is set to xMinYMax and the bottom edge of the rectangle is then aligned with the bottom of the display window.

Shapes

A number of shapes can be drawn with SVG. Rectangles are drawn using the rect element. The position, width, height, and other properties of the rectangle can be specified. It might look like this:

```
<?xml version="1.0" standalone="yes"?>
<!DOCTYPE svg PUBLIC "-//W3C//DTD SVG 20001102//EN"
"http://www.w3.org/TR/2000/CR-SVG-20001102/DTD/svg-20001102.dtd">

<svg width="150px" height="100px" viewBox="0 0 150 100">
<title>An SVG example.</title>
<desc>The application renders some cool objects onto a 150x100 screen.</desc>
<rect x="50" y="25" width="50" height="50"
      fill="#0000ff" stroke="#ff0000 " stroke-width="1"/>
</svg>
```

The previous example draws a rectangle. Here, the view box is set to the same dimensions as the width and height of the display area. The point (0,0) is located at the upper-right corner of the display area and the point (150, 150) is located at the lower-right corner of the display area. Consequently, the previous rectangle would have all its sides, located 25 pixels from the middle of the display area.

Fill

With the *fill* attribute, you can specify an RGB (Red, Green, and Blue) color. If the fill attribute is present, the rectangle is filled with the specified color, but if the attribute is left out, the rectangle isn't filled at all.

If the stroke-width attribute is given, then the rectangle can be drawn with an arbitrary thickness. You can also specify the color of the stroke, using the stroke attribute. More SVG shapes are shown in Chapter 16.

Paths

Many shapes don't have a name. SVG would be useless if you had to refer to a certain name, like rectangle, as soon as you need to draw a shape. Real-world objects usually aren't that easy to describe, and location-based mobile Internet services, which are supposed to help users find a certain place, need constructs to describe arbitrary paths in the geography.

The Path Element

With the *path* element, you can draw arbitrary paths using straight lines, elliptical arcs, and Bézier curves. *Bézier curves* are curves that need only a few points to define a large number of shapes. Closed paths can be filled. The following example draws a path created from a straight line and an arc. The path is closed, causing it to form an object, which is painted blue:

```
<?xml version="1.0" standalone="yes"?>
<!DOCTYPE svg PUBLIC "-//W3C//DTD SVG 20001102//EN"
"http://www.w3.org/TR/2000/CR-SVG-20001102/DTD/svg-20001102.dtd">

<svg width="150px" height="100px" viewBox="0 0 150 100">
<title>An SVG example.</title>
<desc>The application renders a closed path onto a 150x100 screen.</desc>
<path d="M 25,0 L 75,50 A 5,5 0 0,0 150,25 Z"
      style="fill:blue; stroke:red; stroke-width=10"/>
</svg>
```

The path element has an attribute—*d*—which stands for "data." It should be set to a list of commands that describe how the path should be drawn. In the previous example, you can see the path data start with M 25, 0. This means the drawing will start at point (25, 0). Then the command L 75, 50 will draw a line between the current point, which is (25, 0) and (75, 50). The next command is A, which means "arc." The arc command has seven parameters. First, the *x* radius and the *y* radius of the arc are specified (that's (5, 5) in our example). Then, you should specify a number, which indicates how much the arc should be rotated around the *x* axis. The next two parameters indicate the direction and size of the arc's sweep and the last two coordinates indicate the end position for the arc on the *x* and *y* axis. You have seven parameters to keep track of here, so the best way to learn how to draw arcs is to experiment with different values and watch the result.

Text

Text messages are displayed using the *text* element. Arbitrary font size can be used and the text can be positioned anywhere in the view box. Even transformations, like scaling, rotations, and skew, can be applied to the text.

The following example shows how the text attributes font-size, fill, *x,* and *y* can be used.

```
<?xml version="1.0" standalone="yes"?>
<!DOCTYPE svg PUBLIC "-//W3C//DTD SVG 20001102//EN"
"http://www.w3.org/TR/2000/CR-SVG-20001102/DTD/svg-20001102.dtd">

<svg width="3cm" height="6cm" viewBox="0 0 150 100">
<title>An SVG example.</title>
<desc>The application renders a closed path onto a 150x100 screen.</desc>
<text x="0cm" y="3cm" style="fill:blue; font-size:8pt">Blue Text
</text>
</svg>
```

The 8-pt font is rendered so it starts to the far left of the display area. Many additional settings can be supplied in the style attribute. One is font-family. I recommend you avoid rare fonts, however, because the application will be executed on a handheld and, in that environment, the number of installed fonts is usually smaller than on a traditional desktop computer.

The Map in SVG

Now, when you're familiar with SVG, let's look at the map we created in the GML section. The map contains a house, a road, and a marker that points at the house. Here's an SVG implementation of the geometry elements:

```
<?xml version="1.0" standalone="yes"?>
<!DOCTYPE svg PUBLIC "-//W3C//DTD SVG 20001102//EN"
"http://www.w3.org/TR/2000/CR-SVG-20001102/DTD/svg-20001102.dtd">

<svg width="150px" height="150px" viewBox="0 0 300 300">

  <title>A simple map.</title>
  <desc>The map contains a road, a house and a marker.</desc>

  <!-- **************** Background **************** -->
  <rect x="0" y="0" width="300" height="300"
      style="fill:green; stroke:green"/>

  <!-- *************** Marker definition *************** -->
  <defs>
  <polyline id="Marker"
      points="0,0 20,4 0,8 0,0"
      transform="translate(-20, -4)"
      fill="yellow" stroke="yellow" stroke-width="1"/>
  </defs>
```

```
<!-- *************** The road *************** -->
<path d="M 30,30 L 30,290"
    style="stroke:red; stroke-width=1"/>

<!-- *************** The house *************** -->
<!-- Inner bound -->
<path d="M 100,100 L 120,100 L 120,120 L 100,120 Z"
    style="fill:black; stroke:black"/>

<!-- Outer bound -->
<path d="M 105,105 L 115,105 L 115,115 L 105,115 Z"
    style="fill:green; stroke:black"/>

<!-- *************** The marker *************** -->
<use xlink:href="#Marker" transform="translate(110,110)"/>

</svg>
```

We've used the title, desc, and path elements earlier in this chapter, so they needn't be explained. The rect element draws a rectangle. We use that element to draw a green background.

The marker is first defined, using the defs elements, and then it's used at the end of the document. A def element can be used to define a geometry object, which is used often. This is similar to how we defined feature types in the GML schema, and then referred to the types when the feature elements were specified. In this case, we defined a marker used via the use element and an xlink. If we need to insert more markers on the map, we insert the use element in the code and set the coordinates in the transform attribute. The *transform* attribute can be used to make transformations like scaling and adding offsets. In our case, we've done two translations. A translation simply adds an offset to the x and y axis. The translation in the def element is used to move the marker so it points at 0,0. This is achieved by subtracting 20 from the x axis and 4 from the y axis. When the marker is used, it points at the coordinates supplied in the translate section, in the transform attribute.

In Chapter 16, we create a more detailed model in GML, which is mapped to an SVG implementation using an XSL style sheet. You'll also get a feeling for how SVG can be executed on Java-compatible devices.

CHAPTER

8

Translations and Optimizations

IN THIS CHAPTER:

Binary XML

A Few Words About WAX

171

WAX and WBXML are two translation technologies you can use to optimize your application from several points of view. With WBXML, you can optimize your XML application with respect to transfer times. The tokenization functionality is part of a WAP gateway/proxy and is carried out automatically on-the-fly. Because the process usually takes some time, however, you might experience a slight latency for some applications. Should this occur, you can use development tools to tokenize your XML code and put it on your server in a tokenized form and the gateway/proxy will pass it through.

With Morphis WAX, you can target many different types of devices by writing your application in the Wireless Abstract XML language. Thus, your application will be optimized to display on as many devices as possible. This translation technology is slightly different from, say, XSLT, which only maps an XML document to another based on a style sheet. WAX can consider nontextual content. For example, it can resize or crop pictures so they display well on the target device. If you don't want to spend endless hours writing style sheets for every possible language and device, this is another reason to look at WAX.

Binary XML

The average developer doesn't need to know how the WBXML process works. You might simply use the development tools available for tokenization. If you're into programming, however, it might be fun and tempting to write an XML to WBXML converter, which optimizes your code as much as possible. In addition, developers, in general, who design wireless XML applications, will get a good feeling for how a WAP network works by examining binary XML in detail. Note, in this case, WAP network doesn't necessarily mean the application, is based on WML and WMLScripts. Because WBXML works with all XML applications, it can be applied on a wide range of languages, such as SVG, GML, SMIL, WML, XHTML, XML-RPC, and XML documents in general that were created according to your own DTD. The only requirement is that the device have support for the WAP protocol stack.

Because the WBXML document is retrieved by a WAP gateway/proxy as an ordinary web document, you need to configure your web server with the right content type. The file extension for a WBXML document is wbxml and the MIME type (content type) that should be associated with this extension is application/vnd.wap.wbxml.

Files represented in WBXML should be packed efficiently for transfer over the air. This isn't only because the documents should be able to be sent relatively quickly over a narrow band connection, such as a 2G GSM network. It's also because no matter how much bandwidth you have, there's always a need for more. Consequently, the packing of information using WBXML certainly isn't only relevant for 2G and 2.5G networks, but also for the third and even fourth generation of wireless networks. The file structure for WBXML documents is based on minimizing the representation, with respect to the code size. Codes and tables are used to refer to elements, attributes, and text. Thus, a string that's used frequently can be replaced by a short code, which represents that string.

Let's encode a simple XHTML Basic document. It could look like this:

```
<?xml version="1.0" encoding="UTF-8"?>
<!DOCTYPE html PUBLIC "-//W3C//DTD XHTML Basic 1.0//EN"
    "http://www.w3.org/TR/xhtml-basic/xhtml-basic10.dtd">
<html xmlns="http://www.w3.org/1999/xhtml">
  <head>
    <title>Encode
    </title>
  </head>
  <body>
    <p>My <em>table</em>
    </p>
    <table>
      <tr>
        <td>Left</td>
        <td>Right</td>
      </tr>
    </table>
  </body>
</html>
```

A WBXML representation for the previous, and all XML documents, starts with a version number and additional metainformation, such as a character set specification. Then the string table is listed. We'll return to the string table. It's more or less the core of WBXML. The WBXML file then ends with the document body.

The Start of a WBXML Document

Before the string table starts, the version number, document public identifier, and character set are specified.

WBXML Version Number

The file begins with the WBXML version number and it's handled in a slightly unusual way. There's only one byte, which indicates the version, so it needs to be split into two parts—each four bits. The most significant bits are the major version and the least significant bits are the minor version. Because the latest version of WBXML is 1.3, the major version is 1 and the minor version is 3. The major version is represented as the version minus 1, so it becomes 0. Thus, the 1-byte code for the WBXML version number 1.3 would be 3.

Formal Public Identifier

The Formal Public Identifier (FPI) follows the version number. It's a section of the DOCTYPE declaration, which specifies the XML application, the language being used and the company or organization responsible for maintaining the language. For example, the DOCTYPE declaration for XHTML Basic might look like this:

```
<!DOCTYPE html PUBLIC "-//W3C//DTD XHTML Basic 1.0//EN"
    "http://www.w3.org/TR/xhtml-basic/xhtml-basic10.dtd">
```

The FPI in the previous document type declaration is the following string:

```
-//W3C//DTD XHTML Basic 1.0//EN
```

Consequently, a portion of the document type declaration is removed and not represented in WBXML. For example, the URL to the DTD isn't part of the WBXML document. The meaning is that the document should be validated before it's converted to WBXML, however, so it would be somewhat redundant information if it were part of the WBXML document.

The FPI can be represented as a string of characters and the previous FPI could be represented like this using UTF-8 character encoding:

```
UTF-8 Character codes          Text

45 47 47 87 51 67              "-//W3C"
47 47 68 84 68 32              "//DTD "
88 72 84 77 76 32              "XHTML "
66 97 115 105 99 32            "Basic "
49 46 48 47 47 69 78           "1.0//EN"
0                              End of string (null)
```

All codes are 8 bits and correspond to ordinary ASCII or UTF-8 codes. The string ends with a zero, which indicates the end of the string. This is how the actual FPI is encoded in the string table. However, this encoding is just pointed out as an index, after the version number, and before the character set. Later on, you'll notice that we have encoded the FPI as index number 38 in the string table. The byte stream, which represents the FPI, looks like this.

```
Hexadecimal byte stream   Decimal byte stream   Comment

x0                        0                     FPI is indexed.
x26                       38                    Index to string table
                                                is 38.
```

Thus, the byte stream points at a string table, which will include the previous character encoding, as you will soon see . It comes after the character set declaration.

Character Set

The character set is specified after the previous character sequence and it's based on the character set specified in the XML prologue. Usually the XML prologue looks like this.

```
<?xml version="1.0" encoding="UTF-8"?>
```

In XML, the prologue might be left out, although most structured documents include it. If no XML prologue is specified, the default character encoding should be UTF-8. The character encoding is carried out using a code. These codes are assigned by IANA and for UTF-8 it is the hexadecimal value 6A.

```
Hexadecimal byte stream   Decimal byte stream   Comment

x6A                       106                   Code for UTF-8
```

To summarize, the version number, public identifier and character set could be represented the following way for an XHTML Basic document, which uses UTF-8 character encoding. All codes are 8 bits each.

```
Hexadecimal byte stream   Decimal Byte stream   Explanation

0x3                       3                     WBXML version 1.3
0x0 0x26                  0 38                  Index in string table for FPI.
x6A                       106                   UTF-8 character encoding.
```

This would be a valid start for a WBXML file. However, it would have to be followed by a string table and the document body to be a WBXML 1.3 conformant document. So far, the XML document hasn't been packed that much, other than the removal of redundant information in the document type declaration.

The String Table

Here comes the string table. The string table contains a number of strings that the code can refer to by giving an offset to the table. Each string is terminated with a zero that indicates the end of the string. Consequently, a string, such as "table," which contains 5 characters, occupies 6 bytes in the string table, since there is a trailing zero.

The string table could contain a number of strings that represent elements or the FPI, like this.

Encoded	Index in the string table	Positions	Length
table	0	0 - 5	6 (incl. 0)
em	6	6 - 8	3
td	9	9 - 11	3
tr	12	12 - 14	3
html	15	15 - 19	5
p	20	20 - 21	2
head	22	22 - 26	5
title	27	27 - 32	6
body	33	33 - 37	5
"-//W3C//DTD XHTML Basic 1.0//EN"	38	38 - 69	32

The total length of the string table would then be 70 characters and the first string would be referred to using the offset 0 and the second string would be referred to using the offset 6 because it starts on position 6, and so forth. Thus, in this case, the byte stream, which represents the previous sample table, would be the following:

Hexadecimal byte stream	Decimal Byte stream	Explanation
x46	70	Length
x74 x61 x62 x6c x65 x0	116 97 98 108 101 0	"table"
x65 x6d x0	101 109 0	"em"
x74 x64 x0	116 100 0	"td"
x74 x72 x0	116 114 0	"tr"
x68 x74 x6d x6c x0	104 116 109 108 0	"html"
x70 x0	112 0	"p"
x68 x65 61 x64 x0	104 101 97 100 0	"head"

```
x74 x69 x74 x6c x65 x0        116 105 116 108 101 0    "title"
x62 x6f x64 x79 x0            98 111 100 121 0         "body"
x2d x2f x2f x57 x33 x43       45 47 47 87 51 67        "-//W3C
x2f x2f x44 x54 x44 x20       47 47 68 84 68 32        //DTD "
x58 x48 x54 x4d x4c x20       88 72 84 77 76 32        XHTML "
x42 x61 x73 x69 x63 x20       66 97 115 105 99 32      Basic "
x31 x2e x30 x2f x2f x45 x4e   49 46 48 47 47 69 78 0   1.0//EN"
```

Thus, the encoding of an XHTML Basic document, which uses UTF-8 character encoding and the table, em, td, tr, html, p, head, title, and body elements could begin like this:

```
Hexadecimal byte stream       Decimal Byte stream      Explanation

0x3                           3                        WBXML version 1.3
0x0 0x26                      0 38                     Index in string table for FPI.
x6A                           106                      UTF-8 character encoding.
x46                           70                       Length
x74 x61 x62 x6c x65 x0        116 97 98 108 101 0      "table"
x65 x6d x0                    101 109 0                "em"
x74 x64 x0                    116 100 0                "td"
x74 x72 x0                    116 114 0                "tr"
x68 x74 x6d x6c x0            104 116 109 108 0        "html"
x70 x0                        112 0                    "p"
x68 x65 61 x64 x0             104 101 97 100 0         "head"
x74 x69 x74 x6c x65 x0        116 105 116 108 101 0    "title"
x62 x6f x64 x79 x0            98 111 100 121 0         "body"
x2d x2f x2f x57 x33 x43       45 47 47 87 51 67        "-//W3C
x2f x2f x44 x54 x44 x20       47 47 68 84 68 32        //DTD "
x58 x48 x54 x4d x4c x20       88 72 84 77 76 32        XHTML "
x42 x61 x73 x69 x63 x20       66 97 115 105 99 32      Basic "
x31 x2e x30 x2f x2f x45 x4e x0   49 46 48 47 47 69 78 0   1.0//EN"
```

However, the WBXML document would need its final section, the document body, to be complete. So far, the byte stream does not describe the actual document body. It describes only the elements used: the character encoding and FPI.

The Document Body

All tags and attributes are specified using special codes. Each code describes if the element has an end tag or if it only contains a single tag, such as the img element in XHTML. In other words, each code specifies whether the element has an empty content model. In addition, these codes are used to specify if the start tag for the element contains one or more attributes. The following codes are used.

Content and Attributes

An element, which has content and attributes, could be used like this.

```
<html xmlns="http://www.w3.org/1999/xhtml">
   ...
</html>
```

This type of code, which has content and at least one attribute, has the code xC4 (decimal 196). The element is referred to as a LITERAL_AC because it has both content and attributes.

No Content and No Attributes

The following type of element has the code 4.

```
<br/>
```

Because br has an empty content model and is used without any attributes, this type of element is referred to as a LITERAL. It has the code 4.

Content but No Attributes

The following element has content but no attributes.

```
<p>Hello!
</p>
```

This element has the code x44 (decimal 68) and should occur with content but without attributes. The element is referred to as a LITERAL_C because it has content.

No Content but Attributes

Finally, this element has no content but does have attributes.

```
<img src="car.gif" alt="My car."/>
```

This element has an empty content model but contains two attributes. The element is referred to as a LITERAL_A because it has attributes and has the code x84 (decimal 132).

Index to the String Table

All the previous codes are provided with an index to the element in the string table. By combining that information, with one of the previous codes, you can specify which of the language tags you're describing, and if it's a start tag, an end tag, and with or without attributes. Here's the code again, in augmented form, without the XML prologue and the document type declaration.

```
Code                                       Comment

<html xmlns="http://www.w3.org/1999/xhtml">  LITERAL_AC
  <head>                                     LITERAL_C
    <title>Encode                            LITERAL_C
    </title>                                 END of title
  </head>                                    END of head
  <body>                                     LITERAL_C
    <p>My                                    LITERAL_C
      <em>table                              LITERAL_C
      </em>                                  END of em
    </p>                                     END of p
    <table>                                  LITERAL_C
      <tr>                                   LITERAL_C
        <td>Left                             LITERAL_C
        </td>                                END oftd
        <td>Right                            LITERAL_C
        </td>                                END of td
      </tr>                                  END of tr
    </table>                                 END of table
  </body>                                    END of body
</html>                                      END of html
```

As you can see, there are almost only LITERAL_C tags in our code, except the first element, which is a LITERAL_AC tag. This element has content and an attribute.

The previous code could be encoded like this. Because html has index number 15, counting from zero, in the string table, its start tag would be referred to as a LITERAL_AC with index 15 in the string table. Here is a complete listing with all the codes for the preceding markup. Closing tags have the code 1.

```
Code                                       Hexadecimal token number etc.

<html xmlns="http://www.w3.org/1999/xhtml">  xc4 (decimal 196), index 15
```

```
<head>                          x44 (decimal 68), index 22
  <title>Encode                 x44 (decimal 68), index 27
  </title>                      x1
</head>                         x1
<body>                          x44 (decimal 68), index 33
  <p>My                         x44 (decimal 68), index 20
    <em>table                   x44 (decimal 68), index 6
    </em>                       x1
  </p>                          x1
  <table>                       x44 (decimal 68), index 0
    <tr>                        x44 (decimal 68), index 12
      <td>Left                  x44 (decimal 68), index 9
      </td>                     x1
      <td>Right                 x44 (decimal 68), index 9
      </td>                     x1
    </tr>                       x1
  </table>                      x1
</body>                         x1
</html>                         x1
```

If the previous code were encoded as a stream of bytes, then it would look something like this:

Hexadecimal encoding	Explanation
xc4 x0e	html, LITERAL_AC with index 15
x3	STR_I, an inline string follows
"xmlns='http://www.w3.org/1999/xhtml" x0	The attribute as an inline text string.
x1	END of html attribute list
x44 x16	head, LITERAL_C with index 22
x44 x1b	title, LITERAL_C with index 27
x3	STR_I, an inline string follows.
"Encode" x0	The null terminated text string "Encode".
x1	END, closing </title>
x1	END, closing </head>
x44 x21	<body>, LITERAL_C with index 33
x44 x14	p, LITERAL_C with index 20
x3	STR_I, inline string follows
"My" 0	Null terminated string "My".
x44 x6	, LITERAL with index 6
x3	STR_I, inline string follows.
"table" x0	Null terminated string "table".
x1	END, closing
x1	END, closing </p>
x44 x0	<table>, LITERAL_C with index 0.
x44 x0c	<tr>, LITERAL_C with index 12.

```
x44 x09                                <td>, LITERAL_C with index 9.
x1                                     END, closing </td>
x44 x09                                <td>, LITERAL_C with index 9.
x1                                     END, closing </td>
x1                                     END, closing </tr>
x1                                     END, closing </table>
x1                                     END, closing </body>
x1                                     END, closing </html>
```

The special END code is used to indicate the end of either an element or an attribute list. For elements, the special END code represents the closing tag, and for attributes, it represents the end of the start tag in which all attributes have been listed. An inline string can be used as a replacement for a string table index. A string, which is only used once, might be sufficient to refer to as an inline string. Then the code STR_I, or 3, indicates a string will follow. As you can see, XML code can be coded efficiently if the string table is used correctly. Even if the string table isn't used, you'll get a reasonably compact code because all end tags are represented using only a single byte.

Summary

To summarize, the complete WBXML code would look like this.

```
Hexadecimal byte stream              Explanation

0x3                                  WBXML version 1.3
0x0 0x26                             Index in string table for FPI.
x6A                                  UTF-8 character encoding.
x46                                  Length
x74 x61 x62 x6c x65 x0              "table"
x65 x6d x0                          "em"
x74 x64 x0                          "td"
x74 x72 x0                          "tr"
x68 x74 x6d x6c x0                  "html"
x70 x0                              "p"
x68 x65 61 x64 x0                   "head"
x74 x69 x74 x6c x65 x0              "title"
x62 x6f x64 x79 x0                  "body"
x2d x2f x2f x57 x33 x43             "-//W3C
x2f x2f x44 x54 x44 x20            //DTD "
x58 x48 x54 x4d x4c x20            XHTML "
x42 x61 x73 x69 x63 x20            Basic "
x31 x2e x30 x2f x2f x45 x4e 49 46 48 47 47 69 78 0        1.0//EN"
xc4 x0f                             html, LITERAL_AC with index 15
```

x3	STR_I, an inline string follows
"xmlns='http://www.w3.org/1999/xhtml" x0	The attribute as an inline text string.
x1	END of html attribute list
x44 x16	head, LITERAL_C with index 22
x44 x1b	title, LITERAL_C with index 27
x3	STR_I, an inline string follows.
"Encode" x0	The null terminated text string "Encode".
x1	END, closing </title>
x1	END, closing </head>
x44 x21	<body>, LITERAL_C with index 33
x44 x14	p, LITERAL_C with index 20
x3	STR_I, inline string follows
"My" 0	Null terminated string "My".
x44 x06	, LITERAL with index 6
x3	STR_I, inline string follows.
"table" x0	Null terminated string "table".
x1	END, closing
x1	END, closing </p>
x44 x0	<table>, LITERAL_C with index 0.
x44 x0c	<tr>, LITERAL_C with index 12.
x44 x09	<td>, LITERAL_C with index 9.
x1	END, closing </td>
x44 x09	<td>, LITERAL_C with index 9.
x1	END, closing </td>
x1	END, closing </tr>
x1	END, closing </table>
x1	END, closing </body>
x1	END, closing </html>

In this brief example, elements aren't referred to more than once, so putting each element in the string table doesn't save much space. You notice the effect more when many occurrences of an element are in the code and when many occurrences of a certain string are in the code.

So, now you should know how WBXML works. You should also know that if you have strings in your code, which are duplicated at several places in the document, they could be inserted into the string table and referred to using an index only. If they aren't, then this is the time to write your own optimal XML tokenizer. As you might have noticed, our encoding could have saved a couple of bytes by replacing the inline string "table" with a pointer to the string table, so there's room for optimization even in the preceding small code.

A Few Words About WAX

The intention and strengths of XML are that the instance document can be written in a format that's independent of how it's rendered on a device. Many markup languages, such as XHTML, WML, and SVG, however, do have elements and attributes closely related to a specific user interface paradigm. For example, in HTML, XHTML, and WML, the i and b elements specify that the text should be rendered with italics and a bold face font. XSL Transformations can overcome this problem if you create a style sheet from a device-independent language to the target language, such as XHTML or WML. Then you would have to define your own super language, however, which works with the most used languages and devices. If you don't need to use XSLT and if you aren't forced to use XSLT because of infrastructure constraints, then there's an alternative called Morphis WAX, which does the job. *Morphis WAX* converts from WAX to a number of different target languages and devices. We won't spend much time with this technology. I simply want to point out that Morphis WAX is available for you if you don't have the time or the skills to write XSL style sheets.

One Language

The purpose of WAX is to let you write your application in a markup language that's as generic as possible. The code would then be translated to WAP devices, Palm devices that use Avant Go, ordinary web browsers and i-mode phones using cHTML, and so forth. WAX can be downloaded from **http://www.morphis.org/**.

The application might look like this.

```
<?xml version="1.0" encoding="UTF-8"?>
<wax:wax xmlns:wax="http://www.morphis.org/wax" version="1.0">
  <wax:doc>
      <wax:title>Welcome
      </wax:title>
      <wax:background bgcolor="#887788"/>
      <wax:block>
         <wax:p>Hello
         </wax:p>
      </wax:block>
  </wax:doc>
</wax:wax>
```

Thus, the elements used are quite generic, which makes generating code for a number of different devices possible. This has many benefits. The translator can not only generate code, which is optimized for a certain device or browser. It can also make it possible for you to specify a number of characteristics for a number of devices. For example, specifying which image formats a device can display is possible. Then the WAX code refers to a symbolic name in the code and, when the system translates to the target language, it uses an additional XML file to look up which format is most suitable for that device.

Alternatives to WAX exist when it comes to translating the XML code and optimizing it for a certain device. XSLT has been popular lately. In fact, WAX uses XSLT technology to implement the translation mechanism. If you want to have full control over what happens, however, then you might want to implement the style sheets yourself. In that case, though, you won't have any translation of the images, so you would also have to implement such functionality. One solution is your XSL style sheet maps generic names to a number of different image files, which have been optimized manually for different types of devices. Another solution is you create a piece of software that takes an image, resizes it, and adjusts the colors automatically, based on a description of the device (for example, its User Agent Profile).

CHAPTER
9
Profiles

IN THIS CHAPTER:

RDF—Resource Description Framework

CC/PP

UAProf

Using the Profile

Composite Capability/Preference Profile (CC/PP) is a framework to specify a user's personal preferences and the capabilities for a device or application. With the CC/PP exchange protocol, these properties can be transferred between a server that provides content and the client.

The idea is this: the server should be able to check which capabilities the device has and which preferences the user has selected. Then the server can transfer the right content to the device regarding these settings. Because so many different types of small handheld devices exist, there's a need to express capabilities, such as color display, physical display size, or if the device supports audio. In addition, personal preferences, such as accepting cookies and using the application with the sound switched off, can make the experience much more tailored for a user's personal taste and needs. Based on these premises, a server can optimize the content for a particular device and the user's personal preferences before it's transferred to the device.

The information about the device and the user's personal preferences are sent in the HTTP get request. A URL is sent in the get request and the URL points at the profile. Or, the profile can be sent in the HTTP message, instead of sending a pointer. In most cases, though, a better idea is to send a URL, which points at the profile because it saves bandwidth.

The request is sent from the device and is transferred—possibly over the air—to the server and, when the server has received the request, it finds out which document should be sent back. This is where CC/PP comes in. The information can be used to determine which of several documents will be sent back in the get response. Or, the information might be used to decide how the document, associated with the URL in the get request, will be processed before it's sent back to the device.

CC/PP isn't a W3C recommendation yet, so I'll only give you a brief introduction on it and we'll concentrate on *UAProf,* which is a similar technology based on the work that's been done with CC/PP. UAProf is used today in the Wireless Application Protocol (WAP).

RDF—Resource Description Framework

To understand how you can specify properties for a handheld device, you must have some basic understanding about the Resource Description Framework (RDF). RDF is used by CC/PP and User Agent Profiles (UAProf) to specify properties of the devices, such as hardware characteristics and software settings.

The basic idea of RDF is that the resources—in this case, handheld devices—should be possible to describe in terms of subjects, predicates, and objects. Look at the following phrases:

```
The device can display images.
The device can display colors.
The device supports GPRS.
The device accepts the application/xml+xhtml content type.
The device accepts SMIL presentations.
```

If these device properties should be represented in RDF, then you would have to translate each sentence to a subject, predicate, and object. You could end up with the following subjects, predicates, and objects:

```
Subject: the device
Predicate: displays
Object: images

Subject: the device
Predicate: displays
Object: color

Subject: the device
Predicate: supports
Object: GPRS

Subject: the device
Predicate: accepts
Object: the application/xml+xhtml content type

Subject: the device
Predicate: accepts
Object: SMIL presentations
```

These subjects, predicates, and objects would then have to be mapped to a representation using the RDF syntax. RDF documents are XML documents. They begin with the XML header followed by the top-level element, which has a number of XML namespaces provided as attributes. Here's the general structure:

```
<? xml version="1.0"?>
<rdf:RDF xmlns:rdf="http://www.w3.org/1999/02/22-rdf-syntax-ns#">
  <rdf:Description ...>
    ...
```

```
  </rdf:Description>
  <rdf:Description ...>
    ...
  </rdf:Description>
  <rdf:Description ...>
    ...
  </rdf:Description>
</rdf:RDF>
```

Thus, an RDF document contains a sequence of description elements or, in other words, an *RDF document* is a collection of descriptions. For example, the software characteristics of a device can be specified in one description element, and the hardware characteristics in another. To model the previous sentences in RDF, the RDF document can, but doesn't have to, look like this:

```
<? xml version="1.0"?>
<rdf:RDF xmlns:rdf="http://www.w3.org/1999/02/22-rdf-syntax-ns#"
         xmlns:ex="http://www.mynspace.com/features">
  <rdf:Description about="http://www.xyzdevices.com/deviceType1/">
    <ex:DisplayCapabilities>
      <rdf:Bag>
        <rdf:li>image</rdf:li>
        <rdf:li>color</rdf:li>
      </rdf:Bag>
    </ex:DisplayCapabilities>
    <ex:Bearer>GPRS
    </ex:Bearer>
    <ex:AcceptedContentTypes>
      <rdf:Bag>
        <rdf:li>application/xml+xhtml</rdf:li>
        <rdf:li>application/smil</rdf:li>
      </rdf:Bag>
    </ex:AcceptedContentTypes>
  </rdf:Description>
</rdf:RDF>
```

In this example, all characteristics described in the sentences were provided in a single description element. The about attribute works as a unique identifier for the device that's described. RDF defines a number of data types that can be used to describe the data. In the previous example, the bag type has been used. It can include a number of literal elements and each item is an element in the bag. Note, this example is by no means a standard to specify characteristics of wireless devices. This is only an example that shows how RDF can be used.

CC/PP

While RDF is a framework that can be used to describe data in general, CC/PP uses RDF for a specific application. Thus, CC/PP can be seen as an application of RDF. CC/PP uses RDF to describe the capabilities and user preferences for web browsers. CC/PP is even used by UAProf in WAP. So, before jumping to that section, let's look at CC/PP.

CC/PP is needed because it provides a framework to specify capabilities and preferences without being product-specific. In an ideal situation, it shouldn't matter which browser is used. The server shouldn't have to check the browser name and version in the HTTP message. Instead, the capabilities of the browser and the preferences, set by the user, should be transferred to the server. The latter is a far better solution because then the server doesn't have to support all browsers and browser versions on the market. Instead, it maintains browser characteristics and user preferences.

With CC/PP, properties are specified using RDF, almost like in the previous example, but with some additional elements called components. *Components* describe important components of the device, such as the browser, hardware, and software platform. Characteristics of these components are described using a set of properties. Here's an example to clarify this.

```
<?xml version="1.0"?>
<rdf:RDF xmlns:rdf="http://www.w3.org/1999/02/22-rdf-syntax-ns#"
            xmlns:ccpp="http://www.w3.org/2000/07/04-ccpp#"
            xmlns:prf="www.myprof.com/schema#">
    <rdf:Description rdf:about="someCoolHandheldProfile">
        <ccpp:component>
            <rdf:Description rdf:about="TerminalHardware">
                <rdf:type rdf:resource="HardwarePlatform"/>
                <prf:memory>512KB</prf:memory>
                <prf:display>96x64</prf:display>
                <prf:cpu>Z80</prf:cpu>
            </rdf:Description>
        </ccpp:component>
        <ccpp:component>
            <rdf:Description rdf:about="TerminalSoftware">
                <rdf:type rdf:resource="SoftwarePlatform"/>
                <prf:name>Funky OS</prf:name>
                <prf:version>1.0</prf:version>
                <prf:vendor>Wiz-Tech Inc.</prf:vendor>
            </rdf:Description>
```

```
        </ccpp:component>
     </rdf:Description>
</rdf:RDF>
```

As you can see, the profile contains a description of a fictive handheld device. This device has two components: the terminal hardware and software. Each of these components has a type that indicates what kind of description it is. The description for the component has a number of properties, such as name and version.

You can create new properties, but a set of recommended attributes, such as memory, display, and CPU, exists. These should be used as much as possible because this way the specification will be more in line with other devices' CC/PP specifications and compatibility will increase.

UAProf

UAProf defines a specific vocabulary for CC/PP, which is tailor-made for WAP devices. For WAP 2.0 and UAProf, the following components have been defined.

- ▶ HardwarePlatform
- ▶ SoftwarePlatform
- ▶ NetworkCharacteristics
- ▶ BrowserUA
- ▶ BrowserCharacteristics
- ▶ PushCharacteristics

Thus, each of the previous components can be specified as a component element in the RDF document. Consequently, for a fully compliant WAP 2.0 device, it's possible to profile the device according to its hardware, the installed software, and the characteristics of the networks it should be used with. Features and characteristics of the browser, and all the features related to push, such as the reception of e-mail, SMS, and MMS messages can also be profiled.

To get a feeling for what you can include in such a profile, here's an example:

```
<?xml version="1.0"?>
<RDF xmlns="http://www.w3.org/1999/02/22-rdf-syntax-ns#"
    xmlns:rdf="http://www.w3.org/1999/02/22-rdf-syntax-ns#"
```

```
xmlns:prf="http://www.wapforum.org/profiles/UAPROF/ccppschema-20010430#">

<rdf:Description ID="someDevice">

  <prf:component>
    <rdf:Description ID="HardwarePlatform">
      <rdf:type resource="http://www.wapforum.org/profiles/UAPROF/
ccppschema-20010430#HardwarePlatform"/>
      <prf:BitsPerPixel>2</prf:BitsPerPixel>
      <prf:ScreenSize>96x64</prf:ScreenSize>
      <prf:Model>Z1</prf:Model>
      <prf:Keyboard>PhoneKeypad</prf:Keyboard>
      <prf:OutputCharSet>
        <rdf:Bag>
          <rdf:li>US-ASCII</rdf:li>
          <rdf:li>SHIFT_JIS</rdf:li>
        </rdf:Bag>
      </prf:OutputCharSet>
    </rdf:Description>
  </prf:component>

  <prf:component>
    <rdf:Description ID="SoftwarePlatform">
      <rdf:type resource="http://www.wapforum.org/profiles/UAPROF/
ccppschema-20010430#SoftwarePlatform"/>
      <prf:AcceptDownloadableSoftware>Yes
      </prf:AcceptDownloadableSoftware>
      <prf:JavaEnabled>Yes</prf:JavaEnabled>
    </rdf:Description>
  </prf:component>

  <prf:component>
    <rdf:Description ID="NetworkCharacteristics">
      <rdf:type resource="http://www.wapforum.org/profiles/UAPROF/
ccppschema-20010430#NetworkCharacteristics"/>
      <prf:SupportedBearers>
        <rdf:Bag>
          <rdf:li>GPRS</rdf:li>
          <rdf:li>CSD</rdf:li>
          <rdf:li>SMS</rdf:li>
```

```
        </rdf:Bag>
      </prf:SupportedBearers>
    </rdf:Description>
  </prf:component>

  <prf:component>
    <rdf:Description ID="BrowserUA">    .
      <rdf:type resource="http://www.wapforum.org/profiles/UAPROF/
ccppschema-20010430#BrowserUA"/>
        <prf:XhtmlVersion>1.0</prf:XhtmlVersion>
        <prf:FramesCapable>No</prf:FramesCapable>
    </rdf:Description>
  </prf:component>

  <prf:component>
    <rdf:Description ID="WapCharacteristics">
      <rdf:type resource="http://www.wapforum.org/profiles/UAPROF/
ccppschema-20010430#WapCharacteristics"/>
      <prf:WapVersion>2.0</prf:WapVersion>
    </rdf:Description>
  </prf:component>

  <prf:component>
    <rdf:Description ID="PushCharacteristics">
      <rdf:type resource="http://www.wapforum.org/profiles/UAPROF/
ccppschema-20010430#PushCharacteristics"/>
      <prf:Push-Accept>
        <prf:Bag>
          <prf:li>text/html</prf:li>
          <prf:li>application/smil</prf:li>
          <prf:li>text/plain</prf:li>
        </prf:Bag>
      </prf:Push-Accept>
    </rdf:Description>
  </prf:component>

</rdf:Description>
</RDF>
```

All the components listed, before the example, are included in the previous profile, with some properties. As you can see, the device has a monochrome display, 64×96 pixels, and is equipped with a phone type keyboard. The phone accepts both the American US-ASCII character set, as well as the Japanese SHIFT-JIS character set, which is used in the i-mode service. The device is Java-enabled and accepts downloadable software. It has GPRS, but can also use Circuit Switched Data communication and even the Simple Messaging Service to transfer information. The browser supports version 1.0 of XHTML. Because the display is quite small—only 64×96 pixels—the browser doesn't support frames. WAP version 2.0 is supported and the device can also receive SMIL presentations, HTML, and plain text in messages that are pushed onto the device.

All properties defined in UAProf are listed in Appendix B of the Wireless Application Group (WAG) UAProf document, proposed version May 30, 2001. This can be downloaded from http://www.wapforum.org. If you need to write a profile for a device, you should read this specification to become familiar with all the properties that might be specified. For you to have to write a profile would be rare, though. Using and interpreting a profile, however, would be much more common.

Using the Profile

A web server script can check the incoming HTTP get request message to see at which URL the UAProf is located. It can then retrieve the profile, which is located at that URL. An XML parser could then parse the information and extract the information that's necessary either to select a document at the server or to process the requested document so it fits the user agent.

In the previous example, the browser doesn't support frames. The server script could then translate documents that use frames to some other format. If a document is coded with a character set that the user agent doesn't understand, then all occurrences of characters that aren't compatible with the device's character set could be removed, or the document could be replaced with an error document. Another document could also be transferred to the user that lets her select if she wants to retrieve the requested document despite the fact that it contains characters that will be incompatible with the device.

CHAPTER
10

Synchronization

IN THIS CHAPTER:

The Source and Target Elements

SyncML Commands

Synchronization can be carried out in many situations, depending on which problems must be solved. Systems might have to be locked at the same speed, perform tasks at the same time, or they might have to provide a result at the same time or in a certain order. Thus, they're synchronized. When *synchronization* is mentioned in this book, the term mean information should be at the right place, at the right time. If many devices need to share information, they should be synchronized.

Many people own a cellular phone and a small organizer, and they have a desktop computer at home, one at the job, and maybe even a laptop at work. In this case, which isn't uncommon, the user's information is distributed over five computers. If an important address is added to the handheld organizer, wouldn't it be nice if the address could be transferred more or less automatically to the laptop or whichever machines the user prefers?

SyncML is the synchronization markup language developed by the SyncML Initiative. Hundreds of companies are members of the forum to support and develop a common standard, which can be used to synchronize different types of devices. A software manufacturer shouldn't have to implement many different protocols simply to be compatible with as many devices as possible.

One of the strengths of SyncML is it's based around XML. Information transferred between devices can be specified in XML. In addition, metainformation and the device's capabilities can be expressed in XML. These files can be sent over the HTTP or WSP protocols, the same way Web and WAP documents are sent. It's also possible to use OBEX over a Bluetooth or IrDA connection to transfer the files and perform the synchronization.

The SyncML architecture is based on the *client-server paradigm,* which means a client initiates the communication with a server and the server serves the client with the request. Typically, a *SyncML client* is a small and limited device, such as a handheld PC, phone, or PDA, and the server is usually a computer, such as a PC. The client usually initiates the activity. When the client starts synchronization, it first has to send information to the server, which describes the device. This is referred to as *device information* in SyncML. When the server has the device information and all the commands that are part of the message, it can do modifications on the server, and then reply with a code. These codes are based on the codes used by the HTTP and OBEX protocols. For example, code 404 means Not found and 200 means OK. But codes also exist with SyncML specific semantics, such as code 512, which means synchronization failed.

SyncML Messages

In SyncML, you specify messages, or SyncML documents, which perform the actual synchronization. A server replies with the result of the operation. A synchronization message contains a number of commands and the message is followed by a result. Both are XML documents, written in SyncML. The general structure for a synchronization message is this:

```
<?xml version="1.0" encoding="UTF-8"?>
<SyncML xmlns="SYNCML:SYNCML1.0">
  <SyncHdr>
    ...
  </SyncHdr>
  <SyncBody>
    ...
  </SyncBody>
</SyncML>
```

The namespace SYNCML:SYNCML1.0 should be used with the top-level element, SyncML. It contains a header with metainformation, such as the version of SyncML being used, as well as information about the sender and the receiver. The body of the message contains a number of commands, like the following:

```
<?xml version="1.0" encoding="UTF-8"?>
<SyncML xmlns="SYNCML:SYNCML1.0">
  <SyncHdr>
    <VerDTD>1.0</VerDTD>
    <VerProto>SyncML/1.0</VerProto>
    <SessionID>42</SessionID>
    <MsgID>1</MsgID>
    <Target>
        <LocURI> ... </LocURI>
    </Target>
    <Source>
        <LocURI> ... </LocURI>
    </Source>
    ...
  </SyncHdr>
  <SyncBody>
```

```
    <Put>
      <CmdID>2305</CmdID>
      <Item>
        ...
      </Item>
    </Put>
    <Get>
      <CmdID>2308</CmdID>
      <Item>
        ...
      </Item>
    </Get>
    <Copy>
      <CmdID>2307</CmdID>
      <Item>
        ...
      </Item>
    </Copy>
  </SyncBody>
</SyncML>
```

The VerDTD element is used to specify which version of the SyncML DTD is used. SyncML documents don't have an actual DOCTYPE declaration. Instead, information about which DTD is used is specified like this, which makes the instance document slightly less verbose. If you write SyncML documents and you want to validate the documents according to the DTD, then you can use the following URL:

```
http://www.syncml.org/docs/syncml_represent_v10_20001207.dtd
```

VerProto indicates which version of the SyncML specification is used. In this case, 1.0. SessionID is an identifier that relates the message to a particular session.

The command identity (CmdID) is an identity generated by the device that performs the command. If some of the commands cannot be executed, then these command IDs can be used to specify which commands failed.

NOTE

It's possible to perform atomic commands with SyncML. This means either all or none of the commands succeed. In the previous skeleton code, individual commands might fail or succeed.

The Source and Target Elements

In the previous code example, you can see the header isn't complete. What's missing are the target and source elements. You should always choose an identifier which specifies the entities that are part of the synchronization. If you extend the example with that information, it can look like this:

```
<?xml version="1.0" encoding="UTF-8"?>
<SyncML xmlns="SYNCML:SYNCML1.0">
  <SyncHdr>
    <VerDTD>1.0</VerDTD>
    <VerProto>SyncML/1.0</VerProto>
    <SessionID>42</SessionID>
    <MsgID>
      ...
    </MsgID>
    <Target>
      <LocURI>http://www.somecompany.example.com/cooldevice</LocURI>
    </Target>
    <Source>
      <LocURI>http://www.servercompany.example.com/serverPro</LocURI>
    </Source>
  </SyncHdr>
  <SyncBody>
    <Put>
      <CmdID>2305</CmdID>
      <Item>
        ...
      </Item>
    </Put>
    <Get>
      <CmdID>2308</CmdID>
      <Item>
        ...
      </Item>
    </Get>
    <Copy>
      <CmdID>2307</CmdID>
      <Item>
        ...
```

```
        </Item>
      </Copy>
    </SyncBody>
  </SyncML>
```

A target and a source have been added to the header using the target and source elements. Both elements contain the LocURI element. The LocURI can contain an ordinary URL, which works as a unique identifier for the equipment used to perform the synchronization. URIs can be used for devices that are constantly connected to the Internet, such as servers. Handheld devices are occasionally switched off, which disqualifies them for this type of identification mechanism. Then, handheld devices can use International Mobile Equipment Identity (IMEI) for the identification. IMEI is a code that can be used to identify mobile devices using a 15-digit code.

SyncML Commands

In the previous code snippet, you can see the message contains a get, put, and copy command. More commands are available for you, some of which follow.

Add

With the *add* command, the target will become aware of what data the source has added to its local database.

```
<?xml version="1.0" encoding="UTF-8"?>
<SyncML xmlns="SYNCML:SYNCML1.0">
  <SyncHdr>
    <VerDTD>1.0</VerDTD>
    <VerProto>SyncML/1.0</VerProto>
    <SessionID>42</SessionID>
    <MsgID>1</MsgID>
    <Target>
      <LocURI>http://www.somecompany.example.com/cooldevice</LocURI>
    </Target>
    <Source>
      <LocURI>IMEI:123456789012345</LocURI>
    </Source>
  </SyncHdr>
    <SyncBody>
        <Sync>
            <CmdID>1</CmdID>
```

```
                <Add>
                     <CmdID>2</CmdID>
                     <Item>
                          <Source>
                               <LocURI>./adr</LocURI>
                          </Source>
                          <Data>begin:vcard
fn:Carl Smith
n:Smith;Carl
email;type=internet:carl@carlsmithsdomain.com
tel;type=work:+46 8 112 23456789
end:vcard
                          </Data>
                     </Item>
                </Add>
           </Sync>
      </SyncBody>
</SyncML>
```

If the add command was successful, the server responds with a document that
contains a status code, such as the following:

```
<?xml version="1.0" encoding="UTF-8"?>
<SyncML xmlns="SYNCML:SYNCML1.0">
  <SyncHdr>
    <VerDTD>1.0</VerDTD>
    <VerProto>SyncML/1.0</VerProto>
    <SessionID>42</SessionID>
    <MsgID>1</MsgID>
    <Target>
      <LocURI>IMEI:123456789012345</LocURI>
    </Target>
    <Source>
      <LocURI>http://www.servercompany.example.com/serverPro</LocURI>
    </Source>
  </SyncHdr>
  <SyncBody>
    <Status>
        <CmdID>1</CmdID>
        <MsgRef>1</MsgRef>
        <CmdRef>1</CmdRef>
        <Cmd>Add</Cmd>
        <Data>200</Data>
```

```
      </Status>
    </SyncBody>
  </SyncML>
```

A virtual business card is added using the add command. The command contains an identity that's used to identify individual commands within a SyncML document.

Delete

If an item is deleted from the handheld device, a delete command and the following synchronization message might be sent from the client to the server.

```xml
<?xml version="1.0" encoding="UTF-8"?>
<SyncML xmlns="SYNCML:SYNCML1.0">
  <SyncHdr>
    <VerDTD>1.0</VerDTD>
    <VerProto>SyncML/1.0</VerProto>
    <SessionID>42</SessionID>
    <MsgID>1</MsgID>
    <Target>
      <LocURI>http://www.somecompany.example.com/cooldevice</LocURI>
    </Target>
    <Source>
      <LocURI>IMEI:123456789012345</LocURI>
    </Source>
  </SyncHdr>
  <SyncBody>
    <Sync>
      <CmdID>1</CmdID>
      <Delete>
        <CmdID>2</CmdID>
        <Item>
          <Source>
            <LocURI>./adr</LocURI>
          </Source>
        </Item>
      </Delete>
    </Sync>
  </SyncBody>
</SyncML>
```

The server could then return the following response:

```xml
<?xml version="1.0" encoding="UTF-8"?>
<SyncML xmlns="SYNCML:SYNCML1.0">
```

```
<SyncHdr>
  <VerDTD>1.0</VerDTD>
  <VerProto>SyncML/1.0</VerProto>
  <SessionID>42</SessionID>
  <MsgID>1</MsgID>
  <Target>
    <LocURI>IMEI:123456789012345</LocURI>
  </Target>
  <Source>
    <LocURI>http://www.servercompany.example.com/serverPro</LocURI>
  </Source>
</SyncHdr>
<SyncBody>
  <Status>
    <CmdID>1</CmdID>
    <MsgRef>1</MsgRef>
    <CmdRef>1</CmdRef>
    <Cmd>Delete</Cmd>
    <SourceRef>./adr</SourceRef>
    <Data>200</Data>
  </Status>
</SyncBody>
</SyncML>
```

The sync body contains a status element, which refers to the message and command. The command was successful because the data element contains the status code 200, which means OK.

Command Groups

Commands can be grouped to avoid having only one of several commands executed. For example, you might want to delete an entry and add a new one only if the deletion succeeded. Here's how such a scenario could be implemented using the atomic element.

```
<?xml version="1.0" encoding="UTF-8"?>
<SyncML xmlns="SYNCML:SYNCML1.0">
  <SyncHdr>
    <VerDTD>1.0</VerDTD>
    <VerProto>SyncML/1.0</VerProto>
    <SessionID>42</SessionID>
    <MsgID>1</MsgID>
    <Target>
      <LocURI>http://www.somecompany.example.com/cooldevice</LocURI>
    </Target>
    <Source>
```

```
            <LocURI>IMEI:123456789012345</LocURI>
        </Source>
    </SyncHdr>
      <SyncBody>
          <Sync>
              <CmdID>1</CmdID>
              <Atomic>
                  <CmdID>2</CmdID>
                  <Add>
                      <CmdID>3</CmdID>
                      <Item>
                          <Target>
                              <LocURI>./adr</LocURI>
                          </Target>
                          <Data>begin:vcard
name:Carl Smith
fn:Carl Smith
n:Smith;Carl
email;type=internet:carl@carlsmithsdomain.com
tel;type=work:+46 8 112 23456789
end:vcard
                          </Data>
                      </Item>
                  </Add>
                  <Delete>
                      <CmdID>4</CmdID>
                      <Item>
                          <Target>
                              <LocURI>./planning</LocURI>
                          </Target>
                      </Item>
                  </Delete>
              </Atomic>
          </Sync>
      </SyncBody>
</SyncML>
```

Because the atomic element has been used, the planning item is only deleted if the
virtual business card was added successfully and vice versa.

Low-level Communication

IN THIS CHAPTER:

Distributed Wireless Systems

XML-RPC

Using Data Types

Further Reading

Even low-level communication routines in wireless systems and applications can be designed using XML. Not too long ago, systems that contained multiple computers or devices connected in a network had to use application protocols, such as remote procedure call (RPC) to exchange data. One of the drawbacks with these protocols was that reading the values sent from one computer to another was nearly impossible because this was written into the program and exchanged on a low level.

With XML-RPC, it's possible to design systems that communicate over any type of network and it's still possible for a person to read data exchanged between the nodes in the network.

Wireless applications can communicate directly over the WSP, OBEX, HTTP, and other proprietary protocols because data can be sent as an HTTP get or post request. If data is sent as an HTTP get request, the parameters can then be appended to the URL, like this:

```
http://www.receivingNetworkNode.example.com?para=CE
```

However, if the exchange of data is carried out this way or as a post request, which behaves similarly to the get request, a number of problems arise. There's no typing. What does the value, CE, of para mean? Is this a hexadecimal number or a text string? No support exists for types when you transfer parameters like this and you don't have access to ordinary data structures, but there is a long sequence of parameters.

In addition, this would only solve half the problem because you're only transferring parameters from one device or computer to another. With XML-RPC, a function or procedure is called at the receiving side. As the procedure is executed, it might access data in a database or make computations based on the values received through the call from the caller. Then the result is transferred back. As a result, the caller won't notice the call to the procedure was remote. Thus, a RPC is meant to look, more or less, like a call to a local procedure.

Distributed Wireless Systems

A benefit of some wireless systems is that clients can be added dynamically to the network as the user switches on the device or enters the proximity of the network. To transport information on such a network, however, the system needs to consider that the devices connecting to the network might use different types of microprocessors that use different ways of representing numbers. Thus, numbers sent as arguments to a procedure call need to be represented in a processor-independent way.

XML-RPC is another way of doing what has previously been done with technologies, such as CORBA and DCOM. But because CORBA and DCOM don't use text files and the HTTP protocol, watching the traffic to see which values are transmitted between the nodes can be hard. Values are represented in a processor-independent way, which isn't suitable for reading by a human. With XML-RPC, you can check the logs of your web server to see what the caller sent in the body of the HTTP post request and which document the web server sent in the response. So, in a certain way, XML-RPC can, but doesn't have to, make debugging of distributed systems easier because it's readable. Another benefit is XML-RPC can be used over an HTTP-compatible protocol, such as WSP, because the call is encoded as an ordinary post request.

Procedure Calls

Distributed wireless systems make heavy use of intercommunication, so a number of calls are made to retrieve information from other nodes in the network or to execute programs on other nodes. When a call is made to a procedure, stub code for the procedure makes sure the parameters are encapsulated in a message and sent to the receiving computer. Encapsulating the data in the message so it can be transported over the network is often referred to as *marshalling*. The receiving computer executes the actual procedure using the received parameters. The result is passed back to the stub code on the sending side and the stub code returns the result to the caller. This is why XML-RPC is a remote procedure call, as opposed to an ordinary procedure call.

When should you use XML-RPC? If you only need to transfer a few parameters over the air between, say, a mobile phone and a script that runs on a web server, then you won't need it. In that case, using XML-RPC is overkill and a much better idea is to append the parameters to the URL. However, if you're implementing a comprehensive wireless system, which has many nodes that can be connected to and disconnected from the network at arbitrary points in time, then XML-RPC might be the right solution. You might find XML-RPC especially useful if you need to track the messages sent over the air. These documents can be collected in web server logs and transformed, for example, using XSLT to arbitrary formats for storage in, say, billing systems or databases in general.

If you're building a system that needs to provide a high degree of integrity and privacy for the end user, then XML-RPC might be a less-appropriate solution because it's easy to read the arguments to procedure calls on a server. On the other hand, additional security protocols can be used for such solutions.

XML-RPC

The XML document, which is sent by the stub code to the receiver, has the following structure:

```
<?xml version="1.0"?>
<methodCall>
  <methodName> ... </methodName>
  ...
</methodCall>
```

An HTTP post is used to transport the document to the receiving side. The XML header is followed by the mandatory element methodCall. Each HTTP post message contains one document, which contains one methodCall element. The *methodCall* element represents the procedure call with respect to its name and the parameters to the procedure. Thus, the document needs to transfer the name of the procedure, which the receiver will execute. The name is specified using the methodName element. Typically, it contains a text string that provides the name of the procedure. Depending on which language is used, the syntax can look different. A call on the server side, using the C programming language, can look like this:

```
<?xml version="1.0"?>
<methodCall>
  <methodName>getNumber</methodName>
</methodCall>
```

Here, a call is made to the procedure that has the name getNumber. If getNumber doesn't take any parameters, then this is it. The XML code won't contain any more information because the only thing that needs to be transferred to the other side is the name of the procedure that will be called.

In many cases, however, procedures do take input parameters and this is where the XML-RPC technology shines. One of the many purposes of providing an XML-based implementation of XML-RPC is to make transferring typed data over HTTP easier using the RPC mechanism. If the getNumber procedure would have taken a parameter as input—say, a text string—then the XML code could have looked like this:

```
<?xml version="1.0"?>
<methodCall>
  <methodName>getNumber</methodName>
  <params>
      <param>
```

```
        <value>
            <string>str
            </string>
        </value>
    </param>
  </params>
</methodCall>
```

The methodName element is provided because it's mandatory for all calls. In addition, the params element is used to specify all parameters that go with the procedure call. In this case, only one parameter exists, so the params element contains only one param element.

The param element should have a value. In the previous example, the value is a text string, so the value element contains a string element. The actual value of the string is set to str. The str string can be different each time the procedure is called because it represents the argument to the procedure. The procedure call on the client side can look like this, using the XML-RPC for C, and C++ library, which is available at http://xmlrpc-c.sourceforge.net.

```
xmlrpc_env xmlRpcEnv;
xmlrpc_env_init(&xmlRpcEnv);
value = xmlrpc_client_call(&xmlRpcEnv,
        "http://www.serveradr.com/RPC2",
        "server.getNumber", "(s)", "str");
  ...
```

In this implementation of XML-RPC, faults are handled using the xmlrpc_env type. For example, if the server can't be contacted, then information about the fault is stored in that variable. The fourth argument, "(s)", indicates one argument exists and it's a string. The call to the server side is completely transparent. It isn't visible for the programmer, but is encapsulated into the xml-rpc_client_call. When the call is made, an XML-RPC document is sent over the HTTP protocol to the server. The server executes the call and returns the result, in this case, an integer. The response, which contains the integer, then looks like this:

```
<?xml version="1.0"?>
<methodResponse>
  <params>
    <param>
        <value>
            <int>4711
```

```
        </int>
      </value>
    </param>
  </params>
</methodResponse>
```

Note, the response message doesn't contain the methodName element because this isn't a method call, but is the result of a method or, to be more precise, a procedure call. Consequently, the methodResponse element is used by the response message, sent from the server to the caller. Because the result of the call to the procedure getNumber is an integer, the int element is used to encapsulate the actual result. The server-side code can look like this:

```
xmlrpc_value*
getNumber(xmlrpc_env *faults, xmlrpc_value theString, void *user_data) {
  char str[64];
  xmlrpc_parse_value(faults, theString, "(s)", &str);
  if( !strcmp(str, "str") ) {
    return xmlrpc_build_value(faults, "i", (xmlrpc_int32)4711);
  }
  return xmlrpc_build_value(faults, "i", (xmlrpc_int32)42);
}
```

This is an ordinary C function, which returns an integer. The integer must be packaged for transport over the network and the xmlrpc_build_value procedure is used to achieve that.

Using Data Types

Depending on which language you're working with on the client and server sides, the data types available for you can vary. Most programming languages, however, such as C/C++ and Java, support integers and strings. In the previous example, an integer was transferred back as the result of the call to the getNumber procedure. Assume you want to implement a remote procedure, which appends two strings. The procedure could then be implemented like this on the server side:

```
xmlrpc_value*
appendStrings(xmlrpc_env *faults, xmlrpc_value theStrings, void *user_data) {
  char str1[64];
  char str2[64];
  char res[128];
```

```
    xmlrpc_parse_value(faults, theStrings, "(ss)", &str1, &str2);
    sprintf(res, "%s%s", str1, str2);
    return xmlrpc_build_value(faults, "s", (char*)res);
}
```

The client code could look like this:

```
xmlrpc_env xmlRpcEnv;
xmlrpc_env_init(&xmlRpcEnv);
value = xmlrpc_client_call(&xmlRpcEnv, "http://www.serveradr.com/RPC2",
                        "server.appendStrings", "(ss)", "abc", "def");
  ...
```

The XML code that would be sent over the network would then look something like this:

```
<?xml version="1.0"?>
<methodCall>
  <methodName>appendStrings</methodName>
  <params>
      <param>
          <value>
              <string>abc
              </string>
              <string>def
              </string>
          </value>
      </param>
  </params>
</methodCall>
```

And the response would look like this:

```
<?xml version="1.0"?>
<methodResponse>
  <params>
      <param>
          <value>
              <string>abcdef
              </string>
          </value>
      </param>
  </params>
</methodResponse>
```

A document is sent back as the result of the HTTP post request, which contains the previous code. One methodResponse element exists, which contains a params element and the params element contains only one param element because there's only one result from the procedure call. The result has the value abcdef and it's a string.

To give yet another example, a procedure, which adds two floating point numbers, could be implemented like this on the server side:

```
xmlrpc_value*
addNumbers(xmlrpc_env *faults, xmlrpc_value theNumbers, void *user_data) {
  double num1;
  double num2;
  double res;
  xmlrpc_parse_value(faults, theNumbers, "(dd)", &num1, &num2);
  res = num1 + num2;
  return xmlrpc_build_value(faults, "d", (double)res);
}
```

The client code could look like this:

```
xmlrpc_env xmlRpcEnv;
xmlrpc_env_init(&xmlRpcEnv);
value = xmlrpc_client_call(&xmlRpcEnv,
"http://www.serveradr.com/RPC2",
                            "server.addNumbers", "(dd)", 2.5, 75);
  ...
```

The XML code sent across the network would then look something like this:

```
<?xml version="1.0"?>
<methodCall>
  <methodName>computeValue</methodName>
  <params>
      <param>
          <value>
              <double>2.5
              </double>
          </value>
      </param>
      <param>
          <value>
              <double>75
              </double>
```

```
        </value>
      </param>
  </params>
</methodCall>
```

The previous message is sent in an HTTP post request and, as usual with HTTP, the result is an HTTP response, which is sent back from the server. In this case, the response would look like the following:

```
<?xml version="1.0"?>
<methodResponse>
  <params>
      <param>
          <value>
              <double>77.5
              </double>
          </value>
      </param>
  </params>
</methodResponse>
```

The value, which is returned in the HTTP response, is a double and the result of the addition of the two numbers: 2.5 and 75.

Further Reading

XML-RPC has been implemented for many programming languages, such as C, C++, and Java and scripting languages, such as Python and Perl. We won't spend time with details of the programming features of XML-RPC because this book focuses on the XML side of things and XML-RPC is available for such a wide range of languages. The principles are the same, though. The call to the client procedure or method sends the XML-RPC document across the network. The procedure is executed on the server and the result is passed back to the client, which returns the result to the caller. On the network it is XML only. At the client and server sides, programming languages, such as C, Java, and Perl, are used.

This chapter is an introduction to the subject of XML-RPC. For developers who work mostly with markup, the use of XML-RPC might be limited. If you're a programmer who needs to find a technology for distributed computing where XML plays a central role, however, then take a deeper look at what XML-RPC has to offer. A number of open source projects are going on that aim to implement XML-RPC on a variety of platforms and for a large number of programming languages. The site http://sourceforge.net/ might be useful. There, you can find projects that implement or use XML-RPC in C/C++, PHP, Python, and Tcl environments, to name a few.

PART
III

Use Cases: The Developer's Detailed Guide

OBJECTIVES

► Translate back and forth between XHTML Basic and i-mode HTML

► Create a simple game for i-mode and XHTML Basic

► Use different methods to send information from a phone to a server

► Build a game that uses voice recognition and voice systhesis

► Build VoiceXML applications that synthesize speech, and recognizes words

► Be aware of the limitations of MMS SMIL 1.0, as compared to SMIL 2.0

► Transform maps from GML to SVG

► Use ECML fields in XHTML Basic to automate the fill-in process for forms

Building XHTML Applications

IN THIS CHAPTER:

Examples in XHTML

Examples in XHTML Basic

Development Tools

Thich chapter is devoted to the creation of applications using XHTML. Because XHTML is a markup language based on HTML4, it can provide all the functions you're familiar with from HTML4—graphical user interfaces, embedded objects and scripts, plus the advantage that the language is based on XML. To add dynamics to a web page, you still need to use server-side technology, like ASP, JSP, Perl scripts, and so forth. Because you can use so many technologies and because it's up to you to choose the server-side technology depending on which project you're involved in, we'll focus on the XHTML part of the applications.

First, let's look at web pages implemented using HTML4, which can be converted to XHTML pages. Then we'll focus on XHTML Basic. You learn how to adapt and transform code from arbitrary formats to XHTML Basic for viewing on small handheld devices that support XHTML Basic with additional modules, like presentation and style sheets. Finally, yet also important, you learn about some of the tools that can be used to edit and test XHTML code.

Examples in XHTML

XHTML Basic is the foundation for future mobile Internet services because it's supported in WAP 2.0 and, most likely, also in the next generation of i-mode services. Because manufacturers can choose to support more than the modules in XHTML Basic, a good idea is to learn XHTML as a whole, and not only the modules in XHTML Basic. For example, in WAP 2.0, the style sheet and presentation modules are supported, in addition to the modules in XHTML Basic.

An ordinary HTML page can easily be converted to XHTML, but a few practical steps are worth a closer look.

Converting HTML to XHTML

As you probably know by now, all XHTML documents begin with an XML header because XHTML is an XML application. The XML header is followed by the DOCTYPE declaration where the URL to the XHTML DTD is added, so the document can be validated. These lines must be added to the HTML document, as in the following example:

```
<!DOCTYPE HTML PUBLIC "-//W3C//DTD HTML 4.0 Strict//EN">
<html>
<head>
<title>My title</title>
</head>
<body>
```

```
   <p>Some text.
   </p>
</body>
</html>
```

The HTML code can be converted to the following XHTML representation:

```
<?xml version="1.0" encoding="UTF-8"?>
<!DOCTYPE html PUBLIC "-//W3C//DTD XHTML 1.0 Strict//EN"
    "http://www.w3.org/TR/xhtml1/DTD/xhtml1-strict.dtd">
<html xmlns="http://www.w3.org/1999/xhtml">
<head>
<title>My title</title>
</head>
<body>
   <p>Some text.
   </p>
</body>
</html>
```

The XML header has been added to the XHTML version of the code and the DOCTYPE declaration has been changed. In the DOCTYPE declaration, the SYSTEM identifier points at the DTD for XHTML 1.0 Strict, rather than HTML4.

The XHTML namespace has been added to the HTML element to indicate it's the default namespace. If another XML-based language is embedded in the XHTML code, XHTML is then regarded as the default namespace. Consequently, all the XHTML elements won't require a namespace prefix.

Slash

A common mistake is to forget the slash at the end of the elements that have an empty content model, such as br and img. Look at the following translation from HTML to XHTML:

```
<!DOCTYPE HTML PUBLIC "-//W3C//DTD HTML 4.01 Strict//EN">
<html>
<head>
  <meta name="Author" content="Mikael Hillborg">
  <base href="http://www.mypics.com">
  <link href="stylesheet.css" rel="stylesheet" type="text/css">
  <title>Untitled
  </title>
</head>
<body>
```

```
   <p>Have a look at this picture.<br>
     <img src="portrait.gif">
   </p>
</body>
</html>
```

The XHTML equivalent would be:

```
<?xml version="1.0" encoding="UTF-8"?>
<!DOCTYPE html PUBLIC "-//W3C//DTD XHTML 1.0 Strict//EN"
    "http://www.w3.org/TR/xhtml1/DTD/xhtml1-strict.dtd">
<html xmlns="http://www.w3.org/1999/xhtml">
<head>
  <meta name="Author" content="Mikael Hillborg"/>
  <base href="http://www.mypics.com"/>
  <link href="stylesheet.css" rel="stylesheet" type="text/css"/>
  <title>Untitled
  </title>
</head>
<body>
  <p>Have a look at this picture.<br/>
    <img src="portrait.gif" alt="Mona Lisa"/>
  </p>
</body>
</html>
```

During the conversion process, a slash has been inserted at the end of the br, img, meta, base, and link elements. In addition, the XML header and the DOCTYPE declaration have been added. In XHTML, the alt attribute is mandatory for the img element, so you need to add this attribute, which was missing in the HTML code.

The p Element

Some HTML developers have a tendency to use only the start tag of the paragraph element to introduce an empty line. This gives a slightly bigger line break than what's created by the br element, but it's a less appropriate way to use HTML because the paragraph element wasn't meant to be used in this manner. Here's an example:

```
<!DOCTYPE HTML PUBLIC "-//W3C//DTD HTML 4.01 Strict//EN">
<html>
<head>
  <title>My title
  </title>
</head>
<body>
```

```
    <h1>My collection of video game consoles.</h1>
        <p>- Atari 2600 (rules)
        <p>- ColecoVision
        <p>- Henderson Gameomatic
        <p>- PlayStation
</body>
</html>
```

In the previous code, the author has used the paragraph element to format the text so a line break is introduced. When this type of code is converted to XHTML, in most cases, it should be converted so an end tag is inserted just before the next paragraph start tag. In that case, the same vertical spacing will be achieved. However, the text will then be put in different paragraphs and that might not have been the intention from the beginning. An alternative conversion is to encapsulate the content in a new p element and replace each p start tag with a br element and an accompanying style attribute. Here are two alternative conversions:

```
<?xml version="1.0" encoding="UTF-8"?>
<!DOCTYPE html PUBLIC "-//W3C//DTD XHTML 1.0 Strict//EN"
    "http://www.w3.org/TR/xhtml1/DTD/xhtml1-strict.dtd">
<html xmlns="http://www.w3.org/1999/xhtml">
<head>
  <title>My title
  </title>
</head>
<body>
    <h1>My collection of video game consoles</h1>
    <p>- Atari 2600 (rules)</p>
    <p>- ColecoVision</p>
    <p>- Henderson Gameomatic</p>
    <p>- PlayStation</p>
</body>
</html>

<?xml version="1.0" encoding="UTF-8"?>
<!DOCTYPE html PUBLIC "-//W3C//DTD XHTML 1.0 Strict//EN"
    "http://www.w3.org/TR/xhtml1/DTD/xhtml1-strict.dtd">
<html xmlns="http://www.w3.org/1999/xhtml">
<head>
  <title>My title
  </title>
</head>
<body>
    <h1>My collection of video game consoles</h1>
```

```
    <p style="margin-top: 12pt">- Atari 2600 (rules)
    <br style="margin-top: 12pt"/>- ColecoVision
    <br style="margin-top: 12pt"/>- Henderson Gameomatic
    <br style="margin-top: 12pt"/>- PlayStation
    </p>
</body>
</html>
```

In the first of the two different conversions, all p tags have been given a corresponding end tag. No start tag occurs before the previous one is closed. In the second conversion, line breaks have been used in combination with the style attribute. The style attribute makes sure the size of the vertical space is equal to the size the p tag would cause.

Discarded Elements

Most desktop browsers are forgiving when it comes to providing all the mandatory elements of HTML. Here's an example:

```
<!DOCTYPE HTML PUBLIC "-//W3C//DTD HTML 4.01 Strict//EN">
<html>
    <h1>My collection of video game consoles</h1>
        <p>- Atari 2600 (rules)</p>
        <p>- ColecoVision</p>
        <p>- Henderson AutoPlay</p>
        <p>- PlayStation</p>
</html>
```

In this case, the author has simply discarded the header and body elements, a big violation of the HTML specification. But still, most browsers for desktop computers will display the markup and render the remaining elements as you'd expect them to be rendered. A perfect conversion to XHTML is impossible because some information, like the title of the document, has been left out (you could leave it empty, though). Tools that perform HTML to XHTML need to check if mandatory elements, even the fundamental ones, were left out.

The Element's Context

Sometimes the authors supply the HTML elements in the wrong context. Because XHTML documents are written and validated with respect to a DTD that contains strict rules concerning the hierarchy of the elements, some HTML code might have to be rewritten to convert it to XHTML. For example, the heading elements (h1, h2, and so forth) must only occur outside, and not inside, a paragraph, as in the following example. The HTML4 code is followed by the equivalent code implemented in XHTML 1.0.

```
<!DOCTYPE HTML PUBLIC "-//W3C//DTD HTML 4.01 Strict//EN">
<html>
<head>
  <title>My title
  </title>
</head>
<body>
  <p>
    <h1>My colleagues</h1>
    <ul>
      <li>Martin</li>
      <li>Linda</li>
      <li>Peter</li>
      <li>Anna</li>
    </ul>
  </p>
</body>
</html>


<?xml version="1.0" encoding="UTF-8"?>
<!DOCTYPE html PUBLIC "-//W3C//DTD XHTML 1.0 Strict//EN"
    "http://www.w3.org/TR/xhtml1/DTD/xhtml1-strict.dtd">
<html xmlns="http://www.w3.org/1999/xhtml">
<head>
  <title>My title
  </title>
</head>
<body>
<h1>My colleagues</h1>
<p>
  <ul>
    <li>Martin</li>
    <li>Linda</li>
    <li>Peter</li>
    <li>Anna</li>
  </ul>
</p>
</body>
</html>
```

If the h1 element is used inside the paragraph element, the browser will display the code, even though it's wrong. In the XHTML case, the code cannot be validated and most XHTML-compliant browsers can't, and shouldn't, display the code. In addition, the unordered list cannot be put inside a paragraph.

Quoted Attribute Values

With XHTML, all attribute values must be single or double quoted. Here's a translation that deals with quoted attribute values. In addition, a second problem exists with the HTML file. Try to determine what the problem is before you study the converted code.

```
<!DOCTYPE HTML PUBLIC "-//W3C//DTD HTML 4.01 Strict//EN">
<html>
<head>
  <title>Employees
  </title>
</head>
<body>
<p align=center>Employees
<table width=100%>
  <tr><td>Employee number</td><td>Name</td></tr>
  <tr><td>1</td><td>Martin</td></tr>
  <tr><td>2</td><td>Linda</td></tr>
  <tr><td>3</td><td>Peter</td></tr>
  <tr><td>4</td><td>Anna</td></tr>
</table>
</p>
</body>
</html>


<?xml version="1.0" encoding="UTF-8"?>
<!DOCTYPE html PUBLIC "-//W3C//DTD XHTML 1.0 Strict//EN"
    "http://www.w3.org/TR/xhtml1/DTD/xhtml1-strict.dtd">
<html xmlns="http://www.w3.org/1999/xhtml">
<head>
<title>Employees</title>
</head>
<body>
<p align="center">Employees</p>
<table width="100%">
  <tr><td>Employee number</td><td>Name</td></tr>
  <tr><td>1</td><td>Martin</td></tr>
  <tr><td>2</td><td>Linda</td></tr>
  <tr><td>3</td><td>Peter</td></tr>
  <tr><td>4</td><td>Anna</td></tr>
```

```
</table>
</body>
</html>
```

Quotes must be used for center, cols, and rows. Also, note the table had to be moved outside the paragraph. Thus, in the HTML code, the end tag for the p element occurred after the end tag for the table. In the XHTML code, it occurs after the text Employees.

Dealing with Frames

Even if some browsers support frames, some handheld devices aren't optimized to display such content. Usually, a set of navigation buttons is placed in one of the frames, which leaves less space for the actual content. With an already small display, the logical display for the content simply becomes too small. Instead, many handheld devices are equipped with smart input devices to make navigation easier on a web page for the mobile Internet. Sony has a Jog Dial located at the side of some of their phones. Nokia has used a scroll wheel, for example, on the 7110 phone. On Ericsson's T68, there's a joystick. These navigation devices are supposed to make navigating easier through a mobile Internet web page, often a number of input fields the user needs to jump between or a page of text that's scrolled on the screen. Frames aren't suitable for these types of input devices because they're best used within a single display area. If you use frames, then you need some mechanism to jump between the frames and how this would be done isn't obvious to the user.

In most cases, a frameset is used to provide navigation facilities in one of the frames and traditional content in the remaining frames. If you need to translate the frameset to a frameless web page, then each frameset can be translated to a link. The result is a hierarchic navigation, which usually works for a small set of frames. One might be dedicated to a number of buttons to the left or right side of the screen, and another is the actual content frame. For complicated nested frames, however, the navigation might become too awkward. In that case, this type of conversion should be avoided. Here's an HTML page that contains a number of frames that need to be converted to frameless XHTML:

```
<!DOCTYPE HTML PUBLIC "-//W3C//DTD HTML 4.01 Frameset//EN">
<html>
<head>
  <title>Start page
  </title>
</head>
<frameset cols="10%, 90%">
  <frame src="left.html" id="left"/>
  <frameset rows="10%, 90%">
    <frame src="top.html" id="top"/>
```

```
      <frame src="main.html" id="main"/>
   </frameset>
</frameset>
</html>
```

The page is divided into two columns and the right column is divided into two rows. In the best case, the HTML code contains the noframes element that describes an alternative layout for browsers that don't support frames. Because most desktop-based browsers support frames, however, you can find lots of HTML code that doesn't include this element. Then a translation to frameless XHTML needs to be carried out. Here's one way to do this:

```
<?xml version="1.0" encoding="UTF-8"?>
<!DOCTYPE html PUBLIC "-//W3C//DTD XHTML 1.0 Strict//EN"
     "http://www.w3.org/TR/xhtml1/DTD/xhtml1-strict.dtd">
<html xmlns="http://www.w3.org/1999/xhtml">
<head>
  <title>Start page
  </title>
</head>
<body>
  <p>
    <a href="left.html">left</a>
    <a href="top.html">top</a>
    <a href="main.html">main</a>
  </p>
</body>
</html>
```

Note, it's not a frameset document any longer, but a strict document, so the DOCTYPE declaration has been changed. A paragraph has been inserted, replacing the outermost frameset element, and each frame element has been replaced by an anchored link. Each file, pointed out by the frame element's src attribute, must also be traversed to remove all the references to the frame identities. Also, in each of these files, a link to the main file is inserted, so the user can navigate back to the previous file. If a tool performs this conversion, then the text between the *a* tags can be the filename without the html extension, as in the previous example. However, it's easy to watch the result afterwards and do some adjustments, such as providing better descriptions for the links' text.

Things to Avoid

Even if a browser would support all the modules and most of the elements and attributes of XHTML, constructs exist that make little sense on a small handheld device.

Applets

The applets you see executing on mobile phones aren't really applets, but MIDlets. A *MIDlet* is a Java program created for the Java 2 Micro Edition (J2ME) according to the Mobile Information Device Profile (MIDP), defined by Sun Microsystems. In the future, as the microprocessors in cellular phones become much more powerful, it's possible the Java 2 Standard Edition (J2SE) will be used not only for desktop computers, but also for cellular phones.

Most applets created for the Internet use a byte code instruction set, which is a super set of the byte code instruction set defined for J2ME configurations, such as the Connected Limited Device Configuration (CLDC). Thus, applets created for the traditional Internet browsers running J2SE cannot be executed on mobile devices that run J2ME MIDlets without modification.

File Upload

Forms sometimes have file upload facilities that enable you to browse the hard disk for a file. The file is then sent with the form when the Submit button is pressed. Here's an example:

```
<?xml version="1.0" encoding="UTF-8"?>
<!DOCTYPE html PUBLIC "-//W3C//DTD XHTML 1.0 Strict//EN"
    "http://www.w3.org/TR/xhtml1/DTD/xhtml1-strict.dtd">
<html xmlns="http://www.w3.org/1999/xhtml">
<head>
  <title>Form</title>
</head>
<body>
  <form action="/cgi/receive.pl"
        enctype="multipart/form-data"
        method="post">
    <input type="file" name="theFile" />
    <input type="submit" value="Submit" />
  </form>
</body>
</html>
```

This feature, to use the type attribute set to file, was defined when only desktop computers could interpret web pages and forms. With XHTML and XHTML Basic, you see a variety of devices that can browse the Web. Only a few of them will probably have disk access, however, which makes the previous code less suitable for handheld devices.

Plug-ins

Plug-ins exist for wireless handheld devices, in particular for the Pocket PC platform, which inherits many of its concepts from the Windows platform. Many of the phones with built-in browsers don't accept plug-ins, however, so you should avoid plug-ins if you need to stay compatible with as many devices as possible.

Functions Associated with Colors

Be careful with colors because many handheld devices have monochrome or gray scale screens. The following example uses color codes to identify certain functions.

```xml
<?xml version="1.0" encoding="UTF-8"?>
<!DOCTYPE html PUBLIC "-//W3C//DTD XHTML 1.0 Strict//EN"
    "http://www.w3.org/TR/xhtml1/DTD/xhtml1-strict.dtd">
<html xmlns="http://www.w3.org/1999/xhtml">
<head>
  <title>Menu
  </title>
</head>
<body>
  <p>Click on the red icon to retrieve company information.<br/>
    <a href="intro.html"><img src="greenIcon.gif" alt="Green icon"/>
    </a>
    <a href="financialInfo.html"><img src="redIcon.gif" alt="Red icon"/>
    </a>
    <a href="about.html"><img src="yellowIcon.gif" alt="Yellow icon"/>
    </a>
    <a href="latestNews.html"><img src="blueIcon.gif" alt="Blue icon"/>
    </a>
    <a href="links.html"><img src="pinkIcon.gif" alt="Pink icon"/>
    </a>
  </p>
</body>
</html>
```

Never design your web page so colors identify certain functions, such as "click the green icon." Two problems exist with the previous code. First, viewing the page on a device that has a limited monochrome display won't make sense because the user doesn't know which button is green. In addition, the alt attribute shouldn't contain information that describes characteristics of the bitmap file itself. Here, the alt attribute tells us which color the bitmap has. Instead, it should describe the picture.

Although you can see devices from Nokia and Compaq that have excellent color screens, simple mobile phones with monochrome LCD screens will still be on the market. Unless you're targeting a specific device, use colors and color codes with care.

One way to provide a good-looking user interface for color devices at the same time as the code is compatible with monochrome devices is to avoid color-related functions, such as the one previously mentioned. Then, most monochrome devices will simply discard the color information or represent different colors as different raster patterns. Some devices might leave out pictures completely and replace them with text. This is why the img element's alt attribute is a required attribute in XHTML.

Also, remember some users are blind or color-blind. They have a tremendous help from the alt attribute and sites that aren't making use of colors to identify certain functions, links, or pictures on the site.

Hard Coding for a Specific Screen Size

Web designers who are used to the creation of web sites for desktop computers can make the mistake that lines of text are broken deliberately, using the br element. This can create problems because the screen size of handheld devices varies a great deal. The following code illustrates this:

```
<?xml version="1.0" encoding="UTF-8"?>
<!DOCTYPE html PUBLIC "-//W3C//DTD XHTML 1.0 Strict//EN"
    "http://www.w3.org/TR/xhtml1/DTD/xhtml1-strict.dtd">
<html xmlns="http://www.w3.org/1999/xhtml">
<head>
  <title>Menu
  </title>
</head>
<body>
  <p>Click on the red icon
    <br/>to retrieve company information.<br/>
    <a href="intro.html"><img src="greenIcon.gif" alt="Green icon"/>
    </a>Introduction to the company, who we are
       <br/>and how it all started.
    <br/>
    <a href="financialInfo.html"><img src="redIcon.gif" alt="Red icon"/>
    </a>Financial info for investors. Here you<br/>
       <br/>find our quarterly reports.
    <br/>
    <a href="about.html"><img src="yellowIcon.gif" alt="Yellow icon"/>
    </a>Read about our products, who we are, <br/>
       <br/>the development crew and the steering board.
    <br/>
    <a href="latestNews.html"><img src="blueIcon.gif" alt="Blue icon"/>
```

```
    </a>Latest news, distribution, product updates<br/>
        <br/>online sales and FAQs.
    <br/>
    <a href="links.html"><img src="pinkIcon.gif" alt="Pink icon"/>
    </a>Links to our colleagues.
  </p>
</body>
</html>
```

Although this code was implemented in XHTML 1.0 Strict, it contains elements and attributes from XHTML Basic 1.0 only. One problem with the previous code is the author assumes a certain screen size and adapts the layout with that size in mind. Line breaks are inserted on a more-or-less random basis to make the lines almost equal in length. If the page is browsed with an XHTML 1.0 Strict-compatible browser and a 20×5 character display, most of the text in the links would be broken and rendered on more than two lines.

```
Click the red
 icon
to retrieve
company
information.
```

The author has inserted line breaks, but the browser breaks the text into lines as well. This causes the text to be displayed as shown in the previous example.

Examples in XHTML Basic

Let's look at some examples implemented in XHTML Basic that have been adapted for small handheld devices.

Creating a Site for Small Devices and Desktop Computers

In Chapter 4, two simple examples in XHTML Basic were shown. Usually, information wants to be published for as many users as possible, no matter if they're using a desktop computer or a wireless handheld device. Let's look at two examples that illustrate how this can be achieved.

Custom Navigation and Shared Content

The following example is a site that can be accessed from handheld devices supporting XHTML Basic, as well as desktop computers. To provide a more sophisticated layout for desktop computers, two different navigation facilities are provided. For desktop computers, the site is navigated using a set of buttons in a frame. For mobile devices, the site is navigated using a set of links. Thus, these controls aren't shared. The content itself remains the same for desktop computers, as well as for mobile phones, however. By providing the site this way, it's possible to add content on a regular basis without having to do any conversions. The controls remain the same: for desktop computers, a set of buttons in a frame and, for mobile devices, a set of links. Here's the implementation. See the comments after the listing.

This is the start page and the top logo for the desktop computer:

```
<?xml version="1.0" encoding="UTF-8"?>
<!-- ********** File: start.html ********** -->
<!DOCTYPE html PUBLIC "-//W3C//DTD XHTML 1.0 Strict//EN"
    "http://www.w3.org/TR/xhtml1/DTD/xhtml1-frameset.dtd">
<html xmlns="http://www.w3.org/1999/xhtml">
    <head>
        <title>Start page</title>
    </head>
    <frameset cols="10%, 90%">
        <frame src="left.html" name="left"/>
        <frameset rows="10%, 90%">
            <frame src="top.html" name="top"/>
            <frame src="main.html" name="main"/>
        </frameset>
    </frameset>
</html>

<?xml version="1.0" encoding="UTF-8"?>
<!-- ********** File: top.html ********** -->
<!DOCTYPE html PUBLIC "-//W3C//DTD XHTML 1.0 Strict//EN"
    "http://www.w3.org/TR/xhtml1/DTD/xhtml1-strict.dtd">
<html xmlns="http://www.w3.org/1999/xhtml">
    <head>
        <title>Top</title>
    </head>
    <body>
        <p><img src="logo.gif" alt="Company logo"/>
        </p>
    </body>
</html>
```

One of the frames, main.html, contains arbitrary content that's displayed the first time the user retrieves the web page. The following code is left.html, referred to in the previous frameset.

```
<?xml version="1.0" encoding="UTF-8"?>
<!-- ********** File: left.html ********** -->
<!DOCTYPE html PUBLIC "-//W3C//DTD XHTML 1.0 Strict//EN"
    "http://www.w3.org/TR/xhtml1/DTD/xhtml1-transitional.dtd">
<html xmlns="http://www.w3.org/1999/xhtml">
    <head>
        <title>Navigation</title>
    </head>
    <body>
        <p><a href="about.html" target="main">
                <img src="about.gif" alt="About us"/>
            </a>
                <br/><a href="news.html" target="main">
                    <img src="news.gif" alt="Latest news"/>
                </a>
                <br/><a href="links.html" target="main">
                    <img src="links.gif" alt="Links"/>
                </a>
        </p>
    </body>
</html>
```

Left.html contains all the links for navigation. Notice you use the target attribute, so the linked content appears in the main frame.

The start page contains a frameset. Each document in the frameset conforms to XHTML 1.0 Strict, as opposed to the wireless version that conforms to XHTML Basic 1.0. For the desktop version, you use a simple nested frameset that contains three frames: left, top, and main. The left frame is used for navigation, so all the links in that document have the target attribute set to the main document. Handheld devices won't have access to the start (frameset) document, the main.html, the left.html, or the top.html files. The version for limited handheld devices shares about.html, news.html and links.html with the version for desktop computers. In addition, a new start page is implemented. All pages are implemented in XHTML Basic 1.0. This is the mobile version of the start page.

```
<?xml version="1.0" encoding="UTF-8"?>
<!-- ********** File: starthandheld.html ********** -->
<!DOCTYPE html PUBLIC "-//W3C//DTD XHTML Basic 1.0//EN"
    "http://www.w3.org/TR/xhtml-basic/xhtml-basic10.dtd">
<html xmlns="http://www.w3.org/1999/xhtml">
    <head>
        <title>Top</title>
    </head>
    <body>
```

```
        <p><a href="about.html">About</a>
            <br/><a href="news.html">News</a>
            <br/><a href="links.html">Links</a>
        </p>
    </body>
</html>
```

The following files are shared: about.html, news.html, and links.html. Note, they're implemented in XHTML Basic 1.0.

```
<?xml version="1.0" encoding="UTF-8"?>
<!-- ********** File: about.html ********** -->
<!DOCTYPE html PUBLIC "-//W3C//DTD XHTML Basic 1.0//EN"
    "http://www.w3.org/TR/xhtml-basic/xhtml-basic10.dtd">
<html xmlns="http://www.w3.org/1999/xhtml">
    <head>
        <title>About us</title>
    </head>
    <body>
        <p>We started this company in 1975. </p>
    </body>
</html>
```

The following listing is news.html:

```
<?xml version="1.0" encoding="UTF-8"?>
<!-- ********** File: news.html ********** -->
<!DOCTYPE html PUBLIC "-//W3C//DTD XHTML Basic 1.0//EN"
    "http://www.w3.org/TR/xhtml-basic/xhtml-basic10.dtd">
<html xmlns="http://www.w3.org/1999/xhtml">
    <head>
        <title>News</title>
    </head>
    <body>
        <p>In January, we signed a deal with Zaka Inc.
        </p>
    </body>
</html>
```

The following file is links.html:

```
<?xml version="1.0" encoding="UTF-8"?>
<!-- ********** File: links.html ********** -->
<!DOCTYPE html PUBLIC "-//W3C//DTD XHTML 1.0 Strict//EN"
    "http://www.w3.org/TR/xhtml1/DTD/xhtml1-strict.dtd">
```

```
<html xmlns="http://www.w3.org/1999/xhtml">
    <head>
        <title>Links</title>
    </head>
    <body>
        <p><a href="http://www.bknet.com">Our friends at BK-net.</a>
            <br/><a href="http://www.zaka.com">Zaka Inc.</a>
        </p>
    </body>
</html>
```

To navigate back to the start page, the device's backward navigation button is used. If you want to insert a link, which is used to navigate back to the start page, then you need to change the shared content. Because the version for desktop computers uses frames and doesn't need a backwards navigation, this is the best solution. Then you needn't change news.html, links.html, or about.html, and these files can be shared. When new content is uploaded, it will be available immediately both for ordinary users and mobile users.

Because the start page is different, you need to use two different addresses for the site: one for the desktop version and one for the mobile version. Or, you can have a server-side script or use a function in the web server that checks the HTTP header. In the header, you can find information about which browser is used, and then you can (at least in theory) find out if a desktop computer or handheld device is being used. In Chapter 2, you can see how the user-agent parameter is set to the name and version of the browser. In practice, using this information in a successful way is a difficult task. A number of mobile browsers are on the market and the code would have to consider that. It's more common that online applications for mobile devices use separate addresses.

Another solution is to look at the accept header in the HTTP message. The accept header should contain an ordered list of the content types the browser accepts. In WAP 2.0, User Agent Profiles (UAProfs) are supposed to solve the problem by implementing a framework, which makes it possible to specify the capabilities of the device. The CC/PP profile has been a basis for that work. UAProfs and CC/PP were discussed in Chapter 9.

Shared Navigation and Content

An alternative is to go for the most common denominator and implement the whole site in XHTML Basic 1.0. Then you would have to skip features, like complicated tables, forms, image maps, and plug-ins. The previous solution, when only a subset of the documents is implemented in XHTML Basic 1.0, can be a good working solution. This is the only feasible answer if you want to make use of sophisticated graphics using, for example, Flash or Java applets for navigation or company logos, but still keep a part of the site compatible with limited handheld devices.

Converting i-mode HTML to XHTML Basic

Compact HTML (cHTML) has been used for a couple of years by the i-mode service. In i-mode, however, NTT DoCoMo chose to provide some extensions to HTML—for example, to make setting up telephone calls possible. The prefix tel: can be used in the href attribute of the *a* element. When the user activates the link, the device sets up a telephone call to the number specified after the tel: prefix.

Converting cHTML documents to XHTML Basic documents is much more simple than converting HTML4 documents to XHTML Basic. HTML4 was created for desktop computers, but what cHTML and XHTML Basic have in common is the languages were created for limited handheld devices. Thus, many constructs are the same and the two languages have excluded support for similar constructs that are part of HTML4 only.

If you're a programmer, then you might want to try to write a server-side script—for example, a Perl or JSP script—which converts cHTML pages to XHTML Basic 1.0. This isn't too hard, and here are the main differences between cHTML and XHTML Basic 1.0.

Tables

Compact HTML doesn't support any tables at all. XHTML Basic 1.0 supports simple tables. Two table modules have been defined in XHTML and one of them, the simple one, is used in XHTML Basic 1.0. You can't use the table heading and the body element, but ordinary rows and table cells can be used. This isn't much of a problem for conversions from cHTML to XHTML Basic 1.0. If you need to do a conversion the other way around, things get more complicated. You'd either have to represent a table as simple text or you'd have to create a picture of the table and implement the table as a picture. Here's a piece of cHTML that you're going to give a suitable representation to in XHTML Basic 1.0:

```
<html>
<head>
  <meta http-equiv="Content-Type" content="text/html; charset=SHIFT_JIS">
  <title>High score list</title>
</head>
<body>
  <p>Name and score
    <br>Liza Stone 24
    <br>Ben Smith 22
```

```
    <br>Joe Lewis 19
    <br>Anne Dudley 12
  </p>
</body>
</html>
```

The Japanese SHIFT_JIS character encoding must be used by i-mode services. This character is specified using the metaelement. In XHTML Basic 1.0, the previous presentation can be given a much more attractive layout.

```
<?xml version="1.0" encoding="UTF-8"?>
<!DOCTYPE html PUBLIC "-//W3C//DTD XHTML Basic 1.0//EN"
    "http://www.w3.org/TR/xhtml-basic/xhtml-basic10.dtd">
<html xmlns="http://www.w3.org/1999/xhtml">
<head>
  <title>High score list</title>
</head>
<body>
    <table>
      <tr><td>Name</td><td>Score</td>
      </tr>
      <tr><td>Liza Stone</td><td>24</td>
      </tr>
      <tr><td>Ben Smith</td><td>22</td>
      </tr>
      <tr><td>Joe Lewis</td><td>19</td>
      </tr>
      <tr><td>Anne Dudley</td><td>12</td>
      </tr>
    </table>
</body>
</html>
```

Because the previous code isn't cHTML anymore and we don't use any Japanese characters, the metaelement has been removed. Note, the code isn't suitable for very small screens because the table has two columns. Devices with less than 16 characters per line will show the text in each column with line breaks. It can look like Figure 12-1.

What you see is a snapshot from the Nokia mobile Internet development kit 3.0, which supports XHTML Basic 1.0. Note, the names in the left column are broken because the device has too few characters per line to display each name and score on a single line.

Figure 12-1   *The High score list is displayed on a Nokia XHTML browser and emulator*

Input Style

The input element has been given a new attribute in i-mode, called *istyle,* which can be used to select the input mode (for example, numeric characters or alphabetic characters). Here's an example:

```
<html>
<head>
  <meta http-equiv="Content-Type" content="text/html; charset=SHIFT_JIS">
  <title>Submit name & phone number</title>
</head>
<body>
  <p>Please submit your name and telephone number!
  </p>
  <form action="cgi/receiver.pl">
    Name:<input type="text" name="theName">
    <br>Tel:<input type="text" name="theNumber" istyle="4">
    <br><input type="submit" value="Submit">
  </form>
</body>
</html>
```

The istyle attribute has been set to 4, which means the input is numeric. No similar attribute is in XHTML Basic 1.0. Usually, discarding this attribute isn't a problem, though, because handheld devices have some built-in mechanism to toggle between different input modes, such as numeric and alphabetic, and possibly other modes that use big letters.

Menus

In i-mode, menus can be provided using the menu element. The *menu* element is part of the legacy module in XHTML and the legacy module isn't part of XHTML Basic 1.0. Thus, if you're converting an i-mode site to XHTML Basic 1.0, then you have to provide a suitable replacement for this element. Here's an example that illustrates one way of solving the problem:

```
<html>
<head>
  <meta http-equiv="Content-Type" content="text/html; charset=SHIFT_JIS">
  <title>Employees</title>
</head>
<body>
  <p>The crew</p>
  <menu>
    <li>Liza Stone</li>
    <li>Ben Smith</li>
    <li>Joe Lewis</li>
    <li>Anne Dudley</li>
  </menu>
</body>
</html>
```

The i-mode code can be converted to the following representation in XHTML Basic 1.0.

```
<?xml version="1.0" encoding="UTF-8"?>
<!DOCTYPE html PUBLIC "-//W3C//DTD XHTML Basic 1.0//EN"
    "http://www.w3.org/TR/xhtml-basic/xhtml-basic10.dtd">
<html xmlns="http://www.w3.org/1999/xhtml">
<head>
  <title>Employees</title>
</head>
<body>
  <p>The crew</p>
  <ul>
    <li>Liza Stone</li>
    <li>Ben Smith</li>
    <li>Joe Lewis</li>
    <li>Anne Dudley</li>
```

```
    </ul>
  </body>
</html>
```

In addition to the XML header, DOCTYPE declaration, and XHTML namespace, the menu element has been replaced by the ul element. An unordered list is usually rendered almost the same way as the menu element.

Dir

In i-mode, you can create a list of items using the dir element. The *dir* element was put in the legacy module when HTML was modularized, so it isn't available in XHTML Basic 1.0. Similar to the menu element, which is also part of the legacy module, this element can be replaced by the ul element if you need to convert an i-mode site to XHTML.

Anchored Links

As previously mentioned, NTT DoCoMo uses a special prefix (protocol specifier) in the href attribute of the *a* element, which makes setting up telephone calls possible by activating a link in a cHTML document. XHTML Basic 1.0 doesn't support this type of link. In those cases, this kind of link can be replaced with a piece of text that says, "Call us at . . ." followed by the telephone number. Here's an example:

```
<html>
<head>
  <meta http-equiv="Content-Type" content="text/html; charset=SHIFT_JIS">
  <title>Hello</title>
</head>
<body>
  <p><a href="tel:0123456790">Call me!</a>
  </p>
</body>
</html>
```

Note, cHTML isn't an XML application, so no XML header exists. The previous file could be converted to the following XHTML Basic 1.0 code:

```
<?xml version="1.0" encoding="UTF-8"?>
<!DOCTYPE html PUBLIC "-//W3C//DTD XHTML Basic 1.0//EN"
    "http://www.w3.org/TR/xhtml-basic/xhtml-basic10.dtd">
<html xmlns="http://www.w3.org/1999/xhtml">
<head>
  <title>Hello</title>
</head>
<body>
```

```
  <p>Call us at tel:0123456790<br/>
  </p>
</body>
</html>
```

The XML header and the DOCTYPE declaration for XHTML Basic 1.0 have been added. In XHTML Basic 1.0, the xhtml namespace must be used, so it was added to the html element. Because the tel prefix is unique for i-mode, it cannot be used and must be replaced with something else. We chose to remove the link and make the value of the href attribute a piece of text preceded by the words "Call us at." This isn't too difficult to implement as an XSL transformation. Also, note a slash had to be inserted at the end of the br and metaelements to make the code well formed.

In addition, i-mode has support for computer telephone integration (CTI). A cti attribute can be used with the *a* element, like this:

```
<html>
<head>
  <meta http-equiv="Content-Type" content="text/html; charset=SHIFT_JIS">
  <title>Hello</title>
</head>
<body>
  <p>
     <a href="error.html" cti="0123456790/,,,5">Call the tele-bank.
     </a>
  </p>
</body>
</html>
```

The telephone number 0123456790 will be called and, when the receiver answers, the DTMF tone for "5" will be sent after three seconds. Thus, a comma denotes one second. If the device doesn't support CTI, the web page error.html, indicated by the value of the href attribute, is displayed. No equivalent to the cti attribute is in XHTML Basic 1.0. The only way to provide a mapping for XHTML Basic 1.0 is to render the actual codes to the screen and instruct the user as to which key presses she should execute to access the service.

```
<?xml version="1.0" encoding="UTF-8"?>
<!DOCTYPE html PUBLIC "-//W3C//DTD XHTML Basic 1.0//EN"
    "http://www.w3.org/TR/xhtml-basic/xhtml-basic10.dtd">
<html xmlns="http://www.w3.org/1999/xhtml">
<head>
  <title>Hello</title>
</head>
```

```
<body>
  <p> Call the tele-bank at 0123456790, wait three seconds
     and then press 5.
  </p>
</body>
</html>
```

The link has been replaced by an instruction for how the service can be accessed manually.

Marquee

A feature in i-mode makes it possible to use scrolling text on your web page. This is achieved using the marquee element and a number of attributes associated with that element. Text can also "slide" into the web page, as in the following example:

```
<html>
<head>
  <meta http-equiv="Content-Type" content="text/html; charset=SHIFT_JIS">
  <title>My Page</title>
</head>
<body>
  <marquee behavior="slide" direction="left">Hello!
  </marquee>
</body>
</html>
```

When the behavior attribute is set to "slide", the text moves in, and then stops when the last character is visible on the screen. The marquee element isn't available in XHTML Basic 1.0. Thus, if you're converting an i-mode page to XHTML Basic 1.0, you might have to replace this element with something else, like this:

```
<?xml version="1.0" encoding="UTF-8"?>
<!DOCTYPE html PUBLIC "-//W3C//DTD XHTML Basic 1.0//EN"
    "http://www.w3.org/TR/xhtml-basic/xhtml-basic10.dtd">
<html xmlns="http://www.w3.org/1999/xhtml">
<head>
  <title>My Page</title>
</head>
<body>
  <p>Hello!
  </p>
</body>
</html>
```

The marquee element has been replaced by the p element. Because no support exists for moving text in XHTML Basic 1.0, this is a working solution. It won't provide moving text, but the actual content won't be removed. In i-mode, you can only provide up to 64 characters of text for the marquee element, so displaying the text using the p element isn't a problem. The text will be readable even on the smallest screens by scrolling down a few rows.

In version 2.0 of WAP, marquees are supported using cascading style sheets or Wireless CSS (WCSS), to be precise. In that case, the "display" property can be set to the value "-wap-marquee." Loop, style, speed, and functions for the direction have been defined. If you want to create a style sheet for a WAP 2.0-enabled phone that supports marquees, then you should read the WCSS specification from WAP-forum. This can be downloaded from **http://www.wapforum.org/**.

Picture Symbols

You can use SHIFT-JIS character codes to refer to a set of simple pictures in i-mode. 196 pictures are available. There are simple geometric figures like squares and arrows, but most are service-related figures, such as weather symbols, bank, and ATM symbols. Note, the pictures are stored in the device's read-only memory and aren't downloaded over the air. The following example illustrates how an author might refer to such figures:

```
<html>
<head>
  <meta http-equiv="Content-Type" content="text/html; charset=SHIFT_JIS">
  <title>My Page</title>
</head>
<body>
  <p>Weather report
    <br>Monday &#63647;
    <br>Tuesday &#63649;
  </p>
</body>
</html>
```

The first character code is a sun and the second is an umbrella. In XHTML Basic 1.0, the standard character encoding isn't SHIFT-JIS, but UTF-8, and no symbols are in this character set. If the device supports another Unicode character set, which includes small icons or illustrations, however, then it's possible to refer to characters in this character set the same way using the Unicode syntax. The previous code could be translated to the following representation in XHTML Basic 1.0:

```
<?xml version="1.0" encoding="UTF-8"?>
<!DOCTYPE html PUBLIC "-//W3C//DTD XHTML Basic 1.0//EN"
    "http://www.w3.org/TR/xhtml-basic/xhtml-basic10.dtd">
<html xmlns="http://www.w3.org/1999/xhtml">
<head>
  <title>My Page</title>
</head>
<body>
  <p>Weather report
    <br>Monday &#x2600;
    <br>Tuesday &#x2602;
  </p>
</body>
</html>
```

The code refers to two Unicode characters that are part of the "Miscellaneous symbols" (U2600) character set. Therefore, this XHTML code is hard coded for devices that support this character set. Because XHTML Basic 1.0 doesn't require that devices should store these particular bitmaps in memory, a lesser idea might be to use pictures like this, unless you're targeting a specific device. If you need to use pictures, using the img element is probably a better idea and you can download the graphics over the air. With 2.5G and 3G coming, the speed will be sufficient that you won't even notice the icons are being downloaded. As a bonus, you can also provide an alternate text for disabled people who might use a voice synthesizer to listen to the web page and for people who use devices that don't support graphics.

Plaintext

In i-mode, you can provide a piece of text that uses the screen in an efficient way. Here's an example:

```
<html>
<head>
  <meta http-equiv="Content-Type" content="text/html; charset=SHIFT_JIS">
  <title>My Page</title>
</head>
<body>
  <plaintext>Welcome to my homepage. When this text is displayed
      on the screen, some words may be broken to minimize the
      space the text occupies.
  </plaintext>
</body>
</html>
```

Displaying the text on a device that has 16 characters on each line can look like the following:

```
Welcome to my ho
mepage. When thi
s text is displa
yed on the scree
n, some words ma
y be broken to m
inimize the spac
e the text occup
ies.
```

As you can see, the text occupies only nine lines. A word can be broken into a new line if it hits the end of the line, rather than moving the whole word to the new line. From a usability perspective, this is a poor way of providing information. The text might become hard to read and confusing. On the other hand, the user doesn't have to scroll so much because the text will consume as little of the display's space as possible. This usually isn't a problem, though, because many of the new handheld devices have smart navigation devices, like joysticks and scroll wheels.

XHTML Basic 1.0 doesn't support the plaintext element. Alternative elements have to be used. Here's one solution:

```
<?xml version="1.0" encoding="UTF-8"?>
<!DOCTYPE html PUBLIC "-//W3C//DTD XHTML Basic 1.0//EN"
    "http://www.w3.org/TR/xhtml-basic/xhtml-basic10.dtd">
<html xmlns="http://www.w3.org/1999/xhtml">
<head>
  <title>My Page</title>
</head>
<body>
  <p>Welcome to my homepage. When this text is displayed
       on the screen, some words may be broken to minimize the
       space the text occupies.
  </p>
</body>
</html>
```

On a device that uses 16 characters per line, it can look like this:

```
Welcome to my
homepage. When
this text is
```

```
displayed on the
screen, some
words may be
broken to
minimize the
space the text
occupies.
```

This text consumes ten lines. Thus, the difference is only one line more, compared to the i-mode representation that used the plaintext element. In addition, the text becomes much more easy to read.

Emphasis and Strong Text

The em and strong elements are supported in XHTML Basic 1.0, but not in cHTML. This isn't a problem when you're converting from cHTML to XHTML Basic 1.0. When you're doing conversions the other way around, the elements can be discarded in many cases.

Center

An i-mode page might look like this:

```
<html>
<head>
  <meta http-equiv="Content-Type" content="text/html; charset=SHIFT_JIS">
  <title>My Page</title>
</head>
<body>
  <center>
    <p>Welcome
    </p>
  </center>
  <p align="center">to my homepage!
  </p>
</body>
</html>
```

Because the center element and the align attribute are both part of the XHTML legacy module, no support exists for it in XHTML Basic 1.0. Thus, if you need to use centered text, you can use an external style sheet to achieve that or you can use a table, in which text can be centered. The following is a mapping of the previous code to XHTML Basic 1.0.

```
<?xml version="1.0" encoding="UTF-8"?>
<!DOCTYPE html PUBLIC "-//W3C//DTD XHTML Basic 1.0//EN"
    "http://www.w3.org/TR/xhtml-basic/xhtml-basic10.dtd">
<html xmlns="http://www.w3.org/1999/xhtml">
<head>
  <title>My Page</title>
</head>
<body>
  <table>
    <tr><td align="center">Welcome</td></tr>
  </table>
  <table>
    <tr><td align="center">to my homepage!</td></tr>
  </table>
</body>
</html>
```

The p and center elements, as well as the align attribute, have been replaced
by the table, tr, and td elements. Using the align attribute, you can specify center
alignment for the text.

External Style Sheets and Links

An external style sheet can be associated to an XHTML Basic 1.0 document using the
link element. The element isn't supported in cHTML. Thus, it only affects conversions
the other way around. Because formatting only affects the styling and not the actual
content, this shouldn't be a problem.

Font Colors

Fonts can have different colors in i-mode, but there's only one font style. The following
code illustrates how the font element is used in i-mode:

```
<html>
<head>
  <meta http-equiv="Content-Type" content="text/html; charset=SHIFT_JIS">
  <title>Blue and red</title>
</head>
<body>
  <p>
    <font color="blue">Welcome
    </font>
    <br>
    <font color="#FF0000">This is my simple home page.
    </font>
```

```
  </p>
</body>
</html>
```

Font colors can be specified using the color names that have been defined for HTML, or they can be specified using RGB color codes. Because the font element and the color attribute are part of the XHTML legacy module, no support exists for fonts or font colors in XHTML Basic 1.0. If a specific device supports color, however, then colors can be used via an external style sheet. Because the actual content won't be affected, it's also quite safe to remove the font element from the code.

Blinking Text

In i-mode, it's possible to include blinking text, such as this:

```
<html>
<head>
  <meta http-equiv="Content-Type" content="text/html; charset=SHIFT_JIS">
  <title>My page</title>
</head>
<body>
  <p><blink>Welcome!</blink>
    <br>to our web page.
  </p>
</body>
</html>
```

In XHTML Basic 1.0, no support exists for blinking text. In most cases, the element can be discarded and the text is displayed on the screen the usual way, like this:

```
<?xml version="1.0" encoding="UTF-8"?>
<!DOCTYPE html PUBLIC "-//W3C//DTD XHTML Basic 1.0//EN"
    "http://www.w3.org/TR/xhtml-basic/xhtml-basic10.dtd">
<html xmlns="http://www.w3.org/1999/xhtml">
<head>
  <title>My page</title>
</head>
<body>
  <p>Welcome!
    <br>to our web page.
  </p>
</body>
</html>
```

The blink element has been removed.

Horizontal Ruler

The hr element, which is used to create a horizontal ruler, is available in cHTML and the i-mode service, but not in XHTML Basic 1.0. You can replace the element with an image, though, as in the following example:

```
<html>
<head>
  <meta http-equiv="Content-Type" content="text/html; charset=SHIFT_JIS">
  <title>Employees</title>
</head>
<body>
  <p>Carl Smith
    <br>General Manager
    <br><a href="tel:0123456790">Call Carl!</a>
    <br>Hobbies: fishing, chess and playing oboe.
    <hr>Liza Stone
    <br>Secretary
    <br><a href="tel:0123456700">Call Liza!</a>
    <br>Hobbies: square dance.
  </p>
</body>
</html>
```

A translation to XHTML Basic 1.0 can look something like this:

```
<?xml version="1.0" encoding="UTF-8"?>
<!DOCTYPE html PUBLIC "-//W3C//DTD XHTML Basic 1.0//EN"
    "http://www.w3.org/TR/xhtml-basic/xhtml-basic10.dtd">
<html xmlns="http://www.w3.org/1999/xhtml">
<head>
  <title>Employees</title>
</head>
<body>
  <p>Carl Smith
    <br/>General Manager
    <br/>tel: 0123456790
    <br/>Hobbies: fishing, chess and playing oboe.
    <br/><img src="horizontalRuler.gif" alt="horizontal ruler">Liza Stone
    <br/>Secretary
    <br/>tel: 0123456700.
    <br/>Hobbies: square dance.
  </p>
</body>
</html>
```

The hr element was replaced by the img element. Be careful about how wide the image is, though, because the screen sizes can vary. In addition, the XML header and DOCTYPE declaration was added. Note, a slash is added to the br elements. Because the link was the type of link only available in i-mode, the XHTML Basic 1.0 implementation only provides the content of the href attribute.

Covering all cases for the hr element, like different settings for the size, width, and noshade attributes, is difficult. In many cases, however, they can be discarded and a single GIF file of a horizontal ruler usually works as intended. Note, a line break was introduced before the image, to have the image drawn on a line of its own.

A Sample XHTML Basic 1.0 and i-mode Site

By now, you should know the basic differences between the HTML used in i-mode and XHTML Basic 1.0. Let's look at a complete site, which is implemented for i-mode terminals, as well as XHTML Basic 1.0-compatible terminals. This is a site that lets you play a game and read the news. Let's start with the requirements, and then check out the implementations.

Requirements

The site should have a start page, where a simple logo is displayed. The user can choose one of the options from this start page: a game or news. When the user chooses one of the options, she is taken to the new page and the information is displayed. Each of these pages has a link back to the main page.

The game is a simple "Guess the word" activity and the news service is given to you from a news agency, in a simple XML format. This means you have to make a transformation to i-mode and XHTML Basic 1.0.

Implementation of the Start Page

The start page, start.html, is implemented only once because it doesn't change. The services, though, change when you receive news or want to change the secret word. Here is the i-mode implementation of the start page.

```
<html>
<head>
  <meta http-equiv="Content-Type" content="text/html; charset=SHIFT_JIS">
  <title>m-info</title>
</head>
<body>
    <p align="center">
        <img src="pics/logo.gif">
        <br>*** m-info ***
```

```
    </p>
    <hr>
    <p>Please choose
      <br><a href="guess.html" accesskey="1">1.Guess the word</a>
      <br><a href="news.html" accesskey="2">2.News</a>
    </p>
</body>
</html>
```

This is straightforward and not complex. The SHIFT-JIS charset is used because it's required for all i-mode pages. The body contains two paragraphs that are separated by a horizontal ruler. Note, if the previous page would be displayed in an ordinary web browser, such as Netscape Navigator or Internet Explorer, they would insert an extra space between the two paragraph blocks, but in i-mode, this isn't the case. A new block doesn't result in an extra line. In the second paragraph, we've used access keys for quick navigation. The user can press keys 1, 2, or 3 to access the desired function. For maximum compatibility, the GIF file is noninterlaced. There are devices that support other graphics formats—like JPEGs and interlaced GIFs—but if you use some of those formats, then all devices wouldn't be able to display the page properly.

Here's a translation of the i-mode page to XHTML Basic 1.0:

```
<?xml version="1.0" encoding="UTF-8"?>
<!DOCTYPE html PUBLIC "-//W3C//DTD XHTML Basic 1.0//EN"
    "http://www.w3.org/TR/xhtml-basic/xhtml-basic10.dtd">
<html xmlns="http://www.w3.org/1999/xhtml">
<head>
  <title>m-info</title>
</head>
<body>
    <table><tr><td align="center">
        <img src="pics/logo.gif"/>
        <br/>*** m-info ***
    </td></tr></table>
    <img src="pics/horizontalRuler.gif"/>
    <p>Please choose
      <br/><a href="guess.html">Guess the word</a>
      <br/><a href="news.html">News</a>
    </p>
</body>
</html>
```

The alignment attribute for the p element isn't supported in XHTML Basic 1.0, so it's been replaced with a simple table. A slash was inserted at the end of the img and br elements, to make them well formed. Because the hr element is part of the presentation module, it's outside the scope of XHTML Basic 1.0. This is why we replaced it with an image, using the img element.

That was the start page. Now let's move on to the game.

Implementation of the Game

Because we want to change the word without redesigning the i-mode and XHTML Basic pages each time, we'll write the secret word in an XML file we created ourselves. Two XSL transformations generate the i-mode and XHTML Basic pages. Here's the format for our XML file in a simple format:

```
<?xml version="1.0" encoding="UTF-8"?>
<word letters="behknooop">phonebook</word>
```

The file contains a word, written between the word tags and all letters provided with the letters attribute. An i-mode file and an XHTML Basic file are generated from this file, using two different XSL transformations.

For each of the i-mode and XHTML Basic files, there's one main file that displays how many characters the word contains. All unique characters that occur in the word are also displayed. It looks something like Figure 12-2.

The user can see how many letters the word has and which letters are there. A simple form lets the user guess the word. When the user submits the form, it's sent to a CGI server script. The first parameter is the guess typed in by the user and the second parameter is a hidden parameter, which is the secret word. The hidden parameter and the guess are input elements in a form.

Figure 12-2   *The main page for the game*

Server-side Scripts   The script checks if the guess is correct or not and generates a reply depending on the outcome of the guess. Because the scope of this book isn't to teach any of the available server-script technologies, the script has been made as simple as possible. Here's how it looks for the i-mode version of the game:

```perl
#!/usr/bin/perl

$query = $ENV{'QUERY_STRING'};
($corr, $gs) = split(/&/, $query);

($correct, $correctVal) = split(/=/, $corr);
($guess, $guessVal) = split(/=/, $gs);

if( $correctVal eq $guessVal ) {
    print "Content-type: text/html\n\n";
    print "<html>";
    print "<head>";
    print "<meta http-equiv='Content-Type' content='text/html; charset=SHIFT_JI\

S'>";
    print "<title>Congratulations!</title>";
    print "</head>";
    print "<body>";
    print "<p>Well done! You guessed this week's secret word.";
    print " <a href='start.html'>Main page.</a>";
    print "</p>";
    print "</body>";
    print "</html>";
    exit;
}

print "Content-type: text/html\n\n";
print "<html>";
print "<head>";
print "<meta http-equiv='Content-Type' content='text/html;charset=SHIFT_JIS'>";
print "<title>Wrong!</title>";
print "</head>";
print "<body>";
print "<p>Sorry, that was wrong. <a href='guess.html'>Try again!</a>";
print "</p>";
print "</body>";
print "</html>";
exit;
```

If you don't know anything about programming, don't fear. This is how it works. All scripts, like Perl, begin with a hash bang. That's the first line, which indicates this file is a Perl script. The first line should always be like that. Then there's an if statement, which checks if the first parameter is the same as the second parameter. If they're the same, everything inside the curly brackets is written to stand out. This means it will be sent back as a web page. Server scripts must always send the content type first, followed by two new lines. The "\n" is the code for a new line.

```perl
#!/usr/bin/perl

$query = $ENV{'QUERY_STRING'};
($corr, $gs) = split(/&/, $query);

($correct, $correctVal) = split(/=/, $corr);
($guess, $guessVal) = split(/=/, $gs);

if( $correctVal eq $guessVal ) {
  print "Content-type: application/xhtml+xml\n\n";
  print "<?xml version='1.0' encoding='UTF-8'?>";
  print "<!DOCTYPE html PUBLIC '-//W3C//DTD XHTML Basic 1.0//EN'";
  print "'http://www.w3.org/TR/xhtml-basic/xhtml-basic10.dtd'>";
  print "<html xmlns='http://www.w3.org/1999/xhtml'>";

  print "<head>";
  print "<title>Congratulations!</title>";
  print "</head>";
  print "<body>";
  print "<p>Well done! You guessed the secret word.";
  print " <a href='start.html'>Main page.</a>";
  print "</p>";
  print "</body>";
  print "</html>";
  exit;
}

print "Content-type: application/xhtml+xml\n\n";
print "<?xml version='1.0' encoding='UTF-8'?>";
print "<!DOCTYPE html PUBLIC '-//W3C//DTD XHTML Basic 1.0//EN'";
print "'http://www.w3.org/TR/xhtml-basic/xhtml-basic10.dtd'>";
print "<html xmlns='http://www.w3.org/1999/xhtml'>";
print "<head>";
print "<title>Wrong!</title>";
print "</head>";
print "<body>";
print "<p>Sorry, that was wrong. <a href='guess.html'>Try again!</a>";
print "</p>";
print "</body>";
print "</html>";
exit;
```

Note, the content type—application/xhtml+xml—is sent back for the XHTML Basic version of the script. An XML header and a DOCTYPE declaration were added and the metaelement was removed. The xmlns attribute is used by the html element, according to the XHTML Basic 1.0 specification. The rest of the code is the same as for the i-mode version.

The Transformations to i-mode HTML and XHTML Basic   Let's return to the XML file that contains the secret word. From this XML file, generate the i-mode source and the XHTML Basic source. Here's how the generated i-mode document will look:

```
<html>
<head>
  <meta http-equiv="Content-Type" content="text/html; charset=SHIFT_JIS">
  <title>Guess the word!</title>
</head>
<body>
    <p>Guess the word!
      <br>Letters: behknooop
    </p>
    <form action="check_imode.pl"><p>
      Guess:<input type="text" name="guess">
      <input type="hidden" name="correct" value="phonebook"></p>
    </form>
    <p><a href="start.html">Back to start page</a>
    </p>
  </body>
</html>
```

The letters are displayed for the user and the correct answer is sent together with the user's guess in the form. The second input field, which sends the correct answer, is hidden for the user. There's also a link back to the start page. Here's how the generated XHTML Basic document will look.

```
<?xml version="1.0" encoding="UTF-8"?>
<!DOCTYPE html PUBLIC "-//W3C//DTD XHTML Basic 1.0//EN"
    "http://www.w3.org/TR/xhtml-basic/xhtml-basic10.dtd">

<html xmlns="http://www.w3.org/1999/xhtml">
  <head>
    <title>Guess the word!</title>
  </head>
  <body>
    <p>Guess the word!
```

```
        <br/>Letters: behknoooop
      </p>
      <form action="check_xhtml.pl"><p>
        Guess:<input type="text" name="guess"/>
        <input type="hidden" name="correct" value="phonebook"/></p>
      </form>
      <p><a href="start.html">Back to start page</a>
      </p>
    </body>
</html>
```

The difference is that the input fields and the br element have a slash at the end to make them well formed. In addition, there's an XML header, a DOCTYPE declaration, and the XML namespace for XHTML.

Now let's look at how the transformations are implemented. One transformation is from the XML file with the word element to the i-mode file and another transformation is from the same XML file, but to the XHTML Basic format. Here's how the XML to i-mode transformation looks.

```
<?xml version="1.0"?>
<xsl:stylesheet version="1.0" xmlns:xsl="http://www.w3.org/1999/XSL/Transform">

  <xsl:output method="html"/>

  <xsl:template match="/">
    <html>
      <head>
        <meta http-equiv="Content-Type" content="text/html; charset=SHIFT_JIS">
        <title>Guess the word!</title>
      </head>
      <body>
        <p>Guess the word!
          <br>Letters: <xsl:value-of select="@letters"/>
        </p>
        <form action='check_imode.pl'><p>
          Guess:<input type='text' name='guess'>
          <input type='hidden' name='correct' value='<xsl:apply-templates/>'>
        </p></form>
        <p><a href='start.html'>Back to start page</a>
        </p>
      </body>
    </html>
  </xsl:template>

</xsl:stylesheet>
```

The correct answer is inserted as the value attribute's value and all the letters are included in the first paragraph. A bit similar, but not identical, is the transformation to XHTML Basic:

```
<?xml version="1.0"?>
<xsl:stylesheet version="1.0"
xmlns:xsl="http://www.w3.org/1999/XSL/Transform">

  <xsl:output
      method="xml"
      doctype-public = "-//W3C//DTD XHTML Basic 1.0//EN"
      doctype-system = "http://www.w3.org/TR/xhtml-basic/xhtml-basic10.dtd"/>

  <xsl:template match="/">
    <html xmlns='http://www.w3.org/1999/xhtml'>
      <head>
        <title>Guess the word!</title>
      </head>
      <body>
        <p>Guess the word!
          <br/>Letters: <xsl:value-of select="@letters"/>
        </p>
        <form action='check.pl'><p>
          Guess:<input type='text' name='guess'/>
          <input type='hidden' name='correct' value='<xsl:apply-templates/>'/>
        </p></form>
        <p><a href-'start.html'>Back to start page</a>
        </p>
      </body>
    </html>
  </xsl:template>
</xsl:stylesheet>
```

Compared with the i-mode transformation, you had to add an XML header, a DOCTYPE declaration, and the slashes for the br and input elements.

Now the game is complete. All you have to do when you change the secret word is to apply the two XML transformations on the XML file. The documents for the i-mode version and the XHTML Basic version should be generated automatically.

Implementation of the News Page

So far, you have the start page and the game. Now, it's time to look at the implementation of the news page. The purpose of the news page is that you should be able to receive a news message in a simple XML format. The content is then transformed to i-mode HTML and XHTML Basic, so the output can be uploaded to the server. The content provider sends the news to you in this format:

```
<?xml version="1.0"?>
<!-- Article 1 -->
<h>The first headline</h>
<p>Text in the first paragraph.
</p>
<p>Text in the second paragraph.
</p>
<!-- Article 2 -->
<h>The second headline</h>
<p>Text in the first paragraph.
</p>
<!-- Article 3 -->
<h>The third headline</h>
<p>Text in the first paragraph.
</p>
<p>Text in the second paragraph.
</p>
```

The file contains one of more articles. Each article has a heading, and one or more paragraphs. An XSL style sheet, which transforms the content to i-mode HTML can be implemented like this:

```
<?xml version="1.0"?>
<xsl:stylesheet version="1.0" xmlns:xsl="http://www.w3.org/1999/XSL/Transform">

  <xsl:output method="html"/>

  <xsl:template match="/">
    <html>
      <head>
        <meta http-equiv='Content-Type' content='text/html; charset=SHIFT_JIS'>
        <title>News</title>
      </head>
      <body>
        <marquee behavior='slide' direction='left'>News
        </marquee>
        <xsl:apply-templates/>
        <hr>
        <a href='start.html'>Main menu</a>
      </body>
    </html>
  </xsl:template>

  <xsl:template match="h">
      <hr>
      <h1>
```

```
        <xsl:apply-templates/>
      </h1>
  </xsl:template>

  <xsl:template match="p">
      <p>
        <xsl:apply-templates/>
      </p>
  </xsl:template>

</xsl:stylesheet>
```

The hr element is used to separate each news article and a "news" heading is slid into the display from the right to the left, using the marquee element. The h1 element has been used, but with compact HTML, which number is written after the *h* doesn't matter. All headings are equal in size to h4.

The XSL style sheet, which performs a transformation to the corresponding XHTML Basic 1.0 code, might look like this:

```
<?xml version="1.0"?>
<xsl:stylesheet version="1.0" xmlns:xsl="http://www.w3.org/1999/XSL/Transform">

  <xsl:output
      method="xml"
      doctype-public = "-//W3C//DTD XHTML Basic 1.0//EN"
      doctype-system = "http://www.w3.org/TR/xhtml-basic/xhtml-basic10.dtd"/>

  <xsl:template match="/">
    <html xmlns='http://www.w3.org/1999/xhtml'>
      <head>
        <title>News</title>
      </head>
      <body>
        <h1>News
        </h1>
        <xsl:apply-templates/>
        <p><img src='horizontalRuler.gif'/>
          <br/><a href='start.html'>Main menu</a>
        </p>
      </body>
    </html>
  </xsl:template>

  <xsl:template match="h">
      <img src='horizontalRuler.gif'/>
      <h2>
        <xsl:apply-templates/>
      </h2>
```

```
    </xsl:template>

    <xsl:template match="p">
        <p>
          <xsl:apply-templates/>
        </p>
    </xsl:template>

</xsl:stylesheet>
```

In the HTML Basic version, the h1 and h2 elements were used. H1 replaces the marquee used in the i-mode version and h2 works as a heading for each article. Devices might exist that don't make a difference between the two headings and render them using the same font size. The hr element hasn't been used because it's part of the presentation module. Instead, an image works as a separator for the articles.

Working with XHTML Basic, the Presentation, and Style Sheet Modules

No matter if you're translating from languages, such as HTML4 or compact HTML, or creating sites from scratch, you might want to work with XHTML Basic 1.0 in combination with the presentation and style sheet modules for several reasons. One reason is these modules contain the most necessary elements and attributes to produce sites with a good layout and room for formatting. XHTML Basic 1.0, which doesn't include the presentation and style sheet modules, doesn't provide the elements for creating horizontal rulers, italics, and boldfaced text, for example. Because these elements are used quite a lot on the traditional Internet, it might become hard to translate ordinary web sites to versions for handheld devices. Another reason is WAP 2.0 is based on these modules, in combination with XHTML Basic 1.0.

Here's a short description of some of the elements and attributes in the presentation and style sheet modules.

Horizontal Ruler

The hr element is part of the presentation module. Thus, one added value of using the presentation module in combination with XHTML Basic 1.0 is it becomes slightly easier to port cHTML pages to this configuration of XHTML. This is because many i-mode pages tend to use the hr element. Here's an example:

```
<html>
<head>
  <meta http-equiv="Content-Type" content="text/html; charset=SHIFT_JIS">
  <title>Employees</title>
</head>
```

```
<body>
  <p>Carl Smith
    <br>General Manager
    <br><a href="tel:0123456790">Call Carl!</a>
    <br>Hobbies: fishing, chess and playing oboe.
    <hr>Liza Stone
    <br>Secretary
    <br><a href="tel:0123456700">Call Liza!</a>
    <br>Hobbies: square dance.
  </p>
</body>
</html>
```

Using the XHTML Basic 1.0 and the presentation module, the code would look like the following (and be almost identical to the i-mode code):

```
<?xml version="1.0" encoding="UTF-8"?>
<!DOCTYPE html PUBLIC "-//W3C//DTD XHTML 1.0 Strict//EN"
    "http://www.w3.org/TR/xhtml1/DTD/xhtml1-strict.dtd">
<html xmlns="http://www.w3.org/1999/xhtml">
<head>
  <title>Employees</title>
</head>
<body>
  <p>Carl Smith
    <br/>General Manager
    <br/>tel: 0123456790
    <br/>Hobbies: fishing, chess and playing oboe.
    <hr/>Liza Stone
    <br/>Secretary
    <br/>tel: 0123456700.
    <br/>Hobbies: square dance.
  </p>
</body>
</html>
```

We added the XML header and the DOCTYPE declaration, and made the br elements well formed by inserting the slash. Note, in XHTML, the hr element must be well formed.

Boldface and Italics

Part of the XHTML presentation module are the i and b elements for italics and boldface fonts, respectively. These elements should be used with care, though, because some devices support one font and the regular font style only. However, they do make porting traditional HTML pages easier, like the following, to this configuration of XHTML:

```
<html>
<head>
  <title>Employees</title>
</head>
<body>
  <p><i>Employees at the corporation. Local contact persons are
      marked with boldface.</i>
    <br><b>Carl Smith</b>
    <br>General Manager
    <br>Tel:0123456790
    <br>Hobbies: fishing, chess and playing oboe.
    <hr>Liza Stone
    <br>Secretary
    <br>Tel:0123456700
    <br>Hobbies: square dancing.
    <hr>Steve Pearce
    <br>Web designer
    <br>Tel:0123456787
    <br>Hobbies: Mountain biking
  </p>
</body>
</html>
```

The code can be translated to the following representation in XHTML:

```
<?xml version="1.0" encoding="UTF-8"?>
<!DOCTYPE html PUBLIC "-//W3C//DTD XHTML Basic 1.0//EN"
    "http://www.w3.org/TR/xhtml-basic/xhtml-basic10.dtd">
<html xmlns="http://www.w3.org/1999/xhtml">
<head>
  <title>Employees</title>
</head>
<body>
  <p><i>Employees at the corporation. Local contact persons are
      marked with boldface.</i>
    <br/><b>Carl Smith</b>
    <br/>General Manager
    <br/>Tel:0123456790
    <br/>Hobbies: fishing, chess and playing oboe.
    <hr/>Liza Stone
    <br/>Secretary
```

```
    <br/>Tel:0123456700
    <br/>Hobbies: square dancing.
    <hr/>Steve Pearce
    <br/>Web designer
    <br/>Tel:0123456787
    <br/>Hobbies: Mountain biking
  </p>
</body>
</html>
```

Because the b element is being used, the code can only be used on devices that support the presentation module, in addition to the modules in XHTML Basic 1.0. However, devices that don't support the presentation module might choose to discard the b element and display the code anyway. Then the code becomes meaningless because it becomes impossible for the user to identify the local contact persons who were supposed to be marked with boldface. It can look like Figure 12-3 on such a browser.

The b element has been discarded. This is one of the reasons you should be careful using elements related to the actual rendering to screen. The b and i elements are such elements. The following elements can create similar problems.

Big and Small Text

These elements, especially the latter, are useful on small handheld devices, but they require that the device supports more than one font size and this isn't always the case.

Figure 12-3   *This is a display on a device that doesn't support the presentation module*

Superscripts and Subscripts

The sup and sub elements are part of the presentation module; also, use them with care. If the target device is known, then you can use these elements if the device supports them. If you're creating a site in general, and you don't know which devices will be used to browse the pages, you should then avoid these elements because they require that the browser support this type of font styling, which is quite rare.

Style Sheets

The style sheets module makes styling content easier for a particular handheld device using the style element. Note, the style attribute is part of the separate style attribute module. Here's an example that uses an internal style sheet:

```
<?xml version="1.0" encoding="UTF-8"?>
<!DOCTYPE html PUBLIC "-//W3C//DTD XHTML Basic 1.0//EN"
    "http://www.w3.org/TR/xhtml-basic/xhtml-basic10.dtd">
<html xmlns="http://www.w3.org/1999/xhtml">
<head>
  <style>td {font-family: Courier}
  </style>
  <title>High score list</title>
</head>
<body>
    <table>
      <tr><td>Name</td><td>Score</td>
      </tr>
      <tr><td>Liza Stone</td><td>24</td>
      </tr>
      <tr><td>Ben Smith</td><td>22</td>
      </tr>
      <tr><td>Joe Lewis</td><td>19</td>
      </tr>
      <tr><td>Anne Dudley</td><td>12</td>
      </tr>
    </table>
</body>
</html>
```

External style sheets can be used with the link element, which is part of the link module. In this case, an internal style sheet is used. Note, you should only use this type of formatting if you know the device supports the specified font.

Development Tools

Compared with the HTML used in i-mode, XHTML has the advantage of being an XML application. This opens a world of possibilities when it comes to editing and storage because a number of more or less standard tools can be used to edit the code and perform a number of checks. An XML editor needn't be tailor made for XHTML, but the code can still be validated or checked using that tool if it's well formed. Here's a survey over a number of tools that can be used to produce XHTML code.

First, you'll look at an editor for general XML applications. Then you'll become familiar with an HTML editor, which is available free and has support for the development of wireless Internet applications. Finally, you'll learn about the features of an XHTML editor for mobile devices.

XML Spy

XML Spy is an editor for XML applications in general. One of the key strengths of XML Spy is it can validate an instance document according to a schema, in addition to the more common document type definition (DTD). Many freeware or shareware XML editors only have support for the validation of an instance document according to a DTD and not with respect to a schema. Because XHTML and XHTML Basic use DTDs only, so far, you'll have most use for the DTD validation.

XHTML Projects

When you're working on an XHTML site, you often end up with a set of files, say, a start page and several subpages. XML Spy has support for projects, which means that a project file contains a list of the files that are part of your site. A click in the project window opens the file for editing. For each project, you can define which DTD you should use for validation (see Figure 12-4).

Changing to a file on disk can be useful if you want to validate your XHTML code, but you're working on a laptop, which isn't always connected to the Internet. Then you can download the flat DTD, put it on disk, and point at the file in the project settings. Consequently, the XHTML files' DOCTYPE declarations needn't be changed during the development process and changed back when everything's finished. Instead, they can still point at the official DTD at http://www.w3.org, although a local file is used during the development.

Graphical Editing

In addition, you can edit XML files graphically using the enhanced grid view. This is an alternative to the text-based editing, which XML Spy also allows. In fact, the browser supports four different views. The enhanced grid view can be useful if you're

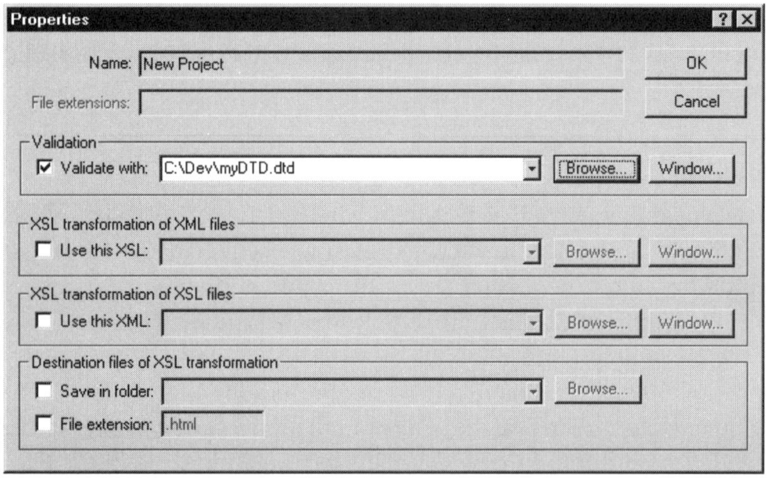

Figure 12-4 *Setting the DTD in XML Spy 3.5*

working with a big document or a document which has a complex nesting of elements, such as nested tables in XHTML (see Figure 12-5).

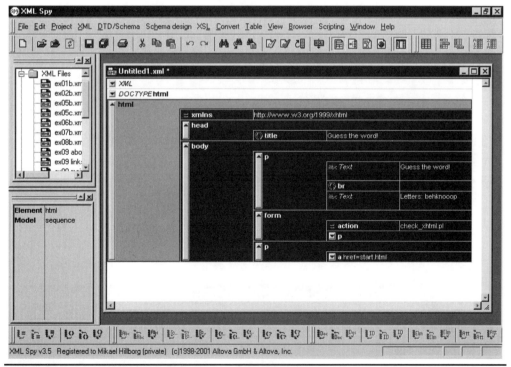

Figure 12-5 *The enhanced grid view in XML Spy 3.5*

Clicking an element expands or collapses the content of that element. Thus, you can see all details of a particular piece of the code without losing the feel of the overall structure.

Entry Helpers

XML Spy has a useful entry helper feature, which can be switched off when you don't want to use it. The tool checks the DTD to determine which attributes are allowed for each element. After you type an element, a drop-down menu appears and you can choose some of the attributes that can be provided with the element. Figure 12-6 shows how the entry help feature looks.

This is a neat feature if you have a hard time remembering all the XHTML attributes. You can easily browse the allowed attributes for a particular element. In addition, mandatory children to new elements can be added automatically. This is also useful when you're learning a new XML-based language because the tool tells you which elements you need to provide.

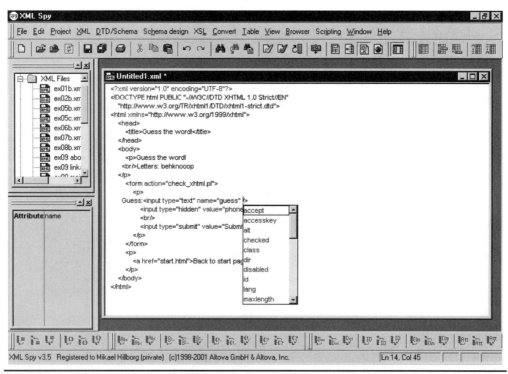

Figure 12-6   *The entry helper function in XML Spy 3.5*

TIP

More information about XML Spy can be obtained from **http://www.xmlspy.com.**

HTML-Kit

While XML Spy is for professional editing of XML files in general, HTML-kit focuses on HTML and HTML-related languages, such as XHTML.

Conversion

HTML-Kit can convert HTML documents to XHTML. However, the final document might have to be edited because HTML documents quite commonly contain errors. When you convert an HTML document to XHTML using HTML-Kit, then the window is split into two sections: the source document is displayed to the left and the new document to the right (see Figure 12-7).

You can compare the two documents to see how the document was converted. At the bottom, you can click items in a list of errors or informative text.

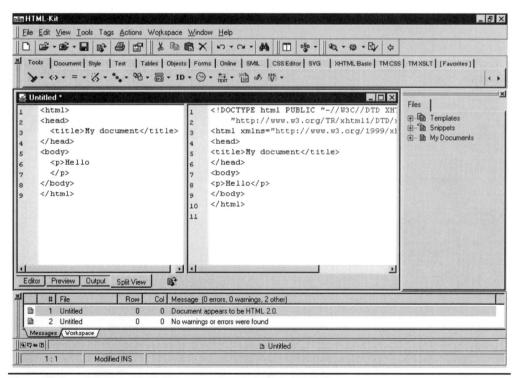

Figure 12-7   *HTML to XHTML conversion in HTML-Kit 1.0*

Plug-ins

One of the key strengths of the HTML-Kit is the enormous amount of free third-party plug-ins available for the tool. The plug-ins are usually simple—only an extra menu of choices that appear as a number of tabs below the standard menu—but many are available. Editing and development become fun and easy when you have all the elements and attributes, as well as combinations of elements and attributes, available on simple and often nicely laid-out menus.

A plug-in is available for XHTML Basic that can be downloaded from the HTML-Kit site. The URL is http://www.chami.com/html-kit/.

XHTML Support in the Nokia Mobile Internet Toolkit

A couple years ago, Nokia released one of the first professional and free development kits for WAP. This is now called the Nokia Mobile Internet Toolkit and it's out in version 3.

XHTML Editing

One of the best features of this development kit is it now supports XHTML, and not only editing of the source code, but emulation of XHTML-compatible handheld devices. Figure 12-8 shows how it can look.

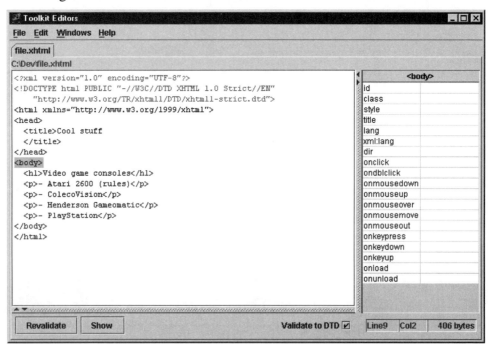

Figure 12-8   *Editing XHTML content in the Nokia Mobile Internet Toolkit editor*

You edit the code in a simple, but easy to use, editor. The code can be validated, and when it is valid, it can be displayed on the emulated handheld device. A nice feature of the editor is it shows the attributes, similar to the entry helpers in XML Spy. When you move the cursor in the editor and position it over an element, all possible attributes are displayed in the window to the right.

Simulating Different Types of Devices

By changing the device settings in the Nokia Mobile Internet Toolkit, you can easily simulate different types of devices by changing to a different screen size. You can also enable and disable colors. These features might seem simple at first sight, but they make it easy to test your application for two of the most important characteristics of many handheld devices: the lack of colors and no standard screen size.

CHAPTER

13

Building WML 2.0 Applications

IN THIS CHAPTER:

Basics

Making Navigation Easier

Using Variables

Jumps

Using the Timer

Integrating Phone Functionality

Using Scripts

Building WML 1.*x*-compliant Sites

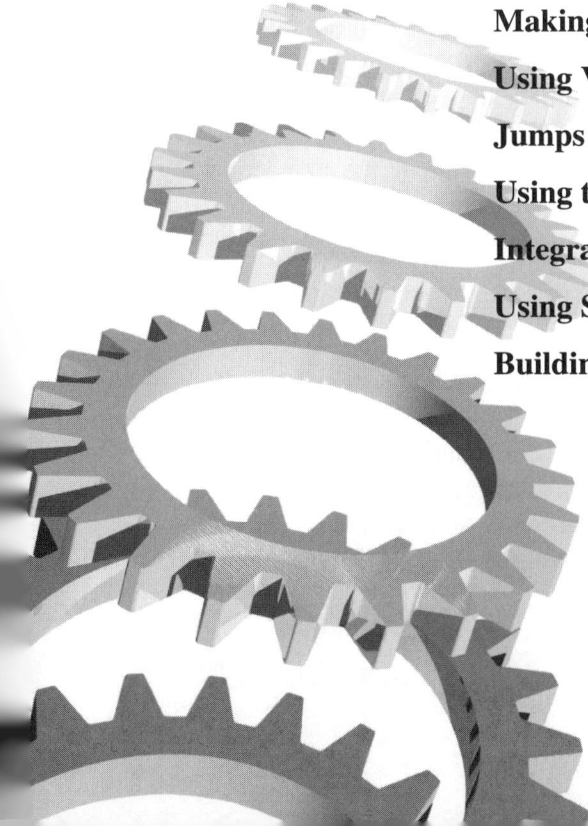

The Wireless Markup Language versions 1.1 and 1.2 has been used for several years now all over the world in 2G and 2.5G networks. Unfortunately, it wasn't the success the industry expected, so the manufacturers, operators, service providers, and software development companies joined forces and released WAP 2.0 at the end of July 2001.

Many opinions exist about WML 1.1 and 1.2 and why it never became a success. Here are a few thoughts. You might disagree but, because no one has the answer, feel free to draw your own conclusions. WML 1.*x* was a completely new language. Developers who created web pages weren't interested in learning the language because it had no support for color graphics and the sites that could be created with the language weren't good enough for the developer community. Basic tables looked ugly on the limited handsets out at that time and some didn't even support the simplest elements, such as em, and b. The language used a metaphor of decks and cards with which developers weren't familiar. Working with timers, jumps, and variables was more like programming than formatted markup. In addition, 2G networks and circuit-switched connections required that the user wait around 20 seconds simply to establish a connection with the network. That wasn't fast enough to motivate the access to such limited pages.

With WML 2.0, things are about to change. Developers can write all their code in XHTML if they want to, and most of the elements and attributes will be familiar to them. In addition, they can use some of the more complex functions, such as timers, pictograms, cards, jumps, and phone functionality if they want to explore that side of WML. Today, handsets are coming out on the market with a color display, as well as support for the GIF and JPG formats. These formats add lots of opportunities compared to the limited and monochrome WBMP type 0 format. 2.5G packet switched networks are also becoming common. They more or less eliminate the connection phase people are used to from the circuit-switched 2G networks.

Basics

WML 2.0 is a mix of XHTML and a number of elements and attributes unique for Wireless Markup Language (WML). The idea is to provide compatibility with XHTML and, at the same time, extend the language with functions that are useful for Mobile Internet applications. Service providers can then choose to develop applications using XHTML only—to make the sites compatible with ordinary web browsers—or to include some of the unique WML features, such as variables and timer functionality.

A page implemented in WML 2.0 begins with the standard XML header, followed by the DOCTYPE declaration. The actual code can be implemented using two different paradigms: a standard HTML body or a set of cards, often referred to as a *deck*.

HTML Body vs. a Deck of Cards

Pages implemented using the standard HTML body have the following structure:

```
<?xml version="1.0"?>
<!DOCTYPE html PUBLIC "-//WAPFORUM//DTD WML 2.0//EN"
  "http://www.wapforum.org/dtd/wml20.dtd">
<html xmlns="http://www.w3.org/1999/xhtml"
      xmlns:wml="http://www.wapforum.org/2001/wml">
  <head>
    <title>Title
    </title>
    ...
  </head>
  <body>
    ...
  </body>
</html>
```

The default namespace is the XHTML namespace. In addition, you have access to the WML elements and attributes using the WML namespace identifier.

The head element can contain the usual head information, as in HTML and XHTML, such as metainformation or a link to an external style sheet.

Using the Body Element

Depending on which type of site you're implementing, you might want to use either a deck of cards, after the head element, or a body element, as in HTML and XHTML. If you need to stay compatible with ordinary desktop computers and web browsers, you should use the body element. If you're making a site that's meant to be used with mobile phones only, then you could go for a deck of cards, which you'll become acquainted with soon. Here's how the code might look if you choose to use the body element:

```
<?xml version="1.0"?>
<!DOCTYPE html PUBLIC "-//WAPFORUM//DTD WML 2.0//EN"
  "http://www.wapforum.org/dtd/wml20.dtd">
<html xmlns="http://www.w3.org/1999/xhtml"
```

```
  xmlns:wml="http://www.wapforum.org/2001/wml">
<head>
  <title>Hello
  </title>
</head>
<body>
  <p>Hello!
  </p>
</body>
</html>
```

You should be familiar with this code because it resembles ordinary HTML. In this case, you've only used elements from the XHTML language, which is one of the features of WML 2.0. It supports a number of modules from XHTML.

The second alternative is to use a deck of cards instead of the body element.

Using a Deck of Cards

Cards can be listed after the head element. Each card represents a screen view on a handheld device, but each card might contain text that doesn't fit the display, so the user might have to scroll to read all the text. Using cards has some benefits. You can perform jumps in the code between cards. For example, one card might display a welcome message for a second or two, and then the user could be redirected automatically to another card. An additional card might handle user input and so forth. Here's the basic structure of a WML 2.0 document that's implemented using a number of cards.

```
<?xml version="1.0"?>
<!DOCTYPE html PUBLIC "-//WAPFORUM//DTD WML 2.0//EN"
  "http://www.wapforum.org/dtd/wml20.dtd">
<html xmlns="http://www.w3.org/1999/xhtml"
      xmlns:wml="http://www.wapforum.org/2001/wml">
  <head>
    <title>Cards
    </title>
    ...
  </head>
  <wml:card id="startCard">
    ...
  </wml:card>
  <wml:card id="secondCard">
    ...
```

```
    </wml:card>
      ...
    <wml:card id="card_N">
      ...
    </wml:card>
</html>
```

Instead of using a body that contains the code, a number of cards are provided. Each card can implement arbitrary functionality, such as managing input, communication with a server, displaying text, images, tables, and so forth.

Mixing XHTML and WML

Check the previous example and you'll see the elements that aren't available in XHTML use the WML prefix. If you're creating a site that's going to be browsed on ordinary HTML (or more precise XHTML) browsers, then you must use the correct DOCTYPE declaration. Otherwise, the WAP gateway might refuse to tokenize the code into WBXML and it won't reach the mobile devices.

If you're going to make use of all the elements in WML 2.0 that are tailor made for mobile devices, however, you'll have to prefix these elements and attributes with the XML namespace called WML.

Here's another example that illustrates how WML 2.0 uses a mix of XHTML with WML unique elements and attributes.

```
<?xml version="1.0"?>
<!DOCTYPE html PUBLIC "-//WAPFORUM//DTD WML 2.0//EN"
  "http://www.wapforum.org/dtd/wml20.dtd">
<html xmlns="http://www.w3.org/1999/xhtml"
      xmlns:wml="http://www.wapforum.org/2001/wml">
  <head>
    <title>Hello</title>
  </head>
  <body>
    <p wml:mode="nowrap">Uncle Joe owns an ARP 2600 (a black).
    </p>
  </body>
</html>
```

In this example, XHTML is used almost exclusively with one exception: the wml:mode attribute. The wml:mode attribute is used to tell the browser that if the text can't be displayed on a single line, then the words at the end should be truncated and not wrapped to a new line.

Formatting

The p element is used in the previous example to provide a piece of text. As you can see, the wml:mode attribute, which is optional, can be used to provide instructions for the interpreter about the text wrapping mode. The default is *wrap*, which means the text will continue on the next line. Some of the common formatting elements you probably know from HTML are also available in WML 2.0.

Boldface, Italics, Strong, and Emphasis

Boldface text, italics, strong text, and text with emphasis can be provided using the b, i, strong, and em elements, respectively. In WML 1.2, these elements should be used with care because the phones and the generation of browsers used didn't necessarily have support for these elements. Things have changed since then, though, and the browsers and phones that use WML 2.0 are more sophisticated. Text which is marked up using these elements will probably be rendered to the screen as you would expect.

Text Sizes

The small and big elements can be used in WML 2.0 to create text that's smaller than the default and larger than the default size, as the following example demonstrates.

```
<?xml version="1.0"?>
<!DOCTYPE html PUBLIC "-//WAPFORUM//DTD WML 2.0//EN"
  "http://www.wapforum.org/dtd/wml20.dtd">
<html xmlns="http://www.w3.org/1999/xhtml"
      xmlns:wml="http://www.wapforum.org/2001/wml">
  <head>
    <title>Hello</title>
  </head>
  <body>
    <p><big>Hello!</big>
    </p>
  </body>
</html>
```

How much larger and smaller the text is rendered depends on the user agent. Some user agents might discard the information and always render with the default size.

Using WCSS to Format the Markup

Although WML 2.0 contains a number of elements that can be associated with the actual formatting on screen, such as the small, big, i, and b elements, cascading style sheets (CSS) is the best way to format content according to a certain user agent's capabilities. For example, a user agent with a limited display might leave out the borders of a table. Another user agent equipped with a color screen might render the b element with another color instead of making it boldface. Things like the amount of space inserted between paragraphs can also be adjusted using CSS or, to be more precise, WCSS, which is the WAP implementation of cascading style sheets. WAP CSS is similar to CSS2 style sheets with some limitations and extensions. The scope of this book isn't to list all possible properties and values. You should read the WCSS specification (downloaded from http://www.wapforum.org) if you need to learn the details about this. You should be familiar with how WCSS can be used, however, so here's an example:

```
<?xml version="1.0"?>
<!DOCTYPE html PUBLIC "-//WAPFORUM//DTD WML 2.0//EN"
  "http://www.wapforum.org/dtd/wml20.dtd">
<html xmlns="http://www.w3.org/1999/xhtml"
      xmlns:wml="http://www.wapforum.org/2001/wml">
  <head>
    <meta name="Author" content="Joe Smith"/>
    <style type='text/css'>p a { font-size: 8pt}
    </style>
    <title>Bob
    </title>
  </head>
  <wml:card id='bob'>
    <p>Not too long ago, Uncle Bob acquired two vintage machines,
        an ARP 2500 and a Fairlight CMI IIx.
        <br/><a href='more.wml'>Read more about it.</a>
    </p>
  </wml:card>
</html>
```

An internal style sheet is used in the previous example. It sets the font size for the a and p elements to 8 points. External style sheets are also possible to use in WML 2.0. In that case, the file resides in a file of its own. The style sheet file looks like the following:

```
p a { font-size: 8pt}
```

WML 2.0 then has to refer to this file, like this:

```
<?xml version="1.0"?>
<!DOCTYPE html PUBLIC "-//WAPFORUM//DTD WML 2.0//EN"
```

```
      "http://www.wapforum.org/wml20.dtd">
<html xmlns="http://www.w3.org/1999/xhtml"
      xmlns:wml="http://www.wapforum.org/2001/wml">
  <head>
    <meta name="Author" content="Joe Smith"/>
    <link href='style.css' type='text/css' rel='stylesheet'/>
    <title>Bob
    </title>
  </head>
  <wml:card id='bob'>
    <p>Not too long ago, Uncle Bob acquired two vintage machines,
       an ARP 2500 and a Fairlight CMI IIx.
       <br/><a href='more.wml'>Read more about it.</a>
    </p>
  </wml:card>
</html>
```

The link element is used to point at the style.css file. Because the link element can be used for things other than pointing at style sheets, the rel attribute must be set to 'stylesheet'. Because the value of the href attribute is a relative link in this example, the style.css file must reside in the same directory as the WML 2.0 file.

As opposed to the previous type of link, which deals with linked style sheets, two other elements that can be used to create hypertext links are in WML 2.0. One of those elements is *a*.

Links

In WML 2.0, you can use the *a* element to introduce a link from one card to another or from a card in one deck (file) to a card in another deck.

Linking to a Card

Linking to a card in the same deck is implemented using a fragment identifier, followed by the ID of the card. The following example illustrates this:

```
<?xml version="1.0"?>
<!DOCTYPE html PUBLIC "-//WAPFORUM//DTD WML 2.0//EN"
  "http://www.wapforum.org/dtd/wml20.dtd">
<html xmlns="http://www.w3.org/1999/xhtml"
      xmlns:wml="http://www.wapforum.org/2001/wml">
  <head>
    <title>Links</title>
```

```
  </head>
  <wml:card id='start'>
    <p>Choose<br/>
      <a href='#news'>Latest news</a>
      <a href='#wf'>Weather forecast</a>
    </p>
  </wml:card>
  <wml:card id="news">
    <p>Lower prices on donuts!
       <br/><a href='#start'>Back</a>
    </p>
  </wml:card>
  <wml:card id='wf'>
    <p>Mostly sunshine, but cloudy in the west and snow in the
       northern parts of the country.
       <br/><a href='#start'>Back</a>
    </p>
  </wml:card>
</html>
```

As you can see, you can link between cards in the same file, using a # followed by the ID of the card. In the previous example, the first card, called 'start', is displayed when the file has been downloaded from the server to the phone. The user can follow one of the two links to the second card called 'news' or the third card called 'wf'. From these cards, there's a link back to the first card. A better alternative exists for implementing backwards navigation, though, which you learn about in the section "Enter Backward."

Linking to a Deck

Linking to another file that contains a new set of cards or a document implemented using an HTML body can be achieved in the following way:

```
<?xml version="1.0"?>
<!DOCTYPE html PUBLIC "-//WAPFORUM//DTD WML 2.0//EN"
  "http://www.wapforum.org/dtd/wml20.dtd">
<html xmlns="http://www.w3.org/1999/xhtml"
      xmlns:wml="http://www.wapforum.org/2001/wml">
  <head>
    <title>Links</title>
  </head>
  <wml:card id='start'>
```

```
    <p>Choose<br/>
      <a href='http://www.example.com/news.wml'>Latest news</a>
      <a href='http://www.example.com/wf.wml'>Weather forecast</a>
    </p>
  </wml:card>
</html>
```

In the previous example, new files are downloaded from the network, depending on which choice the user makes. These files might contain either new sets of cards or they can be implemented in pure XHTML only.

Linking to a Card in Another Deck

If you want to link to a new file, as in the previous example, but still refer to individual cards in this file, you could use the following syntax.

```
<?xml version="1.0"?>
<!DOCTYPE html PUBLIC "-//WAPFORUM//DTD WML 2.0//EN"
  "http://www.wapforum.org/dtd/wml20.dtd">
<html xmlns="http://www.w3.org/1999/xhtml"
      xmlns:wml="http://www.wapforum.org/2001/wml">
  <head>
    <title>Links</title>
  </head>
  <wml:card id='start'>
    <p>Choose<br/>
      <a href='http://www.example.com/content.wml#news'>Latest news</a>
      <a href='http://www.example.com/content.wml#wf'>Weather forecast</a>
    </p>
  </wml:card>
</html>
```

Here, the links lead to another file, named content.wml, which contains at least two cards with the IDs, news, and wf. Thus, it is possible to jump from a file to individual cards in another file using this syntax.

In the previous example, the links are used in a paragraph only. Links can also be provided in a table.

Tables

In WML 2.0, tables can't be nested and the wml:columns attribute must be used to specify the number of columns in the table. The following example presents a list of products:

```
<?xml version="1.0"?>
<!DOCTYPE html PUBLIC "-//WAPFORUM//DTD WML 2.0//EN"
  "http://www.wapforum.org/dtd/wml20.dtd">
<html xmlns="http://www.w3.org/1999/xhtml"
      xmlns:wml="http://www.wapforum.org/2001/wml">
  <head>
    <title>Links</title>
  </head>
  <wml:card id='main'>
    <table wml:columns="3">
      <tr>
        <td>Prod.#</td>
        <td>Name</td>
        <td>Price</td>
      </tr>
      <tr>
        <td>1.</td>
        <td>FluxCam Pro</td>
        <td>$$199</td>
      </tr>
      <tr>
        <td>2.</td>
        <td>USB mate</td>
        <td>$$29</td>
      </tr>
    </table>
  </wml:card>
</html>
```

The previous table contains two rows and three columns. The elements you're familiar with from ordinary HTML are used, except for a few attributes, such as the wml:columns attribute. This attribute must be provided and specifies the number of columns in the table. Note, the table occurs in a card. If you want to increase the compatibility with nonmobile devices, then you should replace the wml:card with a body element. In the example, this wouldn't make any difference because only one card is used and no jumps occur in the code between cards. An ordinary web browser for a desktop computer would simply discard the wml:columns attribute and render the table correctly because no need exists to specify the number of columns for that type of browser.

Note, two $ characters are provided. As you see later, in the section "Using Variables," the dollar character has a special meaning in WML. To make the WML interpreter understand you mean the dollar character and nothing else, you must provide two consecutive characters.

In the table, each table cell contained a piece of text, but you can also use images in tables.

Images

Images can be used in tables or paragraphs. In WML 2.0, the alt attribute is mandatory. In pure XHTML or HTML, it's also mandatory, but browsers tend not to enforce this requirement and, consequently, many developers don't use it.

Alternative Text

The alt attribute fills two purposes. First, devices that don't have graphic capabilities can present the content of the alt attribute instead of the image. Although almost all new WAP devices introduced on the market do have support for graphics, they might not display all pictures well, such as extremely large WBMP files, GIF, or JPEG files. The second reason is blind people are helped so much when the alt attribute is used properly. Graphic-intensive applications that aren't designed with alternative presentations in mind are painful for this group of people.

Transferring WML code to WAP devices isn't possible without supplying the alt attribute for the image element. The WML code won't validate successfully according to the DTD and this is carried out by the WAP gateway when the WML code is tokenized into a compact binary representation called Wireless Binary XML (WBXML). Here's an example, which illustrates the use of the alt attribute and another attribute called wml:type.

```
<?xml version="1.0"?>
<!DOCTYPE html PUBLIC "-//WAPFORUM//DTD WML 2.0//EN"
  "http://www.wapforum.org/dtd/wml20.dtd">
<html xmlns="http://www.w3.org/1999/xhtml"
      xmlns:wml="http://www.wapforum.org/2001/wml">
  <head>
    <title>Gallery</title>
  </head>
  <wml:card id='one'>
    <p><img src='porsche.jpg' alt='A red Porsche 911' wml:type='image/jpeg'/>
    </p>
  </wml:card>
  <wml:card id='two'>
    <p><img src='buick.gif' alt='My Buick' wml:type='image/gif'/>
    </p>
```

```
    </wml:card>
    <wml:card id='three'>
        <p><img src='Merc.wbmp' alt='A Mercedes Benz'
wml:type='image/vnd.wap.wbmp'/>
        </p>
    </wml:card>
</html>
```

To give the user agent a hint about which content type the graphical object has, the wml:type attribute has been used. The alt attribute must be provided and, in the previous example, it's even more important that it contains a suitable textual description. This is because three different graphic formats are used and the user agent might be unable to handle all three of them. The User Agent Profile (UAProf) can be used to examine this, though.

Pictograms

A *feature,* which is unique for WML, is the option to use a local source for graphics. There's a core of graphics, which all phone manufacturers must install to be WAP 2.0 compatible, as well as an optional additional set of graphics.

The core contains arrows, buttons, actions like stop and back signs, message-related graphics such as envelopes, state graphics like trademark and copyright symbols, media symbols such as book, CD, and video illustrations, as well as general info graphics like a sign that indicates a toll-free call. Pictograms in WML 2.0 are used like this:

```
<?xml version="1.0"?>
<!DOCTYPE html PUBLIC "-//WAPFORUM//DTD WML 2.0//EN"
    "http://www.wapforum.org/dtd/wml20.dtd">
<html xmlns="http://www.w3.org/1999/xhtml"
        xmlns:wml="http://www.wapforum.org/2001/wml">
    <head>
        <title>Stop!</title>
    </head>
    <body>
        <p><img wml:localsrc='pict:///core/action/stop'
                src='http://www.example.com/pics/stop.wbmp'
                alt='Stop!'/>
        You did not enter the address!
        <br/><a href='main.wml'>Go back</a>
        </p>
    </body>
</html>
```

The attribute wml:localsrc contains the local address to the pictogram. A special scheme, pict, is used in the address to indicate it's a pictogram. An additional external address is provided if the pictogram can't be retrieved. In the previous example, the core/action/stop bitmap must be supported, though, so the user agent shouldn't have to fetch the external bitmap.

The Wireless Bitmap

In the previous example, the src attribute referred to a wbmp file. Since the first version of WML was released, the Wireless Bitmap format—type 0—has been the graphics format of choice. In fact, type 0 has been the only graphics format for WAP. This is about to change, though, now that more sophisticated devices have hit the market and UAProf can be used to sense which graphics formats a user agent is compatible with. WAP phones are on the market that can display not only WBMP images, but also GIF87a, GIF89a, and JPEG images.

If you want to be compatible with as many handsets as possible, however, WBMP is the best choice because it's the only image format that must be supported by devices with graphics capabilities.

WBMP images are monochrome and, in most cases, are displayed as black images with a white background, although this can be adjusted in some handsets. The file extension should be wbmp and the content type (MIME format) is image/vnd.wap.wbmp.

Making Navigation Easier

Spending time with user interface aspects is an essential part of WAP services. You can use many of the elements from XHTML but also elements and attributes in the WML namespace, which are tailored for small handheld devices.

In WML 2.0, a number of elements and attributes are available for you to make navigation easier for the end user. Access key can be used to provide shortcuts.

Using Access Keys

Access keys are available in ordinary HTML, but they're seldom used for ordinary web pages. In WAP, though, quick and easy navigation is even more important because it usually takes longer to follow a link and input text on a WAP device than on a desktop computer, which has a QWERTY keyboard. This is the case if access keys aren't used. One of the reasons access keys haven't been used much for WAP services is they weren't part of WML 1.1, but were introduced in WML 1.2.

When access keys are used correctly, they can greatly enhance a WAP service. One of the drawbacks of many WAP services is they require too many clicks. Using a phone keyboard can be tedious and the user often gets tired quickly if too many clicks are needed to use a service. Imagine the following service:

```
<?xml version="1.0"?>
<!DOCTYPE html PUBLIC "-//WAPFORUM//DTD WML 2.0//EN"
  "http://www.wapforum.org/dtd/wml20.dtd">
<html xmlns="http://www.w3.org/1999/xhtml"
      xmlns:wml="http://www.wapforum.org/2001/wml">
  <head>
    <title>Content Portal</title>
  </head>
  <body>
    <p>Content Portal
      <br/><a href='ec.wml'>Economy News</a>
      <br/><a href='na.wml'>International News</a>
      <br/><a href='int.wml'>National News</a>
      <br/><a href='we.wml'>Weather Forecast</a>
      <br/><a href='games.wml'>Fun &amp; Games</a>
    </p>
  </body>
</html>
```

The cursor is positioned at the first link, and if the user wants to access the fifth link from the top, he or she must press the down key four times to move the cursor down to the link and a fifth time to activate it. If access keys are used, your application could look like the following:

```
<?xml version="1.0"?>
<!DOCTYPE html PUBLIC "-//WAPFORUM//DTD WML 2.0//EN"
  "http://www.wapforum.org/dtd/wml20.dtd">
<html xmlns="http://www.w3.org/1999/xhtml"
      xmlns:wml="http://www.wapforum.org/2001/wml">
  <head>
    <title>Content Portal</title>
  </head>
  <body>
    <p>Content Portal
      <br/><a href='ec.wml' accesskey='1'>1.Economy News</a>
      <br/><a href='na.wml' accesskey='2'>2.International News</a>
      <br/><a href='int.wml' accesskey='3'>3.National News</a>
      <br/><a href='we.wml' accesskey='4'>4.Weather Forecast</a>
```

```
        <br/><a href='games.wml' accesskey='5'>5.Fun &amp; Games</a>
    </p>
  </body>
</html>
```

To get access to the fifth link from the top, the user could press the number 5 on the phone's keyboard. As you can imagine, access keys dramatically reduce the number of key presses required to access a WAP service.

Using Variables

Variables can be used in many situations in WML. When the user types in text, a variable is set to the result. A single-choice or multiple-choice selection sets a variable, the value of which can then be used, for example, in a WMLScript or transferred to a server script.

Reading the Value of a Variable

A variable can be read using the $ character. As you know from a previous example, you then need to provide two $ characters if you want to display a $. In the following code, a variable is read using the $ syntax:

```
<?xml version="1.0"?>
<!DOCTYPE html PUBLIC "-//WAPFORUM//DTD WML 2.0//EN"
  "http://www.wapforum.org/dtd/wml20.dtd">
<html xmlns="http://www.w3.org/1999/xhtml"
      xmlns:wml="http://www.wapforum.org/2001/wml">
  <head>
    <title>Result</title>
  </head>
  <body>
    <p>You got $(val) points.
        <br/><a href='main.wml'>Back</a>
    </p>
  </body>
</html>
```

In the previous code, $(val) is substituted with the value of the variable val. All WML variables are global. WML variables are resident in the device's memory and can be used even if a new WML file is loaded. This is the case with the previous example because no place exists in the code where the variable is set. Instead, it was set in another file and this page simply shows the result to the user.

In WML 2.0, there's a second way of reading the variable. The getvar element results in a variable substitution and the previous example could look like the following if the getvar element is used instead of the $ character:

```
<?xml version="1.0"?>
<!DOCTYPE html PUBLIC "-//WAPFORUM//DTD WML 2.0//EN"
  "http://www.wapforum.org/dtd/wml20.dtd">
<html xmlns="http://www.w3.org/1999/xhtml"
      xmlns:wml="http://www.wapforum.org/2001/wml">
  <head>
    <title>Result</title>
  </head>
  <body>
    <p>You got <wml:getvar name='val'/> points.
       <br/><a href='main.wml'>Back</a>
    </p>
  </body>
</html>
```

The getvar element was used to refer to the val variable. Note, the WML namespace was used because the getvar element isn't part of any XHTML module; it's an element, which is unique for WML.

Writing Parameterized Code Using Variable References

The main difference between $ and the getvar element is that the $ character can be used in attribute values. This means you can set a variable in a card and, for example, jump to another card or file where the variable is used in an attribute value. The WML code then becomes parameterized of dynamic in the sense that the code itself might change, depending on which values certain variables have. These variables can be set as the result of user input or some computation in a WMLScript. Before going into that, let's see how variables are assigned values.

Setting a Variable

A variable can be assigned a value using the setvar element. The *setvar* element has two attributes: name and value. The name attribute contains the name of the variable and the value attribute contains the value the variable should be assigned. It might look like the following:

```
<setvar name='items' value='0'/>
<setvar name='month' value='Jan'/>
```

The variable item is set to the value 0 and the variable month is set to the value Jan. Note, although 0 is quoted and meant to be the number zero, WML doesn't make any distinction between numbers and text strings. Everything is text strings. In WMLScript, though, a number of data types are used and a distinction exists between numbers and text strings, as you will see in the section "Using Scripts," in this chapter.

Free Text Input

Another way of setting a variable is to use some of the elements for user input. With some applications, you might want to query the user for a piece of text, such as the user's full name, a street name, or anything that requires text input rather than choosing an item in a selection list. In this case, the input element is what you should use. It has an attribute—name—that should be set to the name of the variable, which is assigned the text message the user types in. The input element can be used like this:

```
<?xml version="1.0"?>
<!DOCTYPE html PUBLIC "-//WAPFORUM//DTD WML 2.0//EN"
  "http://www.wapforum.org/dtd/wml20.dtd">
<html xmlns="http://www.w3.org/1999/xhtml"
      xmlns:wml="http://www.wapforum.org/2001/wml">
  <head>
    <title>Gallery</title>
  </head>
  <wml:card id="inp">
    <p>First name:
     <input name='firstname'/>
     <br/><a href='#display'>Next</a>
    </p>
  </wml:card>
  <wml:card id="display">
    <p>Hello <getvar name='firstname'/>!
       <br/>Welcome to the mobile shop.
    </p>
  </wml:card>
</html>
```

The user must provide his first name, and then can follow the link to the next card, which displays the name. If the user were to follow the link without inputting the name first, then the variable would contain an empty string. If you want to provide a default value (just in case the user skips the input procedure), then the value attribute can be used and it should be set to the default value.

You should think about a few things when you use the input element to input text. Most WAP services are accessed with phones, which have a limited keyboard. Some keys must be pressed several times to obtain a certain character, or text prediction technologies, such as T9, can be used, but the prediction software doesn't always give the user what she expects. If possible, avoid asking for long text messages. If you want the user to input his full name, ask yourself if it's enough to retrieve the first name, the surname, or a short user-defined name. Long text inputs generally scare people away from using the service because it might take minutes to type in the text on a phone keyboard.

Passwords

It's possible to hide the text the user types in; instead, an asterisk is displayed for each character. To achieve this effect, the type attribute should be set to password, as in the following example:

```
<?xml version="1.0"?>
<!DOCTYPE html PUBLIC "-//WAPFORUM//DTD WML 2.0//EN"
  "http://www.wapforum.org/dtd/wml20.dtd">
<html xmlns="http://www.w3.org/1999/xhtml"
      xmlns:wml="http://www.wapforum.org/2001/wml">
  <head>
    <title>Info</title>
  </head>
  <body>
    <p>Social security number:
     <input name='num' type='password'/>
     <br/><a href='next.wml'>Next</a>
    </p>
  </body>
</html>
```

The type attribute is set to 'password', which means the interpreter shouldn't display the actual characters onscreen. However, the 'num' variable will contain the value in plain text. The type attribute fills only one purpose: to hide the characters when they're presented onscreen.

Formats

In some cases, you might want the user to type in information according to a certain format. For example, you might ask for the month followed by a slash, followed by the day, such as 03/14 or 12/25. To be sure the user types in numbers and not letters, and to be sure a slash is between the month and the day, you can use the format attribute, like this:

```
<?xml version="1.0"?>
<!DOCTYPE html PUBLIC "-//WAPFORUM//DTD WML 2.0//EN"
  "http://www.wapforum.org/dtd/wml20.dtd">
<html xmlns="http://www.w3.org/1999/xhtml"
      xmlns:wml="http://www.wapforum.org/2001/wml">
  <head>
    <title>Input Date</title>
  </head>
  <body>
    <p>Month and day:
     <input name='date' wml:format='NN\/NN'/>
     <br/><a href='processDate.wml'>Next</a>
    </p>
  </body>
</html>
```

Note, the format attribute needs to be prefixed with the WML namespace because it's an attribute, which is unique for WML. A capital *N* represents a numeric character, such as 0 or 9. A backslash means the character after the backslash should be displayed. So, if you're asking for two numeric characters, the device will then insert a slash. How this is carried out is device-dependent. After the slash, the user is prompted to input two additional numeric characters. Most devices implement this, so it becomes impossible for the user to press any alphanumeric characters. For example, if the device is an ordinary phone, it becomes impossible to press a key several times to obtain an alphanumeric character. Only the number is obtained, no matter how many times the user presses the key to toggle between the number and the other characters related to that key.

Other codes that work the same way as *N* are *a*, which means lowercase letters, and symbols, but not numbers. If you want to allow any type of character, you can use the code *m*. The code *M* means the same, but defaults to uppercase, as opposed to *m*, which defaults to lowercase letters.

Sending Variable Values to a Server Script

In many cases, the user is asked to input some information, and then the information is passed on to a server, which stores the data in a database, on disk, or simply performs some computation, and then replies with a new WML document. A CGI script can receive parameters, which have been input by the user, the following way:

```
<?xml version="1.0"?>
<!DOCTYPE html PUBLIC "-//WAPFORUM//DTD WML 2.0//EN"
  "http://www.wapforum.org/dtd/wml20.dtd">
<html xmlns="http://www.w3.org/1999/xhtml"
      xmlns:wml="http://www.wapforum.org/2001/wml">
  <head>
    <title>Name And Date</title>
  </head>
  <body>
    <p>Name:
      <input name='fullname'/>
      <br/>Month and day:
      <input name='date' wml:format='NN\/NN'/>
      <br/><a
href='process.cgi?name=$(fullname)&amp;date=$(date)'>Send</a>
    </p>
  </body>
</html>
```

The variables are then sent in an HTTP get request to the server, as parameters in the URL. As you can see, the variable substitution syntax is used to refer to the variables "name" and "date." The parameters in the URL are separated by the & character and it must be provided using the Unicode syntax, which is &amp. On the server side, the script is implemented, so it always expects two parameters—name and date—that can be processed further. The server script must reply with a new WML document and the content of the responded document might be dependant on the values of the variables.

Using Postfields

The previous example can also be implemented using the postfield element. For example, if you want to pass on the parameters to a server script using the HTTP post request method, rather than appending the parameters to the URL, then you must use the postfield elements. With the *postfield element,* you can specify which method should be used: get or post. *Post* is a bit different because, with that method, the parameters are transferred in the body of the HTTP message rather than in the address. This is much safer because the address basically ends up everywhere on the Internet in server and router logs. Here is the same example as the previous one, but it's implemented using the postfield element and the post method.

```
<?xml version="1.0"?>
<!DOCTYPE html PUBLIC"-//WAPFORUM//DTD WML 2.0//EN"
  "http://www.wapforum.org/wml20.dtd">
<html xmlns="http://www.w3.org/1999/xhtml"
      xmlns:wml="http://www.wapforum.org/2001/wml">
  <head>
    <title>Name And Date</title>
  </head>
  <body>
    <p>Name:
     <input name='fullname'/>
     <br/>Month and day:
     <input name='date' wml:format='NN\/NN'/>
     <br/>
     <wml:anchor>Send
       <wml:go href='process.cgi' wml:method='post'>
         <wml:postfield name='theName' value='$(fullname)'/>
         <wml:postfield name='theDate' value='$(date)'/>
       </wml:go>
     </wml:anchor>
    </p>
  </body>
</html>
```

Two postfield elements exist: one for each parameter. You might notice there are two other elements we haven't discussed yet—wml:go and wml:anchor. A postfield element must occur inside a task element, such as wml:go. The wml:go element goes to an address. The *wml:go* element is similar to a link, but it can't occur in an *a* element and must be provided in the wml:anchor element. So, the *wml:anchor* element is similar to the *a* element, but it can contain a go task, which, in turn, can contain an arbitrary amount of postfields. With the wml:go element, you can specify which HTTP method should be used: get or post. Post is a bit safer and you can also transfer larger amounts of data using the post method. With the *get* method, you're restricted to the maximum length of a URL.

Notice how the variable substitution works. The variables fullname and date are input using the input elements, just above the wml:anchor element. In the wml:postfield elements, the names of the variables sent to the server are provided with the name attribute. This isn't necessarily the same name as the variables that were input earlier. Instead, they're referred to in the value attributes. The values of the name attributes are the names of the parameters transferred in the post and it's simply a matter of how the server script has been implemented. These parameters might require special names, such as theName and theDate.

Setting Variables to Change Attribute Values

In WML 2.0, you can use the variable substitution syntax to change the values of variables. Depending on what the user inputs, attributes can be set to certain values, as demonstrated in the following code:

```
<?xml version="1.0"?>
<!DOCTYPE html PUBLIC "-//WAPFORUM//DTD WML 2.0//EN"
  "http://www.wapforum.org/dtd/wml20.dtd">
<html xmlns="http://www.w3.org/1999/xhtml"
      xmlns:wml="http://www.wapforum.org/2001/wml">
  <head>
    <title>Archive</title>
  </head>
  <wml:card id='main'>
    <p>Picture name:
     <input name='picname'/>
     <br/><a href='#show'>Show it</a>
    </p>
  </wml:card>
  <wml:card id='show'>
    <p><img src='$(picname).gif' alt='$(picname)'/>
      <br/><a href='#main'>Back</a>
    </p>
  </wml:card>
</html>
```

There are two cards: main and show. In the first card, the name of a picture can be provided. When the user then follows the link, the image with that name is downloaded from the server and displayed on the phone. To implement this feature, you use variable substitution in the src and alt attributes of the img element. The characters ".gif" are appended to the value of the picname variable to obtain the image's filename.

Selection Lists

An element, which is similar to the input element, is select. This element doesn't let the user input free text, but she can choose among a number of options. The behavior, though, is similar to the input element. The select element sets a variable, specified with the name attribute, and you can give it with a default value, using the value attribute. Each option in the list of selections is specified with the option element.

Single Choice

A single choice selection can be implemented like the following:

```
<?xml version="1.0"?>
<!DOCTYPE html PUBLIC "-//WAPFORUM//DTD WML 2.0//EN"
    "http://www.wapforum.org/dtd/wml20.dtd">
<html xmlns="http://www.w3.org/1999/xhtml"
      xmlns:wml="http://www.wapforum.org/2001/wml">
  <head>
    <title>Select Size</title>
  </head>
  <body>
    <p>Select size:
      <select wml:name='theValue' wml:iname='theIndex'>
        <option value='S'>Small</option>
        <option value='M'>Medium</option>
        <option value='L'>Large</option>
        <option value='XL'>XLarge</option>
        <option value='XXL'>XXLarge</option>
      </select>
      <br/><a href='next.wml'>Next</a>
    </p>
  </body>
</html>
```

The select element includes an arbitrary number of option elements. Each *option* element represents an option that can be chosen. When the user selects one of the options, the variables provided in the wml:name and wml:iname attributes are set to that particular option. If the user chooses the second option in the previous example, then the variable 'theValue' is set to 'M' and 'theIndex' is set to 2 because the user chose the second option. If you want to provide default values for the name and iname variables, the wml:value and wml:ivalue attributes can be used.

Multiple Choices

Multiple choices are implemented almost the same way as single-choice selection lists. The only difference is you must add the multiple attribute to the selection element and set it to true. If you want to change the previous example to make it possible for the user to select more than one option, then the code would look like this:

```
<?xml version="1.0"?>
<!DOCTYPE html PUBLIC "-//WAPFORUM//DTD WML 2.0//EN"
  "http://www.wapforum.org/dtd/wml20.dtd">
<html xmlns="http://www.w3.org/1999/xhtml"
      xmlns:wml="http://www.wapforum.org/2001/wml">
  <head>
    <title>Select Size</title>
  </head>
  <body>
    <p>Select size (you may select more than one):
      <select wml:name='theValue' wml:iname='theIndex'
multiple='true'>
        <option value='S'>Small</option>
        <option value='M'>Medium</option>
        <option value='L'>Large</option>
        <option value='XL'>XLarge</option>
        <option value='XXL'>XXLarge</option>
      </select>
      <br/><a href='next.wml'>Next</a>
    </p>
  </body>
</html>
```

You might be wondering what the variables contain if the user selects more than one option. The answer is a semicolon-separated list. For example, if the user selects the first and second options, 'theValue' would be set to 'S;M' and 'theIndex' would contain the value 1;2'. This is a practical representation for several reasons. Server scripts, such as JSP and Perl, have functions that can easily traverse this representation. WMLScripts, which execute on the client side, on the handheld device, can be called from the WML code and the language has a comprehensive set of functions that operate on such a structure. In the section "Using Scripts," you learn how to implement your own WMLScript functions and call them from WML.

Grouping Options

Sometimes, you need to group options in selection lists. For example, some of the options might require a further explanation or you might want to group them together to make things more clear for the user. In that case, you can use the *optgroup* element, which is a container for option elements. Here, some sizes are grouped to tell the user which ones are always in stock and which aren't.

```xml
<?xml version="1.0"?>
<!DOCTYPE html PUBLIC "-//WAPFORUM//DTD WML 2.0//EN"
  "http://www.wapforum.org/dtd/wml20.dtd">
<html xmlns="http://www.w3.org/1999/xhtml"
      xmlns:wml="http://www.wapforum.org/2001/wml">
  <head>
    <title>Select Size</title>
  </head>
  <body>
    <p>Select size:
      <select wml:name='theValue' wml:iname='theIndex'>
        <optgroup label='Always in stock'>
          <option value='S'>Small</option>
          <option value='M'>Medium</option>
          <option value='L'>Large</option>
        </optgroup>
        <optgroup label='In limited amounts'>
          <option value='XL'>XLarge</option>
          <option value='XXL'>XXLarge</option>
        </optgroup>
      </select>
      <br/><a href='next.wml'>Next</a>
    </p>
  </body>
</html>
```

The optgroup has a mandatory attribute, called *label,* which should be set to the text displayed on the screen. User agents often render this text in another type of font or color and, possibly, with some additional graphics—such as a horizontal ruler—to clarify it's not an option.

Jumps

In a previous example, you saw it's possible to execute a wml:go in the wml:anchor element, and that the wml:go can contain a number of postfields. Let's look at the wml:go element more closely.

Jumping Forward

With the wml:go elements, a jump is executed from one place in the code to another. The destination can be located in the same file or in another file, and even at a particular place in another file.

Jumping When a Menu Item Is Chosen

As you saw in a previous example, the wml:go element can be used in the wml:anchor element. In this case, the text provided with the wml:anchor element is usually rendered as the *a* element, underlined. The wml:go element can exist in another element as well: the wml:do element. The *wml:do* element is used to provide a menu selection, which isn't meant to be rendered into the ordinary text flow as with links, but to appear in the device's menu system. An important attribute—role—is used with the wml:do element, as in the following example:

```
<?xml version="1.0"?>
<!DOCTYPE html PUBLIC "-//WAPFORUM//DTD WML 2.0//EN"
  "http://www.wapforum.org/dtd/wml20.dtd">
<html xmlns="http://www.w3.org/1999/xhtml"
      xmlns:wml="http://www.wapforum.org/2001/wml">
  <head>
    <title>Archive</title>
  </head>
  <wml:card id='start'>
    <wml:do title='Help' role='help'>
      <go href='#help'/>
    </wml:do>
    <p>Picture name:
     <input name='picname'/>
     <br/><a href='#show'>Show it</a>
    </p>
  </wml:card>
  <wml:card id='show'>
    <p><img src='$(picname).gif' alt='$(picname)'/>
```

```
    <br/><a href='#main'>Back</a>
  </p>
</wml:card>
<wml:card id='help'>
  <p>Type in the name and then follow the link
     to display the image.
     <br/><a href='#start'>Back</a>
  </p>
</wml:card>
</html>
```

The *role* attribute specifies which role the item should have, for example, positive for a positive acceptance, help for a help function or escape when the wml:do element represents an escape function. These are hints for the interpreting user agent to use the wml:do element at the most suitable place in the phone's menu system.

Note, in the previous example, the short form of the wml:go element, which doesn't have any content, is used. In a previous example, where the wml:go element contained a number of postfield elements, it had a start tag and an end tag. In this case, neither postfields elements nor other elements are used.

Many user agents will insert the wml:do element in the device's menu system. Typically, you might have to press and hold down the yes button on a phone to access the wml:do element.

Some people might argue that the wml:do element fills an important function for small handheld devices. Personally, I recommend you use the *a* and wml:anchor elements as much as possible instead. Users know what a link is when they see it. Many users, though, don't know how to access the wml:do element because it usually doesn't appear with the card's text on the display. In addition, different devices handle the wml:do elements differently, but all devices handle and render the *a* and anchor elements the same way. The *a* element is part of the XHTML framework and the wml:do element isn't. If you need to create XHTML-compatible sites, this is yet another reason to avoid the wml:do element.

From a Card to a New Deck

In the previous example, the wml:do element was used to jump from one card to another in the same document. You can jump from one card to another where the destination is a new document, like this:

```
<?xml version="1.0"?>
<!DOCTYPE html PUBLIC "-//WAPFORUM//DTD WML 2.0//EN"
   "http://www.wapforum.org/dtd/wml20.dtd">
<html xmlns="http://www.w3.org/1999/xhtml"
```

```
        xmlns:wml="http://www.wapforum.org/2001/wml">
    <head>
      <title>Archive</title>
    </head>
    <wml:card id='start'>
      <wml:do title='Help' role='help'>
        <go href='help.wml'/>
      </wml:do>
      <p>Picture name:
       <input name='picname'/>
       <br/><a href='#show'>Show it</a>
      </p>
    </wml:card>
    <wml:card id='show'>
      <p><img src='$(picname).gif' alt='$(picname)'/>
        <br/><a href='#main'>Back</a>
      </p>
    </wml:card>
</html>
```

A more comprehensive help section is provided here, which is implemented in a new document, 'help,wml'. When the user activates the wml:do element, then the wml:go element is executed and the 'help.wml' document is downloaded from the same directory as the one previously documented.

Widgets

So the user agent can determine more easily how the wml:do element should be handled, an additional element is provided for you to simplify that process. Widgets can be specified in a wml:do element, which can contain a number of wml:widget elements. The device should pick one of the widgets as the preferred way of handling the wml:do. Consequently, the *widget* represents a type of widget and the device should scan the list from top-to-bottom, then pick the first one capable of proper handling. For example, if the user agent can't use soft keys, a feature most PDAs are equipped with, then it would skip such a widget and pick the next one in the list. An example is the best way to illustrate how widgets can be used.

```
<?xml version="1.0"?>
<!DOCTYPE html PUBLIC "-//WAPFORUM//DTD WML 2.0//EN"
  "http://www.wapforum.org/dtd/wml20.dtd">
<html xmlns="http://www.w3.org/1999/xhtml"
      xmlns:wml="http://www.wapforum.org/2001/wml">
  <head>
```

```
    <title>Archive</title>
  </head>
  <wml:card id='start'>
    <wml:do title='Help' role='help'>
      <widget type='softkey'>
        <img src='btn1.gif' alt='Help'/>
      </widget>
      <widget type='menu'>Help
      </widget>
      <go href='help.wml'/>
    </wml:do>
    <p>Picture name:
     <input name='picname'/>
     <br/><a href='#show'>Show it</a>
    </p>
  </wml:card>
  <wml:card id='show'>
    <p><img src='$(picname).gif' alt='$(picname)'/>
      <br/><a href='#main'>Back</a>
    </p>
  </wml:card>
</html>
```

The wml:do element contains two wml:widget elements. The first one is for user agents that can use *soft keys,* a button rendered outside the ordinary document, for example, above or below the browser window. Note, an image is provided for the soft key. The second widget is for devices that can provide a menu of choices. Most WAP devices handle the wml:do event this way.

Jumping When an Option Is Selected

In some cases, you might want to jump to a new card or document immediately as the user chooses an option in a selection list. Then you can use the onpick attribute:

```
<?xml version="1.0"?>
<!DOCTYPE html PUBLIC "-//WAPFORUM//DTD WML 2.0//EN"
  "http://www.wapforum.org/dtd/wml20.dtd">
<html xmlns="http://www.w3.org/1999/xhtml"
      xmlns:wml="http://www.wapforum.org/2001/wml">
  <head>
    <title>Select Size</title>
  </head>
  <body>
    <p>Select size:
```

```
    <select wml:name='theValue' wml:iname='theIndex'>
      <option value='S' onpick='next.wml'>Small</option>
      <option value='M' onpick='next.wml'>Medium</option>
      <option value='L' onpick='next.wml'>Large</option>
      <option value='XL' onpick='next.wml'>XLarge</option>
      <option value='XXL' onpick='next.wml'>XXLarge</option>
    </select>
    <br/><a href='next.wml'>Next</a>
  </p>
 </body>
</html>
```

When an option is selected, the document next.wml is then loaded and executed. Note, the variables 'theValue' and 'theIndex' remain in memory and can be used in the document next.wml.

There's a technique to erase all variables, though. If the document next.wml would use the attribute wml:newcontext with the body element, then the variables would be erased. To achieve that effect, the attribute should be set to "true". You can also use the wml:newcontext attribute on card level.

Setting Variables in a Jump

You can assign values to variables when the wml:go element is executed. For example, you might want to keep track of which card a user came from. Then you can write your code like the following:

```
<?xml version="1.0"?>
<!DOCTYPE html PUBLIC "-//WAPFORUM//DTD WML 2.0//EN"
  "http://www.wapforum.org/dtd/wml20.dtd">
<html xmlns="http://www.w3.org/1999/xhtml"
      xmlns:wml="http://www.wapforum.org/2001/wml">
  <head>
    <title>Archive</title>
  </head>
  <wml:card id='start'>
    <p>Picture name:
     <input name='picname'/>
     <br/><a href='#show'>Show it</a>
     <br/>
     <wml:anchor>Help
       <go href='#help'>
         <setvar name='hlpText'
           value='Type in the name of the image and then show it.'/>
```

```
      </go>
    </wml:anchor>
  </p>
</wml:card>
<wml:card id='show'>
  <p><img src='$(picname).gif' alt='$(picname)'/>
    <br/><a href='#main'>Back</a>
  <br/>
  <wml:anchor>Help
    <go href='#help'>
      <setvar name='hlpText'
        value='Follow the back link to input a new name.'/>
    </go>
  </wml:anchor>
  </p>
</wml:card>
<wml:card id='help'>
  <p>$(hlpText)
    <br/>
    <a href='#main'>Back</a>
  </p>
</wml:card>
</html>
```

The variable 'hlpText' holds the current help text. Depending on which card the user jumps from to the help card, a different text is displayed because the text is set using the wml:setvar and wml:go elements.

Jumping Back

In all examples so far, only forward jumps have been shown. *Forward jumps* are carried out using the wml:go or *a* elements. The handheld device uses a stack to remember which cards and documents have been visited, and the user can use the device's built-in back button to return to previously visited pages, as with an ordinary web browser.

Previous Card or Document

Sometimes, you might want to navigate back as the result of the user activating a link or invoking a wml:do element. For example, you might have several cards in your document and there might be many cards that all lead to a particular card—say, a help card. In that case, the help card doesn't know from which card the user came and you would need a basic mechanism to navigate back if the user followed a link or invokes a wml:do element.

The wml:prev element can be used to achieve this and it can occur on all places where the wml:go element can be provided. For example, you can use the prev element inside a wml:anchor element or you can use it within a wml:do element. The following example shows how the wml:prev element can be used to navigate back from a help page.

```
<?xml version="1.0"?>
<!DOCTYPE html PUBLIC "-//WAPFORUM//DTD WML 2.0//EN"
  "http://www.wapforum.org/dtd/wml20.dtd">
<html xmlns="http://www.w3.org/1999/xhtml"
      xmlns:wml="http://www.wapforum.org/2001/wml">
  <head>
    <title>Archive</title>
  </head>
  <wml:card id='start'>
    <p>Picture name:
     <input name='picname'/>
     <br/><a href='#show'>Show it</a>
     <br/><a href='#help'>Help</a>
    </p>
  </wml:card>
  <wml:card id='show'>
    <p><img src='$(picname).gif' alt='$(picname)'/>
      <br/><a href='#main'>Back</a>
     <br/><a href='#help'>Help</a>
    </p>
  </wml:card>
  <wml:card id='help'>
    <p>Type in the name and then follow the link
       to display the image.
      <br/>
      <wml:anchor>Back
        <wml:prev/>
      </wml:anchor>
    </p>
  </wml:card>
</html>
```

Three cards exist and it's possible to follow a link from the first and second cards to the third. The third card implements the navigation back, using the prev element.

Then you needn't keep track of which card the user came from, but you can invoke a navigation back to the last visited card or document.

The wml:prev element can contain wml:setvar elements if a need exists to assign values to variables when the user navigates back.

Detecting Forward and Backward Jumps

In some cases, you might want to discover how the user navigated to a specific card or document. If the user comes back to it, using the wml:prev element, then he or she has obviously been there before. You might want to display another text or do something else, just because the user has been there before. The wml:onevent element can be used to implement such functionality.

Enter Forward

Forward navigation can be carried out using the *a,* anchor, or go elements, and this type of navigation can be caught by setting the type attribute to 'onenterforward', as this example does.

```
<?xml version="1.0"?>
<!DOCTYPE html PUBLIC "-//WAPFORUM//DTD WML 2.0//EN"
  "http://www.wapforum.org/dtd/wml20.dtd">
<html xmlns="http://www.w3.org/1999/xhtml"
      xmlns:wml="http://www.wapforum.org/2001/wml">
  <head>
    <title>Archive</title>
  </head>
  <wml:card id='start'>
    <wml:onevent type='onenterforward'>
      <wml:go href='#help'/>
    </wml:onevent>
    <p>Picture name:
     <input name='picname'/>
     <br/><a href='#show'>Show it</a>
     <br/><a href='#help'>Help</a>
    </p>
  </wml:card>
  <wml:card id='show'>
    <p><img src='$(picname).gif' alt='$(picname)'/>
      <br/><a href='#main'>Back</a>
     <br/><a href='#help'>Help</a>
    </p>
```

```
  </wml:card>
  <wml:card id='help'>
    <p>Type in the name and then follow the link
       to display the image.
      <br/>
      <wml:anchor>Back
        <wml:prev/>
      </wml:anchor>
    </p>
  </wml:card>
</html>
```

In the previous example, the user is taken to the help page the first time the application starts. Because the prev element is used to navigate back to the first card, the wml:onevent won't execute because it only catches forward navigation.

Enter Backward

You can detect *backward navigation* with the wml:onevent, similar to the previous example, but then the type attribute should be set to 'onenterbackward'. If the user navigates back using the wml:prev element or the device's built-in backward navigation function, those events will be caught and the element inside wml:onevent will be executed. The following example catches a backward navigation triggered by the WML browser's built-in backward navigation function.

```
<?xml version="1.0"?>
<!DOCTYPE html PUBLIC "-//WAPFORUM//DTD WML 2.0//EN"
  "http://www.wapforum.org/dtd/wml20.dtd">
<html xmlns="http://www.w3.org/1999/xhtml"
      xmlns:wml="http://www.wapforum.org/2001/wml">
  <head>
    <title>Archive</title>
  </head>
  <wml:card id='start'>
    <p>Picture name:
     <input name='picname'/>
     <br/><a href='#show'>Show it</a>
     <br/><a href='#help'>Help</a>
    </p>
  </wml:card>
  <wml:card id='show'>
    <p><img src='$(picname).gif' alt='$(picname)'/>
      <br/><a href='#main'>Back</a>
     <br/><a href='#help'>Help</a>
```

```
      </p>
    </wml:card>
    <wml:card id='help'>
      <wml:onevent type='onenterbackward'>
        <wml:go href='#help2'/>
      </wml:onevent>
      <p>Type in the name and then follow the link
        to display the image.
        <br/>
        <wml:anchor>Back
          <wml:prev/>
        </wml:anchor>
      </p>
    </wml:card>
    <wml:card id='help2'>
      <!-- User comes back to the help so provide user with more info. -->
      <p>You should type in the name of a file without its file extension.
        Then the GIF file with that name, stored on the server, will be
        displayed.
        <br/>
        <wml:anchor>Main
          <wml:go href='#prev'/>
        </wml:anchor>
      </p>
    </wml:card>
</html>
```

The application detects if the user goes back to the help text after having been there. In that case, another help text is displayed in the 'help2' card. Using the wml:onevent element, the card named 'help' catches a backward navigation and immediately passes the user on to 'help2'.

Using the Timer

In WML, a built-in timer can generate events. All user agents must support this timer functionality, so it's not a rare function that requires special hardware, although it might sound like one. The timing is specified in tenths of a second, so 50 means five seconds. Similar to events generated as the result of forward and backward navigation, events generated by the timer are also caught using the wml:onevent element. The timer is set using the wml:timer element.

A Start Page

Because an event is generated when the timer reaches zero, you can design card or documents that are valid only for a certain time, and then the user is automatically redirected to another card or document. The following code shows a welcome message for two seconds, and then the user is redirected to another document.

```
<?xml version="1.0"?>
<!DOCTYPE html PUBLIC "-//WAPFORUM//DTD WML 2.0//EN"
  "http://www.wapforum.org/dtd/wml20.dtd">
<html xmlns="http://www.w3.org/1999/xhtml"
      xmlns:wml="http://www.wapforum.org/2001/wml">
  <head>
    <title>Archive</title>
  </head>
  <wml:card id='start'>
    <wml:onevent type='ontimer'>
      <wml:go href='newpage.wml'/>
    </wml:onevent>
    <wml:timer value='20'/>
    <p><img src='welcome.gif' alt='Welcome!'/>
    </p>
  </wml:card>
</html>
```

The type attribute is set to 'ontimer', to indicate the wml:onevent catches the event generated when the timer expires.

Simple Animations

Because the timer displays a card or document for a specific time period, simpler forms of animation can be created, such as the following simple text message:

```
<?xml version="1.0"?>
<!DOCTYPE html PUBLIC "-//WAPFORUM//DTD WML 2.0//EN"
  "http://www.wapforum.org/dtd/wml20.dtd">
<html xmlns="http://www.w3.org/1999/xhtml"
      xmlns:wml="http://www.wapforum.org/2001/wml">
  <head>
    <title>Welcome</title>
```

```
      </head>
      <wml:card id='first'>
        <wml:onevent type='ontimer'>
          <wml:go href=#'second'/>
        </wml:onevent>
        <wml:timer value='5'/>
        <p>Welcome
        </p>
      </wml:card>
      <wml:card id='second'>
        <wml:onevent type='ontimer'>
          <wml:go href='#third'/>
        </wml:onevent>
        <wml:timer value='5'/>
        <p>to
        </p>
      </wml:card>
      <wml:card id='third'>
        <wml:onevent type='ontimer'>
          <wml:go href='#fourth'/>
        </wml:onevent>
        <wml:timer value='5'/>
        <p>our
        </p>
      </wml:card>
      <wml:card id='fourth'>
        <wml:onevent type='ontimer'>
          <wml:go href='main.wml'/>
        </wml:onevent>
        <wml:timer value='5'/>
        <p>shop!
        </p>
      </wml:card>
</html>
```

The application displays the words "welcome to our shop!" one by one, in a sequence. Each word is displayed for 0.5 seconds.

Integrating Phone Functionality

One of the best features of WAP is that you can add phone functionality to your sites. For example, you can create online phone books and contact lists. When you activate a link, the phone automatically dials the number to the person associated with the link.

Dialing a Number

A useful function is Make call. It enables you to create WML applications that can execute phone calls when the user follows a link or executes a wml:go. The following example lets the user make phone calls by activating some of the links.

```
<?xml version="1.0"?>
<!DOCTYPE html PUBLIC "-//WAPFORUM//DTD WML 2.0//EN"
  "http://www.wapforum.org/dtd/wml20.dtd">
<html xmlns="http://www.w3.org/1999/xhtml"
      xmlns:wml="http://www.wapforum.org/2001/wml">
  <head>
    <title>Online dialer</title>
  </head>
  <body>
    <p>ONLINE DIALER
      <br/><a href='wtai://wp/mc;018123456'>Joe</a>
      <br/><a href='wtai://wp/mc;938205984'>Kate</a>
      <br/><a href='wtai://wp/mc;229944032'>Mary</a>
    </p>
  </body>
</html>
```

A special scheme—Wireless Telephony Application Interface (WTAI)—is used in WAP. WTAI is the scheme used to enable telephone functionality on your WML pages. In the previous example, the WTA Public library (wp) is used. It contains a function, mc, which means Make Call. The function takes an argument, the phone number.

Note, you can't create applications that dial numbers without the user's knowledge. When the mc function is executed, a prompt appears and the user must confirm that she wants to dial the number.

Managing the Phone Book

Another function in the WTA Public library lets you add entries to the phone book in the following way.

```
<?xml version="1.0"?>
<!DOCTYPE html PUBLIC "-//WAPFORUM//DTD WML 2.0//EN"
  "http://www.wapforum.org/dtd/wml20.dtd">
<html xmlns="http://www.w3.org/1999/xhtml"
      xmlns:wml="http://www.wapforum.org/2001/wml">
  <head>
    <title>Online phone book</title>
  </head>
  <body>
    <p>ONLINE PHONEBOOK
      <br/>Name:
      <input name='fullname'/>
      <br/>Number:
      <input name='num' wml:format='*n'/>
      <br/>
      <a href='wtai://wp/addPBEntry;$(num);$(fullname)'>Add
      </a>
    </p>
  </body>
</html>
```

Entries are added to the phone book using the addPBEntry function. Two input fields enable the user to type in the name and number. When the link is followed, the addPBEntry function is executed and the data is added. Note, the format attribute is used to force the user to input numbers only.

In addition, the functions Make call and addPBEntry can be called from a WMLScript. The WTAI scheme is easy to use in your WML code, however, so there's no need to do it. Both functions return a result and, if you need to retrieve the result to check if the function call was carried out without problems, simply add the ! character at the end of the call, followed by a variable name. That variable is then assigned the return value.

Using Scripts

WMLScripts are useful when you need to perform simple checks. For example, the user might input something, and then you might want to check if the input contains something that makes sense. For example, if you call some of the previous WTA Public functions, you might want to assign the result to a variable, and then check the result in a WMLScript function.

If you collect information from a user, then sooner or later you'll probably want to send it to a server to store in a database or use it to retrieve other information. In this case, though, you can reduce the load on your server equipment if you check that the user hasn't typed in information incorrectly or hasn't selected all the alternatives he must select.

On the handheld device, WMLScripts execute on the client side. Some people might argue there's no need for client scripts because you can use much more powerful technologies, such as JSP, Perl, and ASP on a Windows or UNIX server. Of course, these technologies are powerful, but the meaning with WMLScripts isn't to be useful in terms of CPU power. WMLScripts can perform simple calculations and examine lists that are the result of multiple-choice selections in WML, *before* the data is sent to a server. Thus, you can execute program code without sending any packets at all over the network. That's the power of WMLScripts and they should be used for such functionality. Because a single WMLScript file can contain an arbitrary number of functions, you can load them once over the wireless network for a specific application and then you might be able to reduce the traffic on the network dramatically. After all, no matter how much bandwidth you have, there will always be room for optimizations. The latency in, for example, a 2.5G GPRS network, can be quite noticeable.

Functions

Although WMLScript is about programming and not so much about working with markup, we'll look at it because it's so tightly coupled with WML documents. You can retrieve WML variables from your WML code and use them in WMLScripts. You can also change the values of WML variables from a WMLScript function.

A simple WMLScript function might look like this:

```
function funcName() {
  var a, b, c;
  a = 1;
  b = 2;
  c = a + b;
  return c;
};
```

The keyword function always comes first, followed by the function name. In the previous function, three variables have been used, *a, b,* and *c.* A simple addition is performed and the result is returned.

Variables

The variables are local for each function, which means they can be used only in that function. If you need to use the value of a variable, which you defined in WML, then you can use a special library function to retrieve that variable, like the following:

```
function changeWmlVar() {
  var value;
  value = WMLBrowser.getVar("theDate");
  if( !String.compare(value, "12/25") )
      WMLBrowser.setVar("theDate", "12/27");
};
```

All the library functions are presented later on, but here you have used three special library functions: compare, getvar, and setvar. Compare examines two text strings and returns zero if they're the same. GetVar reads a WML variable and assigns the value to a WMLScript variable, so the value can be used in the function for calculations. SetVar assigns a value to a WML variable. In the previous example, the function checks if the variable "theDate" was set to "12/25". If this is the case, then it's changed to "12/27".

Function Calls

In the previous example, you can see how library functions are called. But you can also call one of your own WMLScript functions from another or you can call a WMLScript function from the WML code.

Calling a WMLScript Function from Another   When one WMLScript function calls another, it might look like this.

```
function change() {
  var d;
  d = "theDate";
  changeWmlVar(d);
};

function changeWmlVar(v) {
  var value;
  value = WMLBrowser.getVar(v);
  if( !String.compare(value, "12/25") )
      WMLBrowser.setVar(v, "12/27");
};
```

The first function calls the second. All functions are listed in the WMLScript document.

Calling a WMLScript Function from the WML Code   If the function change is going to be called from WML, then you must provide the keyword extern before function, which looks like this:

```
extern function change() {
  var d;
  d = "theDate";
  changeWmlVar(d);
};

function changeWmlVar(v) {
  var value;
  value = WMLBrowser.getVar(v);
  if( !String.compare(value, "12/25") )
      WMLBrowser.setVar(v, "12/27");
};
```

The second function needn't be declared extern because it isn't called from WML, but from the first function only. The WML code, which calls the function change, might look like the following:

```
<?xml version="1.0"?>
<!DOCTYPE html PUBLIC "-//WAPFORUM//DTD WML 2.0//EN"
   "http://www.wapforum.org/dtd/wml20.dtd">
<html xmlns="http://www.w3.org/1999/xhtml"
      xmlns:wml="http://www.wapforum.org/2001/wml">
  <head>
    <title>Name And Date</title>
  </head>
  <wml:card id='start'>
    <p>Name:
     <input name='fullname'/>
     <br/>Month and day:
     <input name='date' wml:format='NN\/NN'/>
     <br/>
     <wml:anchor>Send
       <wml:go href='scripts.wmls#change()'/>
     </wml:anchor>
    </p>
```

```
    </wml:card>
    <wml:card id='checked'>
      <wml:onevent type='onenterforward'>
        <wml:anchor>
          <wml:go
href='process.cgi?name=$(fullname)&amp;date=$(date)'/>
        </wml:anchor>
      </wml:onevent>
    </wml:card>
</html>
```

In the start card, the WMLScript function change is called in the wml:go element. As you can see, the syntax to call a certain function in a certain WMLScript file is to provide the URL to the document and to use the # character to specify the name of the function. In this case, however, you need to change the second WMLScript function, changeWmlVar, a bit. You need to jump to the card, which is named 'checked', immediately after the change function has been executed. Then the function must be changed like this:

```
function changeWmlVar(v) {
  var value;
  value = WMLBrowser.getVar(v);
  if( !String.compare(value, "12/25") ) {
      WMLBrowser.setVar(v, "12/27");
  }
  WMLBrowser.go("#checked");
};
```

The code is extended, so a jump is performed from the WMLScript function to a card in the WML code immediately when the check has been performed. To achieve this, the WMLBrowser library contains a function, which works as the wml:go element, but it can be executed from a WMLScript.

The Standard Libraries

In the previous example, a number of library functions have been used to implement various types of functionality. As you might have understood, it's possible to reduce the code size dramatically if these libraries are used extensively. The libraries can be used to simplify the creation of more-advanced WAP services than the traditional services implemented in pure WML.

Typically, a card in the WML code calls a WMLScript function and the function calls a number of standard WMLScript functions to compute something. The result is then passed back to the WML browser and displayed on the screen. Thus, the WMLScript libraries are, to a high degree, designed to perform common computations, such as the rounding of floating point numbers, taking the root of a number, substituting string elements, or checking the syntax of a URL that the user entered.

Use the libraries as much as possible because they save you time and reduce the complexity of the WMLScript code.

All user agents that conform to WAP 2.0 must support five standard libraries. They are Lang, String, URL, WMLBrowser, and Dialogs. There's a sixth library—Float—which contains floating-point functions. Because some small handheld devices are based on simple microprocessors, supporting all the functions in the Float library can be difficult. Therefore, this library is optional and manufacturers needn't implement all functions. If they aren't supported, they always return an invalid value. You can check if a function returns an invalid value in the following way:

```
if( invalid == Float.round(3.14) )
   . . .
```

Invalid is a special value and data type in WMLScript. If you have the ambition to write robust code, then you should check that critical functions, which might fail, don't return this value. If they do, you should perform the necessary actions either to quit the application or tell the user an error has occurred.

Using the Libraries

We can't go through all the WMScript standard libraries here—that isn't the purpose of the book. If you need to know exactly which functions are available, read the technical specification for the WAP 2.0 WMLScript libraries, which can be downloaded from http://www.wapforum.org. Instead, we'll look at the syntax and semantics of some of the functions contained in each library.

The URL Library

This library has a number of functions associated with it that are meant to manage the syntax of Internet addresses: URLs. Because the word "address" is probably mentioned more often than the word "URL," an explanation is needed here. URL means Uniform Resource Locator and is an ordinary Internet address. A few examples follow.

```
http://www.example.com/index.wml
http://wap.example.net/page.html
http:://comm.example.com/buyhere
ftp://get.it.here.example.com/doc/
```

Functions in the URL library can, for example, be used to check if an address has a correct syntax or they can perform URL encoding and decoding.

The Syntax of a URL   Let's look at which components make up a UR. This can make understanding the semantics of many of the functions in this library easier. Here's a sample URL.

```
http://wap.example.com/cgi/ab?x=4&y=10
```

HTTP is called the *scheme* and wap.example.com is the *host*. The string cgi/ab is the *path* and *x=4&y=10* are *parameters*.

A URL can be absolute or relative. The previous URL is absolute. *Relative URLs* consists of a path only, like theFile.html or dir/. An *absolute URL* consists of a scheme specifier and a host name. A path, port number, parameters, and queries are also allowed, but optional.

Scheme and Host   The scheme of a URL is the first part before the semicolon and describes which protocol is used to transfer the content. Examples are HTTP and FTP. When web pages are transferred, then Hypertext Transfer Protocol (HTTP) is used. File Transfer Protocol (FTP) is used to transfer files to and from a server. If you're designing a WAP service that lets the user type in an address to an FTP site, the function getScheme can be used to verify that the scheme of the URL is FTP and not HTTP or something else. Here's an example of a call to getScheme, which returns a string.

```
function returnHttp() {
  var s, str;
  str = "http://www.example.com/wap";
  s = URL.getScheme(str);
  return s;
};
```

If, for some reason, you want to check the host name on the server side, then the function getHost could be used. getHost takes one argument, a string that's set to the complete URL, and returns the host name as a string. Here's an example that checks the host name of a URL.

```
function returnHost(theUrl) {
  var hostname;
  hostname = URL.getHost(theUrl);
  return hostname;
};
```

If the function would be called with the argument http://example.com/hello.pl, then it would return the string example.com.

Note, both getScheme and getHost can return *invalid,* the data type in WMLScript that represents an error value. Invalid is returned if the URLs don't follow the formal URL syntax. The following URLs aren't valid URLs:

```
://www.example.com
http::/www.example.com
http://
```

The first URL lacks a scheme. The second has a syntax error (only one colon should be there), and no host was specified in the third URL.

Path and Query   If the path needs to be extracted from a URL, you should use the function getPath, which returns a string that contains the path only, without the host and without possible cgi parameters or queries. Here's an example:

```
function returnPath(theUrl) {
  var p;
  p = URL.getPath(theUrl);
  return p;
};
```

If the function would be called with the argument http://www.example.com/myPath/file.wml?x=1&y=2&z=10, then it would return the string /myPath/file.wml because the function would remove the scheme and host name, and then return the path only, without the query.

If you want to retrieve the path and the parameters, you could first execute getPath to get the path, and then call the function getQuery, which would give you the query part of the URL. The following example illustrates this.

```
function returnPathAndQuery(theUrl) {
  var p, q;
  p = URL.getPath(theUrl);
  q = URL.getQuery(theUrl);
  return p + q;
};
```

The last line of code, before the closing }, appends the two strings and returns the result to the calling function.

The Float Library

The Float library is special because manufacturers don't have to include the library in their WAP-compatible devices. Consequently, if you design a service that can be used by anyone with access to the Internet, then avoiding the functions in this library as much as possible is probably a good idea. All limited handheld devices don't have the capability to perform floating point computations.

Rounding Numbers   The most important function in the Float library is probably the round function. The *round* function takes a number as input and rounds the number to the closest integer. Here's an example of a call to the round function:

```
MyInt = Float.round(3.14);
```

The statement sets myInt to 3 by rounding 3.14 to the closest integer, which is 3.

The Lang Library

The library called Lang contains a number of useful functions that can make programming in WMLScript much easier. All the functions perform important routine tasks common in many programs, such as generating a random number, checking if a variable is a string, choosing the greater of two numbers, and so forth.

Random Numbers   In applications like games, a random number often needs to be generated. Two functions in the Lang library can be used when a pseudorandom number should be generated: seed and random.

The *seed* function is used to set a start value for the pseudorandom number generator and the random function generates the actual number. If *random* is called with the value *N,* then a value between zero and *N* (inclusive) is generated. Consequently, if you need to generate a random number equal to four, five, or six, then the random function should be called with the argument two, and then you should add four to the returned random number. Here's a sample WMLScript function that generates random sentences.

```
function generateRandomSentence() {
  var r1, r2, r3, str;
  r1 = Lang.random(3);
  r2 = Lang.random(3);
  if(r1 == 0) str = "Harry washes";
  if(r1 == 1) str = "Jane drives";
  if(r1 == 2) str = "Joe fixes";
```

```
   if(r1 == 3) str = ""Sarah likes";
   if(r2 == 0) str = "the dishes.";
   if(r2 == 1) str = "the car.";
   if(r2 == 2) str = "computers.";
   if(r2 == 3) str = "a book.";
   return r1 + " " + r2;
};
```

The random function is used twice to generate two different random numbers. Then the if statements check these variables to select which words should be part of either the beginning or the end of the sentence. The last statement in the function puts together the result by appending the beginning of the sentence with a space and the end of the sentence.

Checking and Converting Types   In certain situations, you need to check the type of a WMLScript variable and, sometimes, one type must be converted to another. Maybe you wrote a function that takes a Boolean as input, but another function that computes the value you want to send as the argument is an integer, not a Boolean. Although the WMLScript language was designed to take care of type conversions like these, you might have to force a conversion in some cases, where the type conversion rules won't perform the conversion you expect. If you want to be certain about which type the variable is converted to, you should call one of the conversion functions.

The library function, called *parseInt*, takes a string as input and converts it, if possible, to an integer. If the string can't be converted to an integer, then the function returns invalid. The p*arseFloat* function works the same way, but for floating point numbers. A string that represents a floating point value is given as an argument and a floating point value is returned if the conversion was successful. Otherwise, the function returns invalid.

The functions *isInt* and *isFloat* don't perform any conversion but, instead, return a Boolean value, which is true if the argument can be converted to an integer or a float, respectively.

Here are two WMLScript functions that show how parseInt, parseFloat, isInt, and isFloat can be used.

```
function f1(str) {
  if( Lang.isFloat(str) ) {
     return str / 2.0;
  }
  if( Lang.isInt(str) ) {
     return str * 2;
```

```
    }
    return 0;
};

function f2(str) {
    var x;
    x = Lang.parseFloat( str );
    if( x != invalid ) return x / 2.0;
    x = Lang.parseInt( str );
    if( x != invalid ) return x * 2;
    return 0;
};
```

The functions are two implementations of the same thing. Both take a string as the argument and, depending on whether the string can be converted to an integer or a float, the value is either divided or multiplied by two. Function f1 is implemented using the isFloat and isInt library functions while f2 is implemented using parseFloat and parseInt. Function f1 uses the built-in type conversion rules of the WMLScript language to convert the variable called str to either a float or an integer.

Max and Min   The Lang library includes functions that can be used to compute the maximum or minimum of two numbers. These functions are called *max* and *min,* and they take two arguments, the numbers that are compared. A service often needs to check that the user doesn't exceed a limit, and then max can be used. Implementing these functions from scratch isn't too difficult but, because they're available as library functions, you can reduce the code size and avoid bugs in your code if you use the library functions instead.

Here's a function that uses the min and max library functions.

```
function isInside(num, lower, upper) {
    if( num == Lang.max(lower, num) && num == Lang.min(upper, num) )
        return true;
    else
        return false;
};
```

The code checks that a number, num, is inside the boundaries of lower and upper. If not, the function returns false, otherwise, it returns true.

The Dialogs Library

Input is usually taken care of in the WML code, but functions in the Dialogs library exist as well that result in interactions with the user, such as input or the display of alert messages.

A useful function in the Dialogs library is *prompt,* which takes a message string and a default input string as arguments, and then returns a string. The function displays the message on the screen and lets the user input a character string. The second argument to the function, the default string, is the default input the function will return if the user confirms without deleting the default input and without typing anything.

The following example prints "Name:" on the screen and asks for the user's name. The name is then returned by the WMLScript function.

```
function getName() {
  var inp;
  inp = Dialogs.prompt("Name:", "");
  return inp;
};
```

The variable called inp is set to the result of the call to the prompt function.

The String Library

String handling is a fundamental part of many procedural programming languages and WMLScript is no exception. Using the functions in the String library, the length of a string can be computed, strings can be compared, and it's possible to check if a string is empty, and so forth. Also, the String library has a set of functions that operate on string elements.

Checking the Length of a String   Checking the length of a string can be useful if the user is prompted for input and it's possible the user might enter an empty string. The function isEmpty takes one argument, a string, and returns a Boolean, which is true if the string is empty. The following example uses the function isEmpty to check if a string is empty. If so, it returns a default value:

```
function makeNotEmpty(str) {
  if( String.isEmpty(str) )
     return "default";
  else
     return str;
};
```

Another function in the String library can be used to check if a string is empty. The function called *length* returns an integer that specifies how many characters the string contains. This function can be used to check whether a string is empty or isn't too long. Maybe you're designing a WAP service that asks for the user's surname and the string is supposed to be stored in a database on a server. Maybe this server has allocated room for only 32 characters. The following function asks the user to input his surname. The process is repeated until a string has been entered, which is less than or equal to 32 characters.

```
function getSurname() {
  var str;
  while(1) {
      str = Dialogs.prompt("Surname:", "");
      if( String.length(str) < 33 )
          return str;
  };
};
```

The function getSurname uses two library functions: prompt from the Dialogs library and length from the String library. If String.length doesn't return a length less than 33 characters, then the user is asked to enter the string again.

Comparing Strings   Comparing strings is also one of those common tasks when all kinds of applications are implemented. For example, an e-mail application could ask the user for the name of the receiver and the name could then be compared with entries in an address book and substituted with the e-mail address before the mail is sent.

The library function *compare* takes two strings as arguments and compares them, character by character. If they're equal, then the function returns 0. If the first string comes before the second string, then a negative value is returned. If, on the other hand, the second string comes before the first one, then a positive value is returned.

The following function takes one argument, a string, and checks if the string contains one of three defined names:

```
function isName(str) {
  if( !String.compare(str, "Joe") )
     return true;
  if( !String.compare(str, "Jane") )
     return true;
  if( !String.compare(str, "Lars") )
     return true;
  return false;
};
```

The ! checks the result of the compare function to see if it's equal to zero. If the string is equal to "Joe", "Jane", or "Lars", then the function exits immediately and returns true. Otherwise, the function returns false.

Elements   An *element* is a kind of data type that has a number of related functions defined in the String library. Elements can be used as arrays that are implemented using strings. Consequently, element functions in the String library retrieve an element at a certain index, count the number of elements in the string, and replace an element in a string.

The following example shows a WMLScript function that executes a number of operations on a string of elements:

```
function removeGreens(str) {
  var count, elm;
  for(count=0; count<String.elements(str, ";"); count++) {
      elm = String.elementAt(str, count, ";");
      // Is it green?
      if( !String.compare(elm, "green") )
          String.replaceAt(str, "blue", count, ";");
  };
};
```

The code goes through a string, which is supposed to contain a number of colors separated by a semicolon—for example, "white; blue; green; yellow". The function replaces occurrences of "green" with "blue" by calling the replaceAt function.

The WMLBrowser Library

This library contains functions that can be used to read and write variables in the WML browser. The WML browser has its own set of variables that are strings only and each WMLScript function has its own set of local variables. When a WMLScript function computes something, the final value usually needs to be displayed by a WML card. The function called setVar takes two strings as arguments. The first specifies which WML variable should be set and the second specifies which value it should be set to. If a WMLScript function needs to read a variable from the WML browser, then getVar can be used.

In the following example, getVar and setVar are used to get and set the value of a WML variable:

```
function changeWmlVar(v, to) {
  var value;
```

```
  value = WMLBrowser.getVar(v);
  if( !String.compare(value, "enter") )
      WMLBrowser.setVar(v, "start");
};
```

The function checks if a WML variable has been set to the value "enter". If so, the value is changed to "start". Note, the variables that are retrieved with getVar and set with setVar are WML variables, not WMLScript variables. WML variables have a variable space of their own.

Building WML 1.*x*-compliant Sites

WAP 2.0 and WML 2.0 are much more powerful than version 1—there's no doubt about that. In WML 2.0, you can use XHTML only if you want to or you can mix WML unique elements with XHTML and the deck and cards metaphor. WML 2.0 has support for CSS, which makes creating applications that look good on a wide range of browsers easier.

Still, a huge amount of handheld devices that support only WML 1.1 and 1.2 are being used. Thus, if you create a WAP site today that needs to support as many users as possible, you'd have to write WML 1.1 or 1.2-compliant code. So, let's sort out what you'd have to do to stay compatible with these handheld devices. WML 1.1 and 1.2 will, henceforth, be referred to as WML 1.*x*.

Namespaces and the Header

In WML 1.*x*, all elements and attributes are written without the WML namespace. The code might look like this:

```
<?xml version="1.0"?>
<!DOCTYPE wml PUBLIC "-//WAPFORUM//DTD WML 1.2//EN"
  "http://www.wapforum.org/DTD/wml_1.2.xml">
<wml>
 <card id="start">
  <p>Hello!
  </p>
 </card>
</wml>
```

No namespace qualifier is before the card and wml keywords. Note, the wml element replaces the html element and no namespace declaration is in the wml element.

In addition, the header is different because you're referring to a different language. Consequently, validation is done according to another DTD.

Widgets and Roles

Widgets aren't part of the do element's content model in WML 1.x. In WML 1.x, no role attribute existed. Instead, the role was specified using the type attribute. This could be set to "accept", "help", "options", and so forth, but neither the "positive" nor the "negative" values were used. They were introduced in WML 2.0 with the role attribute. The following code shows how the type attribute could be used:

```
<?xml version="1.0"?>
<!DOCTYPE wml PUBLIC "-//WAPFORUM//DTD WML 1.1//EN"
"http://www.wapforum.org/DTD/wml_1.1.xml">

<wml>
  <card id="menu" newcontext="true">
    <p align="center">Welcome!
      <br/>Use the menu functions.
      <do type="options" label="New">
        <go href="new.wml"/>
      </do>
      <do type="options" label="Update">
        <go href= "update.wml"/>
      </do>
      <do type="options" label="Reset">
        <go href="#menu"/>
      </do>
    </p>
  </card>
</wml>
```

This application has three main options that were specified using the type attribute set to "options". The type attribute was replaced by the role attribute in WML 2.0. No namespace prefix exists for the WML elements and attributes, and the wml element is used instead of the html element in WML 2.0.

Templates

Templates were used in WML 1.*x,* but were removed in WML 2.0. Templates were supposed to make the code smaller, by using reusage and making the code easier to read and understand, but the templates weren't successful from a developer's perspective. They often made the deck of cards even harder to read and understand, and they didn't make the code much smaller. Here's an example that uses a template:

```
<?xml version="1.0"?>
<!DOCTYPE wml PUBLIC "-//WAPFORUM//DTD WML 1.1//EN"
"http://www.wapforum.org/DTD/wml_1.1.xml">

<wml>
  <template>
    <do type='help' label='Help' name='Hlp'>
      <go href='#help'/>
    </do>
  </template>
  <card id="menu">
    <p>Welcome!
       <br/><a href='news.wml'>Read the news</a>
    </p>
  </card>
  <card id="help">
    <p>Just follow the link to read the latest news.
       <br/><a href='menu'>Back to main</a>
    </p>
  </card>
</wml>
```

The purpose was that a template should apply for all the cards in the file. In the previous example, it would be possible to execute the do in both the 'menu' and the 'help' card.

CHAPTER 4

Building a Voice Portal

IN THIS CHAPTER:

Functionality

Implementation

I n this chapter, we're going to implement a voice portal. A *voice portal* is like a traditional portal on the World Wide Web but, instead of using an HTML browser to access the content, you use an ordinary phone to navigate and retrieve content. Chapter 5 covered the basics of VoiceXML. If you haven't read Chapter 5, I suggest you read it now. We'll use VoiceXML to implement our voice portal. VoiceXML is one of the leading markup languages for the creation of voice applications. *VoiceXML forum,* which created the language, has over 500 members, so the support for VoiceXML is great. VoiceXML servers are available for deployment and several development kits, both free and commercial, can be used in the design process. Some of these kits are mentioned in Chapter 5.

When we design the voice portal, we'll first go through a requirement and functional phase, where we list the features and content our portal should include. When all the functions are decided, the core functionality of the portal, such as basic navigation, will be implemented followed by the services, which are available on the portal.

Functionality

A voice portal needs some basic functions. Let's consider which basic functions we'll need to provide the user with a decent set of tools for navigation.

A Welcome Message

As the user dials in, a good idea is to provide a simple welcome message that explains the service in basic terms. The user should be aware that a machine is in the other end, which only responds to and understands a small set of words and sentences. You might be confronted with users who dial in and don't know what speech recognition or DTMF tones are. Most people aren't familiar with the term *DTMF tone,* and few are aware that it's possible for machines to understand spoken words and sentences. DTMF tones are tones generated by a phone when the user presses its keys.

The voice portal might provide this message only once, as the user dials in. If the user returns to the main menu, this message might be skipped. Long tedious messages that explain things the user has already heard can be irritating and might cause the user to hang up in frustration. With VoiceXML, you can design messages that are prompted for the user in a different way (shorter) if they've already been played.

Our welcome message will be "Welcome to the voice portal. Listen to the instructions and then say what you want to do."

A Top Menu of Choices

A good voice portal is simple to use and doesn't contain too many choices. If you provide too many choices, the user might forget some of them. For example, if you use the enumerate element—described in Chapter 5—in combination with too many choices, then the user must concentrate to memorize the first choice while other choices are being spoken. Remember, when you sit in front of your development environment, you see the choices in the code in front of you. Although memorizing seven or eight choices might seem simple, try the menu for real using a phone or a simulator in your SDK. You'll notice that more than seven or eight choices can be confusing. As you hear the eighth choice, you might forget the first or second choice.

See if you can put the services in submenus. This kind of system feels more like a guiding system rather than a system that provides the user with an endless amount of choices. Instead of implementing a flat structure of 12 choices, you might be able to split them into three categories, with four choices in each category.

With the voice portal, you can visit the top menu, use one of the services, ask for help, ask about the services, and exit from individual services or the portal.

Go to the Top Menu

No matter where the user is located on the portal, he or she must always be able to start again from scratch. Because we aren't providing any visual feedback, the user might get lost, and then she must be able to start over again.

Use One of the Services

From the top menu, the user might select one of the services provided via the portal. The user might say the name of the service to use it. When the service is being used, the user might go back to the top menu, ask for help, exit, or ask where he is.

Ask for Help

It must be possible to ask which commands are available. If the user says "help," then all the available voice commands used to navigate and exit are replayed.

Ask About the Current Service

If the user chooses a service by mistake, it must be possible to ask what the active service does or how it's used. This could be part of the previous help command or it could be a special command.

Exit

The user must be able both to exit an individual service and to exit from the voice portal as a whole. This voice dialogue prompts the user further to ask if she wants to exit the particular service currently being used or if she wants to log out from the portal.

Services

The services we're going to provide are a news service, a game, and the option to visit an electronic psychiatrist.

News

The *news service* speaks the news for you. We assume an online news service bureau has signed a deal with our portal as a content provider. However, they provide the news for the portal in a traditional Web format, so we have to create a tool that converts the content to spoken words.

Game

A game—the classic HiLo game—is available on our voice portal. The user guesses a number and the server replies if the guess was too high or too low. You should guess as few times as possible. The interaction between the game engine and the user is carried out entirely using voice synthesis and voice recognition.

Visit Liza, the Robot Psychiatrist

This service is a variant of the famous Eliza program, written by Joseph Weizenbaum in the '60s, to demonstrate basic Artificial Intelligence. Although the vocabulary is a bit simpler, the conversation isn't text-based as the original was, but instead uses only voice recognition and voice synthesis.

Liza simulates a psychiatrist who converses with you, the patient. The program gives you the impression a human is at the other end, although the conversation itself is rather primitive. The dialogue is carried out entirely using voice synthesis and voice recognition.

Implementation

Before we start to implement all the previously mentioned functions, we need to sort out the document structure. There will be one root document. VoiceXML makes it possible to provide a number of documents and to make one of them the root or main document. In our case, there will be a root document that implements the top-level navigation: the help and exit functions. These functions are global and can also be accessed in all other documents. This is how VoiceXML works and this suits us well.

Each service is provided in a separate document to make adding new services to the portal and removing old ones easy. Using the application attribute in the vxml element, as described in Chapter 5, all services refer to the root document.

The Welcome Message

Let's start with the root document:

```
<?xml version="1.0"?>
<vxml version="1.0">
  <!-- ************* Introduction speech ************* -->
  <form id="intro">
    <block>
      Welcome to the voice portal. Please listen to the
      instructions and then say what you want to do.
    </block>
  </form>
</vxml>
```

This root document is stored with the filename voicePortal.vxml. All other documents on the portal must refer to this filename.

We follow the XML convention to provide the XML header on the first line. The VoiceXML code is surrounded by the vxml tags. Only one simple form exists and its purpose is to deliver the text, which is given inside the block element. The block element is used when no need occurs for interaction. If we'd used the prompt element, we'd be forced to use the filled element as well. Because there's no need for user interaction at this point on the portal, the text is provided inside the block element.

The Navigation System

With the navigation system on the voice portal, it's possible to access the services, get help, exit, and ask which service is currently being used.

Services

The navigation system is implemented using a menu of choices. Each choice leads to a separate document, which implements the service. When we've added the navigation controls, which take the user to the services, then the root document looks like this:

```
<?xml version="1.0"?>
<vxml version="1.0">
  <!-- ************ Introduction speech ************ -->
  <form id="intro">
     <block>
       Welcome to the voice portal. Please listen to the
       instructions and then say what you want to do.
       <goto next="#menu"/>
     </block>
  </form>
  <!-- ************ Navigation ************ -->
  <menu id="menu">
     <prompt>
         <break size="medium"/>
         Please say one of the following services.
         <break size="medium"/>
         <enumerate/>
     </prompt>
     <choice next="news.vxml">
         News
     </choice>
     <choice next="hiLo.vxml">
         High low
     </choice>
     <choice next="liza.vxml">
         Psychiatrist
     </choice>
  </menu>
</vxml>
```

Note that we added a goto element to the form. The *goto* element can be used to execute jumps in the code between form items, forms, menus, and even to other documents. Next is a mandatory attribute set to the URI (address) for the jump. In our case, we execute a jump that's document internal, so all we have to provide is the local address, #menu.

The menu system is implemented using the menu element and four enumerated choices. First, the user is prompted with some synthesized speech. It will say, "Please say one of the following services: news, HiLo, or psychiatrist." If the user responds by saying "news," then the news service is activated. Before the choices are enumerated, a short pause occurs in the speech output. The break element is used to achieve that. The *break* element has an attribute—medium—that can be set to none, small, medium, or large. We set it to medium, which creates a pause, around half a second long.

Help

Let's add the help function. The *help* function should always be available, no matter which service is being used. Its purpose is to give help for the menu, as well as for each individual service that's put up on the portal. When the help function is added, the root document looks like this:

```
<?xml version="1.0"?>
<vxml version="1.0">
  <!-- ************* Introduction speech ************* -->
  <form id="intro">
      <block>
        Welcome to the voice portal. Please listen to the
        instructions and then say what you want to do.
        You can always say help to get help.
        <goto next="#menu"/>
      </block>
  </form>
  <!-- ************* Navigation ************* -->
  <catch event="help">
      <prompt>Say exit if you want to exit the portal.
        Say main menu if you want to hear which services are available.
      </prompt>
  </catch>
  <menu id="menu">
      <prompt>
          <break size="medium"/>
          Please say one of the following services.
          <break size="medium"/>

          <enumerate/>
      </prompt>
      <choice next="news.vxml">
          News
      </choice>
      <choice next="hiLo.vxml">
```

```
          High low
      </choice>
      <choice next="liza.vxml">
          Psychiatrist
      </choice>
  </menu>
</vxml>
```

The navigation to the help section is implemented with the catch element. A *catch* element can be inserted on the document level and because it's used in the root document on the application level, it will be available in the application as a whole, no matter which of the other documents is used. For example, if the user replies "news," then the code in the news.vxml file is executed, but the catch element in the root document might still be executed if the user asks for help. The global features in the root document, in this case, the catch, are active until the user navigates to a document that doesn't refer to the root document (using the application attribute in the vxml element).

Exit

As with the help function, the *exit* command should be available wherever the user is on the portal. If he's on the top-level page, uses the weather service, or talks to the psychiatrist, he must be able to exit. For this purpose, a second catch element is added, similar to how the help page was implemented. Here's the code as it looks so far:

```
<?xml version="1.0"?>
<vxml version="1.0">
  <!-- ************* Introduction speech ************* -->
  <form id="intro">
      <block>
        Welcome to the voice portal. Please listen to the
        instructions and then say what you want to do.
        You can always say help to get help or say exit to exit.
        <goto next="#menu"/>
      </block>
  </form>
  <!-- ************* Navigation ************* -->
  <catch event="help">
      <prompt>Say exit if you want to exit the portal.
        Say main menu if you want to hear which services are available.
      </prompt>
  </catch>
  <catch event="exit">
      <goto next="#confirm"/>
  </catch>
```

```
<link next="voicePortal.vxml">
    <grammar type="application/x-jsgf">
      menu | main menu | go back
    </grammar>
</link>
<menu id="menu">
    <prompt>
        <break size="medium"/>
        Please say one of the following services.
        <break size="medium"/>
        <enumerate/>
    </prompt>
    <choice next="news.vxml">
        News
    </choice>
    <choice next="hiLo.vxml">
        High low
    </choice>
    <choice next="liza.vxml">
        Psychiatrist
    </choice>
</menu>
</vxml>
```

The new catch element was inserted after the previous one. The form we jump to when the exit command is executed is called confirm. Note, the text in the block element at the top of the file informs the user that it's possible to say "exit."

Go Back to the Main Menu

Note, in the previous code, yet another element—a link—has been inserted. This leads to the same file as is specified in voicePortal.vxml. This link is supposed to be activated if the user gets lost in one of the services, which we'll provide soon. Then the user can get back to the main menu and choose among the alternatives. The syntax, voicePortal.vxml#menu is used. This means the user will jump back to file voicePortal.vxml and the menu that has the ID "menu." When the user jumps back, the introductory text that's spoken in the form intro is skipped. Instead, the jump leads to the menu and not to the first form. The text block in the form is spoken only the first time the user dials in to the portal.

Exit Confirmation

We need to add the form called confirm: It must ask if the user wants to quit the portal or only the service. If the user only wants to quit an individual service on the portal, then she should be taken back to the main menu. This completes the main file, voicePortal.vxml, which finally looks like this:

```
<?xml version="1.0"?>
<vxml version="1.0">
  <!-- ************* Introduction speech ************* -->
  <form id="intro">
      <block>
        Welcome to the voice portal. Please listen to the
        instructions and then say what you want to do.

        You can always say help to get help or say quit to quit.
        <goto next="#menu"/>
      </block>
  </form>
  <!-- ************* Navigation ************* -->
  <catch event="help">
      <prompt>Say exit if you want to exit the portal.
        Say main menu if you want to hear which services are available.
      </prompt>
  </catch>
  <catch event="exit">
      <goto next="#confirm"/>
  </catch>
  <link next="voicePortal.vxml#menu">
      <grammar type="application/x-jsgf">
        menu | main menu | go back
      </grammar>
  </link>
  <form id="confirm">
      <field name="quitPortal" type="boolean">
          <prompt>Do you want to exit the whole portal?
          </prompt>
      </field>
      <filled>
          <if cond="quitPortal">
              <prompt>Thank you and goodbye.
              </prompt>
              <exit/>
          <else/>
              <goto next="#menu"/>
          </if>
      </filled>
  </form>
  <menu id="menu">
      <prompt>
```

```
        <break size="medium"/>
        Please say one of the following services.
        <break size="medium"/>
        <enumerate/>
    </prompt>
    <choice next="news.vxml">
        News
    </choice>
    <choice next="hiLo.vxml">
        High low
    </choice>
    <choice next="liza.vxml">
        Psychiatrist
    </choice>
  </menu>
</vxml>
```

The confirm form is inserted before the menu. Note, the order of the forms and menus doesn't matter. If the first form in the file doesn't execute a jump to the next, then the interpretation will stop there. The confirm form has one field and when it's filled in, the filled element is executed. Because the field is a Boolean field, we needn't provide a grammar element. The filled element checks include an if-statement, which checks if the user answered "yes." If so, the whole application is exited using the exit element. If the user wants to continue, then he just wanted to exit a service. The execution then continues with the menu.

The Services

Now we've implemented the basic shell around everything: the welcome message, the menu navigation system, the basic help section, and the confirmed exit. Let's move on to the services that reside on the voice portal. From the navigation menu, it's possible to access a news service, so we'll start with that.

News

The news service is deployed on the portal using the file news.vxml. As mentioned earlier, though, we assume a news provider has signed a deal with us to provide the content. The content is delivered to us as an XHTML file because the news bureau publishes the content on its own web site. Converting the XHTML code to VoiceXML each time the news is delivered to us is a less-smart strategy because this takes time and it's easy to make mistakes.

Instead, we must find a way to do it more or less automatically and this is where XSL transformations come in. We'll write an XSL style sheet that's used to transform the XHTML to a VoiceXML file.

The Mapping   The XSL transformation takes only a fraction of a second to execute and this can be carried out as the news is delivered to us.

The final VoiceXML content should look something like this:

```
<?xml version="1.0" encoding="UTF-8"?>
<vxml version="1.0" application="voicePortal.vxml">
  <form>
    <block>Today's News</block>
    <block>
      <prompt>Researchers say that they have built
        a <emp>biological AI computer</emp> in the lab.
        The computer can speak with human beings and
        understand words and sentences ...
      </prompt>
    </block>
    <block>
      <prompt>The elections to the parliament start on
        Monday and the parties are busy with their
        campaigns ...
      </prompt>
    </block>
    <block>
      <goto next="voicePortal.vxml#menu"/>
    </block>
  </form>
</vxml>
```

Here's an example of the input. Each text paragraph is converted to a block, which contains the prompt element and the text inside the prompt element.

```
<p>News text
</p>
```

The previous code will be converted to the following VoiceXML code:

```
<block>
  <prompt>
    News text
  </prompt>
</block>
```

Later on, we'll use elements that can only be specified inside the prompt element. This is the way the text is put in a prompt element and not right under the block.

The text is augmented with the *emp* element, which means *emphasis*. As the interpreter speaks the text and renders the emp element, it puts emphasis on the text inside the emp element. In the XHTML code, the i, b, and em elements are converted to the emp element. This is a simplification, but it works quite well. Because italics and boldface are so tightly coupled to visual formatting, they're hard to map to anything other than the emphasis element. Assume the content provider sends us a news file, which contains the following XHTML code:

```
<p>That is why we <em>must</em> keep on fighting for our rights,
  says the leader who formed the <i>Zonk tribe</i>.
</p>
```

This will be mapped to the following VoiceXML code:

```
<block>
  <prompt>
    That is why we <emp>must</emp> keep on fighting for our rights,
  says the leader who formed the <emp>Zonk tribe</emp>.
  </prompt>
</block>
```

Note, the em and the i elements have been mapped to the emp element, and the paragraph has been replaced by a block followed by a prompt.

The output—the VoiceXML code—must always end with a block that contains a goto. This takes the user back to the portal's main menu and the code looks like this:

```
<block>
  <goto next="voicePortal.vxml#menu"/>
</block>
```

Links won't be mapped at all. Only the content between the *a* tags is kept as is. The same goes for the title element, which isn't mapped to anything special except a prompt section. Here's an example that illustrates how the title and the *a* elements are mapped.

```
<head>
  <title>News</title>
</head>
<p>That is why we <em>must</em> keep on fighting for our rights,
  says the leader who formed
  <a href="www.example.com/zonk.html">the Zonk tribe</a>.
</p>
```

The code corresponds to the following VoiceXML code:

```
<block>
    News
</block>
<block>
  <prompt>
That is why we <em>must</em> keep on fighting for our rights,
  says the leader who formed the Zonk tribe.
  </prompt>
</block>
```

List elements are treated in a special way. Because a list contains a number of items, each item must be read in a special way, so the listener understands that the speaker enumerates something. We'll use the break element to insert a short pause between each list tem, according to the following example:

```
Things to do:
<ul>
  <li>Stay inside.
  </li>
  <li>Check the weather report.
  </li>
  <li>Listen to the radio.
  </li>
</ul>
```

The list is converted to the following VoiceXML code:

```
Things to do:
<break size="medium"/>
Stay inside.
<break size="medium"/>
Check the weather report.
<break size="medium"/>
Listen to the radio.
<break size="medium"/>
```

The break elements are used to create a short pause between the spoken phrases. If we don't use the break element and simply remove the li elements from the XHTML, then the text will be read as if it were a whole sentence and it will be difficult to understand what the voice synthesizer says.

Tables will be mapped almost the same way as list elements. Each table is preceded by a short break and a short break is inserted after each table data element. Here's an example:

```
News headlines.
<table rows="2" cols="2">
  <tr>
    <td>Tomorrow's weather.</td>
    <td>The worst storm ever is approaching your area.</td>
  </tr>
  <tr>
    <td>Low market values on the stock exchanges.</td>
    <td>New markets open up.</td>
  </tr>
</table>
```

The table is mapped to the following VoiceXML code:

```
News headlines.
<break size="medium"/>
Tomorrow's weather.
<break size="medium"/>
The worst storm ever is approaching your area.
<break size="medium"/>
<break size="medium"/>
Low market values on the stock exchanges.
<break size="medium"/>
New markets open up.
<break size="medium"/>
<break size="medium"/>
```

You can map tables and lists in several ways. We've chosen one of them—a simple mapping. An alternative is to look for the values of certain attributes and use them in the transformation process.

Pictures must be mapped to a representation, which can be spoken. Therefore, the img element is mapped to the text Picture:. If the content provider has used the alt attribute to give an alternate description of the image, then that text is inserted after Picture:. Assume the content provider uses the following XHTML element:

```
<img src="./images/pic435.gif" alt="Red Porsche"/>
```

It will be mapped to the following VoiceXML code:

```
Picture: Red Porsche
```

The value of the alt attribute is inserted after Picture:.

The Implementation   The basic shell for the XSL style sheet looks like this:

```
<?xml version="1.0"?>
<xsl:stylesheet version="1.0" xmlns:xsl="http://www.w3.org/1999/XSL/Transform">
  <xsl:output method="xml"/>

<!-- ******** Rules specified here. ******** -->

</xsl:stylesheet>
```

Let's look at some of the rules, which are worth a comment. When the XSL transformation processor starts scanning the top of the XHTML, we should generate the vxml element, the form element, and the last block, which contains the goto element. The XSL rule looks like this:

```
<xsl:template match="/">
  <vxml version="1.0" application="voicePortal.vxml">
    <form>
      <xsl:apply-templates/>
    <block>
        <goto next="voicePortal.vxml#menu"/>
    </block>
    </form>
  </vxml>
</xsl:template>
```

The next attribute is set to the portal's main document and the menu, so when the voice synthesizer has read everything, it enters the last block. We're then directed to the main menu of the portal.

The title element in the XHTML file should result in a block and the text provided between the title tags. Therefore, the following rule is provided in the XSL file:

```
<xsl:template match="title">
  <block>
    <xsl:apply-templates/>
  </block>
</xsl:template>
```

Because the title is usually simple and doesn't require any emphasis or other fancy stuff, we needn't put a prompt element inside a block.

If a table is right under the body element, then we need to generate a block and a prompt, plus everything inside the table. The rule goes like this:

```
<xsl:template match="//html/body/table">
  <block>
    <prompt>
      <xsl:apply-templates/>
    </prompt>
  </block>
</xsl:template>
```

Note the XPath, which matches a table under the body element. Providing a table inside a paragraph is also possible. Then we use the following rule:

```
<xsl:template match="//html/body/p/table">
    <xsl:apply-templates/>
</xsl:template>
```

If the table occurs under the paragraph, then the block and prompt have already been created by the paragraph element. Therefore, we should only apply the templates for the content of the table.

This is the rule for managing the tr element:

```
<xsl:template match="tr">
  <xsl:apply-templates/>
    <break size="medium"/>
</xsl:template>
```

A break is inserted after the row's content, which is an arbitrary number of td elements. Each td element is managed according to the following rule:

```
<xsl:template match="td">
  <xsl:apply-templates/>
    <break size="medium"/>
</xsl:template>
```

The content of each td element, typically a piece of text, ends with a break to create a pause.

Here's how we handle the img element:

```
<xsl:template match="img">
  Picture: <xsl:value-of select="@alt"/>.
</xsl:template>
```

The text Picture: is inserted where an image occurs in the XHTML code. In addition, the value of the img element's src attribute is also provided. As you can see, we use the xsl:value-of element to select the value of the alt attribute. The @ means attribute.

The remaining elements are handled easily without too much transformation or they're simply not supported. You can see which elements I left out. Feel free to refine this transformation and make it more complex. I deliberately skipped many of the elements in the XHTML language, so you can try different styles of transformation. Creating good transformations for elements that were designed for visual renderings only is a challenge. To name several, map and area were designed to describe image maps, so they are, without a doubt, visual elements. The same goes for the hr element, the horizontal ruler, the big, and the small elements.

This is the final XSL sheet:

```
<?xml version="1.0"?>
<xsl:stylesheet version="1.0" xmlns:xsl="http://www.w3.org/1999/XSL/Transform">
  <xsl:output method="xml"/>

  <xsl:template match="/">
    <vxml version="1.0" application="voicePortal.vxml">
      <form>
        <xsl:apply-templates/>
      <block>
          <goto next="voicePortal.vxml#menu"/>
      </block>
      </form>
    </vxml>
  </xsl:template>

  <xsl:template match="head">

    <xsl:apply-templates/>
  </xsl:template>

  <xsl:template match="title">
    <block>
      <xsl:apply-templates/>
    </block>
```

```xsl
</xsl:template>

<xsl:template match="div">
  <block>
    <xsl:apply-templates/>
  </block>
</xsl:template>

<xsl:template match="span">
  <xsl:apply-templates/>
</xsl:template>

<xsl:template match="body">
  <xsl:apply-templates/>
</xsl:template>

<xsl:template match="//html/body/p">
  <block>
    <prompt>
      <xsl:apply-templates/>
    </prompt>
  </block>
</xsl:template>

<xsl:template match="pre">
  <block>
      <xsl:apply-templates/>
  </block>
</xsl:template>

<xsl:template match="cite">
  Cite: <xsl:apply-templates/> End of cite.
</xsl:template>

<xsl:template match="blockquote">
  <block>
    Quote: <xsl:apply-templates/> End of quote.
  </block>
</xsl:template>

<xsl:template match="q">
  Quote: <xsl:apply-templates/> End of quote.
</xsl:template>

<xsl:template match="sub">
  <xsl:apply-templates/>
</xsl:template>
```

```
<xsl:template match="sup">
  <xsl:apply-templates/>
</xsl:template>

<xsl:template match="abbr">
  <xsl:apply-templates/>
</xsl:template>

<xsl:template match="acronym">
  <xsl:apply-templates/>
</xsl:template>

<xsl:template match="em">
  <emp>
    <xsl:apply-templates/>
  </emp>
</xsl:template>

<xsl:template match="strong">
  <emp>
    <xsl:apply-templates/>
  </emp>
</xsl:template>

<xsl:template match="i">
  <emp>
    <xsl:apply-templates/>
  </emp>
</xsl:template>

<xsl:template match="b">
  <emp>
    <xsl:apply-templates/>
  </emp>
</xsl:template>

<xsl:template match="ul">
  <break size="medium"/>
    <xsl:apply-templates/>
</xsl:template>

<xsl:template match="ol">
  <break size="medium"/>
    <xsl:apply-templates/>
</xsl:template>
```

```
<xsl:template match="li">
    <xsl:apply-templates/>
  <break size="medium"/>
</xsl:template>

<xsl:template match="a">
  <xsl:apply-templates/>
</xsl:template>

<xsl:template match="//html/body/table">
  <block>
    <prompt>
      <xsl:apply-templates/>
    </prompt>
  </block>
</xsl:template>

<xsl:template match="//html/body/p/table">
    <xsl:apply-templates/>
</xsl:template>

<xsl:template match="h1">
  <block>
      <xsl:apply-templates/>
  </block>
</xsl:template>

<xsl:template match="h2">
  <block>
      <xsl:apply-templates/>
  </block>
</xsl:template>

<xsl:template match="h3">
  <block>
      <xsl:apply-templates/>
  </block>
</xsl:template>

<xsl:template match="h4">
  <block>
      <xsl:apply-templates/>
  </block>
</xsl:template>

<xsl:template match="h5">
  <block>
```

```
        <xsl:apply-templates/>
      </block>
</xsl:template>

<xsl:template match="h6">
  <block>
      <xsl:apply-templates/>
    </block>
</xsl:template>

<xsl:template match="tr">
  <xsl:apply-templates/>
    <break size="medium"/>
</xsl:template>

<xsl:template match="td">
  <xsl:apply-templates/>
    <break size="medium"/>
</xsl:template>

<xsl:template match="img">
  Picture: <xsl:value-of select="@alt"/>.
</xsl:template>

<xsl:template match="ins">
  The following text has been inserted:
    <xsl:apply-templates/>
  End of inserted text.
</xsl:template>

<xsl:template match="del">
  The following text was deleted:
    <xsl:apply-templates/>
  End of deleted text.
</xsl:template>

<xsl:template match="base"></xsl:template>
<xsl:template match="meta"></xsl:template>
<xsl:template match="link"></xsl:template>
<xsl:template match="style"></xsl:template>
<xsl:template match="script"></xsl:template>
<xsl:template match="noscript"></xsl:template>
<xsl:template match="dl"></xsl:template>
<xsl:template match="address"></xsl:template>
<xsl:template match="hr"></xsl:template>
<xsl:template match="bdo"></xsl:template>
<xsl:template match="br"></xsl:template>
```

```
<xsl:template match="def"></xsl:template>
<xsl:template match="code"></xsl:template>
<xsl:template match="samp"></xsl:template>
<xsl:template match="kbd"></xsl:template>
<xsl:template match="var"></xsl:template>
<xsl:template match="tt"></xsl:template>
<xsl:template match="big"></xsl:template>
<xsl:template match="small"></xsl:template>
<xsl:template match="object"></xsl:template>
<xsl:template match="param"></xsl:template>
<xsl:template match="map"></xsl:template>
<xsl:template match="area"></xsl:template>
<xsl:template match="form"></xsl:template>
<xsl:template match="label"></xsl:template>
<xsl:template match="input"></xsl:template>
<xsl:template match="select"></xsl:template>
<xsl:template match="optgroup"></xsl:template>
<xsl:template match="option"></xsl:template>
<xsl:template match="textarea"></xsl:template>
<xsl:template match="fieldset"></xsl:template>
<xsl:template match="legend"></xsl:template>
<xsl:template match="button"></xsl:template>
<xsl:template match="select"></xsl:template>
<xsl:template match="caption"></xsl:template>
<xsl:template match="thead"></xsl:template>
<xsl:template match="tfoot"></xsl:template>
<xsl:template match="tbody"></xsl:template>
<xsl:template match="colgroup"></xsl:template>
<xsl:template match="col"></xsl:template>
<xsl:template match="th"></xsl:template>
<xsl:template match="iframe"></xsl:template>

</xsl:stylesheet>
```

Note how the cite and quotation elements are transformed. For inline and block quotations, the text string Quote: is inserted before the actual quote. After the quote, the text End of quote is inserted. The cite element is transformed in a similar way.

Example   Let's look at an example. Assume you received the following XHTML code from the news provider:

```
<!DOCTYPE html PUBLIC "-//W3C//DTD XHTML 1.0 Strict//EN"
    "http://www.w3.org/TR/xhtml1/DTD/xhtml1-strict.dtd">
<html xmlns="http://www.w3.org/1999/xhtml">
<head>
```

```
<title>Today's news</title>
</head>
<body>
<h1>World</h1>

<p>An accident occurred yesterday when a guy tried to fly. He
had built his own jet. Unfortunately, it did not work very
well.</p>

<h1>IT</h1>

<p>IT stocks are going up again. After a long period of low market values,
the market for IT stocks looks bright.</p>

<p>New AI software launched. Now it is possible to talk with your
computer. It understands what you say and answers politely.</p>
</body>
</html>
```

Running the file through the XSL transformation processor results in the following output, which can be spoken by a VoiceXML-enabled server:

```
<?xml version="1.0" encoding="UTF-8"?>
<vxml version="1.0" application="voicePortal.vxml"><form>

<block>Today's news</block>

<block>World</block>

<block><prompt>An accident occurred yesterday when a guy tried to fly. He
had built his own jet. Unfortunately, it did not work very
well.</prompt></block>

<block>IT</block>

<block><prompt>IT stock are going up again. After a long period of low market
values, the market for IT stocks looks bright.</prompt></block>

<block><prompt>New AI software launched. Now it is possible to talk with your
computer. It understands what you say and answers politely.</prompt></block>

<block><goto next="voicePortal.vxml#menu"/></block></form></vxml>
```

Note the last block, which includes a link to the main menu on the voice portal. Each block is executed and, when the interpreter reaches the last block, we're taken back to the main menu. Immediately, all the choices on the main menu are spoken.

HiLo

HiLo is one of the classic games that's been implemented on everything from programmable calculators to desktop computers. First, a welcome message is synthesized, and then the voice says "Guess a number between 0 and 100." If the guess is too high, then the voice says, "You guessed ___ and that's too high." A similar message is synthesized if the guess is too low. The process is repeated until the user guesses the right number and the voice says "Bingo! The number is ___. You guessed ___ times."

Once a game ends, the voice asks "Do you want to try again?" If the user doesn't want to continue, he is transferred to the main menu of the portal.

Main Functions of HiLo   The welcome message has to be implemented and it must be possible to ask for help and to quit. If the user wants to quit, she must be asked to confirm. If the answer is no, then yet another game round is started. But the most difficult part of this application is probably to implement the generation of the secret number, to check what the user guesses against the secret number and to repeat these steps until the user wins. The application must also keep track of how many times the user has guessed. Another task that must be solved is the grammar for the user's guesses. Here's how a typical conversation should sound.

```
Voice:   Welcome to HiLo! Guess the number.
User:    Help!
Voice:   Guess a number between 0 and 100. The computer will tell you if
         you guessed too high or too low.
User:    42.
Voice:   You guessed 42 and that's too low.
User:    67.
Voice:   You guessed 67 and that's too high.
User:    58.
Voice:   Bingo! The number is 58. You guessed 3 times.
         Do you want to try again?
User:    No.
Voice:   Please say one of the following services: News ...
```

Let's look at the implementation.

The Implementation   The basic shell for the application looks like this:

```
<?xml version="1.0"?>
<vxml version="1.0" application="voicePortal.vxml">
  <!-- ************* Welcome message. ************* -->

  <!-- ************* Help. ************* -->

  <!-- ************* Play the game. ************* -->

  <!-- ************* Really quit? ************* -->

</vxml>
```

As in all VoiceXML files, the vxml element comes first. HiLo has been divided into four sections: one that synthesizes the welcome message, one that helps the user, one that manages the actual playing of the game, and the last section that confirms the user wants to quit.

Here's the implementation of the welcome message:

```
<?xml version="1.0"?>
<vxml version="1.0" application="voicePortal.vxml">
<var name="num" expr="Math.round( 100 * Math.random() )"/>
<var name="counter" expr="1"/>
<form id="intro">
    <block>
      Welcome to high low.
      <goto next="#theGame"/>
    </block>
</form>
</vxml>
```

Two variables are used: num and counter. *Num* holds the secret number and *counter* keeps track of how many times the user has guessed. When a variable is declared, it can also be given a value using the expr attribute. Counter is assigned the value 1 and num is given the value that's the result of the expression. A random number is generated using the Math.random() function. This is an ECMAScript function that returns a value greater than or equal to 0, but less than 1. This value is multiplied by 100 and the result is rounded to the closest integer value. Consequently, the result of expr is a random number between 0 and 100.

The intro form generates the welcome speech. Immediately, as the text is spoken, the interpreter jumps to the dialogue, which is called "theGame."

In this form, the actual playing of the game is implemented. Each guess is handed in as a field in a form. This is the code for the form:

```
<form id="theGame">
    <field name="guess" type="number">
      <prompt>Guess the number.
      </prompt>
      <filled>
          <if cond="guess &lt; num">
            <prompt>You guessed <value expr="guess"/> and that's too low.
            </prompt>
            <assign name="counter" expr="counter + 1"/>
          <elseif cond="guess &gt; num"/>
            <prompt>You guessed <value expr="guess"/> and that's too high.
            </prompt>
            <assign name="counter" expr="counter + 1"/>
          <else/>
            <prompt>Bingo! The number is <value expr="guess"/>.
              You guessed <value expr="counter"/> times.
            </prompt>
            <goto next="#tryAgain"/>
          </if>
          <goto next="#theGame"/>
      </filled>
    </field>
</form>
```

Note, we specified the type of the field in the form, using the type attribute. This is set to number, which means the server's voice recognition software expects a number and nothing else for that field. Consequently, you needn't provide a grammar (unless you want to) for numbers. Another solution can be to provide a grammar that's hard coded for the numbers you expect: integers between zero and one hundred. With this solution, any number is a valid input, even large decimal numbers, such as 20394.54.

First, the user is asked to guess a number. When the user replies, the filled section is executed. An if-else statement is in the filled section that needs to be explained. The if-statement looks like this:

```
<if cond="guess &lt; num">
```

However, it means:

```
<if cond="guess < num">
```

We must replace the less-than character with the XML encoding of it because these characters cannot be provided in the cond attribute. If you check the else-if element, then you can see the > character has been encoded as >.

Inside the if- and else-if elements, the counter variable is incremented with 1, using the assign element. If the else element is executed, then the user guessed the right number and the value of the secret number is spoken using the value element. When the message has been spoken, there's a jump to try again. In that dialogue, the user is asked to try again or to return to the portal's main menu.

The last element inside the "filled" element is a goto, which works as a loop because the goto leads to the same form as we are in.

Now, let's move on to the help section. The user must have access to a help menu. Help is implemented using the catch element:

```
<catch event="help">
    <prompt>Guess a number between 0 and 100. The computer will tell you
    if you guessed too high or too low.
    </prompt>
</catch>
```

In VoiceXML, it's possible to throw and catch events. If the user says "help," the predefined help event is thrown by the system. So, we simply catch that event and provide the code for giving help inside the catch element.

One section remains: the one that deals with confirmation in case the user wants to quit. Every time a game round ends, the user should be asked if he wants to continue. To implement this behavior, you use a form that contains one field only of type Boolean. Here's the code:

```
<form id="tryAgain">
    <field name="again" type="boolean">
      <prompt>Do you want to try again?
      </prompt>
      <filled>
        <if cond="again">
          <assign name="num" expr="Math.round( 100 * Math.random() )"/>
          <assign name="counter" expr="1"/>
          <goto next="#theGame"/>
        <else/>
          <goto next="voicePortal.vxml#menu"/>
```

```
        </if>
      </filled>
    </field>
</form>
```

Because the field element has the type attribute set to "boolean," the interpreter expects a yes or a no as the reply, so you needn't provide a grammar for the answer. As the user answers, the filled element is executed. If the user answers yes, then the counter variable is reset, a new secret number is generated, and the interpreter jumps to the form called "theGame." If the answer is no, then the user is taken back to the portal's menu.

That's it. Here's the complete implementation:

```
<?xml version="1.0"?>
<vxml version="1.0" application="voicePortal.vxml">
  <!-- ************ Welcome message. ************* -->
  <var name="num" expr="Math.round( 100 * Math.random() )"/>
  <var name="counter" expr="1"/>
  <form id="intro">
      <block>
        Welcome to high low.
        <goto next="#theGame"/>
      </block>
  </form>
  <!-- ************ Help. ************* -->
  <catch event="help">
      <prompt>Guess a number between 0 and 100. The computer will tell you
      if you guessed too high or too low.
      </prompt>
  </catch>
  <!-- ************ Play the game. ************* -->
  <form id="theGame">
      <field name="guess" type="number">
        <prompt>Guess the number.
        </prompt>
        <filled>
            <if cond="guess &lt; num">
              <prompt>You guessed <value expr="guess"/> and that's too low.
              </prompt>
              <assign name="counter" expr="counter + 1"/>
            <elseif cond="guess &gt; num"/>
              <prompt>You guessed <value expr="guess"/> and that's too high.
              </prompt>
              <assign name="counter" expr="counter + 1"/>
            <else/>
```

```
                        <prompt>Bingo! The number is <value expr="guess"/>.
                            You guessed <value expr="counter"/> times.
                        </prompt>
                        <goto next="#tryAgain"/>
                    </if>
                    <goto next="#theGame"/>
            </filled>
        </field>
    </form>
    <!-- ************* Really quit? ************* -->
    <form id="tryAgain">
        <field name="again" type="boolean">
            <prompt>Do you want to try again?
            </prompt>
            <filled>
                <if cond="again">
                    <assign name="num" expr="Math.round( 100 * Math.random() )"/>
                    <assign name="counter" expr="1"/>
                    <goto next="#theGame"/>
                <else/>
                    <goto next="voicePortal.vxml#menu"/>
                </if>
            </filled>
        </field>
    </form>
</vxml>
```

Liza — the Robot Psychiatrist

The last application that resides on the portal is Liza, the robot psychiatrist. As the
user enters "the room" to the psychiatrist, Liza says, "Welcome! Please sit down
and tell me about your problem." The user can then say something and Liza will
reply as if she understands what the user says. If the user says "help," then Liza says
she's there to help you. After a while, Liza asks politely if the user can come back
tomorrow instead. If the answer is yes, the user is transferred back to the portal's
main menu. If the answer is no, the conversation continues. The conversation can
go like this:

```
Liza:  Welcome! Please sit down and tell me about your problem.
User:  I feel sick.
Liza:  And?
User:  Well, my stomach hurts.
Liza:  Tell me more.
User:  I feel cold.
Liza:  Can you give me more details?
```

```
User:   Help!
Liza:   I am here to help you. Just tell me how you feel.
User:   I feel bad.
Liza:   Sorry, but time's up. I suggest that we meet again tomorrow.
        I am sure I can help you. Is it OK with you to stop here?
User:   Yes.
Voice:  Please say one of the following services: News ...
```

The implementation of Liza has similarities with the implementation of HiLo because we're going to reuse the two variables—num and counter—and introduce a third: sent. In this case, *num* holds a random number that decides what Liza is going to say. *Counter* counts how many times Liza has replied. When Liza has replied six times, then it's time to ask the client to leave. *Sent* is used to store Liza's sentences. Here's the basic code shell for everything:

```xml
<?xml version="1.0"?>
<vxml version="1.0" application="voicePortal.vxml">
  <!-- ************ Welcome message. ************ -->
  <var name="num" expr="Math.round( 6 * Math.random() )"/>
  <var name="counter" expr="0"/>
  <var name="sentence" expr="'Welcome! Please sit down and tell me about your
    problem.'"/>
  <form id="conversation">
    ...
  </form>
  <form id="stopTalking">
    ...

  </form>
</vxml>
```

There are two forms: "conversation" and "stopTalking." The first form is the main loop, which speaks a sentence and expects a reply. The second form asks the user if it's okay to quit. If the reply is "yes," the user is transferred back to the portal's main menu. If the reply is "no," the process continues.

The three variables are declared at the top of the file and assigned initial values. As you can see, the Math.random and Math.round functions are used the same way as in the HiLo example. Let's add some code to the conversation form:

```xml
<?xml version="1.0"?>
<vxml version="1.0" application="voicePortal.vxml">
  <!-- ************ Welcome message. ************ -->
  <var name="num" expr="Math.round( 6 * Math.random() )"/>
  <var name="counter" expr="0"/>
```

```
<var name="sentence" expr="'Welcome! Please sit down and tell me about your
    problem.'"/>
<form id="conversation">
    <field name="sent">
        <prompt><value expr="sentence"/>
        </prompt>
        <grammar type="application/x-jsgf">
            quit | stop | [this is] enough | get me out [of here] | I have had
            enough [of this]
        </grammar>
        <catch event="nomatch">
            <!-- ********** Time's up ********** -->
              ...

            <!-- ********** Replies ********** -->
              ...

        </catch>
        <catch event="noinput">
          ...

        </catch>
        <catch event="exit">
          ...

        </catch>
        <catch event="help">
          ...

        </catch>
        <filled>
            <goto next="#stopTalking"/>
        </filled>
    </field>
</form>
<form id="stopTalking">
        ...

</form>
</vxml>
```

You can see the application's basic structure here. There's a form "conversation" that has a field: "sent." The current sentence is spoken, using the value element. Because the value of the variable sent is changed, a new sentence is spoken every time the interpreter executes the prompt statement.

A grammar has been specified using the Java speech API grammar format. The vertical bar denotes an "or" condition and the square brackets enclose optional phrases. For example, the user might say "quit," "stop," "enough," or "this is enough," and the grammar will then parse the input successfully.

The grammar applies to the situation when the user wants to quit. Whatever the user says in addition to that won't be used. In fact, Liza's replies will be totally independent of what the user says. So, all normal sentences spoken by the user will be caught in the catch, which has the event set to "nomatch." Inside that catch element, is a check to see if it's time to stop or if a new sentence should be composed. Here's the code for all the catch statements, except "nomatch":

```xml
<?xml version="1.0"?>
<vxml version="1.0" application="voicePortal.vxml">
  <!-- ************* Welcome message. ************* -->
  <var name="num" expr="Math.round( 6 * Math.random() )"/>
  <var name="counter" expr="0"/>
  <var name="sentence" expr="'Welcome! Please sit down and tell me about your
      problem.'"/>
  <form id="conversation">
      <field name="sent">
        <prompt><value expr="sentence"/>
        </prompt>
        <grammar type="application/x-jsgf">
           quit | stop | [this is] enough | get me out [of here] | I have had
              enough [of this]
        </grammar>
        <catch event="nomatch">
           <!-- ********** Time's up ********** -->
             ...

           <!-- ********** Replies ********** -->
             ...

        </catch>
        <catch event="noinput">
          <prompt>Please tell me how you feel.
          </prompt>
        </catch>
        <catch event="exit">
          <goto next="#stopTalking"/>
        </catch>
        <catch event="help">
          <prompt>I am here to help you. Just tell me how you feel.
          </prompt>
          <goto next="#stopTalking"/>
```

```
        </catch>
        <filled>
            <goto next="#stopTalking"/>
        </filled>
      </field>
  </form>
  <form id="stopTalking">
    ...

  </form>
</vxml>
```

If the user doesn't say anything, then the noinput event is thrown by the system and Liza says, "Please tell me how you feel." If the user says "exit," then the system automatically associates that phrase with the exit event and the catch element that has event set to "exit" is executed. In that element, there's a jump to "stopTalking," so the dialogue that confirms the user wants to stop is then executed. If the user says "help," then the system throws a help event. Because we're catching that event, the text we've provided is spoken, and then there's a goto to the "stopTalking" dialogue. If the user says anything else (such as, "I feel sick"), then the filled element is executed. Let's extend the previous code with the section that deals with the replied sentences. The code, which stops after six sentences, is also provided.

```
<?xml version="1.0"?>
<vxml version="1.0" application="voicePortal.vxml">
  <!-- ************* Welcome message. ************* -->
  <var name="num" expr="Math.round( 6 * Math.random() )"/>
  <var name="counter" expr="0"/>
  <var name="sentence" expr="'Welcome! Please sit down and tell me about your
      problem.'"/>
  <form id="conversation">
      <field name="sent">
        <prompt><value expr="sentence"/>
        </prompt>
        <grammar type="application/x-jsgf">
          quit | stop | [this is] enough | get me out [of here] | I have had
              enough [of this]
        </grammar>
        <catch event="nomatch">
            <!-- ********** Time's up ********** -->
            <if cond="counter == 5 &amp;&amp; num &lt; 3">
              <prompt>Ok. Let's stop here for today. Please come back tomorrow.
                  I am sure that we can continue with the therapy then.
              </prompt>
              <goto next="#stopTalking"/>
```

```
          </if>
          <if cond="counter == 5 &amp;&amp; num &gt;= 3">
            <prompt>Sorry, but time's up. I suggest that we meet again tomorrow.
              I am sure I can help you.
            </prompt>
            <goto next="#stopTalking"/>
          </if>
          <!-- ********** Replies ********** -->
          <if cond="num == 0">
            <assign name="sentence" expr="'Please continue.'"/>
          <elseif cond="num == 1"/>
            <assign name="sentence" expr="'Tell me more.'"/>
          <elseif cond="num == 2"/>
            <assign name="sentence" expr="'Just go on. I am listening.'"/>
          <elseif cond="num == 3"/>
            <assign name="sentence" expr="'Can you please explain why you came
                here?'"/>
          <elseif cond="num == 4"/>
            <assign name="sentence" expr="'How does it make you feel?'"/>
          <elseif cond="num == 5"/>
            <assign name="sentence" expr="'Can you give me more details?'"/>
          <else/>
            <assign name="sentence" expr="'And?'"/>
          </if>
          <assign name="counter" expr="counter + 1"/>
          <assign name="num" expr="Math.round( 6 * Math.random() )"/>

          <goto next="#conversation"/>
      </catch>
      <catch event="noinput">
        <prompt>Please tell me how you feel.
        </prompt>
      </catch>
      <catch event="exit">
        <goto next="#stopTalking"/>
      </catch>
      <catch event="help">
        <prompt>I am here to help you. Just tell me how you feel.
        </prompt>
        <goto next="#stopTalking"/>
      </catch>
      <filled>
          <goto next="#stopTalking"/>
      </filled>
    </field>
  </form>
<form id="stopTalking">
```

```
    ...
  </form>
</vxml>
```

Under the "Time's up" comment, we check how many times the patient has talked with Liza. If the user has asked six questions, then one of two possible sentences is chosen randomly. Either Liza replies, "Okay. Let's stop here …" or she says, "Sorry, but time's up…" Then the user is asked if it's okay to stop. If the user hasn't yet asked six questions, then one of the if-elements under the "Replies" comment is executed. A sentence is chosen according to the random number, num. Then a new random number is generated and the counter that keeps track of how many questions the user has asked is incremented with 1. The new sentence is then spoken for the user and the process repeats.

The "stopTalking" form remains and completes the applications, which follows here:

```
<?xml version="1.0"?>
<vxml version="1.0" application="voicePortal.vxml">
  <!-- ************* Welcome message. ************* -->
  <var name="num" expr="Math.round( 6 * Math.random() )"/>
  <var name="counter" expr="0"/>
  <var name="sentence" expr="'Welcome! Please sit down and tell me about your
      problem.'"/>
  <form id="conversation">
      <field name="sent">
        <prompt><value expr="sentence"/>
        </prompt>
        <grammar type="application/x-jsgf">
           quit | stop | [this is] enough | get me out [of here] | I have had
              enough [of this]
        </grammar>
        <catch event="nomatch">
           <!-- ********** Time's up ********** -->
           <if cond="counter == 5 &amp;&amp; num &lt; 3">
             <prompt>Ok. Let's stop here for today. Please come back tomorrow.
                I am sure that we can continue with the therapy then.
             </prompt>
             <goto next="#stopTalking"/>
           </if>
           <if cond="counter == 5 &amp;&amp; num &gt;= 3">
             <prompt>Sorry, but time's up. I suggest that we meet again tomorrow.
               I am sure I can help you.
             </prompt>
             <goto next="#stopTalking"/>
           </if>
```

```vxml
      <!-- ********** Replies ********** -->
      <if cond="num == 0">
        <assign name="sentence" expr="'Please continue.'"/>
      <elseif cond="num == 1"/>
        <assign name="sentence" expr="'Tell me more.'"/>
      <elseif cond="num == 2"/>
        <assign name="sentence" expr="'Just go on. I am listening.'"/>
      <elseif cond="num == 3"/>
        <assign name="sentence" expr="'Can you please explain why you came
            here?'"/>
      <elseif cond="num == 4"/>
        <assign name="sentence" expr="'How does it make you feel?'"/>
      <elseif cond="num == 5"/>
        <assign name="sentence" expr="'Can you give me more details?'"/>
      <else/>
        <assign name="sentence" expr="'And?'"/>
      </if>
      <assign name="counter" expr="counter + 1"/>
      <assign name="num" expr="Math.round( 6 * Math.random() )"/>
      <goto next="#conversation"/>
    </catch>
    <catch event="noinput">
      <prompt>Please tell me how you feel.
      </prompt>
    </catch>
    <catch event="exit">
      <goto next="#stopTalking"/>
    </catch>
    <catch event="help">
      <prompt>I am here to help you. Just tell me how you feel.
      </prompt>
      <goto next="#stopTalking"/>
    </catch>
    <filled>
        <goto next="#stopTalking"/>
    </filled>
  </field>
</form>
<form id="stopTalking">
    <field name="stopNow" type="boolean">
      <prompt>Is it ok with you to stop here?
      </prompt>
      <filled>
          <if cond="stopNow">
            <goto next="voicePortal.vxml#menu"/>
          <else/>
            <assign name="num" expr="Math.round( 6 * Math.random() )"/>
```

```
            <assign name="counter" expr="0"/>
            <assign name="sentence" expr="'Well ok. So please go on and tell me
               how you feel.'"/>
            <goto next="#conversation"/>
         </if>
      </filled>
    </field>
  </form>
</vxml>
```

The "stopTalking" form is called when it's time to stop. Either Liza doesn't want
to talk anymore with the patient (six questions have been asked) or the user has said
"exit" or "help." If the user wants to quit, then she is taken back to the voice portal's
main menu. Otherwise, the patient may continue therapy with Liza. The num and
counter attributes are then reset and the sentence variable is assigned a new value,
which is spoken in the conversation form.

CHAPTER

15

Building Multimedia Applications

IN THIS CHAPTER:

Preparations

Layouts and Regions

Slide Show Timings

Text Messages

Graphics and Animation

Audio

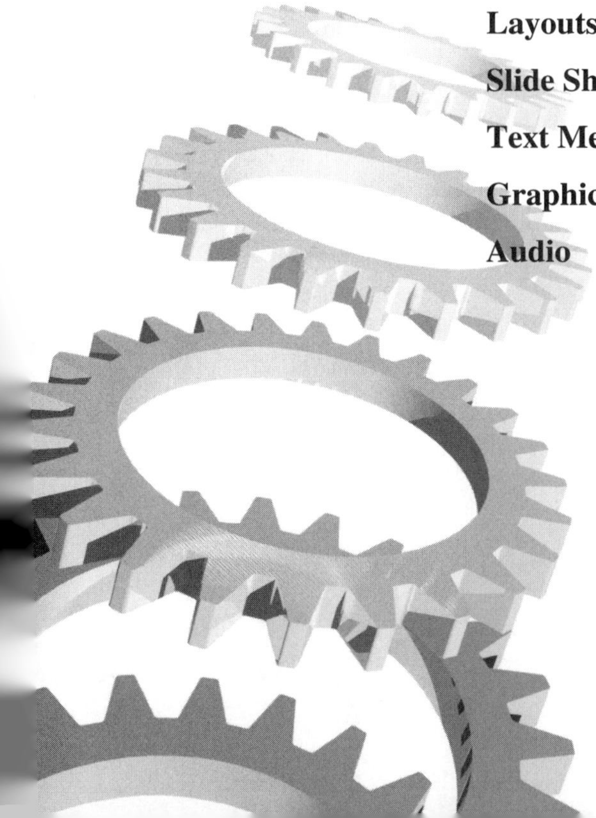

In Chapter 6, the Synchronized Multimedia Integration Language (SMIL) was introduced. This chapter is devoted to some more practical issues of the language and its wireless environment, Multimedia Messaging Service (MMS). Manufacturers are about to release handsets that support MMS using a subset of SMIL 1.0, and Ericsson and Nokia have agreed on a common framework to enhance MMS interoperability. The initial support for elements and attributes in SMIL will be slightly limited, but should increase as the service spreads and more MMS-compatible handsets appear on the market. The major boom for MMS will most likely be in the 3G networks, such as CDMA2000 and WCDMA. MMS can be used in a packet-switched 2.5G network, however, such as GPRS, and even in 2G networks.

Preparations

You need to do a few things before you can start to develop MMS applications. First, you must choose the right development tools for your task. Second, you need to consider which formats you'll use. And third, you might want to use a real server, which works as a MMS Proxy-Relay, or you might settle for a PC emulator. The server receives your documents and forwards them to the actual handsets that interpret the SMIL code. The handset then reads the text, graphics, and audio, which are referenced in the SMIL document.

Development Tools

SMIL documents can be developed using a simple text editor, such as Notepad, in Windows, but you should make sure the XML code is well formed. Then, an arbitrary XML editor, such as XML Spy, makes the job easy. If the code isn't well formed, it won't reach the handheld device because it will travel through a WAP gateway, which forwards the document over the air to the device. WAP gateways tokenize XML documents into WBXML and this is only possible if the content is well formed.

HTML-Kit is a tool mentioned in Chapter 12 and at least one SMIL plug-in is available for that tool. The HTML-Kit makes coding SMIL documents easier because all tags are available from simple drop-down menus.

A good idea is to test your MMS document on a PC before it's sent and tested on a handheld device. Then RealONE Player from RealNetworks is a good choice. RealONE Player has support for SMIL 2.0, which is a superset of SMIL 1.0, used by MMS. If you want to try your document on the handheld immediately, then you need to submit all graphics and text files to a receiving MMS Proxy-Relay.

Consequently, putting all files in a folder on your PC while you write the SMIL document is smarter. Then when everything seems to be working fine, you can send the content to the MMS Proxy-Relay. The content needs to be chosen according to a number of things, such as which formats are most suitable for your application and which content types are supported by the handheld device and your web server.

Formats and Content Types

Text can be provided in an ordinary text file. The text file is referred to in the SMIL document using the text element. Because MMS is part of the WAP infrastructure, it supports the WBMP graphics format. The WBMP graphics format was created so many new types of images can be defined and added to the format. So far, one type has been defined: type 0. It supports only monochrome images and can be used in MMS messages. Many professional image editors support the WBMP format, and plug-ins are available that can convert to this format. The content type (MIME type) for a WBMP graphics file is image/vnd.wap.wbmp; level=0. Make sure the server on which the content is going to be stored is configured to transfer the right content type. How this is done depends on which web server you're using.

For photo-quality images, the JPEG format can be used. The content type for a JPEG image is image/jpeg.

Two versions of the GIF format are used often on the Internet: GIF87a and GIF89. These also can be used by MMS-compatible devices, but a limit on how large the files can be will always exist because wireless handheld devices have limited memory and CPU power. The content type for a GIF image is image/gif.

The MMS Proxy-Relay, which receives your SMIL document and makes sure it's sent over the air to the receiver might choose to adjust the content. For example, if you're providing an image that's too large, the server might delete it or it might compress the image even more. This type of content adaptation can be based on a number of issues, such as which capabilities the devices has. The capabilities are specified by the device in a User Agent Profile (UAProf), see Chapter 9. Other criteria, such as how much bandwidth is available, can decide if the MMS Proxy-Relay will adapt the content for the MMS-compatible device.

Document Submission

The SMIL document and all content, including graphics files, audio, and text files, are transferred to the MMS Proxy-Relay. How this interface is presented for you, as a developer, depends on the MMS Proxy-Relay server implementation and vendor. You should ask your operator or service provider about this. In practice, two methods exist: the content is either posted as a form or sent as an e-mail with attachments.

NOTE

All examples in this chapter use a relative URL as the address to graphics, audio, and text files.

Depending on which MMS Proxy-Relay you use, it might require that a fully resolved URL is used. When documents are transferred *from* one handheld device to another, the multimedia content will be embedded as a MIME multipart message and relative URLs will be used in combination with content identifiers. To see how content identifiers in general can be used, see Chapter 20.

Layouts and Regions

You need to consider two things when you work with SMIL documents that are tailor-made for limited handheld devices that support MMS. Screens are smaller compared to SMIL running on a desktop computer and some restrictions exist concerning the regions available for you, which means you might have to take appropriate actions to make the content fit a particular screen.

In the near future, you'll most likely see a number of different screen types on the market, including phones with portrait-oriented screens and PDAs with landscape-oriented screens.

Image and Text Regions

The first MMS-compatible handheld devices released in 2002 will be slightly limited, and you'll have to follow a few rules for the image and text regions.

Regions

The SMIL presentations will use a maximum of one image region and one text region. The following is an example, which uses one text region only:

```
<?xml version="1.0" encoding="UTF-8"?>
<!DOCTYPE smil PUBLIC "-//W3C//DTD SMIL 1.0//EN"
    "http://www.w3.org/TR/REC-smil/SMIL10.dtd">
<smil xmlns="http://www.w3.org/2001/SMIL20/Language">
    <head>
```

```
        <layout>
            <root-layout width="101" height="80"/>
            <region id="textreg" top="0" left="0" width="101" height="80"/>
        </layout>
    </head>
    <body>
        <par>
            <text region="textreg" src="Text.txt"/>
        </par>
    </body>
</smil>
```

A simple text message is displayed on the handheld device. This isn't much more sophisticated than a simple SMS message, but it has the advantage that the message can be longer. SMS allows for only 150 to 160 characters of text. The following example shows a short text message centered from top to bottom on the screen:

```
<?xml version="1.0" encoding="UTF-8"?>
<!DOCTYPE smil PUBLIC "-//W3C//DTD SMIL 1.0//EN"
    "http://www.w3.org/TR/REC-smil/SMIL10.dtd">
<smil xmlns="http://www.w3.org/2001/SMIL20/Language">
    <head>
        <layout>
            <root-layout width="101" height="80"/>
            <region id="textreg" top="35" left="0" width="101" height="40"/>
        </layout>
    </head>
    <body>
        <par>
            <text region="textreg" src="message.txt"/>
        </par>
    </body>
</smil>
```

The text element is used to refer to the text using its src attribute and a URL. Here's another example, which uses only one image region.

```
<?xml version="1.0" encoding="UTF-8"?>
<!DOCTYPE smil PUBLIC "-//W3C//DTD SMIL 1.0//EN"
    "http://www.w3.org/TR/REC-smil/SMIL10.dtd">
<smil xmlns="http://www.w3.org/2001/SMIL20/Language">
    <head>
        <layout>
            <root-layout width="101" height="80"/>
            <region id="image" top="0" left="0" width="101" height="80"/>
        </layout>
```

```
    </head>
    <body>
        <par>
            <img region="image" src="hello.gif" dur="2s"/>
        </par>
        <par>
            <img region="picOfMe.gif" dur="2s"/>
        </par>
        <par>
            <img region="image" src="seeYou.gif" dur="2s"/>
        </par>
    </body>
</smil>
```

One region is defined and is used to display three pictures for two seconds each in a sequence. The GIF format was used, but you could also have used the WBMP format or the JPEG format.

The previous example would only work properly on a SMIL interpreter on a desktop computer, however. The interpreters in phones and PDAs follow two de facto rules. The dur element cannot be used on media element level—in this case, with the img element. Instead, you'd have to move it up one level and put it on the par element.

In addition, early implementations of MMS will use hard-coded names for the image and text regions. The following example has one text region and one image region, and the names comply with the interoperability agreements made between Ericsson and Nokia.

```
<?xml version="1.0" encoding="UTF-8"?>
<!DOCTYPE smil PUBLIC "-//W3C//DTD SMIL 1.0//EN"
    "http://www.w3.org/TR/REC-smil/SMIL10.dtd">
<smil xmlns="http://www.w3.org/2001/SMIL20/Language">
    <head>
        <layout>
            <root-layout width="101" height="80"/>
            <region id="Image" top="0" left="0" width="101" height="40"/>
            <region id="Text" top="40" left="0" width="101" height="40"/>
        </layout>
    </head>
    <body>
        <par>
            <text region="Text" src="myText.txt"/>
            <img region="Image" src="welcome.gif"/>
        </par>
    </body>
</smil>
```

The name "Text" is used for the text region and the name "Image" is used for the image region. Another constraint you might have noticed is the body of a SMIL document doesn't contain any seq element, but does contain a number of par elements. It's understood these elements are executed in a sequence. In the previous example, though, only one slide was used. Again, note that the dur element, which is used for timing, is limited to the par tag.

Making It Fit Particular Screen Types

In SMIL, several ways exist to make an image fit the display. You can specify how the image will be transformed to fit the display. If an image doesn't have the same aspect ratio as the physical display, then you might have to change the aspect ratio of the image to make it fit. If you must keep the aspect ratio, then the image can be adjusted so it fits the display as much as possible. The display area not covered by the image can be painted with the background color of the image.

NOTE

The fit attribute isn't recommended by the manufacturers for use in MMS SMIL.

As the technology evolves and the MMS service is used more often, however, terminals and servers will probably be on the market to support it. In addition, an MMS Proxy-Relay might process the documents to transform your image according to the "fit" attribute, and then remove the attribute before it's transferred over the air to the handheld device. To benefit from such transformations, check which features the MMS Proxy-Relay has.

Scale with Preserved Aspect Ratio and Do Not Clip

This example displays the image welcome.gif, which is 30 pixels wide × 30 pixels high.

```
<?xml version="1.0" encoding="UTF-8"?>
<!DOCTYPE smil PUBLIC "-//W3C//DTD SMIL 1.0//EN"
    "http://www.w3.org/TR/REC-smil/SMIL10.dtd">
<smil xmlns="http://www.w3.org/2001/SMIL20/Language">
    <head>
        <layout>
            <root-layout width="101" height="80"/>
            <!-- 101x40 image region -->
            <region fit="meet" id="Image" top="0" left="0" width="101"
                height="40"/>
```

```
            <region id="Text" top="40" left="0" width="101" height="40"/>
        </layout>
    </head>
    <body>
        <par>
            <text region="Text" src="myText.txt"/>
            <!-- 30x30 image -->
            <img region="Image" src="welcome.gif"/>
        </par>
    </body>
</smil>
```

The image won't be transformed in any way because it's smaller than the image region. Compare it with the following code. Here, the same image is displayed on a much smaller portion of the screen.

```
<?xml version="1.0" encoding="UTF-8"?>
<!DOCTYPE smil PUBLIC "-//W3C//DTD SMIL 1.0//EN"
    "http://www.w3.org/TR/REC-smil/SMIL10.dtd">
<smil xmlns="http://www.w3.org/2001/SMIL20/Language">
    <head>
        <layout>
            <root-layout width="101" height="80"/>
            <!-- 20x25 image region -->
            <region fit="meet" id="Image" top="0" left="0" width="20"
                    height="25"/>
            <region id="Text" top="40" left="0" width="101" height="40"/>
        </layout>
    </head>
    <body>
        <par>
            <text region="Text" src="myText.txt"/>
            <!-- 20x60 image -->
            <img region="Image" src="welcome.gif"/>
        </par>
    </body>
</smil>
```

The image must be shrunk to fit the image region, which is 20 pixels wide × 25 pixels high. Because the aspect ratio of this region doesn't match the aspect ratio of the picture, the picture will be scaled to 7 pixels wide × 25 pixels high. The aspect ratio of the picture is then maintained and it fits the region, although some white space will appear to the left and to the right of the image. Note, the transformation will be performed only if the MMS Proxy-Relay supports it. Try to avoid the fit attribute.

Scale with Preserved Aspect Ratio and Clip

In the previous example, the image was scaled until both the height and width fit inside the region and the aspect ratio was preserved, which made the picture very small. If you want to keep the aspect ratio, but scale the image only until either the width or height fits, then the fit attribute can be set to slice.

```
<?xml version="1.0" encoding="UTF-8"?>
<!DOCTYPE smil PUBLIC "-//W3C//DTD SMIL 1.0//EN"
    "http://www.w3.org/TR/REC-smil/SMIL10.dtd">
<smil xmlns="http://www.w3.org/2001/SMIL20/Language">
    <head>
        <layout>
            <root-layout width="101" height="80"/>
            <!-- 20x25 image region -->
            <region fit="slice" id="Image" top="0" left="0" width="20"
                height="25"/>
            <region id="Text" top="40" left="0" width="101" height="40"/>
        </layout>
    </head>
    <body>
        <par>
            <text region="Text" src="myText.txt"/>
            <!-- 20x30 image -->
            <img region="Image" src="welcome.gif"/>
        </par>
    </body>
</smil>
```

In this example, the image is scaled with preserved aspect ratio, so the width fits. Thus, the width covers the entire image region, which is 20 pixels wide, but the lower portion of the image is clipped. Because the image is 30 pixels high and the image region is only 25 pixels high, the lower 5 pixels of the image are truncated. Another example follows, which also uses the fit attribute set to slice.

```
<?xml version="1.0" encoding="UTF-8"?>
<!DOCTYPE smil PUBLIC "-//W3C//DTD SMIL 1.0//EN"
    "http://www.w3.org/TR/REC-smil/SMIL10.dtd">
<smil xmlns="http://www.w3.org/2001/SMIL20/Language">
    <head>
        <layout>
            <root-layout width="101" height="80"/>
            <region fit="slice" id="Image" top="0" left="0" width="15"
                height="30"/>
```

```
                <region id="Text" top="40" left="0" width="101" height="40"/>
        </layout>
    </head>
    <body>
        <par>
            <text region="text" src="myText.txt"/>
            <!-- 20x30 image -->
            <img region="image" src="welcome.gif"/>
        </par>
    </body>
</smil>
```

In this case, the image will be truncated to its right because the image is 30 pixels wide, but the display region is only 25 pixels wide. Because the height of the image fits the height of the region, the width will be clipped and it's always clipped to the right. Thus, on each line, pixels 0 to 25, counted from the left, will be visible and will cover the entire image region.

Scale with Nonpreserved Aspect Ratio

Images can be scaled so they fit the region, but without preserving the aspect ratio. This is done using the fit attribute, set to fill. In this case, both the height and width are scaled.

```
<?xml version="1.0" encoding="UTF-8"?>
<!DOCTYPE smil PUBLIC "-//W3C//DTD SMIL 1.0//EN"
    "http://www.w3.org/TR/REC-smil/SMIL10.dtd">
<smil xmlns="http://www.w3.org/2001/SMIL20/Language">
    <head>
        <layout>
            <root-layout width="101" height="80"/>
            <!-- 101x40 image region -->
            <region fit="fill" id="Image" top="0" left="0" width="101"
                height="40"/>
            <region id="Text" top="40" left="0" width="101" height="40"/>
        </layout>
    </head>
    <body>
        <par>
            <text region="Text" src="myText.txt"/>
            <!-- 30x40 image -->
            <img region="Image" src="mypic.gif"/>
        </par>
    </body>
</smil>
```

In this case, the image becomes heavily distorted because the image itself is 30 pixels wide × 40 pixels high. The image region, though, is 101 pixels wide × 40 pixels high. Thus, the image is stretched horizontally to cover the entire region. Here is yet another piece of code, which uses the fit attribute set to fill.

```
<?xml version="1.0" encoding="UTF-8"?>
<!DOCTYPE smil PUBLIC "-//W3C//DTD SMIL 1.0//EN"
    "http://www.w3.org/TR/REC-smil/SMIL10.dtd">
<smil xmlns="http://www.w3.org/2001/SMIL20/Language">
    <head>
        <layout>
            <root-layout width="101" height="80"/>
            <!-- 101x40 image region -->
            <region fit="fill" id="Image" top="0" left="0" width="101"
                height="40"/>
            <region id="Text" top="40" left="0" width="101" height="40"/>
        </layout>
    </head>
    <body>
        <par>
            <text region="Text" src="myText.txt"/>
            <!-- 120x50 image -->
            <img region="Image" src="pic.gif"/>
        </par>
    </body>
</smil>
```

The image region is 101 pixels wide × 40 pixels high. In this case, the image is larger than the image region and the image must be shrunk to make it fit. Note, the aspect ratio will be lost because the proportion of the width and height of the image region isn't the same as the proportion of the width and height of the image.

Fill with Background Color

According to the SMIL specification, the default value for the fit attribute is hidden. Try to avoid the fit attribute in MMS SMIL until the technology has evolved or until MMS Proxy-Relays can transform the content. This is how the fit attribute behaves if it isn't provided in the code.

```
<?xml version="1.0" encoding="UTF-8"?>
<!DOCTYPE smil PUBLIC "-//W3C//DTD SMIL 1.0//EN"
    "http://www.w3.org/TR/REC-smil/SMIL10.dtd">
<smil xmlns="http://www.w3.org/2001/SMIL20/Language">
    <head>
```

```
        <layout>
            <root-layout width="101" height="80"/>
            <!-- 101x40 image region -->
            <region fit="hidden" id="Image" top="0" left="0" width="101"
                height="40"/>
            <region id="Text" top="40" left="0" width="101" height="40"/>
        </layout>
    </head>
    <body>
        <par>
            <text region="Text" src="myText.txt"/>
            <!-- 101x50 image -->
            <img region="Image" src="mygif.gif"/>
        </par>
    </body>
</smil>
```

The height of the image is larger than the height of the image region. Consequently, the image will be truncated. But, because only the height of the image doesn't fit, only the bottom of the image will be clipped. The bottom 10 pixels aren't visible. Note, the aspect ratio is preserved. Another example follows.

```
<?xml version="1.0" encoding="UTF-8"?>
<!DOCTYPE smil PUBLIC "-//W3C//DTD SMIL 1.0//EN"
    "http://www.w3.org/TR/REC-smil/SMIL10.dtd">
<smil xmlns="http://www.w3.org/2001/SMIL20/Language">
    <head>
        <layout>
            <root-layout width="101" height="80"/>
            <!-- 101x40 image region -->
            <region fit="meet" id="Image" top="0" left="0" width="101"
                height="40"/>
            <region id="Text" top="40" left="0" width="101" height="40"/>
        </layout>
    </head>
    <body>
        <par>
            <text region="Text" src="myText.txt"/>
            <!-- 120x60 image -->
            <img region="Image" src="welcome.gif"/>
        </par>
    </body>
</smil>
```

In this case, the height and the width of the image are bigger than the height and the width of the image region. The image is then clipped both horizontally and vertically.

The rightmost 19 pixels on each pixel row and the bottom 20 pixels of the image aren't visible, but are truncated.

Slide Show Timings

Normally, the par element contains attributes that specify the duration, start, and end of the slide associated with the element. However, you can also use attributes on elements inside the par element. The following example uses the dur attribute to specify how long each slide in a sequence of slides will be displayed.

```
<?xml version="1.0" encoding="UTF-8"?>
<!DOCTYPE smil PUBLIC "-//W3C//DTD SMIL 1.0//EN"
    "http://www.w3.org/TR/REC-smil/SMIL10.dtd">
<smil xmlns="http://www.w3.org/2001/SMIL20/Language">
    <head>
        <layout>
            <root-layout width="101" height="80"/>
            <region id="Image" top="0" left="0" width="101" height="40"/>
            <region id="Text" top="40" left="0" width="101" height="40"/>
        </layout>
    </head>
    <body>
        <par dur="3s">
            <text region="Text" src="text1.txt"/>
            <img region="Image" src="pic1.gif"/>
        </par>
        <par dur="3s">
            <text region="Text" src="text2.txt"/>
            <img region="Image" src="pic2.gif"/>
        </par>
        <par dur="3s">
            <text region="Text" src="text3.txt"/>
            <img region="Image" src="pic3.gif"/>
        </par>
    </body>
</smil>
```

Three slides include an image and a piece of text, and each slide is displayed for three seconds before the next one is presented. Here's another variant, which uses the begin attribute.

```
<?xml version="1.0" encoding="UTF-8"?>
<!DOCTYPE smil PUBLIC "-//W3C//DTD SMIL 1.0//EN"
```

```
       "http://www.w3.org/TR/REC-smil/SMIL10.dtd">
<smil xmlns="http://www.w3.org/2001/SMIL20/Language">
    <head>
        <layout>
            <root-layout width="101" height="80"/>
            <region id="Image" top="0" left="0" width="101" height="40"/>
            <region id="Text" top="40" left="0" width="101" height="40"/>
        </layout>
    </head>
    <body>
        <par dur="3s">
            <text region="Text" src="text1.txt" begin="1s"/>
            <img region="Image" src="pic1.gif"/>
        </par>
        <par dur="3s">
            <text region="Text" src="text2.txt" begin="1s"/>
            <img region="Image" src="pic2.gif"/>
        </par>
        <par dur="3s">
            <text region="Text" src="text3.txt" begin="1s"/>
            <img region="Image" src="pic3.gif"/>
        </par>
    </body>
</smil>
```

In this case, three slides are shown for three seconds, but each text file is displayed one second after the image. If only minor changes exist in the text or in an image, this technique can be used to draw the end user's attention to the fact that the text or image is changed.

Text Messages

Even simple text-based MMS messages have advantages over simple SMS messages. SMS is available in 2.5G and 3G networks, but of the two, MMS is the most powerful messaging technology. MMS has a richer multimedia framework than simple SMS, which is text-based only. MMS messages that contain text only can show the text in an animated style. For example, a sentence can be displayed for a second, and then a new sentence can be displayed. As mentioned earlier, MMS also provides room for larger text chunks, as opposed to SMS, which has a limit of around 150 to 160 characters of text, depending on which network is used.

Static Text

When you're producing a message that contains simple text only, you have to create the actual text message, in addition to the SMIL document.

Producing the Text

The text can be encoded using the Unicode UTF-8 character-encoding standard or the simple US-ASCII character encoding. Don't use line breaks, but let the text wrap around to the next line if you're providing a larger piece of text. It you're introducing line breaks, you might end up with strange formatting because you don't know how big the screen is or which font size will be used to display the message.

Use the file extension .txt, unless you know what you're doing. The file will be embedded in the message as a MIME-type attachment and the MMS Proxy-Relay might fail to embed it correctly if you use a strange file extension.

Don't forget that the MMS Proxy-Relay might be case-sensitive and will make a distinction between capitals and small letters in the filename. If you name the file myText.txt, then you should refer to that file in the SMIL document using the same syntax, which is myText.txt, not mytext.txt.

Layout

As mentioned earlier, only one text region should be used for maximum compatibility with the early MMS-compatible devices on the market. The layout section might look like this:

```
<layout>
    <root-layout width="160" height="120"/>
    <region id="Text" top="0" left="0" width="160" height="120"/>
</layout>
```

Only one text region exists: "Text." In this case, the screen size is 160 pixels wide × 120 pixels high.

Point at the Source

Then you need to provide the URL to the text message in the SMIL document. Use the src attribute and the text element. The body might look like this:

```
<body>
  <par>
```

```
        <text region="Text" src="myText.txt"/>
    </par>
</body>
```

The text file is an ordinary text/plain file and the src attribute is used to provide the filename.

Unicode Characters

To spice things up a bit, you can make use of all the characters available in the Unicode framework. This applies only if you know a particular character set is supported—in other words, if you're targeting devices that are compatible with this character set. The characters can be encoded using UTF-8 or UTF-16. An example follows, which inserts a smiley character from the Miscellaneous Symbols character code table.

```
&0x263A; Good news!
```

The character is referred to using the 16-bit code. The prefix 0x means the code is expressed in hexadecimal format, the ampersand indicates a Unicode character, and the code ends with a semicolon. This will be rendered as ☺ if the handheld device has implemented support for the Miscellaneous Symbols character code table.

Example

Here's a final example of static text before we move on to more sophisticated text messages. The following SMIL document displays a simple text message:

```
<?xml version="1.0" encoding="UTF-8"?>
<!DOCTYPE smil PUBLIC "-//W3C//DTD SMIL 1.0//EN"
    "http://www.w3.org/TR/REC-smil/SMIL10.dtd">
<smil xmlns="http://www.w3.org/2001/SMIL20/Language">
    <head>
        <layout>
            <root-layout width="101" height="80"/>
            <region id="Text" top="40" left="0" width="101" height="40"/>
        </layout>
    </head>
    <body>
        <par>
            <text region="Text" src="myText.txt"/>
        </par>
    </body>
</smil>
```

The document refers to the text file myText.txt. The text file looks like this.

```
Hello J&#xF6;rgen!
```

The file contains Unicode characters, most notably the *o* with two dots over it, used in Germany and Sweden. It's called an umlaut and has the hexadecimal Unicode value F6. Note that the Unicode characters will only be rendered correctly if the device supports it and if the correct MIME type has been set on the server.

Animated Text

You can do quite a lot simply using text. Text messages have the advantage of occupying little space. While SMS allows for 150 to 160 characters of static text only, MMS makes it possible to send large texts and also makes presenting the text in different ways possible.

Sentence by Sentence

The duration attribute can be used to display the text sentence by sentence. This becomes almost like a slide show, but without the pictures.

```
<?xml version="1.0" encoding="UTF-8"?>
<!DOCTYPE smil PUBLIC "-//W3C//DTD SMIL 1.0//EN"
    "http://www.w3.org/TR/REC-smil/SMIL10.dtd">
<smil xmlns="http://www.w3.org/2001/SMIL20/Language">
    <head>
        <layout>
            <root-layout width="101" height="80"/>
            <region id="Text" top="0" left="0" width="101" height="80"/>
        </layout>
    </head>
    <body>
        <par dur="1s">
            <text region="Text" src="text1.txt"/>
        </par>
        <par dur="1s">
            <text region="Text" src="text2.txt"/>
        </par>
        <par dur="1s">
            <text region="Text" src="text3.txt"/>
```

```
        </par>
    </body>
</smil>
```

Each text message (file) is displayed for a second. Flashing text is a trick to get the end user's attention and can be implemented like this.

```
<?xml version="1.0" encoding="UTF-8"?>
<!DOCTYPE smil PUBLIC "-//W3C//DTD SMIL 1.0//EN"
    "http://www.w3.org/TR/REC-smil/SMIL10.dtd">
<smil xmlns="http://www.w3.org/2001/SMIL20/Language">
    <head>
        <layout>
            <root-layout width="101" height="80"/>
            <region id="Text" top="0" left="0" width="101" height="80"/>
        </layout>
    </head>
    <body>
        <par dur="1s">
            <text region="Text" src="text1.txt"/>
        </par>
        <par begin="0.5" dur="1s">
            <text region="Text" src="text1.txt"/>
        </par>
        <par begin="0.5s" dur="1s">
            <text region="Text" src="text1.txt"/>
        </par>
    </body>
</smil>
```

The same text message is displayed in all par elements, but a 0.5 second gap between each par element creates a flashing effect.

Word by Word

A similar way to grab the user's attention is to render the text word by word, giving it an animated feeling. Here's an example.

```
<?xml version="1.0" encoding="UTF-8"?>
<!DOCTYPE smil PUBLIC "-//W3C//DTD SMIL 1.0//EN"
    "http://www.w3.org/TR/REC-smil/SMIL10.dtd">
<smil xmlns="http://www.w3.org/2001/SMIL20/Language">
    <head>
```

```
        <layout>
            <root-layout width="101" height="80"/>
            <region id="Text" top="0" left="0" width="101" height="80"/>
        </layout>
    </head>
    <body>
        <par dur="0.2s">
            <text region="Text" src="words1.txt"/>
        </par>
        <par dur="0.2s">
            <text region="Text" src="words2.txt"/>
        </par>
        <par dur="0.2s">
            <text region="Text" src="words3.txt"/>
        </par>
        <par dur="0.2s">
            <text region="Text" src="words4.txt"/>
        </par>
        <par dur="5s">
            <text region="Text" src="words5.txt"/>
        </par>
    </body>
</smil>
```

The text file words1.txt looks like this:

```
Did
```

This is words2.txt:

```
Did you
```

The file words3.txt contains these words:

```
Did you know
```

The file words4.txt has these words in it:

```
Did you know that
```

The final sentence, stored in file words5.txt, looks like this:

```
GarysGear has
cellulars for
sale!
```

This is effective for mobile commercials because the user gets curious and probably waits until the complete message has been displayed. Here's another variant of the same theme.

```xml
<?xml version="1.0" encoding="UTF-8"?>
<!DOCTYPE smil PUBLIC "-//W3C//DTD SMIL 1.0//EN"
    "http://www.w3.org/TR/REC-smil/SMIL10.dtd">
<smil xmlns="http://www.w3.org/2001/SMIL20/Language">
    <head>
        <layout>
            <root-layout width="101" height="80"/>
            <region id="Text" top="0" left="0" width="101" height="80"/>
        </layout>
    </head>
    <body>
        <par dur="0.2s">
            <text region="Text" src="r.txt"/>
        </par>
        <par dur="0.2s">
            <text region="Text" src="ro.txt"/>
        </par>
        <par dur="0.2s">
            <text region="Text" src="roc.txt"/>
        </par>
        <par dur="5s">
            <text region="Text" src="rock.txt"/>
        </par>
    </body>
</smil>
```

Each character is displayed for 0.2 seconds and, finally, the word rock has been created using text from the four text files. Note, you can't have content in the text elements. It's easy to think you could write the code like this:

```xml
<text region="Text">R</text>
```

This isn't legal SMIL, though, because the goal of SMIL is synchronization and integration, not content creation.

Graphics and Animation

It can be tempting to define two or more image regions, and then to create a moving object by displaying different images in these regions, like this:

```
<?xml version="1.0" encoding="UTF-8"?>
<!DOCTYPE smil PUBLIC "-//W3C//DTD SMIL 1.0//EN"
    "http://www.w3.org/TR/REC-smil/SMIL10.dtd">
<smil xmlns="http://www.w3.org/2001/SMIL20/Language">
    <head>
        <layout>
            <root-layout width="101" height="80"/>
            <region id="image1" top="0" left="0" width="101" height="26"/>
            <region id="image2" top="26" left="0" width="101" height="26"/>
            <region id="image3" top="52" left="0" width="101" height="28"/>
        </layout>
    </head>
    <body>
        <par dur="1s">
            <img region="image1" src="firstpic.gif"/>
        </par>
        <par dur="1s">
            <img region="image1" src="background.gif"/>
            <img region="image2" src="secondpic.gif"/>
        </par>
        <par dur="1s">
            <img region="image2" src="background.gif"/>
            <img region="image3" src="thirdpic.gif"/>
        </par>
    </body>
</smil>
```

Remember, MMS SMIL so far supports only one image region, at least on the early devices on the market, so you should use other tricks to achieve animation effects. Here are several solutions.

Animation with Pictures

GIF pictures can include a number of frames that make up an animation. A presentation, which uses such an image, could look like the following:

```
<?xml version="1.0" encoding="UTF-8"?>
<!DOCTYPE smil PUBLIC "-//W3C//DTD SMIL 1.0//EN"
    "http://www.w3.org/TR/REC-smil/SMIL10.dtd">
<smil xmlns="http://www.w3.org/2001/SMIL20/Language">
    <head>
        <layout>
            <root-layout width="101" height="80"/>
            <region id="Image" top="0" left="0" width="101" height="80"/>
        </layout>
```

```
    </head>
    <body>
        <par dur="1s">
            <img region="Image" src="logo.gif"/>
        </par>
        <par dur="5s">
            <img region="Image" src="anim.gif"/>
        </par>
    </body>
</smil>
```

Two images are used. The first displays a logo for a second before the actual animation starts. Then the second image is displayed. It contains a number of frames, which provide the actual animation. Timing for the animation frames is built into the image. Most professional image editors come with a utility or function that can be used to edit individual frames in an animated GIF image.

Animation Using Sequences

An alternative to using animations in the pictures themselves is to animate using a sequence of images, each displayed for a certain time using the dur attribute. Such an implementation can look like this.

```
<?xml version="1.0" encoding="UTF-8"?>
<!DOCTYPE smil PUBLIC "-//W3C//DTD SMIL 1.0//EN"
    "http://www.w3.org/TR/REC-smil/SMIL10.dtd">
<smil xmlns="http://www.w3.org/2001/SMIL20/Language">
    <head>
        <layout>
            <root-layout width="101" height="80"/>
            <region id="Image" top="0" left="0" width="101" height="80"/>
        </layout>
    </head>
    <body>
        <par dur="1s">
            <img region="Image" src="anim1.gif"/>
        </par>
        <par dur="1s">
            <img region="Image" src="anim2.gif"/>
        </par>
        <par dur="1s">
            <img region="Image" src="anim3.gif"/>
        </par>
```

```
    <par dur="5s">
        <img region="Image" src="anim4.gif"/>
    </par>
    </body>
</smil>
```

Four images are shown in a sequence to form a short animation, while the last image is displayed for five seconds.

Combined Text and Graphics Animations

Finally, a mix of text and image effects often produces the best results. The following presentation displays a sequence of sentences and images.

```
<?xml version="1.0" encoding="UTF-8"?>
<!DOCTYPE smil PUBLIC "-//W3C//DTD SMIL 1.0//EN"
    "http://www.w3.org/TR/REC-smil/SMIL10.dtd">
<smil xmlns="http://www.w3.org/2001/SMIL20/Language">
    <head>
        <layout>
            <root-layout width="101" height="80"/>
            <region fit="meet" id="Image" top="0" left="0" width="101"
                height="40"/>
            <region id="Text" top="40" left="0" width="101" height="40"/>
        </layout>
    </head>
    <body>
        <par dur="2s">
            <text region="Text" src="intro.txt"/>
        </par>
        <par dur="4s">
            <text region="Text" src="text.txt"/>
            <!-- Animated GIF -->
            <img region="Image" src="anim.gif"/>
        </par>
        <par dur="4s">
            <text region="Text" src="end.txt"/>
            <img region="Image" src="end.gif"/>
        </par>
    </body>
</smil>
```

First, a text message is displayed for two seconds. Then some text is displayed in parallel with an animation, which is implemented as an animated GIF. Finally, the presentation ends with a text message and an ordinary GIF image.

Optimizations and Adjustments

You can optimize the files used in the SMIL presentation in several ways. GIF files are always compressed using the LZW compression algorithm. This algorithm works so pixels are represented as indexes to a color palette. For example, if you're using 16 colors, including the background color, then each pixel will take up 4 bits because 4 bits are needed to represent the numbers 0 thru 15. If you only use 8 colors instead of 16 in the picture, then you can reduce the image size by 25 percent without losing quality. If the image uses 14 colors, however, you still need 4 bits to represent the numbers 0 thru 13 and there's no room for optimization. Large areas with the same color can be compressed a lot. By replacing complex textures with a single color, you can reduce the image size dramatically.

As MMS is used in 2.5G networks, this type of optimization can improve transfer times because the transfer speed, in practice, is similar to a dial-up connection using a modem and a fixed telephone line.

The SMIL code itself will be tokenized into WBXML because it passes through a WAP gateway before it's sent over the air. Consequently, the SMIL code is being optimized for fast delivery more or less automatically.

Audio

Audio in MMS SMIL is based around a reasonably new audio compression technology, called Adaptive MultiRate Audio (AMR). Many handheld devices will most likely support this audio compression technology in the future because the audio can be compressed to a high degree.

Handheld devices can specify which audio formats they support in the UAProf. If some device wouldn't support the AMR format, or if the source is provided in another format other than AMR, then the MMS Proxy-Relay may translate the source into the supported format. The MMS Proxy-Relay will know the exact capabilities of the handheld device by scanning the UAProf, and can then take the appropriate actions more or less automatically and transparently for the developer.

Embedding Audio

This SMIL presentation doesn't show any text or images, but only plays a sound.

```
<?xml version="1.0" encoding="UTF-8"?>
<!DOCTYPE smil PUBLIC "-//W3C//DTD SMIL 1.0//EN"
    "http://www.w3.org/TR/REC-smil/SMIL10.dtd">
```

```
<smil xmlns="http://www.w3.org/2001/SMIL20/Language">
    <head>
        <layout>
            <root-layout width="101" height="80"/>
            <region id="Text" top="40" left="0" width="101" height="80"/>
        </layout>
    </head>
    <body>
        <par>
            <audio src="welcome.amr" alt="welcome"/>
        </par>
    </body>
</smil>
```

An alternative text is provided if the handheld device doesn't have the capabilities to play the audio clip. The following example shows a slide show and plays a short sound effect as each new slide is displayed.

```
<?xml version="1.0" encoding="UTF-8"?>
<!DOCTYPE smil PUBLIC "-//W3C//DTD SMIL 1.0//EN"
    "http://www.w3.org/TR/REC-smil/SMIL10.dtd">
<smil xmlns="http://www.w3.org/2001/SMIL20/Language">
    <head>
        <layout>
            <root-layout width="101" height="80"/>
            <region id="Image" top="0" left="0" width="101" height="40"/>
            <region id="Text" top="40" left="0" width="101" height="40"/>
        </layout>
    </head>
    <body>
        <par dur="3s">
            <audio src="welcome.amr" alt="welcome"/>
            <text region="Text" src="text1.txt"/>
            <img region="Image" src="pic1.gif"/>
        </par>
        <par dur="3s">
            <audio src="product.amr" alt="product presentation"/>
            <text region="Text" src="text2.txt"/>
            <img region="Image" src="pic2.gif"/>
        </par>
        <par dur="3s">
            <audio src="theEnd.amr" alt="this is the end"/>
            <text region="Text" src="text3.txt"/>
            <img region="Image" src="pic3.gif"/>
        </par>
    </body>
</smil>
```

The slide show contains three sections, which are displayed in a sequence. Two regions have been defined: one for text and one for the images. Each slide section shows some text, an image, and plays an AMR sound.

iMelody

The *iMelody* format is neither part of the MMS nor the SMIL specification, but many handheld devices support this format because its ordinary use is to define ring melodies, which are also rather misleading, referred to as ring tones. In the Enhanced Messaging Service (EMS), iMelody is used to specify the ring tones. *EMS* is a technology that is much more limited than MMS and allows ring tones and small monochrome bitmaps to be embedded in simple text messages. EMS is an evolution of SMS and an intermediate technology, which can be described as more sophisticated than SMS, but far from as full of possibilities as MMS.

The idea is this: it should be possible to have a melody played, similar to a ring tone, as a SMIL document is presented, together with pictures and text. Then applications like electronic postcards that play a cute little melody can be implemented.

An iMelody file should have the file extension .imy, which can be referenced in the src attribute of the audio element. The format supports note durations, different styles, repeats, volumes, loops, and other effects.

Basics

The following iMelody file plays a short and simple melody, which contains seven notes:

```
BEGIN:IMELODY
VERSION:1.2
FORMAT:CLASS1.0
MELODY:c2d2e2f2g2a2b2
END:IMELODY
```

The specified melody is a simple scale, which corresponds to the white keys on a piano. Quarter notes are represented by the number 2. The SMIL code that embeds the previous iMelody file could look like this.

```
<?xml version="1.0" encoding="UTF-8"?>
<!DOCTYPE smil PUBLIC "-//W3C//DTD SMIL 1.0//EN"
    "http://www.w3.org/TR/REC-smil/SMIL10.dtd">
<smil xmlns="http://www.w3.org/2001/SMIL20/Language">
```

```
    <head>
      <layout>
         <root-layout width="101" height="80"/>
         <region id="Text" top="40" left="0" width="101" height="80"/>
      </layout>
    </head>
    <body>
      <par>
         <text region="Text" src="message.txt"/>
         <audio src="scale.imy" alt="a simple melody"/>
      </par>
    </body>
</smil>
```

The ring tone is played using the audio element. Note, iMelody files should have the extension imy. Here's another example, which plays a melody that spans several octaves:

```
BEGIN:IMELODY
VERSION:1.2
FORMAT:CLASS1.0
STYLE:S2
MELODY:*5c2*3d2*4e2*6f2*2g2*3a2*3b2
END:IMELODY
```

Here, the melody has been changed to include octave information. Octaves can be specified using an asterisk followed by a number between zero and eight (inclusive). The style command chooses one of the three styles. Style 2 means the melody will be played *staccato,* a musical term that means the notes are short compared to the rest periods between the notes. Style 1 removes the rest periods between the notes and Style 0 uses a normal rest period. The SMIL code could look the same as in the previous example.

Loops

The iMelody format allows repetition and notes can be repeated, like this:

```
BEGIN:IMELODY
VERSION:1.2
FORMAT:CLASS1.0
MELODY:c2r5c2r5c2r5(c2d2e2@5)
END:IMELODY
```

The key *C* is played three times, with a rest between each note, before you enter a loop that plays the keys *C*, *D*, and *E* five times. The loop is surrounded by parentheses and the @ character indicates how many times the loop should be repeated. Zero means endlessly. Here's another example, which increases the volume for each loop:

```
BEGIN:IMELODY
VERSION:1.2
FORMAT:CLASS1.0
MELODY:V1c2r5c2r5c2r5(c2d2e2@5V+)
END:IMELODY
```

In this example, the ring tone starts with a volume setting, indicated by the *V*. The number that follows after the *V* sets the volume and should be a number between 0 and 15. Consequently, the previous melody starts with a low volume but, as you enter the loop, the volume increases for each time the notes in the loop have been played. The increase is specified with the *V* and + characters.

Effects

A number of effects can be created using staccatos and experimenting with the beats. The following example plays an effect and a simple melody.

```
<?xml version="1.0" encoding="UTF-8"?>
<!DOCTYPE smil PUBLIC "-//W3C//DTD SMIL 1.0//EN"
    "http://www.w3.org/TR/REC-smil/SMIL10.dtd">
<smil xmlns="http://www.w3.org/2001/SMIL20/Language">
    <head>
        <layout>
            <root-layout width="101" height="80"/>
            <region id="Image" top="0" left="0" width="101" height="80"/>
        </layout>
    </head>
    <body>
        <par>
            <audio src="fx.imy" alt="FX"/>
        </par>
        <par dur="2s">
            <img region="Image" src="anImg.gif"/>
        </par>
        <par>
            <audio src="mel.imy" alt="a simple melody"/>
        </par>
    </body>
</smil>
```

The file fx.imy implements an effect, which is played immediately as the SMIL presentation starts. An image is then displayed for two seconds, and then the melody, which is defined in the mel.imy file, is played for the receiver. The implementation of fx.imy looks like this:

```
BEGIN:IMELODY
VERSION:1.2
FORMAT:CLASS1.0
BEAT:200
STYLE:S1
MELODY:*7e5*7f5*7#f5*7g5*7#g5*7a5*7#a5*7b5*8c05*8#"
END:IMELODY
```

A sequence of notes is played on the highest octaves, 7 and 8. The default speed is 120 beats per minute, but the beat command overrides this setting and provides a much faster speed, 200 beats per minute. In addition, the S1 style is used to remove rests between the notes. The effect is a rising pitch. The implementation of mel.imy, the other melody played in the SMIL presentation, looks like this:

```
BEGIN:IMELODY
VERSION:1.2
FORMAT:CLASS1.0
MELODY:c3d3e3f3g3f3e3d3c3r3e3r3c3r3r3r3
END:IMELODY
```

It's a simple melody, which contains notes and rests only. The melody defaults to the speed of 120 beats per minute and the volume level 7.

Using SVG with GML to Represent the Real World

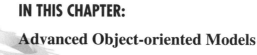

IN THIS CHAPTER:

Advanced Object-oriented Models

A Map

In this chapter, you learn to implement a map in GML. The GML representation is then transformed to a representation in SVG, which can be rendered on an SVG-compatible device. At the end of the chapter, you become familiar with *Batik* which is a Java framework that can be used to display SVG code on Java-enabled devices. Consequently, we go through the whole development chain in this chapter—from using the format geo data providers use, to specify maps, to transforming into an SVG representation, and, finally, viewing the result on a Java virtual machine.

A number of phones and PDAs that support Java, are on the market. The Nokia 9290 communicator is a combined PDA and phone that supports Java. Many Pocket PCs, such as the Compaq iPAQ series of PDAs and the HP Jornada, also have Java support. Before we start the implementation of the map, object-oriented models need to be explained. Chapter 7 only mentions a few of the basic object-oriented concepts in GML.

Advanced Object-oriented Models

GML can be used to represent maps, roads, corridors, or any object possible to describe in terms of lines, points, and shapes. When you use GML to describe these objects, you're creating a model of the real world. However, nothing says you couldn't use the language to create fictive worlds only. GML could be used to represent virtual worlds that don't exist in real life. In combination with SVG or X3D, you have a complete framework that can be used to represent and render virtual worlds.

UML is the standard specification language used by software engineers to describe systems, use cases, and system interactions. The UML and some of the features therein serve as a foundation to the principles of GML. Consequently, going through the basics of object orientation is a good idea before we start with the creation of our model in GML.

Modeling Tools

Real-world objects like streets and buildings can be described as objects that behave in a certain way and contain a number of smaller objects. For example, a street is used by cars and pedestrians. It has a length, a width, and a location. A building can contain a number of offices. It has a length, a certain depth, and height (or a certain number of floors) and, like the street, it also has a location.

Classes

In the real world, buildings can, but don't have to, contain offices. A football stadium counts as a building, but it usually doesn't contain offices. Some common denominators do exist, though. The football stadium and the office building both have a certain length, depth, and height. Both are located somewhere and both have an entrance.

Classes are used to classify objects or to group objects of the same kind into the same class. The football stadium and the office building are both buildings, so you could say both belong to the class Building. GML uses a slightly different vocabulary. A class in GML is referred to as a *type*.

Objects

Objects are created according to a certain class. If you want to create an object that would represent a football stadium, then it could be created using the Building class. In the same way, if you want to create an object to represent the office building, it could also be created using the Building class. The football stadium would have a different length, depth, height, and location compared to the office building, but both would still be objects (or instances) of the same class: the Building class.

In other words, an object is created using a specific description, referred to as the object's class. The class tells us what it contains, which relations it might have, and, in some cases, how it behaves. All objects created according to that class have that behavior, contain exactly what the class specifies them to contain, and may have that set of relations to other objects. In GML, objects are referred to as features and all *features* are instances of a type.

Attributes and Properties

In real life, buildings have a certain length, depth, height, and location. In this case, these things aren't visible but, instead, are properties of the building and we've decided these properties are important, simply because we might be interested in retrieving them later. If you want, you could include yet another property, such as the color of the building, if this were important to you. It's always up to you, the modeler, to decide which properties should be included in the class. Modeling an object, such as a house, in perfect detail is a never-ending task. Therefore, you need to spend some time thinking about the purpose of your model and which properties are of importance to your application.

Properties are sometimes also called attributes, like in UML. With XML-based languages, *attributes* are something that accompany tags. For example, the img element in XHTML has a mandatory attribute called src. Don't confuse this with attributes in object-oriented models, though. To avoid such confusion, GML usually refers to these object-oriented attributes as properties.

Relations

Environments, like cities, contain objects that are related in various ways. For example, a building could be located next to another building. In that case, the building class would contain a relation to another building. When the model is used to retrieve information, relations are used for navigation. If you have access to a representation of one of the buildings and want to know which building is located next to it, you'd follow the "next to" relation and end up at the other office building.

Inheritance

After all, you're trying to build a model of something that exists in real life and buildings are almost never the same. Therefore, it would probably be a less-good solution to build a complete city model using only a single Building class. Instead, the city would most likely contain one or several churches, supermarkets, and factories.

Although these buildings would be different, they would still be buildings with some common denominators. For example, all would contain a number of doors and windows, as well as a floor and a roof. However, only the factory would host a number of manufacturing lines, only the supermarket would contain a number of cashiers, and only the church would contain a pipe organ.

Assume your application had to retrieve all buildings in the city. Then you would be interested to go through your specification line by line and check if each class instance (object) is a building. No matter if it's a church, supermarket, or factory, you'd be interested to retrieve it because it's a building.

Inheritance indicates that a class has certain basic characteristics according to another class, so it inherits these basic characteristics from the base class. In this case, with the buildings, you could define a base class Building, which would be inherited by Factory, Church, and Supermarket. If you want to retrieve all buildings from your specification and find a supermarket, then you'd immediately see that the supermarket is a building because it inherits its basic characteristics from the Building class. Consequently, if your application in certain situations needs to generalize by focusing on a set of the basic characteristics of objects, then inheritance is the mechanism you should use.

Abstract Classes

Abstract classes are used when you want to provide a *general* class, which is always inherited by specialized classes. The base class cannot be used alone to create objects, but objects must always be created according to one of the specialized classes.

If we continue with our examples of buildings, then we could make the Building class abstract. This would mean objects must always be created as churches, factories, or supermarkets, but never only as buildings. This would make sense in our case because an object that is only a building doesn't say too much. On the other hand, if a particular building is a supermarket and another is a factory, then the model says much more.

Models

Remember, a model is an approximation of something. No matter how detailed your model is, properties or behavior will always exist that aren't part of the model. Creating a good model requires you to spend some time thinking about which properties and structures are most important to your model.

If you're making a model to be used by people to find the location of a certain street, then it's probably less important to model exactly how the houses that surround the streets look. It's probably more important to make sure all the houses are included, along with their approximate locations. And most important in this case would be to model how long the streets are, the start and end of each, where the streets cross, what they're called, and how they're numbered.

Always consider if there's a need to use inheritance for generalization and specialization. If you want to use many objects in your model that are of the same type but, at the same time are different, then you can probably use inheritance to model this property. For example, if you're creating a model of an office environment, you could have an abstract base class Room that has a number of specializations, such as Entrance, Kitchen, WorkingRoom, RestingRoom, Bathroom, and so forth. The base class can contain properties such as size and location because all rooms, no matter if they are working rooms or kitchens, must contain that information. Perhaps the model will be drawn on a handheld device that uses the data for a location-based service. In this case, size and location are important properties for your model.

A Map

Let's start with the implementation of our map. The area we're going to model is 160×160 meters, and includes houses, a parking place, streets, a lake, and a bridge. The coordinate system is our own. This is an east-to-south type of coordinate system, which means when you move to the east, then you start at 0 and move toward 160 on the x axis. If you move to the south, then you start at 0 and move toward 160 on the y axis.

First, a schema and a document instance are created in GML. Then a style sheet is implemented, which transforms the GML implementation to an SVG file. Here's the data we're going to use.

There's one parking place, which is shaped like a square. A number of buildings exist: one is L-shaped and the others are shaped like squares. A bridge crosses a lake and a road is on the bridge. Streets are either one-way or two-way streets. All these details have been measured and here's the data we'll use.

```
Parking place

5,10 35,40

Rectangle shaped buildings

40,10 50,30
40,30 50,40
40,40 50,70
40,70 50,90
20,45 35,55
0,70  20,90
25,70 30,90
60,10 70,40
60,40 70,50
80,80 110,90
110,80 120,90
120,80 150,90
0,100 10,110
10,100 40,110
40,100 50,110
50,100 80,110
80,100 90,110
90,100 120,110
120,100 130,110
130,100 160,110

L-shaped building

60,60 70,60
70,80 75,80
75,90 60,90
60,60
```

Two-way streets

```
0,5 100,5
55,5 55,95
0,95 160,95
0,65 35,65
35,65 35,95
155,70 155,95
```

Two-way street over the bridge

```
100,5 155,70
```

One-way streets to and from the parking place

```
10,40 10,65
30,5 30,10
```

Bridge

```
100,5 155,70
```

Lake

```
90,10
80,40
85,70
110,60
140,70
160,65
155,20
140,15
135,5
90,10
```

The first thing you must do is determine how these objects are best represented in GML.

Representation in GML

You need to consider which objects should be present in your model. As usual, all objects in GML will be part of a collection so you need a collection object. Let's call this the StreetModel. The street model contains a number of objects that are part of the model. You can call them StreetModelMember objects. Street model members can be parking places, different types of buildings, different types of streets, bridges, and lakes.

Types

We'll use a number of types that are referred to in the schema.

- ▶ **Parking Place**   The *parking place* has a textual description for its use. It also contains the coordinates for the parking place on the map.

- ▶ **Buildings**   All *buildings* have an address, age, and color. Buildings can have an arbitrary number of floors and can be categorized using a type parameter, which typically contains a textual description, such as warehouse or office.

- ▶ **Complex Buildings and Square Buildings**   Buildings can have a complex shape or they can resemble a square. You can implement these two types of buildings as subclasses of the previous class.

- ▶ **Streets**   All streets have a name and a centerline.

- ▶ **One-way Streets**   One-way streets inherit the previous type and extend it with two properties: reason and meters wide. The first property is used to specify, with text, the reason for making the street a one-way street only. The second property is used to provide the width of the street. We won't model the direction of the one-way street. However, if you want to make your own extensions to the model, just for fun, consider modeling the direction of the one-way street.

- ▶ **Two-way Streets**   Two-way streets also inherit the previous type. They extend the type with a single property, meterswide total, which is used to specify the total street width.

- ▶ **Bridge**   Bridges have a name and a certain width. The location of the bridge is modeled using a description of the bridge's centerline.

- ▶ **Lake**   Lakes have a name. The shape is modeled as a polygon.

The Schema

This is the implementation of the schema. Note how it's divided into a number of sections. First, is the header and the line that imports the standard GML features. The element declarations follow. Also note some of the elements are abstract and used by other feature types only. Finally, yet equally important, all the feature types are defined. The complete listing of the schema follows.

```xml
<!-- The XML header and schema declaration. -->

<?xml version="1.0" encoding="UTF-8" ?>
<schema targetNamespace="http://www.myExample.com/myNameSpace"
xmlns:myModel="http://www.myExample.com/myNameSpace"
xmlns:gml="http://www.opengis.net/gml"
xmlns="http://www.w3.org/2000/10/XMLSchema"
  elementFormDefault="qualified" version="2.03">

    <!-- Import the "standard" GML features. -->
    <import namespace="http://www.opengis.net/gml"
schemaLocation="feature.xsd"/>

    <!-- The elements, which can be used in the street.xml file. -->
    <element name="StreetModel" type="myModel:StreetModelType"
        substitutionGroup="gml:_FeatureCollection"/>
    <element name="StreetModelMember" type="myModel:StreetModelMemberType"
        substitutionGroup="gml:featureMember"/>
    <element name="ParkingPlace" type="myModel:ParkingPlaceType"
        substitutionGroup="myModel:_StreetModelFeature"/>
    <element name="Building" type="myModel:BuildingType" abstract="true"
        substitutionGroup="myModel:_StreetModelFeature"/>
    <element name="SquareBuilding" type="myModel:SquareBuildingType"
        substitutionGroup="myModel:_StreetModelFeature"/>
    <element name="ComplexBuilding" type="myModel:ComplexBuildingType"
        substitutionGroup="myModel:_StreetModelFeature"/>
    <element name="Street" type="myModel:StreetType"
        substitutionGroup="myModel:_StreetModelFeature"/>
    <element name="OneWayStreet" type="myModel:OneWayStreetType"
        substitutionGroup="myModel:_StreetModelFeature"/>
    <element name="TwoWayStreet" type="myModel:TwoWayStreetType"
        substitutionGroup="myModel:_StreetModelFeature"/>
    <element name="Bridge" type="myModel:BridgeType"
        substitutionGroup="myModel:_StreetModelFeature"/>
    <element name="Lake" type="myModel:LakeType"
        substitutionGroup="myModel:_StreetModelFeature"/>

    <!-- The is the association, used by the StreetModelMemberType. -->
    <element name="_StreetModelFeature" type="gml:AbstractFeatureType"
        abstract="true" substitutionGroup="gml:_Feature"/>

    <!-- The elements above use the types below, which define the "content" of the
        elements. -->
```

```xml
<!-- Our "StreetModel" has a name and a description.  -->
<complexType name="StreetModelType">
    <complexContent>
        <extension base="gml:AbstractFeatureCollectionType">
            <sequence>
                <element name="name" type="string"/>
                <element name="desc" type="string"/>
            </sequence>
        </extension>
    </complexContent>
</complexType>

<!-- The type for the association between the container class and
     feature members. -->
<complexType name="StreetModelMemberType">
    <complexContent>
        <restriction base="gml:FeatureAssociationType">
            <sequence minOccurs="0">
                <element ref="myModel:_StreetModelFeature"/>
            </sequence>
        </restriction>
    </complexContent>
</complexType>

<!-- The type for the ParkingPlace class. -->
<complexType name="ParkingPlaceType">
    <complexContent>
        <extension base="gml:AbstractFeatureType">
            <sequence>
                <element name="desc" type="string"/>
                <element ref="gml:Box"/>
            </sequence>
        </extension>
    </complexContent>
</complexType>

<!-- The type for the Building class. Buildings have addresses (text). -->
<complexType name="BuildingType">
    <complexContent>
        <extension base="gml:AbstractFeatureType">
            <sequence>
                <element name="address" type="string"/>
                <element name="age" type="integer"/>
                <element name="type" type="string"/>
                <element name="color" type="string"/>
                <element name="floors" type="integer"/>
            </sequence>
```

```
        </extension>
    </complexContent>
</complexType>

<!-- A square building is a building which has the shape of a square. -->
<complexType name="SquareBuildingType">
    <complexContent>
        <extension base="myModel:BuildingType">
            <sequence>
                <element ref="gml:Box"/>
            </sequence>
        </extension>
    </complexContent>
</complexType>

<!-- A complex building has the shape of an arbitrary polygon. -->
<complexType name="ComplexBuildingType">
    <complexContent>
        <extension base="myModel:BuildingType">
            <sequence>
                <element ref="gml:Polygon"/>
            </sequence>
        </extension>
    </complexContent>
</complexType>

<!-- A street has a name and a shape. -->
<complexType name="StreetType">
    <complexContent>
        <extension base="gml:AbstractFeatureType">
            <sequence>
                <element name="name" type="string"/>
                <element ref="gml:centerLineOf"/>
            </sequence>
        </extension>
    </complexContent>
</complexType>

<!-- One-way streets are streets specified with the total width.
     There is a reason why the street is a one-way street. -->
<complexType name="OneWayStreetType">
    <complexContent>
        <extension base="myModel:StreetType">
            <sequence>
                <element name="reason" type="string"/>
                <element name="meterswide" type="integer"/>
            </sequence>
```

```
            </extension>
        </complexContent>
    </complexType>

    <!-- Two-way streets are streets which have the total width specified. -->
    <complexType name="TwoWayStreetType">
        <complexContent>
            <extension base="myModel:StreetType">
                <sequence>
                    <element name="meterswidetotal" type="integer"/>
                </sequence>
            </extension>
        </complexContent>
    </complexType>

    <!-- A bridge has a name and a shape represented by a polygon. -->
    <complexType name="BridgeType">
        <complexContent>
            <extension base="gml:AbstractFeatureType">
                <sequence>
                    <element name="name" type="string"/>
                    <element name="meterswidetotal" type="integer"/>
                    <element ref="gml:centerLineOf"/>
                </sequence>
            </extension>
        </complexContent>
    </complexType>

    <!-- Lakes have names. A lake is represented by a polygon. -->
    <complexType name="LakeType">
        <complexContent>
            <extension base="gml:AbstractFeatureType">
                <sequence>
                    <element name="name" type="string"/>
                    <element ref="gml:Polygon"/>
                </sequence>
            </extension>
        </complexContent>
    </complexType>
</schema>
```

The traditional XML header is followed by a schema declaration and the import statement, as described in Chapter 7. Then all the element declarations follow. Notice that Building and Street are abstract. They are only used by SquareBuilding, ComplexBuilding, OneWayStreet, and TwoWayStreet. As you can see, all _StreetModelFeature types are gml:AbstractFeatureType types. Otherwise, you couldn't put them in your street model collection, StreetModelType, which inherits gml:_FeatureCollection.

All types are defined using the complexType declaration. This is because they're composed of properties and geometry elements, not just simple properties. The definitions are rather straightforward. You'll get a better feeling for how the instance document might look when we've provided all the data in it.

The Instance Document

The measured data listed earlier is provided in the instance document. The following is how the document looks. It's quite long, but don't worry. We'll go through the more complicated parts of it after the listing.

```
<?xml version="1.0" encoding="UTF-8"?>

<StreetModel xmlns="http://www.myExample.com/myNameSpace"
            xmlns:gml="http://www.opengis.net/gml"
            xmlns:xsi="http://www.w3.org/2000/10/XMLSchema-instance"
            xsi:schemaLocation=". myFeatures.xsd">

    <!-- The bounds, or the box, for the model. All objects in our model are
        inside these coordinates. -->

    <gml:boundedBy>
        <gml:Box srsName="myModel:srs">
            <gml:coord>
                <gml:x>0</gml:x>
                <gml:y>0</gml:y>
            </gml:coord>
            <gml:coord>
                <gml:x>160</gml:x>
                <gml:y>160</gml:y>
            </gml:coord>
        </gml:Box>
    </gml:boundedBy>

    <!-- *************** The parking place. *************** -->
    <StreetModelMember>
        <ParkingPlace>
            <desc>A parking place.</desc>
            <gml:Box>
                <gml:coord>
                    <gml:x>5</gml:x>
                    <gml:y>10</gml:y>
                </gml:coord>
```

```
                <gml:coord>
                    <gml:x>35</gml:x>
                    <gml:y>40</gml:y>
                </gml:coord>
            </gml:Box>
        </ParkingPlace>
</StreetModelMember>

<!-- *********** One-way street into the parking place. *********** -->
<StreetModelMember>
    <OneWayStreet>
        <name>Parking place drive in</name>
        <gml:centerLineOf>
            <gml:LineString>
                <gml:coord>
                    <gml:x>30</gml:x>
                    <gml:y>5</gml:y>
                </gml:coord>
                <gml:coord>
                    <gml:x>30</gml:x>
                    <gml:y>10</gml:y>
                </gml:coord>
            </gml:LineString>
        </gml:centerLineOf>
        <reason>Drive in to parking place only.</reason>
        <meterswide>3</meterswide>
    </OneWayStreet>
</StreetModelMember>

<!-- ********* One-way street out from the parking place. ********* -->
<StreetModelMember>
    <OneWayStreet>
        <name>Parking place drive out</name>
        <gml:centerLineOf>
            <gml:LineString>
                <gml:coord>
                    <gml:x>10</gml:x>
                    <gml:y>40</gml:y>
                </gml:coord>
                <gml:coord>
                    <gml:x>10</gml:x>
                    <gml:y>65</gml:y>
                </gml:coord>
            </gml:LineString>
        </gml:centerLineOf>
        <reason>Drive out from parking place only.</reason>
        <meterswide>3</meterswide>
```

```
        </OneWayStreet>
</StreetModelMember>

<!-- *************** The lake. *************** -->
<StreetModelMember>
    <Lake>
        <name>Lake Chattanoga</name>
        <gml:Polygon>
            <gml:outerBoundaryIs>
                <gml:LinearRing>
                    <gml:coord>
                        <gml:x>90</gml:x>
                        <gml:y>10</gml:y>
                    </gml:coord>
                    <gml:coord>
                        <gml:x>80</gml:x>
                        <gml:y>40</gml:y>
                    </gml:coord>
                    <gml:coord>
                        <gml:x>85</gml:x>
                        <gml:y>70</gml:y>
                    </gml:coord>
                    <gml:coord>
                        <gml:x>110</gml:x>
                        <gml:y>60</gml:y>
                    </gml:coord>
                    <gml:coord>
                        <gml:x>140</gml:x>
                        <gml:y>70</gml:y>
                    </gml:coord>
                    <gml:coord>
                        <gml:x>160</gml:x>
                        <gml:y>65</gml:y>
                    </gml:coord>
                    <gml:coord>
                        <gml:x>155</gml:x>
                        <gml:y>20</gml:y>
                    </gml:coord>
                    <gml:coord>
                        <gml:x>140</gml:x>
                        <gml:y>15</gml:y>
                    </gml:coord>
                    <gml:coord>
                        <gml:x>135</gml:x>
                        <gml:y>5</gml:y>
                    </gml:coord>
                    <gml:coord>
```

```
                    <gml:x>90</gml:x>
                    <gml:y>10</gml:y>
                </gml:coord>
            </gml:LinearRing>
        </gml:outerBoundaryIs>
    </gml:Polygon>
</Lake>
</StreetModelMember>


<!-- *************** Northern West-to-East street. *************** -->
<StreetModelMember>
    <TwoWayStreet>
        <name>Northern West-to-East street</name>
        <gml:centerLineOf>
            <gml:LineString>
                <gml:coord>
                    <gml:x>0</gml:x>
                    <gml:y>5</gml:y>
                </gml:coord>
                <gml:coord>
                    <gml:x>100</gml:x>
                    <gml:y>5</gml:y>
                </gml:coord>
            </gml:LineString>
        </gml:centerLineOf>
        <meterswidetotal>6</meterswidetotal>
    </TwoWayStreet>
</StreetModelMember>

<!-- *************** Southern West-to-East street. *************** -->

<StreetModelMember>
    <TwoWayStreet>
        <name>Southern West-to-East street</name>
        <gml:centerLineOf>
            <gml:LineString>
                <gml:coord>
                    <gml:x>0</gml:x>
                    <gml:y>95</gml:y>
                </gml:coord>
                <gml:coord>
                    <gml:x>160</gml:x>
                    <gml:y>95</gml:y>
                </gml:coord>
            </gml:LineString>
        </gml:centerLineOf>
        <meterswidetotal>6</meterswidetotal>
```

```
        </TwoWayStreet>
</StreetModelMember>


<!-- *************** Mid West-to-East street. *************** -->
<StreetModelMember>
    <TwoWayStreet>
        <name>Mid West-to-East street</name>
        <gml:centerLineOf>
            <gml:LineString>
                <gml:coord>
                    <gml:x>0</gml:x>
                    <gml:y>65</gml:y>
                </gml:coord>
                <gml:coord>
                    <gml:x>35</gml:x>
                    <gml:y>65</gml:y>
                </gml:coord>
            </gml:LineString>
        </gml:centerLineOf>
        <meterswidetotal>6</meterswidetotal>
    </TwoWayStreet>
</StreetModelMember>


<!-- *************** West North-to-South street. *************** -->
<StreetModelMember>
    <TwoWayStreet>
        <name>West North-to-South street</name>
        <gml:centerLineOf>
            <gml:LineString>
                <gml:coord>
                    <gml:x>35</gml:x>
                    <gml:y>65</gml:y>
                </gml:coord>
                <gml:coord>
                    <gml:x>35</gml:x>
                    <gml:y>95</gml:y>
                </gml:coord>
            </gml:LineString>
        </gml:centerLineOf>
        <meterswidetotal>6</meterswidetotal>
    </TwoWayStreet>
</StreetModelMember>


<!-- *************** Mid North-to-South street. *************** -->
<StreetModelMember>
    <TwoWayStreet>
        <name>Mid North-to-South street</name>
```

```
            <gml:centerLineOf>
                <gml:LineString>
                    <gml:coord>
                        <gml:x>55</gml:x>
                        <gml:y>5</gml:y>
                    </gml:coord>
                    <gml:coord>
                        <gml:x>55</gml:x>
                        <gml:y>95</gml:y>
                    </gml:coord>
                </gml:LineString>
            </gml:centerLineOf>
            <meterswidetotal>6</meterswidetotal>
        </TwoWayStreet>
    </StreetModelMember>

    <!-- *************** Bridge street. *************** -->
    <StreetModelMember>
        <TwoWayStreet>
            <name>Bridge street</name>
            <gml:centerLineOf>
                <gml:LineString>
                    <gml:coord>
                        <gml:x>100</gml:x>
                        <gml:y>5</gml:y>
                    </gml:coord>
                    <gml:coord>
                        <gml:x>155</gml:x>
                        <gml:y>70</gml:y>
                    </gml:coord>
                </gml:LineString>
            </gml:centerLineOf>
            <meterswidetotal>6</meterswidetotal>
        </TwoWayStreet>
    </StreetModelMember>

    <!-- *************** East North-to-South street. *************** -->
    <StreetModelMember>
        <TwoWayStreet>
            <name>East North-to-South street</name>
            <gml:centerLineOf>
                <gml:LineString>
                    <gml:coord>
                        <gml:x>155</gml:x>
                        <gml:y>70</gml:y>
                    </gml:coord>
                    <gml:coord>
```

```
                <gml:x>155</gml:x>
                <gml:y>95</gml:y>
            </gml:coord>
        </gml:LineString>
    </gml:centerLineOf>
    <meterswidetotal>6</meterswidetotal>
    </TwoWayStreet>
</StreetModelMember>


<!-- *************** The Bridge. *************** -->
<StreetModelMember>
    <Bridge>
        <name>The Lake bridge</name>
        <meterswidetotal>10</meterswidetotal>
        <gml:centerLineOf>
            <gml:LineString>
                <gml:coord>
                    <gml:x>100</gml:x>
                    <gml:y>5</gml:y>
                </gml:coord>
                <gml:coord>
                    <gml:x>155</gml:x>
                    <gml:y>70</gml:y>
                </gml:coord>
            </gml:LineString>
        </gml:centerLineOf>
    </Bridge>
</StreetModelMember>


<!-- ************ Buildings 1-3 Mid North-toSouth Street ************ -->
<StreetModelMember>
    <SquareBuilding>
        <address>1-3 Mid North-toSouth Street</address>
        <age>10</age>
        <type>home</type>
        <color>#404040</color>
        <floors>5</floors>
        <gml:Box>
            <gml:coord>
                <gml:x>40</gml:x>
                <gml:y>10</gml:y>
            </gml:coord>
            <gml:coord>
                <gml:x>50</gml:x>
                <gml:y>30</gml:y>
            </gml:coord>
        </gml:Box>
```

```
        </SquareBuilding>
    </StreetModelMember>


    <!-- *************** Buildings 5 Mid North-toSouth Street ***************
-->
    <StreetModelMember>
        <SquareBuilding>
            <address>5 Mid North-toSouth Street</address>
            <age>20</age>
            <type>school</type>
            <color>#101010</color>
            <floors>5</floors>
            <gml:Box>
                <gml:coord>
                    <gml:x>40</gml:x>
                    <gml:y>30</gml:y>
                </gml:coord>
                <gml:coord>
                    <gml:x>50</gml:x>
                    <gml:y>40</gml:y>
                </gml:coord>
            </gml:Box>
        </SquareBuilding>
    </StreetModelMember>


    <!-- ************ Buildings 7-11 Mid North-toSouth Street ************ -->
    <StreetModelMember>
        <SquareBuilding>
            <address>7-11 Mid North-toSouth Street</address>
            <age>30</age>
            <type>home</type>
            <color>#F00000</color>
            <floors>2</floors>
            <gml:Box>
                <gml:coord>
                    <gml:x>40</gml:x>
                    <gml:y>40</gml:y>
                </gml:coord>
                <gml:coord>
                    <gml:x>50</gml:x>
                    <gml:y>70</gml:y>
                </gml:coord>
            </gml:Box>
        </SquareBuilding>
    </StreetModelMember>
```

```
<!-- ************ Buildings 13-15 Mid North-toSouth Street ************
-->
    <StreetModelMember>
        <SquareBuilding>
            <address>13-15 Mid North-toSouth Street</address>
            <age>30</age>
            <type>home</type>
            <color>#404040</color>
            <floors>5</floors>
            <gml:Box>
                <gml:coord>
                    <gml:x>40</gml:x>
                    <gml:y>70</gml:y>
                </gml:coord>
                <gml:coord>
                    <gml:x>50</gml:x>
                    <gml:y>90</gml:y>
                </gml:coord>
            </gml:Box>
        </SquareBuilding>
    </StreetModelMember>


<!-- *************** Buildings 4 Mid West-to-East Street ***************
-->
    <StreetModelMember>
        <SquareBuilding>
            <address>4 Mid West-to-East Street</address>
            <age>10</age>
            <type>warehouse</type>
            <color>#909090</color>
            <floors>1</floors>
            <gml:Box>
                <gml:coord>
                    <gml:x>20</gml:x>
                    <gml:y>45</gml:y>
                </gml:coord>
                <gml:coord>
                    <gml:x>35</gml:x>
                    <gml:y>55</gml:y>
                </gml:coord>
            </gml:Box>
        </SquareBuilding>
    </StreetModelMember>


<!-- *************** Buildings 1-3 Mid West-to-East Street ***************
-->
    <StreetModelMember>
```

```xml
    <SquareBuilding>
        <address>1-3 Mid West-to-East Street</address>
        <age>5</age>
        <type>home</type>
        <color>#404040</color>
        <floors>1</floors>
        <gml:Box>
            <gml:coord>
                <gml:x>0</gml:x>
                <gml:y>70</gml:y>
            </gml:coord>
            <gml:coord>
                <gml:x>20</gml:x>
                <gml:y>90</gml:y>
            </gml:coord>
        </gml:Box>
    </SquareBuilding>
</StreetModelMember>

<!-- *************** Buildings 5 Mid West-to-East Street ***************
-->
<StreetModelMember>
    <SquareBuilding>
        <address>5 Mid West-to-East Street</address>
        <age>15</age>
        <type>home</type>
        <color>#00FF80</color>
        <floors>2</floors>
        <gml:Box>
            <gml:coord>
                <gml:x>25</gml:x>
                <gml:y>70</gml:y>
            </gml:coord>
            <gml:coord>
                <gml:x>30</gml:x>
                <gml:y>90</gml:y>
            </gml:coord>
        </gml:Box>
    </SquareBuilding>
</StreetModelMember>

<!-- ************ Buildings 2-6 Mid North-toSouth Street ************ -->
<StreetModelMember>
    <SquareBuilding>
        <address>2-6 Mid North-toSouth Street</address>
        <age>17</age>
        <type>supermarket</type>
```

```
            <color>#404040</color>
            <floors>1</floors>
            <gml:Box>
                <gml:coord>
                    <gml:x>60</gml:x>
                    <gml:y>10</gml:y>
                </gml:coord>
                <gml:coord>
                    <gml:x>70</gml:x>
                    <gml:y>40</gml:y>
                </gml:coord>
            </gml:Box>
        </SquareBuilding>
    </StreetModelMember>


    <!-- *************** Buildings 8 Mid North-toSouth Street ***************
-->
    <StreetModelMember>
        <SquareBuilding>
            <address>8 Mid North-toSouth Street</address>
            <age>35</age>
            <type>home</type>
            <color>#308050</color>
            <floors>2</floors>
            <gml:Box>
                <gml:coord>
                    <gml:x>60</gml:x>
                    <gml:y>40</gml:y>
                </gml:coord>
                <gml:coord>
                    <gml:x>70</gml:x>
                    <gml:y>50</gml:y>
                </gml:coord>
            </gml:Box>
        </SquareBuilding>
    </StreetModelMember>


    <!-- ************ Buildings 12-16 Mid North-toSouth Street ************
-->
    <StreetModelMember>
        <ComplexBuilding>
            <address>12-16 Mid North-toSouth Street</address>
            <age>10</age>
            <type>office</type>
            <color>#AA80AA</color>
            <floors>1</floors>
```

```
        <gml:Polygon>
            <gml:outerBoundaryIs>
                <gml:LinearRing>
                    <gml:coord>
                        <gml:x>60</gml:x>
                        <gml:y>60</gml:y>
                    </gml:coord>
                    <gml:coord>
                        <gml:x>70</gml:x>
                        <gml:y>60</gml:y>
                    </gml:coord>
                    <gml:coord>
                        <gml:x>70</gml:x>
                        <gml:y>80</gml:y>
                    </gml:coord>
                    <gml:coord>
                        <gml:x>75</gml:x>
                        <gml:y>80</gml:y>
                    </gml:coord>
                    <gml:coord>
                        <gml:x>75</gml:x>
                        <gml:y>90</gml:y>
                    </gml:coord>
                    <gml:coord>
                        <gml:x>60</gml:x>
                        <gml:y>90</gml:y>
                    </gml:coord>
                    <gml:coord>
                        <gml:x>60</gml:x>
                        <gml:y>60</gml:y>
                    </gml:coord>
                </gml:LinearRing>
            </gml:outerBoundaryIs>
        </gml:Polygon>
    </ComplexBuilding>
</StreetModelMember>

<!-- ********** Buildings 18-22 Southern West-to-East street **********
-->
<StreetModelMember>
    <SquareBuilding>
        <address>18-22 Southern West-to-East street</address>
        <age>15</age>
        <type>office</type>
        <color>#404040</color>
        <floors>2</floors>
        <gml:Box>
```

```
                <gml:coord>
                    <gml:x>80</gml:x>
                    <gml:y>80</gml:y>
                </gml:coord>
                <gml:coord>
                    <gml:x>110</gml:x>
                    <gml:y>90</gml:y>
                </gml:coord>
            </gml:Box>
        </SquareBuilding>
    </StreetModelMember>


<!-- ********** Buildings 24 Southern West-to-East street ********** -->


<StreetModelMember>
    <SquareBuilding
        <address>24 Southern West-to-East street</address>
        <age>40</age>
        <type>home</type>
        <color>#404040</color>
        <floors>2</floors>
        <gml:Box>
            <gml:coord>
                <gml:x>110</gml:x>
                <gml:y>80</gml:y>
            </gml:coord>
            <gml:coord>
                <gml:x>120</gml:x>
                <gml:y>90</gml:y>
            </gml:coord>
        </gml:Box>
    </SquareBuilding>
</StreetModelMember>

<!-- ********** Buildings 26-30 Southern West-to-East street **********
-->
<StreetModelMember>
    <SquareBuilding
        <address>26-30 Southern West-to-East street</address>
        <age>20</age>
        <type>office</type>
        <color>#404040</color>
        <floors>1</floors>
        <gml:Box>
            <gml:coord>
                <gml:x>120</gml:x>
                <gml:y>80</gml:y>
```

```xml
            </gml:coord>
            <gml:coord>
                <gml:x>150</gml:x>
                <gml:y>90</gml:y>
            </gml:coord>
        </gml:Box>
    </SquareBuilding>
</StreetModelMember>

<!-- ********** Buildings 1 Southern West-to-East street ********** -->
<StreetModelMember>
    <SquareBuilding>
        <address>1 Southern West-to-East street</address>
        <age>12</age>
        <type>home</type>
        <color>#404040</color>
        <floors>2</floors>
        <gml:Box>
            <gml:coord>
                <gml:x>0</gml:x>
                <gml:y>100</gml:y>
            </gml:coord>
            <gml:coord>
                <gml:x>10</gml:x>
                <gml:y>110</gml:y>
            </gml:coord>
        </gml:Box>
    </SquareBuilding>
</StreetModelMember>

<!-- ********** Buildings 3-7 Southern West-to-East street ********** -->

<StreetModelMember>
    <SquareBuilding>
        <address>3-7 Southern West-to-East street</address>
        <age>23</age>
        <type>office</type>
        <color>#404040</color>
        <floors>5</floors>
        <gml:Box>
            <gml:coord>
                <gml:x>10</gml:x>
                <gml:y>100</gml:y>
            </gml:coord>
            <gml:coord>
                <gml:x>40</gml:x>
                <gml:y>110</gml:y>
```

```
            </gml:coord>
        </gml:Box>
    </SquareBuilding>
</StreetModelMember>


<!-- ********** Buildings 9 Southern West-to-East street ********** -->
<StreetModelMember>
    <SquareBuilding>
        <address>9 Southern West-to-East street</address>
        <age>16</age>
        <type>home</type>
        <color>#004040</color>
        <floors>2</floors>
        <gml:Box>
            <gml:coord><gml:x>40</gml:x><gml:y>100</gml:y></gml:coord>
            <gml:coord><gml:x>50</gml:x><gml:y>110</gml:y></gml:coord>
        </gml:Box>
    </SquareBuilding>
</StreetModelMember>


<!-- ********** Buildings 11-15 Southern West-to-East street **********
-->
<StreetModelMember>
    <SquareBuilding>
        <address>11-15 Southern West-to-East street</address>
        <age>29</age>
        <type>home</type>
        <color>#707099</color>
        <floors>2</floors>
        <gml:Box>
            <gml:coord><gml:x>50</gml:x><gml:y>100</gml:y></gml:coord>
            <gml:coord><gml:x>80</gml:x><gml:y>110</gml:y></gml:coord>
        </gml:Box>
    </SquareBuilding>
</StreetModelMember>


<!-- ********** Buildings 17 Southern West-to-East street ********** -->
<StreetModelMember>
    <SquareBuilding>
        <address>17 Southern West-to-East street</address>
        <age>19</age>
        <type>home</type>
        <color>#BB8330</color>
        <floors>2</floors>
        <gml:Box>
            <gml:coord><gml:x>80</gml:x><gml:y>100</gml:y></gml:coord>
            <gml:coord><gml:x>90</gml:x><gml:y>110</gml:y></gml:coord>
```

```
            </gml:Box>
        </SquareBuilding>
    </StreetModelMember>


    <!-- ********** Buildings 19-23 Southern West-to-East street **********
-->
    <StreetModelMember>
        <SquareBuilding>
            <address>19-23 Southern West-to-East street</address>
            <age>15</age>
            <type>office</type>
            <color>#FFC0FF</color>
            <floors>2</floors>
            <gml:Box>
                <gml:coord><gml:x>90</gml:x><gml:y>100</gml:y></gml:coord>
                <gml:coord><gml:x>120</gml:x><gml:y>110</gml:y></gml:coord>
            </gml:Box>
        </SquareBuilding>
    </StreetModelMember>


    <!-- ********** Buildings 25 Southern West-to-East street ********** -->
    <StreetModelMember>
        <SquareBuilding>
            <address>25 Southern West-to-East street</address>
            <age>9</age>
            <type>home</type>
            <color>#707099</color>
            <floors>2</floors>
            <gml:Box>
                <gml:coord><gml:x>120</gml:x><gml:y>100</gml:y></gml:coord>
                <gml:coord><gml:x>130</gml:x><gml:y>110</gml:y></gml:coord>
            </gml:Box>
        </SquareBuilding>
    </StreetModelMember>


    <!-- ********** Buildings 27-31 Southern West-to-East street **********
-->
    <StreetModelMember>
        <SquareBuilding>
            <address>27-31 Southern West-to-East street</address>
            <age>5</age>
            <type>office</type>
            <color>#707099</color>
            <floors>3</floors>
            <gml:Box>
                <gml:coord><gml:x>130</gml:x><gml:y>100</gml:y></gml:coord>
                <gml:coord><gml:x>160</gml:x><gml:y>110</gml:y></gml:coord>
```

```
            </gml:Box>
        </SquareBuilding>
    </StreetModelMember>
    <name>Streetmodel</name>
    <desc>Streets and buildings.</desc>
</StreetModel>
```

You can see how the inheritance works here. OneWayStreet elements and
TwoWayStreet elements contain the name element and the gml:centerLineOf element,
which have been defined in the parent Street. In addition, the SquareBuilding and
ComplexBuilding elements contain elements that were defined in BuildingType, such
as address and age.

Note, the gml:Box element must contain two coord elements. Each *coord* element
contains an *x* and a *y* element to specify the position of the box. The parking place
and square buildings are specified like this.

Streets use the gml:centerLineOf element to provide the data for the line that
models the street. The gml:centerLineOf element contains a gml:LineString and
two gml:coord elements that provide the *x* and *y* data.

The shape of the lake is described using a polygon. No innerBoundary exists for
the lake, so only the gml:outerBoundaryIs element is used for the lake. This element
contains a gml:LinearRing. A *linear ring* is a geometric object that has the same start
and end coordinates (it's closed).

The colors of the buildings have also been modeled. The RGB color code is
provided inside the color tags. This isn't a GML-specific feature but, instead, simply
a definition added to the schema. The next step is to create an XSL style sheet that
maps this description to an SVG format.

Transformation to SVG

For the transformation, you need to determine how the types defined in the schema
will be rendered. You needn't consider the abstract types—Building and Street—
because they can't appear in the instance document. The types you need to consider,
though, are one-way streets, two-way streets, bridges, square buildings, complex
buildings, and lakes. The user can create instance documents that contain dozens of
lakes or several parking places but, as long as you've created a mapping from the
type to a suitable SVG rendering, it's possible to render that representation. The
approach is to use a polygon for the parking place, a path for both types of streets, a
path for the bridge, a polygon for the lake, and a polygon for both types of buildings.

Implementing the XSL Style Sheet

Here's the implementation of the XSL style sheet:

```
<?xml version="1.0" encoding="UTF-8"?>
<xsl:stylesheet
  version="1.0"
  xmlns:gml="http://www.opengis.net/gml"
  xmlns:xsl="http://www.w3.org/1999/XSL/Transform"
  xmlns:fo="http://www.w3.org/1999/XSL/Format">

<xsl:output
    method="xml"
    doctype-public = "-//W3C//DTD SVG 20001102//EN
    http://www.w3.org/TR/2000/CR-SVG-20001102/DTD/svg-20001102.dtd"/>

<!-- ***** Top level, SVG element and the view box's dimensions.***** -->
<xsl:template match="/">
  <xsl:variable name="x1">
    <xsl:value-of
select="/StreetModel/gml:boundedBy/gml:Box/gml:coord/gml:x"/>
  </xsl:variable>
  <xsl:variable name="y1">
      <xsl:value-of
select="/StreetModel/gml:boundedBy/gml:Box/gml:coord/gml:y"/>
  </xsl:variable>
  <xsl:variable name="x2">
    <xsl:value-of
select="/StreetModel/gml:boundedBy/gml:Box/gml:coord[2]/gml:x"/>
  </xsl:variable>
  <xsl:variable name="y2">
    <xsl:value-of
select="/StreetModel/gml:boundedBy/gml:Box/gml:coord[2]/gml:y"/>
  </xsl:variable>

  <svg width="160px" height="160px"
          viewBox="{$x1},{$y1},{$x2},{$y2}" preserveAspectRatio="xMinYMid">

  <polygon style="fill:green; stroke:green"
    points="{$x1},{$y1} {$x2},{$y1} {$x2},{$y2} {$x1},{$y2} {$x1},{$y1}"/>

  <xsl:for-each select="/StreetModel/StreetModelMember">
    <xsl:apply-templates/>
  </xsl:for-each>
  </svg>
</xsl:template>
```

```xsl
<xsl:template match="StreetModelMember">
    <xsl:apply-templates/>
</xsl:template>


<!-- ****************** Parking places ****************** -->
<xsl:template match="ParkingPlace">
  <xsl:variable name="x1">
    <xsl:value-of select="gml:Box/gml:coord/gml:x"/></xsl:variable>
  <xsl:variable name="y1">
    <xsl:value-of select="gml:Box/gml:coord/gml:y"/>
  </xsl:variable>
  <xsl:variable name="x2">
    <xsl:value-of select="gml:Box/gml:coord[2]/gml:x"/>
  </xsl:variable>
  <xsl:variable name="y2">
    <xsl:value-of select="gml:Box/gml:coord[2]/gml:y"/>
  </xsl:variable>
  <polygon style="fill:gray; stroke:black"
    points="{$x1},{$y1} {$x2},{$y1} {$x2},{$y2} {$x1},{$y2} {$x1},{$y1}"/>
</xsl:template>


<!-- ****************** One-way streets ****************** -->
<xsl:template match="OneWayStreet">
  <xsl:variable name="x1"
           select="gml:centerLineOf/gml:LineString/gml:coord[1]/gml:x"/>
  <xsl:variable name="y1"
           select="gml:centerLineOf/gml:LineString/gml:coord[1]/gml:y"/>
  <xsl:variable name="x2"
           select="gml:centerLineOf/gml:LineString/gml:coord[2]/gml:x"/>
  <xsl:variable name="y2"
           select="gml:centerLineOf/gml:LineString/gml:coord[2]/gml:y"/>
  <path d="M {$x1},{$y1} L {$x2},{$y2}" style="stroke:red; stroke-width:2"/>
</xsl:template>


<!-- ****************** Two-way streets ****************** -->
<xsl:template match="TwoWayStreet">
  <xsl:variable name="x1"
           select="gml:centerLineOf/gml:LineString/gml:coord[1]/gml:x"/>
  <xsl:variable name="y1"
           select="gml:centerLineOf/gml:LineString/gml:coord[1]/gml:y"/>
  <xsl:variable name="x2"
           select="gml:centerLineOf/gml:LineString/gml:coord[2]/gml:x"/>
  <xsl:variable name="y2"
           select="gml:centerLineOf/gml:LineString/gml:coord[2]/gml:y"/>
  <path d="M {$x1},{$y1} L {$x2},{$y2}" style="stroke:red; stroke-width:4"/>
</xsl:template>
```

```xml
<!-- ******************* Bridges ******************* -->
<xsl:template match="Bridge">
  <xsl:variable name="x1"
           select="gml:centerLineOf/gml:LineString/gml:coord[1]/gml:x"/>
  <xsl:variable name="y1"
           select="gml:centerLineOf/gml:LineString/gml:coord[1]/gml:y"/>
  <xsl:variable name="x2"
           select="gml:centerLineOf/gml:LineString/gml:coord[2]/gml:x"/>
  <xsl:variable name="y2"
            select="gml:centerLineOf/gml:LineString/gml:coord[2]/gml:y"/>
  <xsl:variable name="wide" select="meterswidetotal"/>
  <path d="M {$x1},{$y1} L {$x2},{$y2}"
       style="opacity:.5; stroke:#CCCCCC; stroke-width:{$wide}"/>
</xsl:template>


<!-- ******************* Square buildings ******************* -->
<xsl:template match="SquareBuilding">
  <xsl:variable name="x1">
    <xsl:value-of select="gml:Box/gml:coord/gml:x"/>
  </xsl:variable>
  <xsl:variable name="y1">
    <xsl:value-of select="gml:Box/gml:coord/gml:y"/>
  </xsl:variable>
  <xsl:variable name="x2">
    <xsl:value-of select="gml:Box/gml:coord[2]/gml:x"/>
  </xsl:variable>
  <xsl:variable name="y2">
    <xsl:value-of select="gml:Box/gml:coord[2]/gml:y"/>
  </xsl:variable>
  <xsl:variable name="colorCode" select="color"/>
  <polygon style="fill:{$colorCode}; stroke:black"
      points="{$x1},{$y1} {$x2},{$y1} {$x2},{$y2} {$x1},{$y2} {$x1},{$y1}"/>
</xsl:template>


<!-- ******************* Complex buildings ******************* -->
<xsl:template match="ComplexBuilding">
    <xsl:variable name="coordList">
    <xsl:for-each
        select="gml:Polygon/gml:outerBoundaryIs/gml:LinearRing/gml:coord">
        <xsl:value-of select="gml:x"/>,<xsl:value-of select="gml:y"/>
        <xsl:text> </xsl:text>
      </xsl:for-each>
    </xsl:variable>
    <xsl:variable name="colorCode" select="color"/>
    <polygon style="fill:{$colorCode}; stroke:black"
        points="{$coordList}"/>
</xsl:template>
```

```
<!-- ****************** Lakes ****************** -->
<xsl:template match="Lake">
      <xsl:variable name="coordList">
        <xsl:for-each
select="gml:Polygon/gml:outerBoundaryIs/gml:LinearRing/gml:coord">
                    <xsl:value-of select="gml:x"/>,<xsl:value-of
select="gml:y"/>
                    <xsl:text> </xsl:text>
        </xsl:for-each>
      </xsl:variable>
      <polygon style="opacity:.5; fill:blue; stroke:blue"
points="{$coordList}"/>
</xsl:template>

</xsl:stylesheet>
```

The template rule that matches the root, /, generates the svg start and end tags. To retrieve the parameters for the view box, a number of xsl:value-of elements are used. Each value-of element retrieves the *x* or *y* coordinate for some of the coord elements in the GML bounding box. These values are stored in four variables: x1, y1, x2, and y2. Using the {$var} syntax, the variables' values can be inserted into the value of the svg viewbox attribute.

The previous values are also used to draw a green background, which covers the whole view box. To achieve this, the polygon element is used.

The parking place, buildings, and the lake are drawn almost the same way as the green background is drawn, using a polygon and a number of value-of elements that retrieve the coordinates.

Streets and the bridge use the path element to draw a colored path. Notice a two-way street is rendered twice as thick as a one-way street.

Lakes and bridges are rendered with 50 percent opacity. This is because GML features can be specified in an arbitrary order, and then the bridge might be rendered before the lake and the lake will cover the bridge. GML doesn't deal with rendering at all, so the provider of the data can specify the features in an arbitrary order.

The color codes provided with the color elements are used when buildings are rendered. In this case, the color code is extracted using a statement like this one:

```
<xsl:variable name="colorCode" select="color"/>
```

In the polygon element's style attribute, the colorCode variable is used to color the building objects.

The coordinates for the polygon that describe complex buildings and lakes are collected in a special way. Because all coordinates are specified in GML using gml:coord, gml:x, and gml:y elements, the data must be looped through and collected in a list. This is done like the following:

```
<xsl:variable name="coordList">
<xsl:for-each
select="gml:Polygon/gml:outerBoundaryIs/gml:LinearRing/gml:coord">
  <xsl:value-of select="gml:x"/>,<xsl:value-of select="gml:y"/>
  <xsl:text> </xsl:text>
</xsl:for-each>
</xsl:variable>
<polygon style="opacity:.5; fill:blue; stroke:blue"
points="{$coordList}"/>
```

All coordinates in the polygon element are provided as a string, where each coordinate pair is separated by a space, and the *x* and *y* coordinates are separated by a comma. The for-each element retrieves all gml:coord elements and, for each of these elements, the *x* and *y* coordinates are put together with a comma in between. The result ends up in the variable coordList, which is specified as an attribute to the surrounding xml:variable element.

Here's the document, the result of the transformation from GML to SVG:

```
<?xml version="1.0" encoding="UTF-8"?>
<svg xmlns:fo="http://www.w3.org/1999/XSL/Format"
xmlns:gml="http://www.opengis.net/gml" width="160px" height="160px"
viewBox="0,0,160,160" preserveAspectRatio="xMinYMid">

  <polygon style="fill:green; stroke:green"
    points="0,0 160,0 160,160 0,160 0,0"/>

  <polygon style="fill:gray; stroke:black" points="5,10 35,10 35,40
5,40 5,10"/>

  <path d="M 30,5 L 30,10" style="stroke:red; stroke-width:2"/>

  <path d="M 10,40 L 10,65" style="stroke:red; stroke-width:2"/>

  <polygon style="opacity:.5; fill:blue; stroke:blue"
    points="90,10 80,40 85,70 110,60 140,70 160,65 155,20 140,15
135,5 90,10 "/>
```

```
<path d="M 0,5 L 100,5" style="stroke:red; stroke-width:4"/>

<path d="M 0,95 L 160,95" style="stroke:red; stroke-width:4"/>

<path d="M 0,65 L 35,65" style="stroke:red; stroke-width:4"/>

<path d="M 35,65 L 35,95" style="stroke:red; stroke-width:4"/>

<path d="M 55,5 L 55,95" style="stroke:red; stroke-width:4"/>

<path d="M 100,5 L 155,70" style="stroke:red; stroke-width4:"/>

<path d="M 155,70 L 155,95" style="stroke:red; stroke-width4:"/>

<path d="M 100,5 L 155,70" style="opacity:.5; stroke:#CCCCCC;
stroke-width:10"/>

<polygon style="fill:#404040; stroke:black"
  points="40,10 50,10 50,30 40,30 40,10"/>

<polygon style="fill:#101010; stroke:black"
  points="40,30 50,30 50,40 40,40 40,30"/>

<polygon style="fill:#F00000; stroke:black"
  points="40,40 50,40 50,70 40,70 40,40"/>

<polygon style="fill:#404040; stroke:black"
  points="40,70 50,70 50,90 40,90 40,70"/>

<polygon style="fill:#909090; stroke:black"
  points="20,45 35,45 35,55 20,55 20,45"/>

<polygon style="fill:#404040; stroke:black"
  points="0,70 20,70 20,90 0,90 0,70"/>

<polygon style="fill:#00FF80; stroke:black"
  points="25,70 30,70 30,90 25,90 25,70"/>

<polygon style="fill:#404040; stroke:black"
  points="60,10 70,10 70,40 60,40 60,10"/>

<polygon style="fill:#308050; stroke:black"
  points="60,40 70,40 70,50 60,50 60,40"/>
```

```
<polygon style="fill:#AA80AA; stroke:black"
   points="60,60 70,60 70,80 75,80 75,90 60,90 60,60 "/>

<polygon style="fill:#404040; stroke:black"
   points="80,80 110,80 110,90 80,90 80,80"/>

<polygon style="fill:#404040; stroke:black"
   points="110,80 120,80 120,90 110,90 110,80"/>

<polygon style="fill:#404040; stroke:black"
   points="120,80 150,80 150,90 120,90 120,80"/>

<polygon style="fill:#404040; stroke:black"
   points="0,100 10,100 10,110 0,110 0,100"/>

<polygon style="fill:#404040; stroke:black"
   points="10,100 40,100 40,110 10,110 10,100"/>

<polygon style="fill:#004040; stroke:black"
   points="40,100 50,100 50,110 40,110 40,100"/>

<polygon style="fill:#707099; stroke:black"
   points="50,100 80,100 80,110 50,110 50,100"/>

<polygon style="fill:#BB8330; stroke:black"
   points="80,100 90,100 90,110 80,110 80,100"/>

<polygon style="fill:#FFC0FF; stroke:black"
   points="90,100 120,100 120,110 90,110 90,100"/>

<polygon style="fill:#707099; stroke:black"
   points="120,100 130,100 130,110 120,110 120,100"/>

<polygon style="fill:#707099; stroke:black"
   points="130,100 160,100 160,110 130,110 130,100"/>
</svg>
```

Notice how the color codes have been extracted from the color element in the GML specification and used in the polygon elements' style attribute. The coordinates in the points attribute were created using the xsl:for-each elements, described earlier.

About Batik

As mentioned earlier in this chapter, Batik is a Java-based framework for managing SVG files. It contains a complete API for Java programmers who want to use SVG in their applications. In addition, a couple stand-alone applications are part of the Batik package, such as an SVG browser. We aren't going to go through the Batik Java API because it's subject is more related to Java than XML. If you plan to design a location-based service that needs to run on many different platforms, such as Windows CE and the Symbian platform, however, Batik is worth a closer look. You can read more about it at http://xml.apache.org/batik.

The Batik SVG Viewer

The requirement for running the SVG browser is to have a Java 1.2 or later compatible virtual machine installed. Here's how our map looks in the Batik SVG browser (see Figure 16-1).

In addition, the SVG browser can be used to convert your SVG file to a JPG image, which can be sent across the wireless network to a Pocket PC and viewed on a web page using the Microsoft Mobile Explorer. From the JPG format, you can do conversions to the WBMP and GIF formats, using some of the many available freeware tools. Then, even the first generation of WAP- and i-mode phones can view the map.

Features   The SVG browser enables you to hook in a style sheet. This can be useful if you want to override some of the SVG defaults settings.

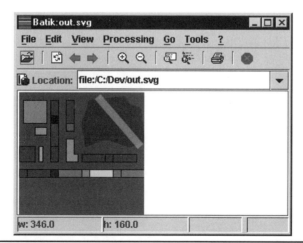

Figure 16-1   *The Batik SVG browser in action*

You can transform the SVG document when it's loaded into the browser. For example, it's possible to translate, scale, and rotate a document the same way as the transform element does.

The document can also be zoomed in and out. After you make the necessary transformations, the document can be exported as a PNG, JPG, or TIFF file.

Other Batik Tools

If you need to convert a batch of files to the PNG, JPG, or TIFF format, the rasterizer can be used. As previously mentioned, you can also convert one file at a time using the Batik SVG browser. The latter has a graphical user interface.

One problem with limited handheld devices is some fonts, you might want to use may be unavailable on the device. Limited handheld devices usually have much less memory available than a desktop computer. A consequence could be that fewer fonts are available. If you're using SVG and Batik, then it's possible to use the Batik Font Converter, which converts True Type Fonts to SVG.

The Batik distribution also includes a pretty printer utility that can be used to print SVG files. You can also print SVG files from the SVG browser utility.

CHAPTER 7

Mobile Commerce

IN THIS CHAPTER:

Digital Signatures

ECML

Mobile commerce involves a number of technologies that solve different problems. For example, consumers won't buy anything using a phone or PDA if they're uncertain about the security. For that purpose, the software and hardware manufacturers developed security solutions for the ordinary Internet, as well as the Mobile Internet. Wireless Transport Layer Security (WTLS) is used in Wireless Application Protocol (WAP) and TSL/SSL (Secure Sockets Layer) on the Internet to provide encryption.

One of the more interesting problems is that sites need to speak the same language for merchants to use software from different manufacturers that process the transactions in various ways, such as managing bills and maintaining customer databases. The Electronic Commerce Modeling Language (ECML) provides a good foundation for the representation of that type of information. ECML can be used in XHTML, WML, and other markup languages that support forms, such as i-mode's Compact HTML.

Hackers shouldn't be able to change the information exchanged between the consumer and the merchant, so the merchant also needs guarantees that the user has decided to buy the products. This problem can be solved using digital signatures, which is, more or less, proof that the consumer has confirmed the transaction. WAP has a crypto library, which contains one function that can be invoked from a WMLScript function. This function creates a digital signature the merchant can use as proof that the consumer wants to proceed and commit the business transaction.

Digital Signatures

A consumer might use his or her phone to sign a document that proves the user agreed to purchase a product. A digital signature doesn't provide encryption, it only signs a document with a code that can be associated with that document and the person who signs it. Operators can deploy equipment that issues certificates to their subscribers. As the subscriber completes a transaction by providing the merchant with a digital signature, the merchant can check if the signature is real or fake. It's practically impossible, though, for the merchant or anyone else to forge a signature because it's based on the certificate, which only the subscriber and the trusted source (the certificate issuer) can access.

Signing a Document and Sending It to a Server

In WAP 2.0, a WMLScript library makes it possible to add a digital signature to a document. The library contains one function only, signText, which takes a piece of text and a set of options as input, and then signs the text. The result can be sent to the merchant, who can check that the signature is real and hasn't changed on its way over the air from the consumer to the merchant.

Here's an application, implemented in WML 2.0 and WMLScript. This application lets the user add products to a shopping cart, go to the cashier, and complete the purchase by signing a purchase order. The purchase order is then transferred to the merchant's server. The WML 2.0 code looks like the following:

```
<?xml version="1.0"?>
<!DOCTYPE html PUBLIC "-//WAPFORUM//DTD WML 2.0//EN"
  "http://www.wapforum.org/dtd/wml20.dtd">
<html xmlns="http://www.w3.org/1999/xhtml"
  xmlns:wml="http://www.wapforum.org/2001/wml">
    <head>
        <title>Shop</title>
    </head>
    <wml:card id="start">
        <!-- Set the variable, which holds all bought items. -->
        <p>Select products:
          <select name="items" multiple="true" iname="num">
                <option value="Headset">Headset</option>
                <option value="FM-radio">FM radio</option>
                <option value="MP3-player">MP3 player</option>
                <option value="Pda">PDA</option>
                <option value="Phone">Phone</option>
          </select>
          <!-- Call the script, which creates the digital signature. -->
          <a href="script.wmls#buy()">Buy the selections</a>
        </p>
    </wml:card>
    <!-- This card is called from the above script if the -->
    <!-- signature was created successfully. -->
    <wml:card id="ok">
        <wml:onevent type="onenterforward">
          <wml:go href="http://www.example.com/receiver" method="post">
            <postfield name="query" value="$(signed)"/>
          </wml:go>
        </wml:onevent>
    </wml:card>
    <!-- This card is called from the script if the signature could -->
    <!-- not be created. -->
    <wml:card id="error">
```

```
        <p>Sorry, the order could not be signed.
        </p>
    </wml:card>
</html>
```

Three cards exist, called start, ok, and error. In the first card, start, the consumer selects the products he wants to buy. How the multiple selections appear on the display is device-dependent. However, most manufacturers represent a multiple selection element as a list, where each option is rendered on a row and a check box is to the left of the text, which can be chosen. Then an *x* appears in the check box. There's a link after the select element, which calls the script without any arguments. Here's the WMLScript code:

```
extern function buy() {
 var res, items, price, str;

 // Get the semicolon separated list of items.
 items = WMLBrowser.getvar("items");

 // Check what the cart contains and compute the sum.
 if( String.find("Headset", items) != -1 ) {
  res += "1 Headset: $99\n ";
  price += 99;
 }
 if( String.find("FM-radio", items) != -1 ) {
  res += "1 FM-radio: $10\n";
  price += 10;
 }
 if( String.find("MP3-player", items) != -1 ) {
  res += "1 MP3-player: $99\n";
  price += 99;
 }
 if( String.find("Pda", items) != -1 ) {
  res += "1 PDA: $199\n";
  price += 199;
 }
 if( String.find("Phone", items) != -1 ) {
  res += "1 Phone: $199\n";
  price += 199;
 }

 // Create the text, presented for the user.
```

```
str = "Bill\n----\n" + res + "\nTotal: $" + price;

// User confirms the transaction.
res = Crypto.signText(str, 0, 0, "");

// Something wrong?
if( res == invalid )
 WMLBrowser.go("#error");
if( !String.compare("error:noCert", res) )
 WMLBrowser.go("#error");
if( !String.compare("error:userCancel", res) )
 WMLBrowser.go("#error");

// Everything ok?
// Then post the result to the server.
WMLBrowser.setvar("signed", str);
WMLBrowser.go("#ok");
};
```

The function is declared using the keyword extern because the calling WML code is located outside the WMLScript file. The function could have been called with the WML variable items as an argument, but instead the standard library function getvar is used to retrieve its value. This variable holds all the items the consumer wants to buy. Because this variable is the result of an input using the select element and the multiple attribute is set to true, it contains a semicolon-separated list of all the values.

The semicolon-separated string is searched using the standard library function find and the function computes how much the consumer should pay. For each item, the price is calculated and a string is created, which displays all bought items and the total sum. This is the string displayed for the user in the call to the signText function. If the text couldn't be signed, then the program jumps back to the "error" card in the WML code and an error message is displayed. If the function returns a successful value, then the signed variable is set to the output of the signText function. That is the signed document. The program then jumps back to the WML code and the "ok" card. In the WML code and the "ok" card, the signed document is posted to a server script using the go and postfield elements.

Note, the code doesn't input any information about the user, such as name, payment method, and shipping address. An application that would be deployed for real should ask for that information and a number of other parameters, which is where ECML comes in.

ECML

If you check the previous application again, you might realize the merchant would have to ask the user about many things simply to complete the transaction. Information about what the user has put in the shopping cart simply isn't enough. The merchant would have to retrieve information, such as the consumer's full name, shipping address, state, region, or country, charging method, telephone number, or e-mail address, and so forth. Wireless handheld devices are less suitable for typing in those amounts of data because they usually have a limited numerical phone keyboard where each digit needs to be toggled to retrieve a letter or they use hand-writing recognition, which also takes some time. If the consumer thinks too much time is required to type in too much administrative information, then she might choose not to complete the transaction.

The ECML is based on the concept of a merchant and a consumer. The merchant offers the consumer a number of products. If the consumer decides to buy some of them, then he must fill in a form, which contains a number of information fields that complete the business transaction. This is administrative information the merchant must obtain to charge the consumer and deliver the products. This information shouldn't be mixed up with security and digital signatures. The merchant can use a secure channel, implemented using SSL/TSL or WTSL. A digital signature might also be required, but information about the consumer must still be supplied.

ECML provides a set of fields that can be built into handheld devices and used on sites. If the software in the device knows how to identify these fields on the sites, the user can type the information in once, and then the device automatically fills in those fields.

Version 2 of ECML is about to become a proposed standard. It contains an XML syntax, which can be used to express all fields, and the IETF Trade working group recommends the parameters be transferred using the XML syntax. The parameters can also be encoded using another syntax, however. For example, if a user is supposed to fill in a form, the parameters will be transferred as parameters in an HTTP get or post request. In version 1.1 of ECML, no XML syntax exists, so the fields must be transferred in an ordinary form.

Forms can be filled in automatically by using a number of different technologies and you can implement this in many ways.

Even the simplest transactions sometimes require the user to provide dozens of fields of information. For example, when the user buys anything other than software, he needs to provide a shipping address and this isn't necessarily the same as the billing address. In many cases, the user wants to receive a receipt, which might be sent physically or as an e-mail, depending on which method the user prefers. If the user buys something that's paid by the consumer's employee, the bill and the receipt need to be sent to the employer, while the product should be shipped to the employee.

Shipping

Shipping fields in ECML include all the necessary fields to send products to the user's home or work address. It's also possible to ship products to an e-mail address or a phone number.

The following XHTML Basic shopping form could be completed without any interaction from the user. All the consumer would have to do is check that all data is okay, and then press the Submit button.

```
<?xml version="1.0" encoding="UTF-8"?>
<!DOCTYPE html PUBLIC "-//W3C//DTD XHTML Basic 1.0//EN"
    "http://www.w3.org/TR/xhtml-basic/xhtml-basic10.dtd">
<html xmlns="http://www.w3.org/1999/xhtml">
    <head>
        <title>Order form</title>
    </head>
    <body>
      <form action="http://www.example.com/order" method="post">
        <p>
        <!-- The product numbers. This is not ECML. -->
        <strong>Type in the product numbers</strong>
        <br/><input name="ProductNumbers" type="text" size="30"/>

        <!-- Shipping information expressed using the ECML syntax. -->
        <strong>Shipping details</strong>
        <br/>First name
        <br/><input name="Ecom_ShipTo_Postal_Name_First" type="text" size="15"/>
        <br/>Last name
        <br/><input name="Ecom_ShipTo_Postal_Name_Last" type="text" size="15"/>
        <br/>Street
        <br/><input name="Ecom_ShipTo_Postal_Street_Line1" type="text" size="20"/>
        <br/><input name="Ecom_ShipTo_Postal_Street_Line2" type="text" size="20"/>
        <br/><input name="Ecom_ShipTo_Postal_Street_Line3" type="text" size="20"/>
        <br/>City
        <br/><input name="Ecom_ShipTo_Postal_City" type="text" size="22"/>
        <br/>ZIP or postal code
        <br/><input name="Ecom_ShipTo_Postal_PostalCode" type="text" size="14"/>
        <br/>Country code
        <br/><input name="Ecom_ShipTo_Postal_CountryCode" type="text" size="2"/>

        <!-- Hidden ECML fields. -->
        <br/><input name="Ecom_SchemaVersion"
```

```
                    value="http://www.ecml.org/version/1.1" type="hidden"/>

        <!-- Send order -->
        <br/><input name="Send" value="Send" type="submit"/>
        </p>
      </form>
    </body>
</html>
```

As you can see, the concept is based around the use of a number of reserved keywords. In the previous example, the last keyword is used as a hidden field. This keyword is the ECML schema version and should appear on all pages that use ECML fields. It provides a reference to which version of ECML has been used. Note, the merchant must decide which fields should be used. Only a few or a dozen may be provided by the merchant.

If the phone recognizes these keywords, then it's easy for the manufacturers to provide system software in the phone, which automatically fills in the fields.

When the previous form has been filled in and the user has clicked the Submit button, the merchant could reply with a new form, such as this one.

```
<?xml version="1.0" encoding="UTF-8"?>
<!DOCTYPE html PUBLIC "-//W3C//DTD XHTML Basic 1.0//EN"
    "http://www.w3.org/TR/xhtml-basic/xhtml-basic10.dtd">
<html xmlns="http://www.w3.org/1999/xhtml">
    <head>
        <title>Transaction completed</title>
    </head>
    <body>
        <form action="http://www.example.com/order/ok">
            <p>Thank you for buying from us. Your order is being processed.
                <br/>Welcome back!
            <!-- Hidden ECML fields -->
            <!-- Version 1.1 -->
            <input name="Ecom_SchemaVersion"
                    value="http://www.ecml.org/version/1.1" type="hidden"/>

            <!-- The ID of the transaction.-->
            <!-- Issued by the merchant to identify the order. -->
            <input name="Ecom_Transaction_ID"
                    value="coolProducts88330xxzu45" type="hidden"/>

            <!-- Cost. -->
            <input name="Ecom_Transaction_Amount" value="150"
type="hidden"/>
```

```
                <!-- Currency for the above cost. -->
                <input name="Ecom_Transaction_CurrencyCode"
                       value="USD" type="hidden"/>

                <!-- Transaction is now completed. -->
                <input name="Ecom_TransactionComplete" type="hidden"/>
            </p>
        </form>
    </body>
</html>
```

The document contains a paragraph that's presented for the consumer and a number of hidden fields, which can be parsed and used by the wallet software in the device. Note, this form can't be submitted because it works as a final reply to the consumer and the digital wallet. The merchant gave the consumer a number of fields to fill in. The consumer, or the wallet software on the device, replied and got a confirmation that the transaction was completed without errors.

The complete procedure is based on the simple naming of fields through the power of ECML. The simplicity of ECML makes it possible to implement on a number of platforms using a number of languages.

Shipping Content to a Mobile Phone Number

E-mail addresses are useful if the user has bought digital content, such as software. Phone numbers are also useful, especially in 3G networks. Multimedia Messaging Service (MMS), which will be deployed in the 2.5G and 3G networks, makes sending audio, video, text, and graphics to a mobile phone possible. Consequently, content can, indeed, be shipped to a phone number. The phone number can be used, not only as something related to the physical shipping address, but also as the charging address because the operator can look up all details about the subscriber using only the telephone number.

The following application lets the user subscribe to a number of MMSs. The operator charges the user via the phone bill, so the only information the user needs to provide is the phone number. It can be filled in automatically because the ECML syntax is used.

```
<?xml version="1.0" encoding="UTF-8"?>
<!DOCTYPE html PUBLIC "-//W3C//DTD XHTML Basic 1.0//EN"
    "http://www.w3.org/TR/xhtml-basic/xhtml-basic10.dtd">
<html xmlns="http://www.w3.org/1999/xhtml">
    <head>
        <title>Order form</title>
```

```
</head>
<body>
    <form action="http://www.example.com/order" method="post">
     <p>
       <strong>Choose services</strong>
       <br/>
            <!-- Let the user choose a set of services. -->
            <input name="stock" type="checkbox"/>Financial info
            <br/>How often
              <select name="stockInterval">
              <option selected="selected">Every day</option>
              <option>Every Monday</option>
            </select>
       <br/>
            <input name="weather" type="checkbox"/>Weather report
            <br/>How often
              <select name="weatherInterval">
              <option selected="selected">Every day</option>
              <option>Every Monday</option>
            </select>
       <br/>
            <input name="weather" type="checkbox"/>Account info
            <br/>How often
              <select name="accountInterval">
              <option selected="selected">Every day</option>
              <option>Every Monday</option>
            </select>
       <br/>
            <input name="comic" type="checkbox"/>Joke of the day
            <br/>How often
              <select name="jokeInterval">
              <option select="selected">Every day</option>
              <option>Every Monday</option>
            </select>
       <br/>
            <input name="ontv" type="checkbox"/>On TV
            <br/>How often
              <select name="tvInterval">
              <option select="selected">Every day</option>
              <option>Every Monday</option>
            </select>
       <br/><b>Phone number</b>
       <br/>
            <!-- Phone number associated with the shipping address. -->
            <input name="Ecom_ShipTo_Telecom_Phone_Number"
                 type="text" size="10"/>
            <!-- Hidden ECML fields -->
```

```
        <br/>
        <input name="Ecom_SchemaVersion"
                value="http://www.ecml.org/version/1.1" type="hidden"/>
        <!-- Send order -->
        <br/>
        <input type="submit"/>
    </p>
    </form>
    </body>
</html>
```

The user can select one or more services that shall be delivered to his or her phone. The schema version is used because it should always be provided and the only ECML in addition to that is the ship-to telecom phone number field. If the user agent doesn't support automatic fill in of ECML fields, then the user can type in the information manually because the field name is handled as an ordinary input field.

In the previous examples, the consumer has provided ship-to information only. In many cases, however, the consumer might want the bill sent to an address that's different than the shipping address and the receipt sent to an entirely different address. Many online shopping sites also let the consumer make a choice concerning the payment method. If the consumer chooses credit card, then a number of fields must be provided about the expiry date, and so forth. Form fields in ECML cover all these scenarios.

Billing

Billing lets the merchant provide the user with fields for the name and address to the person or company that should pay the bill. This application is implemented in WML 2.0 and makes use of billing fields, in addition to the ship-to field.

```
<?xml version="1.0"?>
<!DOCTYPE html PUBLIC "-//WAPFORUM//DTD WML 2.0//EN"
   "http://www.wapforum.org/dtd/wml20.dtd">
<html xmlns="http://www.w3.org/1999/xhtml"
     xmlns:wml="http://www.wapforum.org/2001/wml">
    <head>
        <title>Order form</title>
    </head>
    <body>
        <p>
            <!-- Let the user choose a set of products. -->
            <b>Choose products</b>
              <select name="productList1">
```

```
            <option value="dvdp">DVD player</option>
            <option value="moni">17 inch monitor</option>
            <option value="lapt">2 GHz Laptop</option>
            <option value="lapb">Laptop battery</option>
            <option value="lapc">Laptop battery charger</option>
      </select>
<!-- Ship-to fields -->
<br/><b>Shipping details</b>
<br/>First name
<br/><input name="Ecom_ShipTo_Postal_Name_First"
            type="text" size="15"/>
<br/>Last name
<br/><input name="Ecom_ShipTo_Postal_Name_Last"
            type="text" size="15"/>
<br/>Street
<br/><input name="Ecom_ShipTo_Postal_Street_Line1"
            type="text" size="20"/>
<br/><input name="Ecom_ShipTo_Postal_Street_Line2"
            type="text" size="20"/>
<br/><input name="Ecom_ShipTo_Postal_Street_Line3"
            type="text" size="20"/>
<br/>City
<br/><input name="Ecom_ShipTo_Postal_City" type="text" size="22"/>
<br/>ZIP or postal code
<br/><input name="Ecom_ShipTo_Postal_PostalCode"
            type="text" size="14"/>
<br/>Country code
<br/><input name="Ecom_ShipTo_Postal_CountryCode"
            type="text" size="2"/>

<!-- Bill-to fields -->
<br/><b>Billing details</b> (you may leave these fields blank
      if they are the same as the shipping fields).
<br/>First name
<br/><input name="Ecom_BillTo_Postal_Name_First"
            type="text" size="15"/>
<br/>Last name
<br/><input name="Ecom_BillTo_Postal_Name_Last"
            type="text" size="15"/>
<br/>Street
<br/><input name="Ecom_BillTo_Postal_Street_Line1"
            type="text" size="20"/>
<br/><input name="Ecom_BillTo_Postal_Street_Line2"
            type="text" size="20"/>
<br/><input name="Ecom_BillTo_Postal_Street_Line3"
            type="text" size="20"/>
<br/>City
```

```
<br/><input name="Ecom_BillTo_Postal_City" type="text" size="22"/>
<br/>ZIP or postal code
<br/><input name="Ecom_BillTo_Postal_PostalCode"
            type="text" size="14"/>
<br/>Country code
<br/><input name="Ecom_BillTo_Postal_CountryCode"
            type="text" size="2"/>

<!-- Hidden ECML fields -->
<br/>
<input name="Ecom_SchemaVersion"
       value="http://www.ecml.org/version/1.1" type="hidden"/>
<!-- Send order -->
<br/>
<wml:anchor>Send
    <!-- Post all fields to the server. -->
    <wml:go href="http://www.example.com/order" method="post">
        <wml:postfield name="products" value="$(productList)"/>
        <wml:postfield name="Ecom_ShipTo_Postal_Name_First"
                       value="$(Ecom_ShipTo_Postal_Name_First)"/>
        <wml:postfield name="Ecom_ShipTo_Postal_Name_Last"
                       value="$(Ecom_ShipTo_Postal_Name_Last)"/>
        <wml:postfield name="Ecom_ShipTo_Postal_Street_Line1"
                       value="$(Ecom_ShipTo_Postal_Street_Line1)"/>
        <wml:postfield name="Ecom_ShipTo_Postal_Street_Line2"
                       value="$(Ecom_ShipTo_Postal_Street_Line2)"/>
        <wml:postfield name="Ecom_ShipTo_Postal_Street_Line3"
                       value="$(Ecom_ShipTo_Postal_Street_Line3)"/>
        <wml:postfield name="Ecom_ShipTo_Postal_City"
                       value="$(Ecom_ShipTo_Postal_City)"/>
        <wml:postfield name="Ecom_ShipTo_Postal_PostalCode"
                       value="$(Ecom_ShipTo_Postal_PostalCode)"/>
        <wml:postfield name="Ecom_ShipTo_Postal_CountryCode"
                       value="$(Ecom_ShipTo_Postal_CountryCode)"/>
        <wml:postfield name="Ecom_BillTo_Postal_Name_First"
                       value="$(Ecom_BillTo_Postal_Name_First)"/>
        <wml:postfield name="Ecom_BillTo_Postal_Name_Last"
                       value="$(Ecom_BillTo_Postal_Name_Last)"/>
        <wml:postfield name="Ecom_BillTo_Postal_Street_Line1"
                       value="$(Ecom_BillTo_Postal_Street_Line1)"/>
        <wml:postfield name="Ecom_BillTo_Postal_Street_Line2"
                       value="$(Ecom_BillTo_Postal_Street_Line2)"/>
        <wml:postfield name="Ecom_BillTo_Postal_Street_Line3"
                       value="$(Ecom_BillTo_Postal_Street_Line3)"/>
        <wml:postfield name="Ecom_BillTo_Postal_City"
                       value="$(Ecom_BillTo_Postal_City)"/>
        <wml:postfield name="Ecom_BillTo_Postal_PostalCode"
```

```
                                    value="$(Ecom_BillTo_Postal_PostalCode)"/>
                    <wml:postfield name="Ecom_BillTo_Postal_CountryCode"
                                    value="$(Ecom_BillTo_Postal_CountryCode)"/>
                    <wml:postfield name="Ecom_SchemaVersion"
                                        value="http://www.ecml.org/version/1.1"/>
                </wml:go>
            </wml:anchor>
        </p>
    </body>
</html>
```

The user can enter shipping and billing information, and the server checks if the billing information was left out. If it was, then the billing address should be the same as the shipping address. As you can see, the WML elements anchor, go, and postfield have been used. They transfer the parameters in an HTTP post request.

Receipts

Receipts can work as a complement to the billing information. In some cases, the consumer might want to receive products and to have the bill sent to her employer. The following form, implemented in XHTML Basic, asks for receipt, shipping, and billing details.

```
<?xml version="1.0" encoding="UTF-8"?>
<!DOCTYPE html PUBLIC "-//W3C//DTD XHTML Basic 1.0//EN"
    "http://www.w3.org/TR/xhtml-basic/xhtml-basic10.dtd">
<html xmlns="http://www.w3.org/1999/xhtml">
    <head>
        <title>Order form</title>
    </head>
    <body>
      <form action="http://www.example.com/order" method="post">
        <p>
            <!-- Let the user select products for purchase. -->
            <strong>Choose products</strong>
            <br/><input name="m-player" type="checkbox"/>M-player
            <br/>Model
            <select name="m1">
                <option selected="selected">mz-101</option>
                <option>mz-102</option>
                <option>mz-103</option>
            </select>
            <br/><input name="softwareplus" type="checkbox"/>Software+ package
            <br/>Version
            <select name="swplus">
                <option>Student edition</option>
                <option selected="selected">Standard</option>
```

```
    <option>Enterprise</option>
</select>

<!-- Ship-to fields -->
<br/>
<strong>Shipping details</strong>
<br/>First name
<br/><input name="Ecom_ShipTo_Postal_Name_First"
            type="text" size="15"/>
<br/>Last name
<br/><input name="Ecom_ShipTo_Postal_Name_Last"
            type="text" size="15"/>
<br/>Street
<br/><input name="Ecom_ShipTo_Postal_Street_Line1"
            type="text" size="20"/>
<br/><input name="Ecom_ShipTo_Postal_Street_Line2"
            type="text" size="20"/>
<br/><input name="Ecom_ShipTo_Postal_Street_Line3"
            type="text" size="20"/>
<br/>City
<br/><input name="Ecom_ShipTo_Postal_City"
            type="text" size="22"/>
<br/>ZIP or postal code
<br/><input name="Ecom_ShipTo_Postal_PostalCode"
            type="text" size="14"/>
<br/>Country code
<br/><input name="Ecom_ShipTo_Postal_CountryCode"
            type="text" size="2"/>

<!-- Bill-to fields -->
<br/>
<b>Billing details</b> (you may leave these fields blank if
        they are the same as the shipping fields).
<br/>First name
<br/><input name="Ecom_BillTo_Postal_Name_First"
            type="text" size="15"/>
<br/>Last name
<br/><input name="Ecom_BillTo_Postal_Name_Last"
            type="text" size="15"/>
<br/>Street
<br/><input name="Ecom_BillTo_Postal_Street_Line1"
            type="text" size="20"/>
<br/><input name="Ecom_BillTo_Postal_Street_Line2"
            type="text" size="20"/>
<br/><input name="Ecom_BillTo_Postal_Street_Line3"
            type="text" size="20"/>
<br/>City
```

```
<br/><input name="Ecom_BillTo_Postal_City" type="text" size="22"/>
<br/>ZIP or postal code
<br/><input name="Ecom_BillTo_Postal_PostalCode"
            type="text" size="14"/>
<br/>Country code
<br/><input name="Ecom_BillTo_Postal_CountryCode"
            type="text" size="2"/>

<!-- Receipt-to fields -->
<br/><b>Receipt details</b> (you may leave these fields
        blank if they are the same as the billing fields).
<br/>First name
<br/><input name="Ecom_ReceiptTo_Postal_Name_First"
            type="text" size="15"/>
<br/>Last name
<br/><input name="Ecom_ReceiptTo_Postal_Name_Last"
            type="text" size="15"/>
<br/>Street
<br/><input name="Ecom_ReceiptTo_Postal_Street_Line1"
            type="text" size="20"/>
<br/><input name="Ecom_ReceiptTo_Postal_Street_Line2"
            type="text" size="20"/>
<br/><input name="Ecom_ReceiptTo_Postal_Street_Line3"
            type="text" size="20"/>
<br/>City
<br/><input name="Ecom_ReceiptTo_Postal_City"
            type="text" size="22"/>
<br/>ZIP or postal code
<br/><input name="Ecom_ReceiptTo_Postal_PostalCode"
            type="text" size="14"/>
<br/>Country code
<br/><input name="Ecom_ReceiptTo_Postal_CountryCode"
            type="text" size="2"/>

<!-- Hidden ECML fields -->
<br/>
<input name="Ecom_SchemaVersion"
        value="http://www.ecml.org/version/1.1" type="hidden"/>

<!-- Send order -->
<br/>
<input value="Send" type="submit"/>
        </p>
    </form>
  </body>
</html>
```

Here, the consumer might input separate shipping, billing, and receipt addresses. If the device fills in the fields automatically, then the receipt and shipping fields might be the same. If this is done manually, then the user might leave certain fields, which are the same, blank. Software on the server side—for example, a script—checks if the fields make sense. The script has the address http://www.example.com/order.

Cards Details

ECML makes specifying credit card details possible, such as the expiry date, the name associated with the card, and the card protocol. Here's a WML 2.0 application that asks for shipping details and card information. It's implemented using the XHTML framework in WML, with the exception of the WML unique anchor, go, and postfield elements.

```
<?xml version="1.0"?>
<!DOCTYPE html PUBLIC "-//WAPFORUM//DTD WML 2.0//EN"
  "http://www.wapforum.org/dtd/wml20.dtd">
<html xmlns="http://www.w3.org/1999/xhtml"
      xmlns:wml="http://www.wapforum.org/2001/wml">
    <head>
        <title>Order form</title>
    </head>
    <body>
        <p>
            <strong>Choose products</strong>
            <!-- The variable "productList" holds the result as a -->
            <!-- semicolon separated list. -->
            <select name="productList">
                <option value="dvdp">DVD player</option>
                <option value="moni">17 inch monitor</option>
                <option value="lapt">2 GHz Laptop</option>
                <option value="lapb">Laptop battery</option>
                <option value="lapc">Laptop battery charger</option>
            </select>

            <!-- Ship-to fields -->
            <br/>
            <strong>Shipping details</strong>
            <br/>First name
            <br/><input name="Ecom_ShipTo_Postal_Name_First"
                    type="text" size="15"/>
            <br/>Last name
            <br/><input name="Ecom_ShipTo_Postal_Name_Last"
                    type="text" size="15"/>
```

```
<br/>Street
<br/><input name="Ecom_ShipTo_Postal_Street_Line1"
          type="text" size="20"/>
<br/><input name="Ecom_ShipTo_Postal_Street_Line2"
          type="text" size="20"/>
<br/><input name="Ecom_ShipTo_Postal_Street_Line3"
          type="text" size="20"/>
<br/>City
<br/><input name="Ecom_ShipTo_Postal_City" type="text" size="22"/>
<br/>ZIP or postal code
<br/><input name="Ecom_ShipTo_Postal_PostalCode"
          type="text" size="14"/>
<br/>Country code
<br/><input name="Ecom_ShipTo_Postal_CountryCode"
          type="text" size="2"/>

<!-- Card fields -->
<br/>Name on card
<br/><input name="Ecom_Payment_Card_Name" type="text" size="30"/>
<br/>Expiry date: Month (1-12)
<br/><input name="Ecom_Payment_Card_ExpDate_Month"
          type="text" size="2"/>
<br/>Expiry date: Day (1-31)
<br/><input name="Ecom_Payment_Card_ExpDate_Day"
          type="text" size="2"/>
<br/>Expiry date: Year (YYYY)
<br/><input name="Ecom_Payment_Card_ExpDate_Day"
          type="text" size="4"/>
<br/>Card type
<select name="Ecom_Payment_Card_Type">
    <option value="VISA">VISA</option>
    <option value="AMER">American Express</option>
    <option value="MAST">Mastercard</option>
</select>
<br/>Card number
<br/><input name="Ecom_Payment_Card_Number" type="text" size="19"/>

<!-- Hidden ECML fields -->
<br/>
<input name="Ecom_SchemaVersion"
      value="http://www.ecml.org/version/1.1" type="hidden"/>

<!-- Send order -->
<br/>
<wml:anchor>Send
    <!-- Post the value of the "productList" variable and all -->
    <!-- ECML fields to the server script. -->
```

```
<wml:go href="http://www.example.com/order" method="post">
    <wml:postfield name="products" value="$(productList)"/>
    <wml:postfield name="Ecom_ShipTo_Postal_Name_First"
                   value="$(Ecom_ShipTo_Postal_Name_First)"/>
    <wml:postfield name="Ecom_ShipTo_Postal_Name_Last"
                   value="$(Ecom_ShipTo_Postal_Name_Last)"/>
    <wml:postfield name="Ecom_ShipTo_Postal_Street_Line1"
                   value="$(Ecom_ShipTo_Postal_Street_Line1)"/>
    <wml:postfield name="Ecom_ShipTo_Postal_Street_Line2"
                   value="$(Ecom_ShipTo_Postal_Street_Line2)"/>
    <wml:postfield name="Ecom_ShipTo_Postal_Street_Line3"
                   value="$(Ecom_ShipTo_Postal_Street_Line3)"/>
    <wml:postfield name="Ecom_ShipTo_Postal_City"
                   value="$(Ecom_ShipTo_Postal_City)"/>
    <wml:postfield name="Ecom_ShipTo_Postal_PostalCode"
                   value="$(Ecom_ShipTo_Postal_PostalCode)"/>
    <wml:postfield name="Ecom_ShipTo_Postal_CountryCode"
                   value="$(Ecom_ShipTo_Postal_CountryCode)"/>
    <wml:postfield name="Ecom_Payment_Card_Name"
                   value="$(Ecom_Payment_Card_Name)"/>
    <wml:postfield name="Ecom_Payment_Card_ExpDate_Month"
                   value="$(Ecom_Payment_Card_ExpDate_Month)"/>
    <wml:postfield name="Ecom_Payment_Card_ExpDate_Day"
                   value="$(Ecom_Payment_Card_ExpDate_Day)"/>
    <wml:postfield name="Ecom_Payment_Card_ExpDate_Day"
                   value="$(Ecom_Payment_Card_ExpDate_Day)"/>
    <wml:postfield name="Ecom_Payment_Card_Type"
                   value="$(Ecom_Payment_Card_Type)"/>
    <wml:postfield name="Ecom_Payment_Card_Number"
                   value="$(Ecom_Payment_Card_Number)"/>
    <wml:postfield name="Ecom_SchemaVersion"
                   value="http://www.ecml.org/version/1.1"/>
</wml:go>
        </wml:anchor>
    </p>
  </body>
</html>
```

Note, the card fields will be sent in plain text unless some of the security protocols, like WTLS or SSL, are used. All information is sent to the user using a number of postfields in combination with the go and anchor elements. An alternative is to use the form element but, in this case, it isn't possible to implement the Send button as an ordinary link. A browser that supports WML 2.0 might implement the submit type as a menu choice, the same way most devices implement the do element. Because many users often don't know how these menus are accessed or forget they're available, a better solution is to go for ordinary links as much as possible.

Merchant and Transaction Information

The merchant receives the forms the consumer has completed. The forms contain a number of fields: some might follow the ECML syntax and some might include additional information, such as which products the consumer purchased. When the form is received for processing, the merchant sends back a document to the consumer. This document might contain a URL to the company's web site and fields, which describe the transaction.

Merchant's URL

The following XHTML Basic application asks the user to provide his name and address, and, at the same time, the device gets the URL to the merchant. The software on the client side can save this field, so the consumer can later check on which merchant the transaction was completed with.

```
<?xml version="1.0" encoding="UTF-8"?>
<!DOCTYPE html PUBLIC "-//W3C//DTD XHTML Basic 1.0//EN"
    "http://www.w3.org/TR/xhtml-basic/xhtml-basic10.dtd">
<html xmlns="http://www.w3.org/1999/xhtml">
    <head>
        <title>Order form</title>
    </head>
    <body>
        <form action="http://www.example.com/order/" method="post">
            <p>
                <strong>Choose products</strong>
                <br/><input name="prod_mous" type="checkbox"/>Mouse
                <br/><input name="prod_mpad" type="checkbox"/>Mouse pad
                <br/><input name="prod_usbc" type="checkbox"/>USB cable
                <br/><input name="prod_wlan" type="checkbox"/>WLAN card
                <br/><input name="prod_netc" type="checkbox"/>Network card

                <!-- Ship-to fields -->
                <br/><strong>Shipping details</strong>
                <br/>First name
                <br/><input name="Ecom_ShipTo_Postal_Name_First"
                        type="text" size="15"/>
                <br/>Last name
                <br/><input name="Ecom_ShipTo_Postal_Name_Last"
                        type="text" size="15"/>
                <br/>Street
                <br/><input name="Ecom_ShipTo_Postal_Street_Line1"
```

```
                                    type="text" size="20"/>
            <br/><input name="Ecom_ShipTo_Postal_Street_Line2"
                        type="text" size="20"/>
            <br/><input name="Ecom_ShipTo_Postal_Street_Line3"
                        type="text" size="20"/>
            <br/>City
            <br/><input name="Ecom_ShipTo_Postal_City" type="text" size="22"/>
            <br/>ZIP or postal code
            <br/><input name="Ecom_ShipTo_Postal_PostalCode"
                        type="text" size="14"/>
            <br/>Country code
            <br/><input name="Ecom_ShipTo_Postal_CountryCode"
                        type="text" size="2"/>

            <!-- Hidden ECML fields -->
            <input name="Ecom_SchemaVersion"
                   value="http://www.ecml.org/version/1.1" type="hidden"/>
            <input name="Ecom_Merchant"
                   value="www.example.com" type="hidden"/>

            <!-- Send order -->
            <br/>
            <input value="Send" type="submit"/>
        </p>
    </form>
  </body>
</html>
```

Note, the field that specifies the merchant's home domain is a hidden field, which isn't supposed to be filled in manually or automatically. Instead, the device can present it for the user or store it in the user's list of bookmarks. The server script, which receives this form, checks the names of all the parameters transferred in the post. Some are ECML fields and some aren't. All the parameters that specify if the user selected a product have arbitrary names.

Transactions

The merchant usually has some type of code or number associated with the transaction. If the user phones the merchant and has some questions, the merchant might ask for the code. Often associated with transactions are process codes, approval codes, and a URL, which can be used to retrieve information about the shipment or the transaction in general. A number of transaction fields were used in an example at the beginning of this chapter. Let's look at a more detailed example. Assume the consumer has filled in the form in the latest example and sent it to the merchant. The merchant can then reply with the following document.

```xml
<?xml version="1.0" encoding="UTF-8"?>
<!DOCTYPE html PUBLIC "-//W3C//DTD XHTML Basic 1.0//EN"
    "http://www.w3.org/TR/xhtml-basic/xhtml-basic10.dtd">
<html xmlns="http://www.w3.org/1999/xhtml">
    <head>
        <title>Transaction completed</title>
    </head>
    <body>
        <form action="http://www.example.com/order/ok">
            <p>Thank you for buying from us. Your order is being processed.
            You may visit our site to
                <a href="http://www.example.com?trid=t230983438">
                    check its status
                </a>.
                <br/>Welcome back!
            <!-- Hidden ECML fields -->

            <!-- Version 1.1 -->
            <input name="Ecom_SchemaVersion"
                    value="http://www.ecml.org/version/1.1" type="hidden"/>

            <!-- The ID of the transaction. -->
            <!-- Issued by the merchant to identify the order. -->
            <input name="Ecom_Transaction_ID"
                    value="t230983438" type="hidden"/>

            <!-- Cost. -->
            <input name="Ecom_Transaction_Amount" value="50" type="hidden"/>

            <!-- Currency for the above cost. -->
            <input name="Ecom_Transaction_CurrencyCode"
                        value="USD" type="hidden"/>

            <!-- URL to retrieve information about the transaction. -->
            <input name="Ecom_Transaction_Inquiry"
                    value="http://www.example.com?trid=t230983438"
                    type="hidden"/>

            <!-- Transaction date. -->
            <input name="Ecom_Transaction_Date"
                    value="February 17 2002" type="hidden"/>

            <!-- Credit transaction. -->
```

```
                <input name="Ecom_Transaction_Type" value="credit" type="hidden"/>

                <!-- Transaction is now completed. -->
                <input name="Ecom_TransactionComplete" type="hidden"/>
            </p>
        </form>
    </body>
</html>
```

The merchant sends back a transaction identity, which is specified using the name Ecom_Transaction_ID. In addition, the same transaction identity is provided as a parameter to the URL in the Ecom_Transaction_Inquiry field. If a device doesn't use these hidden fields, the application will work perfectly, even though these fields aren't used. The parameters are only hidden fields in a form, which can't be submitted, and they're there only for informative purposes. This is probably one of the best characteristics of ECML. If the device doesn't support ECML fields, the application will still be useful. The only difference is that the fields, which were supposed to be provided automatically, must now be entered manually, and the informative fields that were hidden won't be used by the consumer or in future transactions.

The Future of XML in Wireless

OBJECTIVES

▶ Express positions with POIX

▶ Specify moving objects, their speed, and direction

▶ Use the vCard and vCalendar format in XML documents

▶ Be familiar with the base for all instant messaging and presence applications, RFC2778

▶ Know which roles watchers and presentities will have for future presence applications

▶ Create simple queries for XQuery

CHAPTER
18

Proximity

IN THIS CHAPTER:

Navigation with NVML

Specifying Points of Interest with POIX

Technologies, such as GML, can be used to describe a map with respect to a spatial reference system. Various technologies based on XML exist that can be used by an application to determine where a person is located or on which route a person is traveling, with respect to a spatial reference system and the representation of a geographical area. It remains to be seen, though, which of these technologies will be used to implement mobile location based services. A number of technologies have been discussed and tested, and a fair chance exists that at least some of the technologies presented in this chapter will play important roles for the representation of geographic positions, guides, and routes in mobile telephony networks.

Navigation Markup Language (NVML) isn't a W3C recommendation, but it might play an important role for location-based services in the future. NVML has been submitted to the W3C as a note, for discussion. When the position has been retrieved, the NVML can be used to describe how the user can travel from her position to a particular place. Typically, the user can type in the name of a shop and the application retrieves the position from the mobile network, finds the address to the shop, and then generates a route—specified in NVML—from the user's position to the shop. This description can then be transformed into a number of different formats, such as VoiceXML, XHTML, Compact HTML, or WML.

Point Of Interest eXchange (POIX) isn't a World Wide Web Consortium (W3C) recommendation, but it has been submitted to the consortium as a note and might become a recommendation in the future. The purpose of POIX is to provide a framework, which can be used to specify the position of an object, so POIX shouldn't be used to specify maps. Instead, POIX can be used when the position, which has been retrieved from a map, is shared with other software modules or nodes in the network. For example, a handheld device might query a server for a position and the server replies with the position and related information in a POIX document. Specifying moving objects with POIX is possible, which makes it suitable for wireless networks in general, and mobile telephony networks in particular. In addition to the location, an instance document can give information about which speed and direction the object moves.

Navigation with NVML

Previously in this book, you saw how maps might be represented using GML and rendered with technologies, such as SVG. Location-based services aren't only about letting the user watch a map over where he is, though. Location-based services might provide information about how the user moves from one point to another and they might work as guides for the user as she moves on a route from one point to another. For those types of services, NVML is a perfect match.

Two important concepts exist in NVML: routes and guides. A *route* is a description of, for example, a road or path between two locations. A route might contain information about points on that route and *metainformation*—information about the route itself, such as name and how long it takes to follow the route.

Guides are meant to guide the user as she navigates a location-based service. For example, a guide might contain images or text messages suitable for display on WAP devices, or a guide might contain voice sections that can be transformed to a VoiceXML representation and synthesized as speech.

Document Structure

A NVML document contains a head element and a body element. The head contains metainformation that's relevant for all routes and guides in the document. Here's the main structure for a representation of routes and guides in NVML:

```xml
<?xml version="1.0" encoding="UTF-8"?>
<nvml>
  <head>
    . . .
  </head>
  <body>
    <navi>
      . . .
    </navi>
    . . .
    <navi>
      . . .
    </navi>
  </body>
</nvml>
```

The head contains information that applies to all navi elements. An NVML document might contain an arbitrary number of navi elements. A *navi* element can contain a description about points at the beginning of a route, the route itself, or guides—for example, text or images related to a particular point. The head can look like this:

```xml
<?xml version="1.0" encoding="UTF-8"?>
<nvml>
  <head>
    <title>From the football stadium to the opera house.
    </title>
```

```
<transport>car
</transport>
<duration>3 minutes
</duration>
<distance>2 km
</distance>
</head>
<body>
<navi>
...
</navi>
...
<navi>
...
</navi>
</body>
</nvml>
```

In this example, the document describes how a pedestrian can get from the local football stadium to the opera house. It would take three minutes to drive the two-kilometer distance, which is described in the nav elements. The elements in the head element—title, transport, duration, and distance—are optional elements. They needn't be provided but, if they are, then they must occur in the previous order.

Routes

A path from one point to another can be described in NVML as a sequence of nvml elements. Each *nvml* element can describe a point on the path, such as a stadium, a gas station, a warehouse, and so forth. In addition, the user can get information about the route itself on which the point occurs. Here's an example:

```
<?xml version="1.0" encoding="UTF-8"?>
<nvml>
  <head>
    <title>From the football stadium to the opera house.
    </title>
    <transport>car
    </transport>
    <duration>3 minutes
    </duration>
    <distance>2 km
    </distance>
  </head>
```

```
<body>
  <navi>
    <point>
      <name>Football stadium</name>
      <address>5 Sample Street</address>
    </point>
    <info>
      <text>The football stadium.</text>
    </info>
  </navi>
  <navi>
    <route>
      <name>Route</name>
      <number>64</number>
    </route>
    <info>
      <text>Route 64 goes from the football stadium to the
            opera house.
      </text>
    </info>
  </navi>
  <n
    <point>
      <name>Verdi Opera house</name>
      <address>42 Blue Avenue</address>
    </point>
    <info>
      <text>The opera house.</text>
    </info>
  </navi>
  </body>
</nvml>
```

The *head* element describes the document in general and specifies the path from the football stadium to the opera house. Three navi elements are in the body element. The first navi element contains the starting point, which is the football stadium. The second has the route from the football stadium to the next point, the opera house, which is specified using the route element. This navi element also has a textual description, which is meant to describe the route. Finally, the third navi element specifies the end point, which is the opera house. As in the first navi element, the point element is used to provide information about its formal name and address. An information element is also provided here to give a textual description about the point.

The *info* element is supposed to be used by the interpreting program. For example, you could use an XSL Transformation to convert this representation to something that can be rendered on to a screen, such as WML, Compact HTML, or XHTML code. If you want to show a graphical representation of the point, the text element could be replaced by the image element or the voice element. The image element can be used as follows:

```
<navi>
  <point>
    <name>Verdi Opera house</name>
    <address>42 Blue Avenue</address>
  </point>
  <info>
    <image src='operaHouse.gif'/>
  </info>
</navi>
```

Here, the info element could be displayed on a device that supports graphics and the GIF format. An alternative could be to represent the point, so it can easily be spoken by a speech synthesizer engine. Typically, the point would then be transformed to say a VoiceXML document. Here's how the NVML code could look then:

```
<navi>
  <point>
    <name>Verdi Opera house</name>
    <address>42 Blue Avenue</address>
  </point>
  <info>
    <voice>The opera house.</voice>
  </info>
</navi>
```

The voice element contains a text, which is supposed to be spoken.

Guides

Guides are different from routes because they aren't supposed to be used for navigation from one point to another. Instead, a *guide* describes the details of a point. For example, a small device with a mobile Internet connection can be mounted into a vehicle. It downloads a NVML document and retrieves the position from the mobile network. The position is continuously compared with the longitude and latitude elements in the NVML document. As the position matches some of the guide and point elements in the document, the text inside the voice element is rendered as synthetic speech. Here's an example:

```
<?xml version="1.0" encoding="UTF-8"?>
<nvml>
  <head>
    <title>The city
    </title>
    <transport>car
    </transport>
  </head>
  <body>
    <guide>
      <point area="100m">
        <name>Football stadium</name>
        <latitude>N23.12.23.3</latitude>
        <longitude>W119.32.41.8</longitude>
        <address>5 Sample Street</address>
      </point>
      <info duration="1min">
        <text>The football stadium.
        </text>
        <voice>You're at the football stadium, built in 1981. Next game
               is Wednesday the 5th of June.
        </voice>
        <image src='stadium.gif'/>
      </info>
    </guide>
    <guide>
      <point area="100m">
        <name>Opera house</name>
        <address>42 Blue Avenue</address>
        <latitude>N23.11.25.4</latitude>
        <longitude>W119.32.41.8</longitude>
      </point>
      <info duration="1min">
        <text>The opera house.
        </text>
        <image src='operaHouse.gif'/>
        <voice>You're at the opera house on Blue Avenue. The premiere of
               Tosca is next month, on Friday the 16th at 8 p.m. Book your
               tickets now.
        </voice>
      </info>
```

```
    </guide>
  </body>
</nvml>
```

An arbitrary number of guide elements can be specified, each of which contains a point element. The info, though, is optional. In the previous example, the duration attribute was used on the info element. The duration attribute specifies for how long the message should be active when the user enters the proximity of the area, which has been specified. The point is specified using the latitude and longitude elements, and the radius of the point is provided with the area attribute on the point element. The body of an NVML document can mix guide elements and navi elements to provide both guidance and routes.

Guides are used to describe points, while other emerging technologies can be used to describe points and locations. POIX, meanwhile, can be used to specify points of interest.

Specifying Points of Interest with POIX

POIX is an XML application that can be used to exchange the position between nodes in a wireless network. Technologies, such as GML, can be used to specify maps. With NVML, routes and guides can be provided for devices mounted in vehicles, such as cars or buses. The position, though, needs to be transferred from a positioning server in the mobile network to the application, which runs on the client device. This server is usually owned by the operator and the service provider buys access to it.

One of the benefits with POIX is it can be used to describe the position of moving objects. For example, a device mounted in a car can send the position, expressed in POIX, to a server. The server can take the vehicle's position, speed, and direction into account, and reply with information, such as how much time it will take to drive to a certain place.

Japan's Mobile Information Standard Technical Committee (MOSTEC) maintains the POIX framework.

The position of an object is transferred in a POIX document, which has a structure like this:

```
<?xml version="1.0" encoding="UTF-8"?>
<!DOCTYPE poix PUBLIC "-//MOSTEC//POIX V2.0//EN"
   "http://www.w3.org/TR/poix/poix.dtd">
```

```
<poix version="2.0">
  <!-- Coordinate system, e.g. wgs84, author, moving etc... -->
  <format>
    ...
  </format>
  <!-- The point of interest. -->
  <poi>
    ...
  </poi>
</poix>
```

The top-level element is the poix element, which must contain a format element followed by a poi element.

Formats

Information about the coordinate system is specified in the *format* element. In addition, the format element can contain a type element, which indicates if the object is moving, gives author information, and a time element, such as in the following document:

```
<?xml version="1.0" encoding="UTF-8"?>
<!DOCTYPE poix PUBLIC "-//MOSTEC//POIX V2.0//EN"
  "http://www.w3.org/TR/poix/poix.dtd">
<poix version="2.0">
  <!-- Coordinate system, author, moving etc... -->
  <format>
    <datum>wgs84</datum>
    <unit>degree</unit>
    <type object="move"/>
    <author>Joe Smith</author>
    <time>2002-02-20T08:30:12+01:00</time>
  </format>
  <!-- The point of interest. -->
  <poi>
    ...
  </poi>
</poix>
```

The coordinate system that has been used is wgs84, one of the more common coordinate systems, to specify the position. The longitude and latitude of the moving object are expressed in degrees. The author of the document is Joe Smith and it was created February 20, 2002.

NOTE

The instance document doesn't specify how the position was retrieved from the mobile network, and it isn't part of the POIX framework at all. Instead, the instance document is used to exchange the position only.

The Position

The actual position (point of interest) is expressed using the poi and the point elements. Note, the point is expressed with respect to the format element:

```
<?xml version="1.0" encoding="UTF-8"?>
<!DOCTYPE poix PUBLIC "-//MOSTEC//POIX V2.0//EN"
  "http://www.w3.org/TR/poix/poix.dtd">
<poix version="2.0">
  <!-- Coordinate system, author, moving etc... -->
  <format>
    <datum>wgs84</datum>
    <unit>degree</unit>
    <type object="move"/>
    <author>Joe Smith</author>
    <time>2002-02-20T08:30:12+01:00</time>
  </format>
  <!-- The point of interest. -->
  <poi>
    <point>
      <pos>
        <lat>23.0000</lat>
        <lon>131.7200</lon>
      </pos>
    </point>
    ...
  </poi>
</poix>
```

Latitude and longitude values are expressed in the *lat* and *lon* elements. The actual syntax of the elements' content depends on the datum, which is provided in the *datum* element.

Because the type element had the object attribute set to "move," you should provide more information about the object, which is obviously mobile.

Mobility

Information about the movement can be provided after the point element. For example, both the speed and the object's movenent can be specified like this:

```xml
<?xml version="1.0" encoding="UTF-8"?>
<!DOCTYPE poix PUBLIC "-//MOSTEC//POIX V2.0//EN"
  "http://www.w3.org/TR/poix/poix.dtd">
<poix version="2.0">
  <!-- Coordinate system, author, moving etc... -->
  <format>
    <datum>wgs84</datum>
    <unit>degree</unit>
    <type object="move"/>
    <author>Joe Smith</author>
    <time>2002-02-20T08:30:12+01:00</time>
  </format>
  <!-- The point of interest. -->
  <poi>
    <point>
      <pos>
        <lat>23.0000</lat>
        <lon>131.7200</lon>
      </pos>
    </point>
    <move>
      <method>onfoot</method>
      <!-- Speed, Always km/h -->
      <speed>5</speed>
    </move>
  </poi>
</poix>
```

The *move* element is optional and can occur, at most, once in a document. In this example, the object in question is obviously someone walking at the speed of five kilometers an hour, which is equivalent to approximately three miles an hour. The method element can contain other values than onfoot, such as car or bus.

Here's another example, which uses an additional element to specify the direction of the object.

```xml
<?xml version="1.0" encoding="UTF-8"?>
<!DOCTYPE poix PUBLIC "-//MOSTEC//POIX V2.0//EN"
```

```
    "http://www.w3.org/TR/poix/poix.dtd">
<poix version="2.0">
  <!-- Coordinate system, author, moving etc... -->
  <format>
    <datum>wgs84</datum>
    <unit>degree</unit>
    <type object="move"/>
    <author>Joe Smith</author>
    <time>2002-02-20T08:30:12+01:00</time>
  </format>
  <!-- The point of interest. -->
  <poi>
    <point>
      <pos>
        <lat>23.0000</lat>
        <lon>131.7200</lon>
      </pos>
    </point>
    <move>
      <!-- A train. -->
      <method>railway</method>
      <!-- Speed, Always km/h -->
      <speed>180</speed>
      <!-- Moving east. -->
      <dir>90</dir>
    </move>
  </poi>
</poix>
```

The direction is calculated from 0 to 360 degrees, starting with zero and north at 12 o'clock, and moving clockwise to 90 degrees at 3 o'clock and 180 degrees at 6 o'clock. Thus, in the previous example, the object is a train, which moves east at 180 kilometers an hour (approximately 112 miles an hour). A motorcycle moving northwest at 90 kilometers an hour could be specified like this:

```
<?xml version="1.0" encoding="UTF-8"?>
<!DOCTYPE poix PUBLIC "-//MOSTEC//POIX V2.0//EN"
   "http://www.w3.org/TR/poix/poix.dtd">
<poix version="2.0">
  <!-- Coordinate system, author, moving etc... -->
  <format>
    <datum>wgs84</datum>
```

```
        <unit>degree</unit>
        <type object="move"/>
        <author>Joe Smith</author>
        <time>2002-02-20T08:30:12+01:00</time>
    </format>
    <!-- The point of interest. -->
    <poi>
        <point>
            <pos>
                <lat>33.0000</lat>
                <lon>119.9400</lon>
            </pos>
        </point>
        <move>
            <!-- A motorcycle. -->
            <method>motorcycle</method>
            <!-- Speed, Always km/h -->
            <speed>90</speed>
            <!-- Moving northwest. -->
            <dir>315</dir>
        </move>
    </poi>
</poix>
```

The methods defined by MOSTEC are car, motorcycle, railway, onfoot, bus, airplane, ship, and others. If you need to specify someone moving on a bicycle, for example, you'd then have to use either motorcycle or others, with a suitable speed. The content of the dir element is 315 because the object moves northwest. That's 45 degrees between west and north, which is 270 degrees plus 45 degrees.

Extending the Point of Interest with Start and End Points

In addition to the previous examples, which have included information about a single point only, it's possible to provide information about the start and end of the object's path. The point of interest is still the focus of the instance document, but it can be augmented with this type of information. After all, a single position, speed, and direction might not be sufficient for all applications. In some cases, you might want to retrieve the position where the object started and where it ends, to sort several objects, which are more or less located at the same place. This can give you a much better picture if the POIX instance document is given a graphical representation in XHTML, WML, SVG, or other formats. For example, the object can then be drawn as a small circle with a solid arrow that points in the direction the object moves. The start and end point can be connected to the object as dotted lines to indicate the start and end points.

A bus, which moves south at 80 kilometers an hour, from an introductory point to a terminal point, could be specified like this:

```xml
<?xml version="1.0" encoding="UTF-8"?>
<!DOCTYPE poix PUBLIC "-//MOSTEC//POIX V2.0//EN"
  "http://www.w3.org/TR/poix/poix.dtd">
<poix version="2.0">
  <!-- Coordinate system, author, moving etc... -->
  <format>
    <datum>wgs84</datum>
    <unit>degree</unit>
    <type object="move"/>
    <author>Joe Smith</author>
    <time>2002-02-20T08:30:12+01:00</time>
  </format>
  <!-- The point of interest. -->
  <poi>
    <point>
      <pos>
        <lat>33.0000</lat>
        <lon>119.9400</lon>
      </pos>
    </point>
    <move>
      <!-- Speed, Always km/h -->
      <speed>80</speed>
      <!-- Moving south. -->
      <dir>180</dir>
    </move>
    <access>
      <!-- A bus. -->
      <method>bus</method>
      <ipoint>
        <iclass>street</iclass>
        <pos>
          <lat>33.0000</lat>
          <lon>119.8900</lon>
        </pos>
      </ipoint>
```

```
      <tpoint>
        <tclass>parking</tclass>
        <pos>
          <lat>33.0000</lat>
          <lon>119.9500</lon>
        </pos>
      </tpoint>
    </access>
  </poi>
</poix>
```

The *access* element contains the start point, called *ipoint* or introductory point, and the end point, called *tpoint* or terminal point. A number of classes have been defined for the introductory points and terminal points. Introductory points can be crossings, streets, stations, airports, harbors, and so forth. Terminal points can be parking lots or entrances. If the terminal points to something other than these two, then you should use other. Finally, the ipoints and tpoints can be augmented with a name that describes the position and the class more in detail. It might look like the following:

```
<?xml version="1.0" encoding="UTF-8"?>
<!DOCTYPE poix PUBLIC "-//MOSTEC//POIX V2.0//EN"
  "http://www.w3.org/TR/poix/poix.dtd">
<poix version="2.0">
  <!-- Coordinate system, author, moving etc... -->
  <format>
    <datum>wgs84</datum>
    <unit>degree</unit>
    <type object="move"/>
    <author>Joe Smith</author>
    <time>2002-02-20T08:30:12+01:00</time>
  </format>
  <!-- The point of interest. -->
  <poi>
    <point>
      <pos>
        <lat>33.0000</lat>
        <lon>119.9400</lon>
      </pos>
    </point>
    <move>
      <!-- Speed, Always km/h -->
      <speed>80</speed>
```

```
      <!-- Moving south. -->
      <dir>180</dir>
    </move>
    <access>
      <!-- A bus. -->
      <method>bus</method>
      <ipoint>
        <iclass>street</iclass>
        <pos>
          <lat>33.0000</lat>
          <lon>119.8900</lon>
        </pos>
        <name><nb>42 Blue Street</nb></name>
      </ipoint>
      <tpoint>
        <tclass>parking</tclass>
        <pos>
          <lat>33.0000</lat>
          <lon>119.9500</lon>
        </pos>
        <name><nb>Parking lot at 19 Yellow Street</nb></name>
      </tpoint>
    </access>
  </poi>
</poix>
```

The name can be used if the instance document is transformed to a graphical representation. In most cases, it will be transformed, and then a name, which can be written on the map, says more than a dot at the position, which is specified in the pos, lat, and lon elements. The name element is optional, though, and, if it's used, the name element should occur after the pos element.

CHAPTER 9

The Future of Personalization

IN THIS CHAPTER:

CSS Mobile Profile 1.0

Virtual Personal Information

A s you know, personalized services let the user adjust a number of settings to adapt the experience to the user's hardware, software, personal preferences, physical location, language, and so forth. The following is a short presentation of a few technologies you might experience in the near future. These technologies could have an impact on how wireless applications are developed.

CSS Mobile Profile 1.0

At press time, the CSS Mobile Profile 1.0 is a working draft. WAP 2.0-compliant devices use Wireless CSS (WCSS), which is compatible with the CSS Mobile Profile 1.0 draft. Because the CSS Mobile Profile 1.0 isn't specified for WAP devices only, it can be a good idea to stay compliant with this draft because it probably will make your applications compatible with as many mobile devices as possible (and not only WAP devices). We hope the CSS Mobile Profile 1.0 will become a W3C recommendation.

Adding Style

As with CSS2 and WCSS in WAP 2.0, the CSS Mobile Profile 1.0 makes it possible to style documents for a particular device or type of device. For example, if the device supports small font sizes, then you can choose a small font size for the p element in XHTML, or you can reduce to a minimum the vertical space that the line break introduces . This can leave more room for text on small displays. To achieve this styling, a number of selectors and properties can be used. Let's look at some of them in the CSS Mobile Profile 1.0 draft. Note that they also apply to CSS2 and WCSS because the CSS Mobile Profile 1.0 draft is a subset of these.

Selectors

In CSS, WCSS, and the CSS Mobile Profile, selectors are used to select the elements that will be affected by the properties you specify. The following example illustrates how the CSS Mobile Profile 1.0 working draft is used to express that all elements in the XHTML document should be rendered with a small, 8-point font.

```
<?xml version="1.0" encoding="UTF-8"?>
<!DOCTYPE html PUBLIC "-//W3C//DTD XHTML 1.0 Strict//EN"
    "http://www.w3.org/TR/xhtml1/DTD/xhtml1-strict.dtd">
<html xmlns="http://www.w3.org/1999/xhtml">
<head>
```

```
   <style type='text/css'>* { font-size: 8pt }
   </style>
   <title>My document</title>
</head>
<body>
    <h1>Hello</h1>
    <p>This is <em>my</em> document.
    </p>
</body>
</html>
```

With the CSS Mobile Profile, you can use the universal selector as in the previous example. You can also refer to individual elements and to a set of elements.

```
<?xml version="1.0" encoding="UTF-8"?>
<!DOCTYPE html PUBLIC "-//W3C//DTD XHTML 1.0 Strict//EN"
    "http://www.w3.org/TR/xhtml1/DTD/xhtml1-strict.dtd">
<html xmlns="http://www.w3.org/1999/xhtml">
<head>
  <style type='text/css'>h1 { font-size: 10pt }
        p em { font-size: 9pt}
  </style>
  <title>My document</title>
</head>
<body>
    <h1>Hello</h1>
    <p>This is <em>my</em> document.
    </p>
</body>
</html>
```

Here the h1 element has been given a slightly larger font size. The p and em elements are referred to in the same selection.

Let's check what you can't do in the CSS Mobile Profile 1.0 working draft. You can't refer to child elements, like this:

```
<?xml version="1.0" encoding="UTF-8"?>
<!DOCTYPE html PUBLIC "-//W3C//DTD XHTML 1.0 Strict//EN"
    "http://www.w3.org/TR/xhtml1/DTD/xhtml1-strict.dtd">
<html xmlns="http://www.w3.org/1999/xhtml">
<head>
  <style type='text/css'>h1 { font-size: 10pt }
```

```
            p:first-child { font-size: 10pt}
            p { font-size: 9pt}
            p > em { font-size: 9pt}
    </style>
    <title>My document</title>
</head>
<body>
    <h1>Hello</h1>
    <p>This is <em>my</em> document.
    </p>
</body>
</html>
```

You can't use the child selector (indicated by the greater-than (>) symbol) declaration, so the previous example wouldn't be compliant with the CSS Mobile Profile 1.0 draft. Another forbidden construct is the following:

```
<?xml version="1.0" encoding="UTF-8"?>
<!DOCTYPE html PUBLIC "-//W3C//DTD XHTML 1.0 Strict//EN"
    "http://www.w3.org/TR/xhtml1/DTD/xhtml1-strict.dtd">
<html xmlns="http://www.w3.org/1999/xhtml">
<head>
    <style type='text/css'>h1 { font-size: 10pt }
            h1 + p { font-size: 10pt}
            p em { font-size: 9pt}
    </style>
    <title>My document</title>
</head>
<body>
    <h1>Hello</h1>
    <p>This is <em>my</em> document.
    </p>
</body>
</html>
```

Here, we used the + character to match the paragraph tag. The code h1 + p indicates the p element should occur immediately after the h1 element. This functionality isn't included and you should, instead, specify the p element individually, like this.

```
<?xml version="1.0" encoding="UTF-8"?>
<!DOCTYPE html PUBLIC "-//W3C//DTD XHTML 1.0 Strict//EN"
    "http://www.w3.org/TR/xhtml1/DTD/xhtml1-strict.dtd">
```

```
<html xmlns="http://www.w3.org/1999/xhtml">
<head>
  <style>h1 { font-size: 10pt }
         p { font-size: 10pt}
         em { font-size: 9pt}
  </style>
  <title>My document</title>
</head>
<body>
    <h1>Hello</h1>
    <p>This is <em>my</em> document.
    </p>
</body>
</html>
```

Then, however, you won't be able to render the first paragraph after the h1 element in a different style compared to all other paragraph elements. If you need to do this, ask yourself if you should use the *p* element. In this case, you could use the h2 element instead.

Often, selectors that aren't allowed, such as the previous, can be replaced with something that gives a similar effect, allowing them to become compatible with the CSS Mobile Profile 1.0.

Properties

Some more or less important properties aren't supported by the CSS Mobile Profile 1.0 working draft. The position, top, bottom, left, and right properties aren't allowed. This makes the following web page incompatible with the profile.

```
<?xml version="1.0" encoding="UTF-8"?>
<!DOCTYPE html PUBLIC "-//W3C//DTD XHTML 1.0 Strict//EN"
    "http://www.w3.org/TR/xhtml1/DTD/xhtml1-strict.dtd">
<html xmlns="http://www.w3.org/1999/xhtml">
<head>
  <style>h1 { font-size: 12pt; position=absolute;  top=80; left=20; }
         p { font-size: 10pt}
         em { font-size: 9pt}
  </style>
  <title>My document</title>
</head>
<body>
    <h1>Hello</h1>
```

```
    <p>This is <em>my</em> document.
    </p>
</body>
</html>
```

In the previous example, the h1 element has been hard coded to appear at position 20, 80. The properties used to achieve this aren't allowed in the CSS Mobile Profile 1.0. Even if those properties were allowed, using them like this isn't a good idea because the page probably wouldn't display well on small devices. The margin-top, margin-bottom, margin-left, and margin-right properties can be used, though. They don't allow the author to work with absolute coordinates. These properties are used for making fine adjustments and only set the margins for a block.

Properties used with aural style sheets aren't supported by the CSS Mobile Profile 1.0 draft. These properties should be used by speech synthesizers rather than applications that show the result on a display.

Virtual Personal Information

An aspect of personalized applications is that some of them might enable you to administrate your own personal contact lists and calendar data. For this purpose, two formats have been around for a while: the vCalendar and vCard formats.

The vCalendar and vCard formats are plain text formats, but RDF/XML versions of these might exist in the future. Suggestions for how this can be done have been submitted to the World Wide Web Consortium (W3C). Until a recommendation is available, learning the plain text versions used today is a good idea for two reasons. First, these documents can be transferred between a handheld device and a computer using the XML-based SyncML format. For an example, see Chapter 10. Second, you can include vCards in documents, such as XHTML pages using the object element. Thus, these formats are often used in an XML environment.

Using the vCard Format

Virtual business cards (vCards) should have the file extension .vcf if they are stored in a file system. The document type is text/x-vCard. If you're storing a vCard file on a web server, you must configure the web server so it sends this content type when the document is retrieved by an application.

A vCard contains a number of properties. A *property* can be an information field, such as a telephone number, but it can also be another vCard. This makes creating a set of business cards possible—for example, a complete phone book. Because everything is text-based, it's easy to incorporate the business cards in XML documents, such as a SyncML file, an MMS message that contains a SMIL presentation, or an XHTML document. Here's a simple example:

```
begin:vcard
fn:Carl Smith
n:Smith;Carl; William; Mr.
tel;type=work:+1 8 112 23456789
tel;type=home:+1 8 999 44 123456
email;type=internet:carl@carlsmithsdomain.com
end:vcard
```

The vCard file starts with the begin:vcard declaration, indicating the start of the business card. At the end of the card, is the text end:vcard. All the fields in the business card are specified between the begin and the end declarations.

The property fn means *formatted name*. It contains the name as it is written, character by character or formatted. This field is usually displayed—at the top or as a default—by the application.

The property n, on the other hand, defines the name as a number of fields to make it possible for applications to extract and use, say, the surname only. The first field is the surname and the second field is the first name. Additional names are specified in the third field, and a title—in this case, Mr.—can be specified in the fourth field.

Telephone numbers can be specified using the tel property, as you can see in the previous example. Here you used two parameters, work and home, to specify the number to the person's home and work. Parameters are provided after the property with a semicolon between the property and the parameter.

The e-mail address can be provided using the e-mail property. Sending e-mail over the Internet is probably most common, but other parameters can be provided, such as AOL or X400. The value for the e-mail property is the e-mail address, using the well-known syntax.

Referring to vCards in an XHTML document is possible. Then it would look something like this:

```
<?xml version="1.0" encoding="UTF-8"?>
<!DOCTYPE html PUBLIC "-//W3C//DTD XHTML Basic 1.0//EN"
"http://www.w3.org/TR/xhtml-basic/xhtml-basic10.dtd">
<html xmlns="http://www.w3.org/1999/xhtml">
<head>
  <title>Hello</title>
</head>
```

```
<body>
  <h1>Welcome!</h1>
  <p>Please read my virtual business card
   when you need to contact me.
   <object data="my_vCard.vcf" type="text/x-vCard">
     Cannot display the virtual business card.
   </object>
  </p>
</body>
</html>
```

Note that the object element is used. The object element is part of the object module, and the object module is part of XHTML Basic 1.0.

Here's another example demonstrating a more comprehensive vCard file that contains more information than the last example:

```
begin:vcard
fn:Carl Smith
n:Smith;Carl; William; Mr.
tel;type=work:+1 8 112 23456789
tel;type=fax:+1 8 999 44 123499
tel;type=home:+1 8 999 44 123456
tel;type=cell:+1 70 5552 1904
tel;type=pref:+1 70 5552 1904
email;type=internet:carl@carlsmithsdomain.com
version:2.1
adr;type=intl,work:p.o. box 42;;5 King Street;New York;NY;19938-2928;USA
photo;value=url;type=gif:http://www.carlsmithsdomain.com/me.gif
bday:19670125
logo;value=url;type=gif:http://www.somecompanydomain.com/companylogo.gif
note:I work with wireless systems and applications.
sound;value=url;type=wave:http://www.carlsmithsdomain.com/pronounce.wav
end:vcard
```

Several telephone numbers are provided here: the fax number, the home number, and the telephone number to the person's cellular phone. In addition, the preferred phone number has been specified using the pref parameter.

The version number 2.1 indicates the properties and parameters in the virtual business card might have been provided with respect to version 2.1 of the vCard specification. Thus, some fields might require a tool that understands vCard version 2.1 to interpret them correctly.

The address (adr) property, which is an international address to the person's work, was used to specify the address of the person. All fields are separated by a semicolon and the value ends with USA because this is an international address. If the parameter dom, as in domestic, was used instead of intl, then it wouldn't have been necessary to specify USA. Applications compliant with version 2.1 of the vCard specification don't have to support the adr property. This is optional.

The same goes for the remaining properties of the vCard. Support for the photo property is optional. With the photo property, a picture of the person can be included. In this case, it points at a URL at the Internet, so the value parameter has been set to the value URL and the URL has been provided.

The birthday (bday) property is also optional for tools to support. Using this property, the person's birthday can be specified using the previous syntax: four-digit year, two-digit month, and two-digit day.

A company logo can be incorporated into the card. In this case, it points at a picture on the Internet. Thus, the value parameter has been set to URL, similar to how it's used with the photo property.

The note property can be used to insert a short note or description. It can contain arbitrary text, but it usually contains a description of the person's job tasks.

The sound property should be used to specify how the person's name should be pronounced. It applies to the fn property, which should be set to the person's formatted name. In this case, the property uses the value parameter, similar to how it's used with the photo and company logo properties. In this example, a .wav file is used, but it's also possible to use .aif files, which are common in the Mac world. AIFF means Audio Interchange File Format.

Using the vCalendar Format

Virtual calendars, or vCalendars, should have the file extension .vcs if they're stored in a file system. The document type is text/x-vCalendar.

The vCalendar begins with begin:vcalendar declaration and it ends with the line end:vcalendar. This is similar to how the vCard format is laid out. A vCalendar can contain events and todo objects.

The *todo* object, or *vTodo* object, describes something the user thinks is important and needs to be done. It might contain a textual description and represent an action point. An *event,* or *vEvent,* represents a period in the calendar. Typically, an event is a booking for a meeting and a todo object represents something personal, such as handing in a form on time or going to the dentist.

The general structure for the vEvents and vTodos in the vCalendar document follows.

```
begin:vcalendar
    ...
begin:vevent
```

```
  ...
end:vevent
  ...
begin:todo
  ...
end:todo
  ...
end:vcalendar
```

The complete vCalendar starts with the begin:vcalendar line and ends with the end:vcalendar line. It contains a number of begin:vevent and end:vevent chunks, and a number of begin:todo and end:todo chunks. Here's an example:

```
begin:vcalendar
version:1.0
begin:vevent
categories:business; meeting
dtstart:20020122T083000
dtend: 20020122T120000
attendee;role=owner;status=confirmed:E. Froese <efroese@the
company.com>
attendee;role=attendee;status=confirmed:S. Vath <svath@the
company.com>
attendee;role=attendee;status=confirmed:D. Sylvian <dsylvian@the
company.com>
summary:Presentation
description: Present the new business model for the team.
class:confidential
end:vevent
begin:todo
summary:Buy a new battery for the cellular.
due:20020123T093000
end:todo
end:vcalendar
```

The version number works exactly the same as for the vCard. It specifies which version tools must be compliant to interpret all properties correctly.

Categories is a property that specifies the category for an event or a todo. Many categories can be specified, as in the previous example, which is a business event and a meeting. Other allowed values are education, holiday, travel, and so forth.

The dtstart and dtend provide the date and time start, and the date and time end, for the event. The format is a bit special: the year followed by the month, the day, and then the character *T* for time, followed by the local time. The two zeroes at the end indicate it's local time.

Several attendees can be listed together with their status. The status usually indicates if they have replied. The role parameter is used to provide a description of each attendee's role for the event. Instead of using the e-mail address to the attendee, it's possible to refer to the attendee's vCard, which usually contains the e-mail address and much more information. Then the value parameter can be used, as it was used for the photo property in the vCard example. It should then be set to URL and, instead of using the e-mail address, a link to the vCard is inserted.

Summary contains a short, descriptive text string, while *description* should contain a longer description of the purpose of the event.

Classifying todos and events is possible. In the previous example, the event has been classified as confidential because important business models are going to be presented and discussed. Other values can be used, such as public and private.

The todo in the calendar is simple. It has a short summary and a due date. The latter provides the expiry date for what must be done, in this case "buy a new battery." The format for the due property is the same as for the dtstart and dtend properties.

Future Representations of Business Cards and Calendars

One suggestion for how to make an XML version of the vCard format is based on RDF and XML name spaces. The vCard format would then be given a name space of its own. All properties, more or less, would be translated to elements with the same name as the properties. For example, the fn property could be specified using a syntax like this:

```
<vCard:fn>Carl Smith</vCard:fn>
<vCard:n>:Smith;Carl; William; Mr.</vCard:n>
```

It remains to be seen, however, how and when a recommendation that deals with the representation of vCards in XML will happen. If an implementation follows for vCalendar, there's a fair chance it will follow the same principles because the format is similar to vCard.

Instant Messaging and Presence Applications

IN THIS CHAPTER:

RFC2778 and RFC2779

The Instant Messaging and Presence Protocol

APEX

Make It SIMPLE

Instant messaging (IM) and presence applications belong to a relatively new category of applications. The need for applications like these goes back to the fact that the Internet, including the Mobile Internet, doesn't have such functionality yet. In the old days, when users connected to a central computer—say, using a vt100 terminal—finding out if a user was online could be relatively easy. Using a UNIX application, such as talk, you could then establish a chat session with the person. Currently, though, users are distributed over the network to an even higher degree. It's difficult to know which computer the user is sitting in front of. Determining this and contacting the person immediately is a nontrivial task. Applications provide this functionality, but the implementations are often proprietary and aren't built on common standards.

The problem is rather complex because, in an ideal situation, you should be able to contact a person, wherever she is, and whichever device and type of network is used. If a person is traveling and only has access to a mobile phone or PDA, then his or her colleague should be able to stay in contact. Sending a message to her phone or PDA should be possible and, in an ultimate situation, the message should be routed to the device automatically. When she's due back at her office, all messages would then be routed automatically to her desktop computer.

A foundation to much of the IM and presence work currently happening has been RFC2778 and RFC2779. The Internet Engineering Task Force (IETF) produces Request for Comments (RFC) and the purpose is to use them as a base for discussion and standardization. So far, not a single standard exists that can be used by all applications that make use of IM or presence functionality. However, the 3G networks for mobile telephony being planned might play an important role for IM and presence applications. The 3GPP organization has a technical group for service and system aspects that works with presence services in 3G networks. Their work is based on RFC2778 and RFC2779.

RFC2778 and RFC2779

Some proposals have been discussed concerning the representation of IM and presence information in XML. To understand the proposals and get a reasonably good idea of what might be released in the future, let's look at some of the principles of these RFCs that serve as the foundation for much of the ongoing work.

A number of objects are part of an IM and presence application. Because the approach to the representation of these services is object-oriented, it becomes relatively easy to discuss possible implementations in languages, such as XML. An object might be implemented as an XML element and other objects that contain these objects might include these elements as child elements.

Most of the presence services are based on a service model where the presence service is the actual service, from which users retrieve the presence information. Watchers retrieve the presence information from the presence service. *Watchers* are entities that use the presence information for arbitrary purposes—for example, to present the information on the screen for a user. On the other hand, presentities are, in some respects, the opposite of watchers. *Presentities* provide the presence information for the watchers by communicating with the presence service.

A watcher can be a subscriber. Subscribers can subscribe to certain presence information and they do it by requesting the information from the presence service. The subscriber receives that request, and then distributes the presence information to the subscriber by sending notifications to it.

An *instant inbox* is a receiver of instant messages. Instant messages are distributed to the instant inbox by the IM service. Ordinary users, or *principals,* use inbox user agents to retrieve the instant messages from the instant inboxes.

The Instant Messaging and Presence Protocol

The IETF is discussing a framework for an IM and presence protocol. A number of proposals have been presented for different parts of such a specification. Similar to the work by 3GPP, IETF's work is based on RFC2778 and RFC2779. A draft exists for a common profile for IM (CPIM), but this is a work in progress and it'll be some time before you can see a full specification.

CPIM Messages

CPIM messages are used to send instant messages between users of IM applications. No final format exists yet, but a framework is being developed and discussed.

The Header

The header is supposed to contain information about the sender and receiver, a bit like ordinary e-mail messages. However, one of the corner stones of IM applications is the user should be contactable wherever he and whichever device he's using. This puts some requirements on the addressing. Using ordinary e-mail addresses might not be enough because IM is another type of messaging than pure e-mail. A proposal is based on the use of ordinary Uniform Resource Identifiers (URIs) where the protocol identifier is im, as in instant messaging. For example, the following type of address might be used in the future for IM applications.

```
To: Michael Cross<im:michael@example.com>
From: Craig Andersson<im:craig@example.com>
```

The address is an ordinary URI or, to be more precise, URL, and the protocol identifier im tells you it's an instant message. In fact, the address is similar to an ordinary mailto: URL syntax, but mailto has been replaced by im.

The use of XML namespaces in the header of instant messages has also been discussed. Namespaces could be used to allow future extensions to IM and make use of features available only on certain devices. It might look like the following:

```
NS: Device42 <http://example.com/device42>
Device42.styling: colorScheme7
```

NS indicates an XML namespace is specified. This is followed by the namespace prefix—in this case, Device42—and the unique URL.

Content

The content of CPIM-compliant messages is probably composed of one or more MIME content types, such as text/html or text/plain. The whole message would also have to be given a content type. The proposal is that the content type should be message/cpim for the Common Profile for Instant Messaging.

So, a complete IM message would then start with the message/cpim content type, and then the to and from fields would follow as previously described. XML namespaces could be used to specify properties of that particular message, and then the content would be encapsulated in the message as ordinary MIME content types are encapsulated in ordinary e-mails.

This solution and layout are currently being discussed and are neither a standard nor a recommendation yet.

CPIM Instant Inboxes

Instant messages are delivered to instant inboxes. An *instant inbox* contains a number of delivery rules, which are specified by the owner of the instant inbox. The owner, a principal, uses an inbox user agent to provide these details.

Sending a message to an IM inbox can be done in several ways, depending on which application is used. So far, no syntax exists for the invocation of such an action. A representation in XML has been discussed, however, and a fair chance exists that an XML-based language might be developed for this. The following syntax has been discussed.

```
<message destination='im:michael@example.com'
        source='im:craig@example.com'
        transID='5'/>
```

NOTE

This format has only been loosely discussed and no standard or recommendation exists yet for how this should be done. The prefix — im — indicates the IM and presence protocol should be used.

The IM service tries to send the message and, if it succeeds, it receives a response that has the same transaction ID: transID. Again, the format hasn't been decided, but the following XML format has been discussed.

```
<response status='success' transID='5'/>
```

Thus, the transaction ID is used by the messaging service to keep track of the message and to know if a successful response was returned.

CPIM Presentities

In CPIM, a presentity is a client that's used with a presence service to provide the presence information. Watchers, on the other hand, receive the presence information from the presence service. Thus, in CPIM and RFC2778, the presence service receives information from presentities and distributes that information to the watchers. This is only a modeling separation, though, and the client could, in fact, provide the presence information. For example, a mobile phone could tell the service where it is and also request information.

Subscriptions

In CPIM, presence services are handled similarly to IM services. A watcher can subscribe to a presence service. A subscribe operation is then invoked. The format is currently being discussed and an XML representation, which is similar to the format for sending instant messages, has been used.

```
<subscribe watcher='pres:michael@example.com'
          target='pres:craig@example.com'
          transID='10'
          duration='432000'/>
```

Here, the pres prefix indicates the entities are part of the presence framework—for example, watchers or presentities. The transaction ID (transID) works as with the IM service. The transID is a unique identification to keep track of which messages the application has received a response for. The duration is in seconds, so the previous subscription would last for five days. This particular message could subscribe Michael to alerts based on the online presence of Craig. How that service works or what kind of notifications are received is purely up to the application.

The application can unsubscribe a presence service by sending an unsubscribe message. The following information would then be provided.

```
<unsubscribe watcher='pres:michael@example.com'
             target='pres:craig@example.com'
             transID='10'/>
```

It works similarly to the subscribe message and also assumes a response is returned.

Notifications

A central concept of CPIM is the use of notifications. The presence service shares the presence information with the watcher using notifications. A notification can, according to RFC2778, contain information, such as if the user is online, offline, busy, or away. In CPIM, this concept has been used and, as soon as a watcher has subscribed to a presence service, a notification is received from the presence service. It might look like this:

```
<notify watcher='pres:bill@billsdomain.com'
        target='pres:presservice@presservice.com'
        transID='10'>
  <presence entityInfo='http://www.example.com/presenceInfoAll'>
    <tuple destination='im:joe@example.com' status='open'/>
    <tuple destination='im:liza@example.com' status='closed'/>
  </presence>
</notify>
```

Note, the CPIM format is only in a draft status and is neither a recommendation nor standard yet, but the principle will probably remain. The notification contains information about the watcher that receives the notification and the target, which is the presence entity. A number of presence tuples specify the status and contact address to each entry in the presence information. Information that applies to all tuples can also be provided.

APEX

Although much of the work going on at the moment that concerns IM and presence over wireless connections is based on RFC2778 and RFC2779, other services and technologies might be used in the future.

Application Exchange (APEX) is a messaging service that can provide presence information. A core provides a basic message-transfer service. On top of the core, additional functionality, such as presence information, executes. The content consists of an XML document and additional arbitrary MIME content types.

NOTE

APEX is only a draft so far and is currently being discussed as an IETF draft. Neither a recommendation nor a standard is out yet.

The APEX Core

In APEX, messages are sent between endpoints. The endpoints that want to send and receive APEX messages must attach to the service. APEX uses a technology called the Blocks Extensible Exchange Protocol (BEEP) to deliver the messages.

To summarize, an application that sends a message to another APEX application invokes a procedure or method that sends a data message. The data message might look like this:

```
<data content='cid:message50@example.com'>
  <originator identity='joe@example.com'/>
  <recipient identity='liza@example.com'/>
</data>
...
```

There's an *originator,* or sender, and a *recipient,* which is the receiver of the message. The message itself is attached as a MIME-content type. That is where the cid comes in. The content-ID (cid) points at the actual message. This means that further down in the previous document, where the MIME content is inserted, it might look like this:

```
...
--boundary-message1
Content-ID: message50@example.com
Content-Type: plain/text
Content-Transfer-Encoding: 7bit

Hello, this is a simple message.
--boundary-message1
```

To obtain the MIME content, the value of the content attribute in the data element is stripped from the cid prefix. The MIME document that has the content ID is the actual content of the data message.

The APEX Presence Service

That was a brief, basic introduction to the heart of the APEX core. On top of this framework of XML-based data messages and MIME-content types is a presence service, which is similar to CPIM. As with the APEX core and CPIM, the presence service in APEX is a draft only and a subject for discussion. Neither a standard nor a recommendation is out yet.

Subscriptions

As with CPIM, it's possible to subscribe to presence information. The presence information is then sent to the subscriber at a certain interval, which is specified when the subscription is started.

```
<data content='#sub'>
  <originator identity='apex=presence@presence.example.com'/>
  <recipient identity='joe@example.com'/>
  <data-content name='sub'>
     <subscribe publisher='mike@example.com'
                duration='432000'
                transID='10'/>
  </data-content>
</data>
```

The syntax apex=presence is used to indicate the message should be related to a presence service. APEX is a message-relay service in general and there are other APEX services than the presence service. *Publisher* is the user publishing the presence information.

Presence Data

When the user has subscribed, the presence data is sent in a data element, which contains a presence subelement.

```
<data content='#pres'>
  <originator
identity='apex=presence@somepresencedomain.example.com'/>
  <recipient identity='joe@foobar42.example.com'/>
  <data-content name='pres'>
    <publish publisher='mike@mikesdomain.com'
```

```
            timestamp='2001-12-01T11:00-01:00'
            transID='10'>
    <presence publisher='mike@mikesdomain.example.com'
            lastUpdate='2001-12-01T10:00-01:00'
            publisherInfo='http://www.foobar42.example.com/mikeh'>
      <tuple
destination='apex:mike/appl=im@mikesdomain.example.com'
            availableUntil='2001-12-01T11:00-01:00'/>
    </presence>
  </publish>
 </data-content>
</data>
```

The presence element can contain a number of tuples, according to the model expressed in RFC2778 and is, more or less, the same concept as in CPIM. The timestamp means December 1, 2001 at 11 A.M. The sub address appl=im indicates the receiver should use this information with an IM application.

NOTE

These formats are only being discussed and remain solely drafts. The APEX presence service has much in common with CPIM and both are influenced by the terminology discussed in RFC2778 and RFC2779.

Make It SIMPLE

SIMPLE is an extension to a protocol, which is called the Session Initiation Protocol (SIP). SIMPLE means Session Initiation Protocol for IM and Presence Leveraging Extensions. Many claim it's the integration of IM, presence, and telephony, in SIMPLE, which makes it such an interesting technology.

Much of the terminology from RFC2778 and RFC2779 is used in CPIM, APEX, and SIMPLE. The details of SIMPLE require some understanding of SIP, which is beyond the scope of this book, so this is only an overview. Watchers are users that receive presence information about other users. An XML-based language to represent watcher information is being discussed for SIMPLE.

Watchers

Information about watchers is specified in XML documents, using the top-level element watcherinfo. A *watcherinfo* can contain a number of presentities, according to the fundamental terminology and concepts, described in RFC2778 and RFC2779. It might look like the following:

```
<watcherinfo>
  <presentity uri='sip:infosource@example.com'>
    <watcher uri='joe@joesdomain.example.com'
             status='pending'
             event='subscribe'>Joe
    </watcher>
    <watcher uri='carl@carlsdomain.example.com'
             status='active'
             event='approved'>
    </watcher>
  </presentity>
</watcherinfo>
```

Carl is generating notifications because he just got approved and now has active status. Joe, on the other hand, is waiting to become active because he recently subscribed. Additional attributes are being discussed, such as the possibility to address duration, when the person first subscribed, who most recently subscribed, and to which address notifications should be sent. It might look like this:

```
<watcherinfo>
  <presentity uri='sip:infosource@example.com'>
    <watcher uri='joe@joesdomain.example.com'
             status='active'
             event='approved'
             duration='3600'>Joe
    </watcher>
  </presentity>
</watcherinfo>
```

Duration is 3,600 seconds or one hour, so it took one hour to get Joe approved and moved into active status.

Note, SIMPLE is still a draft that will probably be revised several times before it becomes reasonably stable, but many of the concepts will most likely remain as they are. For example, the concept of using watchers and presentities is coming back in most technologies for IM and presence. Also, a fair chance exists that the formats will be based on XML. Many of the drafts for all the technologies in this chapter are specified in XML.

IN THIS CHAPTER:

XQuery

XQL

Other Alternatives

Databases are an essential part of wireless applications and systems. In GSM networks, there are Home Location Registers (HLRs) and Visiting Location Registers (VLRs), which store the current location of each subscriber and the services they're allowed to use. Content providers might choose to store the content in databases and generate personalized instance documents. The benefits of storing the content in a database, as opposed to an ordinary file system, is the content can be put together using smaller units or modules. This also makes it possible to store generic XML documents, which are transformed to a version and format that fits the end user's device and software. One problem is this: many databases today aren't prepared for XML-based content and they certainly aren't made for queries via XML instance documents. Some manufacturers have extensions to their original database management system, which make it possible to work with XML content. The query language used is still SQL, however. This is about to change, though, because many database manufacturers seem to adopt the new discussed technology to query databases using an XML syntax. XQuery is still a draft only, but it will probably be used in future versions of some database engines because manufacturers have expressed their support for the initiative.

XQuery

XQuery 1.0 is a working draft that uses a syntax based on XPath 1.0 (XPaths are discussed in Part 1 of this book). The XQuery language extends the syntax with the notion of a document. Queries need to target certain documents, unlike XPaths, which are usually used within a document or with respect to a single document only. A query engine, though, needs a mechanism to select between different documents and to target the query toward a specific document.

A Basic Query

Assume you have the following MMS presentation stored in a database.

```
<?xml version="1.0" encoding="UTF-8"?>
<!DOCTYPE smil PUBLIC "-//W3C//DTD SMIL 1.0//EN"
    "http://www.w3.org/TR/REC-smil/SMIL10.dtd">
<!-- ************ Filename: myPresentation.smil ************ -->
<smil xmlns="http://www.w3.org/2001/SMIL20/Language">
    <head>
        <layout>
            <root-layout width="101" height="80"/>
```

```
            <region fit="meet" id="Image" top="0" left="0" width="101"
                height="40"/>
            <region id="Text" top="40" left="0" width="101" height="40"/>
        </layout>
    </head>
    <body>
        <par dur="2s">
            <text region="Text" src="intro.txt"/>
        </par>
        <par dur="4s">
            <text region="Text" src="text.txt"/>
            <!-- Animated GIF -->
            <img region="Image" src="anim.gif"/>
        </par>
        <par dur="4s">
            <text region="Text" src="end.txt"/>
            <img region="Image" src="end.gif"/>
        </par>
    </body>
</smil>
```

If it would be stored in a database that supports the XQuery language, you could invoke the following command. It would retrieve all URLs in the src attribute of the img and text elements.

```
document("myPresentation.smil")//body//par//(img | text)/src
```

The query begins with the keyword document, followed by the filename and a path. A set of core library functions is in XQuery that can be used to perform a certain function. One of them is document, which retrieves the root of the document. A logical or expression is denoted by a vertical bar. This means the previous query will return all elements that are either img or text elements. Each // collects all elements and attributes that match in a list. The list is then carried on to the next instruction in the path sequence. More advanced queries can also be executed. In the previous example, the result was an unconditional list of URLs. You can also execute a conditional query.

Conditional Queries

Assume you have the following MMS presentation stored in an XQuery-enabled database.

```
<?xml version="1.0" encoding="UTF-8"?>
<!DOCTYPE smil PUBLIC "-//W3C//DTD SMIL 1.0//EN"
```

```
        "http://www.w3.org/TR/REC-smil/SMIL10.dtd">
<!-- ************* Filename: pres.smil ************* -->
<smil xmlns="http://www.w3.org/2001/SMIL20/Language">
    <head>
        <layout>
            <root-layout width="101" height="80"/>
            <region id="Text" top="40" left="0" width="101" height="40"/>
            <region id="Image" top="0" left="0" width="101" height="40"/>
        </layout>
    </head>
    <body>
        <par dur="1s">
            <text region="Text" src="text1.txt"/>
        </par>
        <par dur="1s">
            <text region="Text" src="text2.txt"/>
        </par>
        <par dur="1s">
            <text region="Text" src="text3.txt"/>
            <img region="Image" src="mygif.gif"/>
        </par>
    </body>
</smil>
```

We could remove all image elements in the above MMS presentation, so that only text elements remain. One way to do it would be to test if the region element has been set to "Text." It would also remove all img elements that have set the region attribute to something else than "Image."

```
FOR $m IN document("pres.smil")//body//par
RETURN
  <text-elements>
    {$m/text,
      IF ($m/@region = "Text")
      THEN $m
    }
  </text-elements>
```

The query would return something like this:

```
<text-elements>
<text region="Text" src="text1.txt"/>
<text region="Text" src="text2.txt"/>
<text region="Text" src="text3.txt"/>
</text-elements>
```

Exactly how the XQuery engine returns the result is implementation-dependent, however. It wouldn't necessarily be as a text file, which contains the text as previously formatted. It could be as a number of objects, each representing an element, or it could be as a struct in C.

For, Let, Where, Return Queries

You've already seen how the for loop and return statements work with XQuery. A similar query is the For, Let, Where, Return query (FLWR query). You can use the FLWR query if you have to set a variable in the query and you need to do more advanced testing using a where clause. Assume you have the following MMS presentation stored in a database:

```xml
<?xml version="1.0" encoding="UTF-8"?>
<!DOCTYPE smil PUBLIC "-//W3C//DTD SMIL 1.0//EN"
    "http://www.w3.org/TR/REC-smil/SMIL10.dtd">
<!-- ************ Filename: pr.smil ************ -->
<smil xmlns="http://www.w3.org/2001/SMIL20/Language">
    <head>
        <layout>
            <root-layout width="101" height="80"/>
            <region id="Text" top="40" left="0" width="101" height="40"/>
            <region id="Image" top="0" left="0" width="101" height="40"/>
        </layout>
    </head>
    <body>
        <par dur="2s">
            <text region="Text" src="text1.txt"/>
        </par>
        <par dur="2s">
            <text region="Text" src="text2.txt"/>
        </par>
        <par dur="3s">
            <text region="Text" src="text3.txt"/>
        </par>
        <par dur="3s">
            <text region="Text" src="text4.txt"/>
        </par>
        <par dur="1s">
            <text region="Text" src="text5.txt"/>
            <img region="Image" src="mygif.gif"/>
        </par>
    </body>
</smil>
```

You could retrieve all media objects that have the longest duration, which would be two objects that last for three seconds. Then the following query would be submitted to the XQuery database management system.

```
LET $d := max(document("pr.smil")//body/par/@dur)
FOR $m IN document("myPresentation.smil")//body/par
WHERE $m/@dur = $d
RETURN
  <max-durations>
    {$m}
  </text-durations>
```

The LET clause computes the maximum value for all dur attributes. That's 3s because an alphabetic comparison will be carried out. The for-while statement compares all media objects with the maximum value and returns all that match.

XQL

XQL is yet another query language, which is based on XML. Some of the concepts from XQL were used when XQuery was defined. Which technology, if any, will become a standard and which will become the most widely adopted remains to be seen, though. XQL is only a proposed standard and isn't a W3C recommendation. Assume you have stored the following XHTML Basic document in an XQL-enabled database.

```
<?xml version="1.0" encoding="UTF-8"?>
<!DOCTYPE html PUBLIC "-//W3C//DTD XHTML Basic 1.0//EN"
    "http://www.w3.org/TR/xhtml-basic/xhtml-basic10.dtd">
<html xmlns="http://www.w3.org/1999/xhtml">
<head>
  <title>High score list</title>
</head>
<body>
    <table>
      <tr><td>Name</td><td>Score</td>
      </tr>
      <tr><td>Liza Stone</td><td>24</td>
      </tr>
      <tr><td>Ben Smith</td><td>22</td>
      </tr>
      <tr><td>Joe Lewis</td><td>19</td>
```

```
      </tr>
      <tr><td>Anne Dudley</td><td>12</td>
      </tr>
    </table>
</body>
</html>
```

The following query could then be executed to retrieve all names and results.

```
//td
```

The database management system would then return a list of all td elements.
It could look like this:

```
<td>Name</td>
<td>Score</td>
<td>Liza Stone</td>
<td>24</td>
<td>Ben Smith</td>
<td>22</td>
<td>Joe Lewis</td>
<td>19</td>
<td>Anne Dudley</td>
<td>12</td>
```

The // searches for occurrences of the td element everywhere in the document. If
you want to search through a document depending on the setting of particular attributes,
the square bracket syntax could be used. For example, assume you stored the following
document in the database:

```
<?xml version="1.0" encoding="UTF-8"?>
<!DOCTYPE smil PUBLIC "-//W3C//DTD SMIL 1.0//EN"
    "http://www.w3.org/TR/REC-smil/SMIL10.dtd">
<!-- ************* Filename: pr.smil ************* -->
<smil xmlns="http://www.w3.org/2001/SMIL20/Language">
    <head>
        <layout>
            <root-layout width="101" height="80"/>
            <region id="Text" top="0" left="0" width="101" height="80"/>
        </layout>
    </head>
    <body>
        <par dur="1s">
```

```
            <text region="Text" src="text1.txt"/>
        </par>
        <par dur="2s">
            <text region="Text" src="text2.txt"/>
        </par>
        <par dur="3s">
            <text region="Text" src="text3.txt"/>
        </par>
        <par dur="3s">
            <text region="Text" src="text4.txt"/>
        </par>
        <par dur="4s">
            <text region="Text" src="text5.txt"/>
        </par>
    </body>
</smil>
```

All text elements that have the duration attribute set to one, two, or three seconds could be retrieved using the following query:

```
//par[@dur='1s' or @dur='2s' or @dur='3s']//text
```

The // matches par elements everywhere in the instance document but, in this case, the search is restricted to par elements that have set the dur attribute to 1s, 2s, or 3s. All text elements in these elements are returned.

Other Alternatives

Other alternatives exist to the previously mentioned query languages. In fact, today you'll probably have to use other technologies because the previous query languages haven't been used much. (They've mostly been used in prototype implementations.) Database manufacturers, however, are working on extensive XML support and it remains to be seen if they'll replace, for example, the rather aged SQL with something else. Oracle9i Application Server Wireless has support for XML. IBM has the XML extender, which can be combined with its DB2 database to obtain XML support, and Microsoft is working on XML support in coming releases of its SQL Server platform.

Index

Symbols and Numbers

(?) symbol, 63, 65
(..) symbol, 88
@ symbol, 88
(//) symbol, 88
$ characters, 281-282, 286
> (greater than) symbol, 478
(*) symbol, 63, 65
(*) wildcard, 88
(|) symbol, 65
(+) symbol, 63, 65
2.5G, 21-22
2G (second generation), 21
32 bit addresses, 26
3G, 22-25
    MMS and, 366
    services, 24
    specification organizations, 22-23
    systems, 23-24
    XML and, 24-25
3G Partnership Project (3GPP), 23, 488
4G, 25-26
802.11b (Wireless LANs), 25-26

A

a (anchored links) element, 141, 239-241
A (arc) command, SVG, 168
abstract classes, 398-399
Abstract Specification, OGC, 151
access element, POIX, 473
access keys, WML 2.0, 284-286
accesskey attribute, 143
ACL (Asynchronous Connection-Less)
    links, 44
Active mode, Bluetooth, 45
Adaptive MultiRate Audio (AMR), 388
add command, SyncML, 200-202
addPBEntry, WML 2.0, 310
addressing
    instant messaging and, 6
    IP, 37-38
Advanced Mobile Phone System (AMPS), 21
align attribute, XHTML, 245
alt attribute, WML 2.0, 281-282
alternative text, WML images, 282-283
ampersand @ symbol, 88
AMPS (Advanced Mobile Phone System), 21
AMR (Adaptive MultiRate Audio), 388
anchored links (a) element, 141, 239-241
animated text, 381-384
    sentence by sentence, 381-382
    word by word, 382-384
animation module
    SMIL 2.0, 145-146
    SMIL 2.0 Basic, 147
APEX (Application Exchange), 493-495
    core functions, 493-494
    presence service, 494-495
applets, XHTML, 109-110, 227
Application Exchange. *See* APEX (Application
    Exchange)
application protocols, 27-33
    i-mode, 28
    SyncML, 30-33
    WAP-NG (WAP Next Generation), 28-30

applications, 4-16
    connected all the time, 4
    environments required by, 14-15
    instant messaging and presence
      applications, 4-7
    location-based applications, 11-12
    personalization applications, 7-11
    synchronization applications, 12-14
arc command (A), SVG, 168
aspect ratios
    nonpreserved, 374-375
    preserved, 371-374
    SVG, 166-167
asterisk (*) symbol, 63, 65
asterisk (*) wildcard, 88
Asynchronous Connection-Less (ACL)
  links, 44
attributes
    changing values of, 293
    declaring, 76-77
    HTML to XHTML conversion, 224-225
    object oriented modeling and, 397-398
    specifying in WBXML, 177-178
    XML documents and, 51-52, 67-68
audio, 388-393
    embedding, 389-390
    iMelody, 390-393
    SMIL 2.0, 136-137
    streaming audio, 44
    two-way audio, 42
    VoiceXML, 129-131
authentication, 6

B

Bachus-Naur Form (BNF)
    converting to DTDs, 56-59
    writing grammars with, 52-54
background color, screen types and, 375-377
backward navigation, WML 2.0, 302-306
base module, XHTML, 120-121
basic forms module, XHTML, 111-113

basic tables module, XHTML, 113-116
Batik
    displaying SVG code on Java devices,
      396
    features of, 431-432
    as SVG viewer, 431
    tools, 432
bdo element, XHTML, 110
BEEP (Blocks Extensible Exchange
  Protocol), 493
begin attribute, slide shows, 377-378
BeVocal Cafe, 125
Bézier curves, 168
bidirectional text module, XHTML, 110-111
billing, mobile commerce, 443-446
Binary XML. *See* WBXML (Wireless Binary
  XML)
bitmaps, wireless, 284
blinking text, cHTML to XHTML Basic
  conversion, 247
block elements, CSS, 93-95
Blocks Extensible Exchange Protocol
  (BEEP), 493
Bluetooth, 42-46
    features of, 43-46
    overview of, 42-43
    synchronization support, 13
BNF (Bachus-Naur Form)
    converting to DTDs, 56-59
    writing grammars with, 52-54
body element, HTML, 273-274
bold face fonts
    WML 2.0, 276
    XHTML Basic, 260-262
bounds, GML, 153

C

call control, IrMC, 41-42
CallXML, 131
capability objects, OBEX, 39-40

Capacity/Preference Profile (CC/PP), 186, 189-190

cards, WML. *See* deck of cards approach, WML

cascading style sheets. *See* CSS (cascading style sheets)

categories property, vCalendars, 484

CC/PP (Capacity/Preference Profile), 186, 189-190

CDMA (Code Division Multiple Access), 21-23

cell planning, network topologies, 18-19

center element, XHTML, 245-246

character encoding, XML, 54-55

character set, WBXML, 175-176

chat functionality, 6-7

cHTML (compact HTML), 28, 234-235

cHTML to XHTML Basic conversion, 235-248
    anchored links, 239-241
    blinking text, 247
    center element, 245-246
    dir element, 239
    emphasis and strong text elements, 245
    external style sheets and links, 246
    font colors, 246-247
    horizontal rulers, 248-249
    input style, 237-238
    marquee elements, 241-242
    menus, 238-239
    picture symbols, 242-243
    plaintext element, 243-245
    tables, 235-237

circuit-switched data (CSD), 19-20

classes, object oriented modeling, 397

CLDC (Connected Limited Device Configuration), 227

client-centric solutions, 11-12

client-server architecture, SyncML, 196

closed tags, XHTML, 105-106

Code Division Multiple Access (CDMA), 21-23

collection objects, GML, 401

colors
    background color, 375-377
    font colors, 246-247

RGB values, 98-99, 167, 423

XHTML applications and, 228-229

columns, wml:columns attribute, 281

command groups, SyncML, 203-204

common profile for IM. *See* CPIM (common profile for IM)

communication, low-level, 206-214
    data types, 210-213
    distributed wireless systems, 206-207
    XML-RPC, 208-210

communication protocols, 27

compact HTML (cHTML), 28, 234-235

complex types, schemas, 73-74

Connected Limited Device Configuration (CLDC), 227

consumers, mobile commerce, 438, 453-455

content
    CPIM, 489-490
    multimedia applications, 367
    SMIL, 146, 368
    WBXML, 178
    XHTML Basic, 234-235
    XML, 49-50

conversions. *See* cHTML to XHTML Basic conversion; HTML to XHTML conversion

coord element, GML, 423

CPIM (common profile for IM), 489-492
    content, 489-490
    header, 489-490
    instant inboxes, 490-491
    notifications, 492
    presentities, 491-492

credit card details, ECML, 449-451

CSD (circuit-switched data), 19-20

CSS (cascading style sheets), 92-100. *See also* WCSS (wireless cascading style sheets)
    block and inline elements, 93-95
    CCS Moble Profile 1.0 and, 476
    color specification, 98-99
    font properties, 95-96, 95-96
    matching to XML documents, 99-100
    overview of, 92-93
    space management, 96-97
    units of measurement, 97-98

CSS Moble Profile 1.0, 476-480
    adding style, 476
    properties, 479-480
    selectors, 476-479

D

D-AMPS (Digital-AMPS), 21
d attribute, SVG, 168
data, synchronized, 13
data types, procedure calls and, 210-213
databases
    other choices, 504
    overview of, 498
    XQL, 502-504
    XQuery, 498-502
date representation, personalizing, 10
datum element, POIX, 468
DB2 database, XML extender for, 504
deck of cards approach, WML
    compared with HTML body, 273-275
    jumping back to previous card, 302-303
    jumping from card to deck, 298-299
Dedicated Inquiry Access Codes (DIACs), 44
del element, XHTML, 111
delete command, SyncML, 202-203
description property, vCalendars, 485
desktop computer site. *See* XHTML Basic,
  sample site
development tools, multimedia applications,
  366-367
development tools, XHTML, 264-269
    HTML-Kit, 267-268
    Nokia Mobile Internet Toolkit, 268-269
    XML Spy, 264-266
device information, SyncML, 13, 32-33, 196
device properties, RDF, 186-187
device simulation, Nokia Mobile Internet
  Toolkit, 269
DIACs (Dedicated Inquiry Access Codes), 44
Dialogs library, WML 2.0, 321

Digital AMPS (D-AMPS), 21
digital signatures, mobile commerce, 434-437
dir element, cHTML to XHTML Basic
  conversion, 239
displays. *See* screens
DOCTYPE declarations, 55
    SMIL 2.0, 135
    SMIL 2.0 Basic, 147
    XHTML, 218
    XHTML Basic, 240
documents. *See also* SMIL documents; XML
  documents
    multimedia, 367-368
    NVML, 461-462
    VoiceXML, 125
    WBXML, document body, 177-181
    WBXML, starting elements, 173-176
dollar sign ($) characters, 281-282, 286
dots (..) symbol, 88
drawing board, SVG, 165-167
DTDs
    converting from BNF to, 56-59
    element declarations, 62-67
    rewriting as schemas, 77-80
    schemas as alternative to, 72
    SyncML and, 197-198
    writing, 59-60
    XHTML and, 104-105
DTMF tones, 124, 328
dur element, SMIL, 370, 377

E

ECML (Electronic Commerce Modeling
  Language), 438-455
    billing, 443-446
    credit card details, 449-451
    merchant URLs, 452-453
    overview of, 438-439
    receipts, 446-449

shipping content to mobile phone
numbers, 441-443
shipping fields, 439-441
transactions, 453-455
edit module, XHTML, 110-111
Electronic Commerce Modeling Language.
See ECML (Electronic Commerce
Modeling Language)
ELEMENT keyword, 62-63
elements
GML, 161-162
HTML to XHTML conversion, discarded
elements, 222
HTML to XHTML conversion, element
context, 222-224
WML 2.0, 323
XML, 50-51, 62-67
em element, XHTML, 245
embedded objects module, XHTML, 117-118
embedding audio, multimedia applications,
389-390
emphasis, WML 2.0 formats, 276
empty elements, XML, 51
EMS (Enhanced Messaging Service), 5, 390
encoding attribute, XML, 54
encryption
instant messaging and, 6
mobile commerce and, 434
Enhanced Messaging Service (EMS), 5, 390
entity declarations, XML validation, 68-70
entry helpers, XML Spy, 266
EPOC operating system, 14
extended links, XLink, 82-86
extension element, GML, 162
extensions, GML types, 162-164
external style sheets and links, 246

F

features types, GML, 158, 397
file uploads, XHTML, 227

fill attribute, SVG, 167
first generation mobile telephony, 21
Float library, WML 2.0, 318
flow control, IPv6, 26
FLWR (For, Let, Where, Return) query,
XQuery, 501-502
folder listings, OBEX, 40-41
fonts
colors, cHTML to XHTML Basic
conversion, 246-247
personalizing, 7-8
properties, CSS, 95-96
SVG, 168-169
XHTML Basic, 260-262
For, Let, Where, Return (FLWR) query,
XQuery, 501-502
Formal Public Identifier (FPI), 174-175
format element, POIX, 467
formats
input text and, 290
multimedia, 367
POIX, 467
synchronization and, 13
WML 2.0, 276-278
WML 2.0, boldface, italics, strong, and
emphasis, 276
WML 2.0, marking up with WCSS,
276-278
WML 2.0, text sizes, 276
forms
VoiceXML, 126-127
XHTML, 111-113
forward navigation, WML 2.0, 297-301,
304-305
forward slashes (//) symbol, 88
FPI (Formal Public Identifier), 174-175
frames, XHTML, 118-119, 225-226
frameset XHTML, 105
functions, WMLScripts, 311-314
calling, 312-314
local variables and, 312

G

game implementation, XHTML Basic/i-mode
site, 251-256
    server-side scripts, 252-254
    transformations, 254-256
General Inquiry Access Code (GIAC), 44
General Packet Radio Service (GPRS), 20, 22
generations, mobile telephony
    2.5G, 21-22
    2G, 21
    3G, 22-25
    3G, MMS and, 366
    3G, services, 24
    3G, specification organizations, 22-23
    3G, systems, 23-24
    3G, XML and, 24-25
    4G, 25-26
    first, 21
geometric elements. *See* GML (Geography
    Markup Language); SVG (Scalable Vector
    Graphics)
GET operations, OBEX, 39
GET request, HTTP, 34
getHost, WML 2.0, 316-317
getPath, WML 2.0, 317
getQuery, WML 2.0, 317
getScheme, WML 2.0, 316-317
getvar element, WML 2.0, 287
GIAC (General Inquiry Access Code), 44
GIF files
    i-mode graphics support and, 28
    pictures and, 385
    SMIL presentations and, 136
    XML documents and, 49
Global System for Mobile Communications
    (GSM), 21
GML (Geography Markup Language),
    150-164. *See also* real world models
    (combining SVG with GML)
    bounds specification, 153
    code, sample lines, 155

    compared with SVG, 150
    inner boundaries, 156-157
    objects in, 151-153
    objects, listing, 154
    points, 157
    polygons and outer boundaries, 155-166
    spatial reference systems, 154
    transforming into SVG, 164, 396
GML maps, 169-170
GML schemas
    declarations and import statements,
      160-161
    elements, 161-162
    extensions to GML types, 162-164
    features types in, 158
    inheritance and, 158
    sample, complete listing of, 158-160
gml:_FeatureCollection, 407
gml:AbstractFeatureType, 406
gml:boundedBy element, 153
gml:Box element, 423
gml:LineString elements, 155
gml:polygon, 161
GPRS (General Packet Radio Service), 20, 22
grammars, 52-54
    converting BNF to DTD, 56-59
    JSGF and, 127
    notation for, 52
    VXML documents and, 125
    writing with BNF, 52-54
graphical editing, XML Spy, 265-266
graphics, 384-388
    combining text with, 387
    i-mode support for, 28
    personalizing, 8
    pictures, 385-386
    sequences, 386-387
    SMIL 2.0, 136
    WML 2.0, 283-284
greater than (>) symbol, 478
GSM (Global System for Mobile
    Communications), 21
guides, NVML, 461, 464-466

H

H.323, 25
handheld devices
    colors and, 228-229
    file uploads and, 227
    limitations of, 4
    MIDlets and, 227
    plug-ins and, 227-228
    specifying properties with RDF, 186-187
handover, cells and, 19
handset support, MMS, 366
hardware, specifying properties with RDF, 186
head element, NVML, 463
headers
    CPIM, 489-490
    WML 1.x, 324-325
Hey Anita!, 125
High-Speed Circuit-Switched Data
    (HSCSD), 20
HLRs (Home Location Registers), 498
Hold mode, Bluetooth, 45
Home Location Registers (HLRs), 498
horizontal rulers
    cHTML to XHTML Basic conversion,
        248-249
    XHTML Basic, 259-260
hr element, XHTML Basic, 249
HSCSD (High-Speed Circuit-Switched
    Data), 20
HTML 4, 30, 104, 218
HTML body, 273-275
HTML-Kit, 267-268, 366
HTML platform compatibility, 16
HTML to XHTML conversion
    attribute values, 224-225
    discarded elements, 222
    element context, 222-224
    HTML-Kit and, 267-268
    p element, 220-222
    slash, 219-220
HTTP (Hypertext Transfer Protocol), 33-36
    HTTP requests, 34-35
    HTTP responses, 35-36
    overview of, 33-34
hypertext module, XHTML, 108-109

I

i-mode. *See also* XHTML Basic/i-mode,
    sample site
    features of, 28
    graphics capabilities of, 8
    instant messaging and, 5
i-mode HTML conversion to XHTML Basic.
    See cHTML to XHTML Basic conversion
i-mode phones
    display size of, 7
    fonts, 8
IETF (Internet Engineering Task Force), 488
iframes module, XHTML, 118-119
IM (instant messaging). *See* instant messaging
    (IM)
image maps module, XHTML, 117-118
image regions, SMIL, 368-371
images, WML 2.0, 282-284
    alternative text, 282-283
    pictograms, 283-284
    wireless bitmaps, 284
iMelody, 390-393
    effects, 392-393
    loops, 391-392
    overview of, 390-391
img element
    SMIL 2.0, 136
    XHTML, 117, 118
import statements, GML, 160-161
IMT-2000 (International Mobile
    Telecommunications-2000), 22-23
info element, NVML, 464
Infrared Data Association (IrDA)
    components of, 38
    synchronization support, 14

Infrared Mobile Communications. *See* IrMC
    (Infrared Mobile Communications)
inheritance
        font properties, 95
        GML real world model, 423
        GML schemas, 158
        object oriented modeling and, 398
inline elements, CSS, 93-95
inner boundaries, GML, 156-157
input devices, personalizing, 8-9
input style, cHTML to XHTML Basic
    conversion, 237-238
input text, WML, 287-290
        formats and, 290
        passwords and, 289
ins element, XHTML, 111
instance document, GML, 407-423
instant inboxes, 489, 490-491
instant messaging (IM), 488-496
        APEX, 493-495
        APEX, core, 493-494
        APEX, presence service, 494-495
        applications, 4-7
        CPIM, content, 489-490
        CPIM, header, 489-490
        CPIM, instant inboxes, 490-491
        CPIM, notifications, 492
        CPIM, presentities, 491-492
        RFC2778 and RFC2779, 488-489
        SIMPLE, 495-496
interfaces, 27
International Mobile Equipment Identity
    (IMEI), 200
International Mobile
    Telecommunications-2000 (IMT-2000),
    22-23
Internet Engineering Task Force (IETF), 488
Internet Explorer, version for wireless
    devices, 14
Internet Protocol. *See* IP (Internet Protocol)
intrinsic events module, XHTML, 119-120
IP (Internet Protocol), 37-38
        addressing, 37-38
        packets, 38
        version 6 (IPv6), 26

ipoint, POIX, 473
IPv6, 26
IrDA (Infrared Data Association)
        components of, 38
        synchronization support, 14
IrLAP, 38
IrLMP, 38
IrMC (Infrared Mobile Communications),
    41-42
        call control, 41-42
        real time clock in, 42
        two-way audio, 42
isFloat function, Lang Library, 319
isInt function, Lang Library, 319
istyle, i-mode input style, 237-238
italics
        WML 2.0, 276
        XHTML Basic, 260-262

J

Java 2 Micro Edition (J2ME)
        MIDlets and, 227
        Web site information, 15
        wireless applications and, 14
Java 2 Microedition Wireless Toolkit, 16
Java 2 Standard Edition (J2SE), 227
Java Speech API Grammar Format
    (JSGF), 127
JPEG files
        i-mode, 28
        SMIL, 136
        XML, 49
JSGF (Java Speech API Grammar
    Format), 127
jumps, WML 2.0
        backward, 302-304
        detecting, 304-306
        forward, 297-301
        setting variables, 301-302

K

keywords, ECML, 440

L

label attribute, optgroup element, 296
Lang library, WML 2.0, 318-320
language settings, personalizing, 10
LANs, Wireless (802.11b), 25-26
LAP (Link Access Protocol), 38
lat element, POIX, 468
layout modules, SMIL 2.0, 146
legacy construct module, XHTML, 121-122
LIF (Location Interoperability Forum), 12
linear rings, 156, 423
Link Access Protocol (LAP), 38
Link Management Protocol (LMP), 38
links. *See also* XLink (XML Linking
    Language)
        Bluetooth connections over, 44-45
        cHTML to XHTML Basic
            conversion, 246
        SMIL 2.0, 141-143, 146
        WML 2.0, linking to a card, 278-279
        WML 2.0, linking to a deck, 279-280
        XHTML, 120-121
Linux, Mobile, 14-15
list module, XHTML, 108-109
LMP (Link Management Protocol), 38
location-based applications. *See also* GML
    (Geography Markup Language); NVML
    (Navigation Markup Language); SVG
    (Scalable Vector Graphics)
        GML and SVG and, 150
        instant messaging and, 5
        overview of, 11-12
Location Interoperability Forum (LIF), 12
locators, XLinks, 82
LocURI element, SyncML, 200
lon element, POIX, 468
low-level communication. *See* communication,
    low-level

M

maps
        GML, 169-170
        image maps module, XHTML, 117-118
        real world models (combining SVG with
            GML), 399-401
margin-bottom property, 97
margin-left property, 97
margin-right property, 97
margin-top property, 97
markers, GML, 157
markup, i-mode, 28
marquee elements, cHTML to XHTML Basic
    conversion, 241-242
marshalling, 207
max function, Lang Library, 320
maxOccurs attribute, schemas, 74-75
media object modules, SMIL 2.0, 146
memory capabilities, personalizing, 9
menus
        cHTML to XHTML Basic conversion,
            238-239
        VoiceXML, 128-129
merchants, mobile commerce
        ECML and, 438
        transactions and, 453-455
        URLs for, 452-453
message length, personalizing, 9-10
metaelement, XHTML, 119
metainformation
        NVML, 461
        SMIL 2.0, 146
        SMIL 2.0 Basic, 147
        XHTML, 119-120
methodCall element, XML-RPC, 208
Microsoft Windows, version for wireless
    devices, 14
MIDlets
        J2ME, 14
        platform compatibility of, 16
        XHTML, 227
MIDP (Mobile Information Device
    Profile), 227

MIME (Multipurpose Mail Extensions) types
    CPIM, 490
    SyncML, 13
    WBXML, 172
min function, Lang Library, 320
minOccurs attribute, schemas, 74-75
MMS (Multimedia Messaging Service). *See also* multimedia applications
    3G services and, 24
    compared with SMS, 378
    features of, 29
    handset support for, 366
    image and text regions, 368
    instant messaging and, 5
    shipping content to mobile phone numbers, 441
    SMIL 2.0 and, 134
MMS Proxy-Relay service, 368
Mobile Application Development Kits, Motorola, 125
mobile commerce, 434. *See also* ECML (Electronic Commerce Modeling Language)
Mobile Information Device Profile (MIDP), 227
Mobile Information Standard Technical Committee (MOSTEC), 466
Mobile Linux, 14-15
mobility
    POIX, 469-471
    wireless systems and, 19
modeling tools, object-oriented, 396-399
    abstract classes, 398-399
    attributes and properties, 397-398
    classes, 397
    inheritance, 398
    objects, 397
    relations, 398
models, object oriented, 399
modules
    SMIL 2.0, 145-147
    SMIL 2.0 Basic, 147-148
    XHTML Basic, 107-108

modules, XHTML
    applets and scripts, 109-110
    forms and basic forms, 111-113
    frames, iframes, and targets, 118-119
    image maps and embedded objects, 117-118
    intrinsic events and metainformation, 119-120
    link and base, 120-121
    name identification and legacy constructs, 121-122
    presentation, edit, and bidirectional text, 110-111
    structure, texts, hypertext, and lists, 108-109
    style sheet and style attributes, 120
    tables and basic tables, 113-116
Morphis WAX, 172, 183-184. *See also* WAX (Wireless Abstract XML)
MOSTEC (Mobile Information Standard Technical Committee), 466
Motorola
    Mobile Application Development Kits, 125
    VoxML, 131
move element, POIX, 469
multicast packets, 38
multimedia applications
    animated text, 381-384
    background color, 375-377
    combining text and graphics, 387
    development tools for, 366-367
    document submission, 367-368
    embedding audio, 389-390
    formats and content types, 367
    image and text regions, 368-371
    iMelody, 390-393
    optimizing and adjusting, 388
    pictures, 385-386
    scaling screens with nonpreserved aspect ratio, 374-375

scaling screens with preserved aspect ratio, 371-374
sequences, 386-387
slide shows, 377-378
static text, 379-381
Multimedia Messaging Service. *See* MMS (Multimedia Messaging Service)
multimedia presentations, SMIL 2.0
combining sequential and parallel presentations, 139-141
overlaps and, 138-139
parallel presentations, 138-139
sequential presentations, 137-138
structure of, 135
multimedia synchronization. *See* SMIL (Synchronized Multimedia Integration Language)
Multipurpose Mail Extensions (MIME) types. *See* MIME (Multipurpose Mail Extensions) types

N

name identification module, XHTML, 121-122
namespaces
WML 1.x, 324-325
XML, 71-72
naming conventions, instant messaging, 6
Napa, XSLT processors, 100
nav element, NVML, 461
navigation. *See also* NVML (Navigation Markup Language)
relations and, 398
voice portals and, 331
WML 2.0, 284-286
XHTML Basic, custom, 230-234
XHTML Basic, shared, 234-235
Navigation Markup Language. *See* NVML (Navigation Markup Language)
network elements, Bluetooth, 43

network protocols, 33-46
Bluetooth, 42-46
HTTP, 33-36
IP, 37-38
IrDA, 38
IrMC, 41-42
OBEX, 38-41
WSP, 37
network topologies, 18-20
cells, 18-19
handover, 19
wireless systems and mobility and, 19
news page, XHTML Basic/i-mode site, 256-259
news services, voice portals and, 330
NMT (Nordic Mobile Telephony System), 21
Nokia Mobile Internet Toolkit, 268-269
nonpreserved aspect ratio, 374-375
Nordic Mobile Telephony System (NMT), 21
notifications, CPIM, 492
nvml element, NVML, 462
NVML (Navigation Markup Language), 460-466
document structure, 461-462
guides, 464-466
overview of, 460-461
routes, 462-464

O

OBEX (Object Exchange), 38-41
capability objects, 39-40
folder listings, 40-41
transfers, 39
object orientation, 396-399
GML, 158, 396
modeling tools, 396-399
models, 399
objects
GML, 151-154

modeling and, 397
XHTML, 117
OGC, 150-151
one-way updates, synchronization, 13
onpick attribute, WML 2.0, 300-301
OpenGIS, 150-151
Opera software
Web site information, 15
wireless applications and, 14
optgroup element, WML 2.0, 296
optimization, XML applications. *See* WBXML
(Wireless Binary XML)
Oracle9i, 504
organizations, 3G specifications, 22-23
outer boundaries, GML, 155-166

P

p element. *See* paragraph element (p)
packet-switched networks
compared with circuit-switched data, 20
connected all the time, 4
packets, IP, 38
Palm devices, memory capabilities, 9
Palm OS
platform compatibility of, 16
Web site information, 15
wireless applications and, 15
par element, SMIL 2.0, 138, 139-141
paragraph element (p)
HTML to XHTML conversion, 220-222
selectors and, 478
WML 2.0, 276
XML, 50
parallel presentations, SMIL 2.0, 138-141
param element, XHTML, 117
parameterized code, WML 2.0, 287
Parked mode, Bluetooth, 45
parseFloat function, Lang Library, 319
parseInt function, Lang Library, 319
passwords, input text and, 289

path element, SVG, 167-168
paths, XML. *See* XPath
PDAs
display size of, 7
input devices for, 8-9
support for Java by, 396
virtual menus on, 4
PDC-P (Personal Digital Communications
Packet), 20, 22
Personal Information Management (PIM)
data, 29-30
personalization applications, 7-11
display size, 7
fonts, 7-8
graphics capabilities, 8
input devices, 8-9
memory capabilities, 9
message length, 9-10
region and language settings, 10
standby time, 10-11
time and date representation, 10
personalization technologies, 476-485
CCS Moble Profile 1.0, 476-480
vCalendars, 483-485
vCards, 480-483
phone functionality, WML 2.0, 309-310
dialing numbers, 309
managing phone book, 310
Phone Markup Language (PML), 131
picas, CSS, 97
piconets, Bluetooth, 43
pictograms, WML, 283-284
pictures
cHTML to XHTML Basic conversion,
242-243
graphics animation and, 385-386
PIM (Personal Information Management)
data, 29-30
pipes (l) symbol, 65
plain text formats, vCards and vCalendars, 480
plaintext element, XHTML, 244
plug-ins
HTML-Kit and, 268
XHTML applications and, 227-228

plus (+) symbol, 63, 65
PML (Phone Markup Language), 131
Pocket PC
    application platforms on, 14
    memory capabilities of, 9
    support for Java by, 396
    Web site information, 15
poi element, POIX, 468
point element, POIX, 468
Point Of Interest eXchange. *See* POIX (Point
    Of Interest eXchange)
point of interest, POIX
    extending, 471-474
    position of, 468
point sizes, CSS, 97
points
    GML, 157
    POIX, 466
POIX (Point Of Interest eXchange), 466-474
    extending point of interest, 471-474
    formats, 467
    mobility, 469-471
    overview of, 466-467
    position (point of interest), 468
polygons, GML, 155-166
portals, i-mode, 28
position (point of interest), POIX, 468
postfield element, WML 2.0, 291-293
prefetch element, SMIL 2.0, 143-144
presence applications. *See also* APEX
    (Application Exchange); instant messaging
    (IM)
        instant messaging and, 5, 488
        presence data, 494-495
        presence polling, 5
        watchers and, 489
presentation module, XHTML, 110-111
presentities, 489, 491-492
preserveAspectRatio attribute, SVG, 166-167
preserved aspect ratio, 371-374
procedure calls
    data types and, 210-213
    XML-RPC and, 207

profiles, 186-193
    applying, 193
    CC/PP, 189-190
    RDF, 186-188
    UAProf, 190-193
prompt function, Dialogs library, 321
properties
    CCS Moble Profile 1.0, 479-480
    GML, 397-398
    RDF, 186-187
protocol stacks, 27
protocols. *See* application protocols; network
    protocols
proximity. *See* NVML (Navigation Markup
    Language); POIX (Point Of Interest
    eXchange)
PUBLIC declaration, XML, 55
PUT operations, OBEX, 39

Q

Quartz applications, compatibility of, 16
queries, WML 2.0, 317
queries, XQuery
    basic, 498-499
    conditional, 499-501
    FLWR, 501-502
question mark (?) symbol, 63, 65

R

Radio Access Networks (RANs), 23
radio, short range, 42-43
random numbers, Lang Library, 318-319
RANs (Radio Access Networks), 23
RDF (Resource Description Framework)
    device properties, 186-187
    documents, 187-188
    vCards and vCalendars and, 485

real time clock, IrMC, 42
Real-time Transfer Control Protocol
     (RTCON), 42
real world models (combining SVG with
     GML)
          GML representation, complete schema
               listing, 402-407
          GML representation, instance document,
               407-423
          GML representation, schema types, 402
          implementation of map, 399-401
          tools for, 396-399
          transformation to SVG, 423-430
RealONE Player, 366
receipts, mobile commerce, 446-449
rect element, SVG, 167
regional settings, personalizing, 10
relations, object oriented modeling and, 398
remote procedure call (RPC), 206
representation independence, 69
#REQUIRED attributes, 66
Resource Description Framework. *See* RDF
     (Resource Description Framework)
resources
          RDF specification, 186-187
          XLinks and, 82
RFC2778 and RFC2779, 488-489
RFCs (Request for Comments), 488
RGB values
          color specification, 98-99
          real world model and, 423
          SVG fill attribute and, 167
RIFF format, VoiceXML, 129
role attribute, wml:do element, 297-298
roles, WML 1.x, 325
round function, Float library, 318
routes, NVML, 461, 462-464
RPC (remote procedure call), 206
RTCON (Real-time Transfer Control
     Protocol), 42

S

Saxon, XSLT processors, 100
scatternets, Bluetooth, 43
schemas, 72-80
          as alternative to DTDs, 72
          attributes, 76-77
          complex types, 73-74
          declarations, GML, 160-161
          minOccurs and maxOccurs attributes,
               74-75
          rewriting DTDs as, 77-80
          sequences, 75-76
          simple types, 73
          structure of, 72
schemes, URLs, 316
SCO (Synchronous Connection-Oriented)
     links, 44
screens, 371-377
          background color, 375-377
          personalizing size of, 7
          scaling with nonpreserved aspect ratio,
               374-375
          scaling with preserved aspect ratio,
               277-280
          SMIL documents and, 368
          XHTML applications and, 228-229
scripts
          adding dynamics to web pages, 218
          server-side, 252-254, 291-293
          XHTML, 109-110
scripts, WML 2.0, 310-324
          Dialogs library, 321
          Float library, 318
          functions, calling, 312-314
          functions, local variables, 312
          Lang library, 318-320
          overview, 310-311
          standard libraries, 314-315
          String library, 321-323
          URL library, 315-317

WMLBrowser library, 323-324
WMLScript library, 434-437
Secure Sockets Layer (SSL), 434
security
        instant messaging and, 6
        mobile commerce and, 434
select element, WML 2.0, 294
selection lists, WML 2.0, 294-296
        grouping options, 296
        multiple choices, 295
        single choice, 294
selectors, CCS Moble Profile 1.0, 476-479
        child, 478
        universal, 477
seq element, SMIL 2.0, 137, 139-141
sequences
        of elements, 75-76
        graphics animation and, 386-387
sequential presentations
        combining with parallel presentations,
            139-141
        SMIL 2.0, 137-138
server-centric solutions, 12
server-side scripts, 252-254, 291-293
Session Initiation Protocol for IM and Presence
    Leveraging Extensions (SIMPLE), 495-496
Session Initiation Protocol (SIP), 495
setvar element, WML 2.0, 287-288
shapes, SVG, 167
SHIFT-JIS character codes, 242
shipping, mobile commerce
        fields, 439-441
        shipping content to mobile phone
            numbers, 441-443
Short Message Service. *See* SMS (Short
    Message Service)
sightseeing application, NVML guides,
    464-465
simple links, XLink, 81-82
SIMPLE (Session Initiation Protocol for IM
    and Presence Leveraging Extensions),
    495-496
simple text string, 73, 78-79
simple types, schemas, 73

SIP (Session Initiation Protocol), 495
slash, HTML to XHTML conversion, 219-220
slide shows, 377-378
small device site. *See* XHTML Basic,
    sample site
SMIL documents
        development tools for, 366
        image and text regions, 368-371
        submission of, 367-368
        text formats and content types, 367
SMIL (Synchronized Multimedia Integration
    Language). *See also* multimedia applications
        as feature of MMS, 29
        overview of, 134
SMIL (Synchronized Multimedia Integration
    Language), version 2.0, 135-145. *See also*
    multimedia applications
        audio, 136-137
        Basic profile, 147-148
        combining sequential and parallel
            presentations, 139-141
        graphics, 136
        links, 141-143
        MMS and, 134
        modules, 145-147
        parallel presentations, 138-139
        prefetch application, 143-144
        sequential presentations, 137-138
        structure of SMIL presentations, 135
        system bit rate and, 144-145
SMS (Short Message Service)
        chat and, 6-7
        compared with MMS, 378
        instant messaging and, 5
software, specifying properties with RDF, 186
source elements, synchronization, 199-200
space management, CSS, 96-97
spatial reference systems, 154
SpeechML, 132
SQL databases, 504
SSL (Secure Sockets Layer), 434
standard libraries, WML 2.0, 314-315
        Dialogs library, 321
        Float library, 318

Lang library, 318-320
String library, 321-323
URL library, 315-317
Web site information for, 315
WMLBrowser library, 323-324
standby time, personalizing, 10-11
start page, XHTML Basic/i-mode site, 249-251
static text, 379-380
store-and-forward technique, SMS, 6-7
streaming audio, 44
String library, WML 2.0, 321-323
    comparing strings, 322-323
    element data type and, 323
    length of strings, 321-322
string table, WBXML, 176-177, 179-181
stroke-width attribute, SVG, 167
strong element
    WML 2.0, 276
    XHTML, 245
structure module
    SMIL 2.0, 146
    XHTML, 108-109
style attributes, XHTML, 120
style, CCS Moble Profile 1.0, 476
style sheets
    XHTML, 120
    XHTML Basic, 263
subscriptions
    APEX, 494
    CPIM, 491-492
subscripts, XHTML Basic, 263
subtype, XML, 50
summary property, vCalendars, 485
superscripts, XHTML Basic, 263
SVG (Scalable Vector Graphics), 164-170. *See
    also* real world models (combining SVG
    with GML)
    compared with GML, 150
    drawing board, 165-167
    GML maps and, 169-170
    overview of, 164-165
    paths, 167-168
    shapes, 167
    text, 168-169

transforming GML representation to, 396
    XML and, 50
SVG viewer, Batik, 431
Symbian platform, 14, 15
synchronization, 196-204
    applications, 12-14
    overview of, 196
    SyncML commands, 200-204
    SyncML messages, 197-198
    target and source elements, 199-200
synchronized data, 13
Synchronized Multimedia Integration
    Language. *See* SMIL (Synchronized
    Multimedia Integration Language)
Synchronous Connection-Oriented (SCO)
    links, 44
SyncML forum, 196
SyncML Representation protocol, 31-32
SyncML (synchronization markup
    language), 30-33
    device information document, 32-33
    overview of, 196
    Representation protocol, 31-32
    synchronization with, 12-13
    SyncML commands, 200-204
    SyncML messages, 197-198
syntax, XPath, 88
system-bitrate attribute, SMIL 2.0, 144-145

T

tables
    cHTML to XHTML Basic conversion,
        235-237
    WML 2.0, 280-282
    XHTML, 113-116
TACS (Total Access Communication
    Systems), 21
tags
    WBXML, 177
    XML, 50-51

TalkML, 132

target elements, synchronization, 199-200

targets module, XHTML, 118-119

TCP (Transmission Control Protocol), 38

templates, WML 1.x, 326

text

    animated, 381-384

    combing graphics with, 387

    SMIL, 368-371

    static, 379-381

    SVG, 168-169

    WML 2.0, 276

text containers, XHTML, 109

text, XHTML, 108-109

text, XHTML Basic

    big and small text, 262

    blinking text, 247

    emphasis and strong text, 245

    plaintext, 243-245

time manipulations module, SMIL 2.0, 147

time representation, personalizing, 10

timers, WML 2.0, 306-308

    simple animation, 307-308

    start page, 307

timing modules, SMIL 2.0, 147

todo objects, vCalendars, 483

tokenization, 172

Total Access Communication Systems (TACS), 21

tpoint, POIX, 473

transactions, ECML, 453-455

transformations. *See also* XSLT (XSL transformations)

    GML to SVG, 164, 396, 423-430

    XHTML Basic/i-mode site, 254-256

transition effects module, SMIL 2.0, 147

transitional XHTML documents, 105

translation technologies, 172

Transmission Control Protocol (TCP), 38

tree structure, XPath, 86-87

two-way audio, IrMC, 42

two-way updates, synchronization, 13

types, GML, 397, 402

U

UAProf, 190-193

    components, 190

    example of, 190-192

    Web site information for, 193

UDP (Universal Datagram Protocol), 38

UML object orientation, 396

UMTS Terrestrial Radio Access Networks (UTRANs), 23

UMTS (Universal Mobile Telephony System), 22

Unicode

    cHTML to XHTML Basic conversion, 243

    static text and, 380

    UTF-8 and UTF-16, 54-55, 379

Uniform Resource Identifiers (URIs), 489-490

units of measurement, CSS, 97-98

Universal Datagram Protocol (UDP), 38

Universal Mobile Telephony System (UMTS), 22

updates, synchronization and, 13

URIs (Uniform Resource Identifiers), 489-490

URL library, WML 2.0, 315-317

    path and query, 317

    scheme and host, 316-317

    syntax of URLs, 316

usemap attribute, XHTML, 118

UTF-16, 54-55

UTF-8, 54-55

UTRANs (UMTS Terrestrial Radio Access Networks), 23

V

validation, XML, 55-70

    attribute declarations, 67-68

    DTDs, converting BNF to, 56-59

    DTDs, writing, 59-60

    element declarations, 62-67

entity declarations, 68-70
tool for, 60-62
variable substitution syntax, 293
variables, WML 2.0, 286-296
　　changing attribute values, 293
　　reading values of, 286-287
　　selection lists, 294-296
　　sending values to server scripts, 291-293
　　setting, 287-290
　　setting during jumps, 301-302
　　writing parameterized code, 287
vCalendars, 483-485
vCards, 480-483
.vcf file extensions, 480
.vcs file extensions, 483
vector graphics, 164. *See also* SVG (Scalable
　Vector Graphics)
vEvents, 483
view box, SVG, 165-166
virtual personal information
　　vCalendars, 483-485
　　vCards, 480-483
virtual worlds, GML, 396
VLRs (Visiting Location Registers), 498
voice over IP (VOIP), 131
voice portals, 328-331
　　function of, 124
　　implementation, 331
　　menu of choices, 329-330
　　services, 330
　　VoiceXML and, 328
　　Welcome Message, 328
VoiceXML, 124-131
　　alternatives to, 131-132
　　document structure, 125
　　forms, 126-127
　　menus, 128-129
　　overview of, 124-125
　　playing audio files, 129-131
　　voice portals and, 328
VoiceXML forum, 124, 328
VOIP (voice over IP), 131
Voxeo, CallXML, 131
VoxML, 131
vxml element, 125

W

WAP-NG (WAP Next Generation), 28-30
　　MMS and, 29
　　PIM synchronization and, 29-30
　　XHTML and, 30
WAP phones
　　display size of, 7
　　fonts, 8
　　graphics capabilities of, 8
WAP (Wireless Application Protocol)
　　CCS Moble Profile 1.0 and, 476
　　instant messaging and, 5
　　security and, 434
　　support for XHTML Basic in WAP 2.0,
　　　218
　　UAProf and, 186
watcherinfo element, XML, 495-496
watchers, presence information and, 489
WAV format
　　SMIL, 137
　　VoiceXML, 129
WAX (Wireless Abstract XML)
　　Morphis WAX, 172, 183-184
　　platform compatibility and, 16
WBMP format, 284
wbxml file extension, 172
WBXML (Wireless Binary XML), 172-182
　　code summary, 181-182
　　document body, 177-181
　　documents, starting elements of, 173-176
　　languages, 181-182
　　overview of, 172-173
　　string table, 176-177
　　tokenizing markup into, 106
　　WML 2.0 and, 281-282
WCSS (wireless cascading style sheets)
　　CCS Moble Profile 1.0 and, 476
　　marquee support in, 242
　　WML mark up with, 276-278
web-clipping applications, 16
Welcome Message, voice portals, 328
widgets
　　WML 1.x, 325
　　WML 2.0, 299-300

Windows, version for wireless devices, 14
Wireless Abstract XML. *See* WAX (Wireless Abstract XML)
Wireless Application Protocol. *See* WAP (Wireless Application Protocol)
Wireless Application Protocol Forum, 12
Wireless Binary XML. *See* WBXML (Wireless Binary XML)
wireless bitmaps, WML, 284
wireless cascading style sheets. *See* WCSS (wireless cascading style sheets)
Wireless LANs (802.11b), 25-26
Wireless Markup Language. *See* WML (Wireless Markup Language)
Wireless Session Protocol (WSP)
    functionality and semantics of, 37
    HTTP and, 33-34
wireless systems, distributed, 206-207
Wireless Transport Layer Security (WTLS), 434
WML (Wireless Markup Language) 1.x, 324-326
    lack of success of, 272
    namespaces and headers, 324-325
    templates, 326
    widgets and roles, 325
WML (Wireless Markup Language) 2.0
    formatting, 276-278
    HTML body vs. deck of cards approach, 273-275
    images, 282-284
    jumps, backward, 302-304
    jumps, detecting, 304-306
    jumps, forward, 297-301
    jumps, setting variables in, 301-302
    links, 278-280
    navigation improvements, 284-286
    overview of, 272
    phone functionality, 309-310
    tables, 280-282
    timers, 306-308
WML (Wireless Markup Language) 2.0, scripts, 310-324
    Dialogs library, 321
    Float library, 318
    functions of, 311-314
    Lang library, 318-320
    overview of, 310-311
    standard libraries, 314-315
    String library, 321-323
    URL library, 315-317
    WMLBrowser library, 323-324
WML (Wireless Markup Language) 2.0, variables, 286-296
    changing attribute values with, 293
    selection lists and, 294-296
    sending values to server scripts, 291-293
    setting, 287-290
    values of, 286-287
    writing parameterized code with, 287
WMLBrowser library, 323-324
wml:columns attribute, 281
wml:do element, 297-299
wml:go elements, 297-301, 302
wml:newcontext attribute, 301
wml:onevent element, 304
wml:prev element, 303-304
WMLScript. *See* scripts, WML 2.0
WMLScript library, 434-437
wrap format, WML 2.0, 276
WSP (Wireless Session Protocol)
    functionality and semantics of, 37
    HTTP and, 33-34
WTA Public library, 310
WTLS (Wireless Transport Layer Security), 434

X

XHTML. *See also* HTML to XHTML conversion
    applets and scripting modules, 109-110, 227
    closed tags, 105-106
    colors, 228-229
    DTDs, 104-105
    file uploads, 227
    forms and basic forms modules, 111-113

frames, iframes, and targets modules, 118-119, 225-226
image maps and embedded object modules, 117-118
intrinsic events and metainformation modules, 119-120
link and base modules, 120-121
modules, 106-107
name identification and legacy construct modules, 121-122
plug-ins, 227-228
presentation, edit, and bidirectional text modules, 110-111
screen size, 228-229
structure, texts, hypertext, and lists modules, 108-109
style sheet and style attribute modules, 120
tables and basic tables modules, 113-116
things to avoid, 226-230
WML and, 272, 275
XHTML Basic. *See also* cHTML to XHTML Basic conversion
    forms module, 113
    modules, 107-108
    presentation and style sheet modules, big and small text, 262
    presentation and style sheet modules, bold face and italic fonts, 260-262
    presentation and style sheet modules, horizontal rulers, 259-260
    presentation and style sheet modules, style sheets, 263
    presentation and style sheet modules, superscripts and subscripts, 263
    shopping form, 439
    tables module, 115-116
    WAP-NG and, 30
XHTML Basic/i-mode, sample site, 249-259
    game implementation, 251-256
    game implementation, server-side scripts, 252-254
    game implementation, transformations, 254-256

news page, 256-259
requirement of, 249
start page, 249-251
XHTML Basic, sample site
    custom navigation and shared content, 230-234
    shared navigation and content, 234-235
XHTML development tools, 264-269
    HTML-Kit, 267-268
    Nokia Mobile Internet Toolkit, 268-269
    XML Spy, 264-266
Xlink (XML Linking Language), 80-86
    extended links, 82-86
    simple links, 81-82
xlink:actuate attribute, 85
XML applications
    3G and, 24-25
    Bluetooth, 45-46
    databases, 498
    HTML 4, 104
    optimizing, 172
    POIX, 466
    SMIL, 135
    tools, 100
    vCards and vCalendars, 485
    vector graphics, 164
XML code, well-formed, 105
.xml document, 407-423
XML documents, 48-55. *See also* validation, XML
    attributes, 51-52
    character encoding, 54-55
    content types, 49-50
    declaration, 54
    elements and tags, 50-51
    grammars, 52-54
    matching style sheets to, 99-100
    overview of, 48-49
    public identifiers, 55
XML extender, IBM, 504
XML files, 49-50
XML Linking Language. *See* Xlink (XML Linking Language)
XML namespace, 71-72

XML parsers, 100
XML-RPC
    advantages of, 206, 208
    applying, 208-210
    compared with CORBA and DCOM,
      206-207
    data types and, 210-213
    information resources for, 213-214
    procedure calls, 207
XML schemas. *See* schemas
XML Spy, 264-266
    entry helpers, 266
    graphical editing, 265-266
    SMIL documents and, 366
    XHTML projects, 264
    as XML tool, 100
XML Writer, 100

XPath, 86-88
    syntax for, 86, 88
    tree structures and, 86-87
    XQuery and, 498
XQL database, 502-504
XQuery, 498-502
    basic queries, 498-499
    conditional queries, 499-501
    FLWR queries, 501-502
xsd:attribute declaration, 76
XSLT (XSL transformations), 88-92
    function of, 88
    processor for, 88-90
    structure of, 89-92
    XHTML Basic/i-mode site, 254-256

INTERNATIONAL CONTACT INFORMATION

AUSTRALIA
McGraw-Hill Book Company Australia Pty. Ltd.
TEL +61-2-9417-9899
FAX +61-2-9417-5687
http://www.mcgraw-hill.com.au
books-it_sydney@mcgraw-hill.com

CANADA
McGraw-Hill Ryerson Ltd.
TEL +905-430-5000
FAX +905-430-5020
http://www.mcgrawhill.ca

GREECE, MIDDLE EAST,
NORTHERN AFRICA
McGraw-Hill Hellas
TEL +30-1-656-0990-3-4
FAX +30-1-654-5525

MEXICO (Also serving Latin America)
McGraw-Hill Interamericana Editores S.A. de C.V.
TEL +525-117-1583
FAX +525-117-1589
http://www.mcgraw-hill.com.mx
fernando_castellanos@mcgraw-hill.com

SINGAPORE (Serving Asia)
McGraw-Hill Book Company
TEL +65-863-1580
FAX +65-862-3354
http://www.mcgraw-hill.com.sg
mghasia@mcgraw-hill.com

SOUTH AFRICA
McGraw-Hill South Africa
TEL +27-11-622-7512
FAX +27-11-622-9045
robyn_swanepoel@mcgraw-hill.com

UNITED KINGDOM & EUROPE
(Excluding Southern Europe)
McGraw-Hill Education Europe
TEL +44-1-628-502500
FAX +44-1-628-770224
http://www.mcgraw-hill.co.uk
computing_neurope@mcgraw-hill.com

ALL OTHER INQUIRIES Contact:
Osborne/McGraw-Hill
TEL +1-510-549-6600
FAX +1-510-883-7600
http://www.osborne.com
omg_international@mcgraw-hill.com